Wildflowers *of* NEW BRUNSWICK

TODD BOLAND

Boulder Publications also publishes these field guides:

Birds of Newfoundland
Edible Plants of Atlantic Canada
Edible Plants of Newfoundland and Labrador
Geology of Newfoundland
Geology of Nova Scotia
Trees and Shrubs of the Maritimes
Trees and Shrubs of Newfoundland and Labrador
Whales and Dolphins of Atlantic Canada and Northeast United States
Wildflowers of Newfoundland and Labrador
Wildflowers of Nova Scotia

And these gardening guides:

Atlantic Gardening
Newfoundland Gardening

Wildflowers *of* NEW BRUNSWICK

TODD BOLAND

BOULDER PUBLICATIONS

Library and Archives Canada Cataloguing in Publication

Boland, Todd, author
Wildflowers of New Brunswick : field guide / Todd Boland.

Includes bibliographical references and index.
ISBN 978-1-927099-49-0 (pbk.)

1. Wild flowers--New Brunswick--Identification. 2. Wild flowers--New Brunswick--Pictorial works. I. Title.

QK203.N3B64 2014 582.1309715'1 C2014-901636-0

Published by Boulder Publications
Portugal Cove-St. Philip's, Newfoundland and Labrador
www.boulderpublications.ca

Editor: Stephanie Porter
Copy editor: Iona Bulgin
Design and layout: John Andrews

Printed in Canada

Newfoundland Labrador We acknowledge the financial support of the Government of Newfoundland and Labrador through the Department of Tourism, Culture and Recreation.

We acknowledge the financial support for our publishing program by the Government of Canada and the Department of Canadian Heritage through the Canada Book Fund.

CONTENTS

PREFACE

Wildflowers of New Brunswick will introduce you to more than 700 species of herbaceous wildflowers (plants that die back to the ground in winter) that grow within the province.

I have profiled species that are native to New Brunswick, as well as many introduced species that have become naturalized (and sometimes invasive) by "jumping the fence" from cultivated areas into wild areas or by unintentional introduction, primarily from Europe.

The only recent printed guide to the flora of New Brunswick is my previous book *Trees and Shrubs of the Maritimes*, published in 2012. That pictorial guide covers all the woody plants of the province but does not describe any of the herbaceous wildflowers. Before the release of this book, the only pictorial guide to the wildflowers of New Brunswick was *Wildflowers of Nova Scotia, New Brunswick and Prince Edward Island* by Mary Primrose and Marian Munro (2006). The photography in this coffee-table book is stunning, but it is not set up as a field guide and covers only about 100 of the most common wildflowers of the Maritimes. Harold R. Hinds's second edition of *Flora of New Brunswick* (2000) covers all the flora of the province. *Flora of New Brunswick* is a technical book with line drawings—perfect for the more advanced botanist but perhaps not user-friendly enough for the budding wildflower enthusiast. The book does, however, have maps showing wildflower distributions, which can be helpful; it can be purchased through the University of New Brunswick.

Wildflowers of New Brunswick is designed to help readers who have limited knowledge of botany identify the common wildflowers of the province, along with some of the rare native species. By grouping plants first by flower colour and then by flower shape, and by using other physical plant features such as flower arrangement and leaf shape and arrangement, this guide offers a step-by-step method of plant identification. It is my hope that this guide will help you recognize many of the province's wildflowers.

Concerns about the environment are at the forefront of everyone's mind these days. One way to better understand nature's interconnected web is by learning to recognize and appreciate its plants in their natural habitats. By helping you identify the wildflowers of New Brunswick, I hope that this guide will give you a solid foundation for a thoughtful and observant connection to the natural world around you.

ACKNOWLEDGEMENTS

My thanks to all the photographers who graciously allowed me to use their photographs to fill gaps in my image archive. They are listed by name in the photo credits, page 426.

I note with gratitude the contribution of graphic designer John Andrews for both the book's design and his attention to detail in the layout.

Special thanks go to Stephanie Porter and Iona Bulgin for their care with my prose and grammar, which helped this non-English major write with greater definition and focus.

Finally, I would like to thank Gavin Will and Boulder Publications for having faith that this book would be a successful addition to Boulder's Field Guide series.

INTRODUCTION

New Brunswick is home to about 1,500 species of native and naturalized plants. This guide focuses on the identification of herbaceous wildflowers—plants that die back to the ground in winter. A few sub-shrubs are included; these superficially appear herbaceous but, in fact, contain wood cells and are truly woody plants. Because they are often called "wildflowers," I have included them in this book. For help in identifying woody trees and shrubs (including sub-shrubs), I refer you to my previous publication, *Trees and Shrubs of the Maritimes*, which is also part of Boulder Publications' Field Guide series.

This guide is not all-inclusive. Ferns and their relatives are not covered, nor are any grasses or grass relatives, as they are very challenging to identify. Some very rare native plants and locally introduced exotics with limited distributions are not included due to space constraints.

Many of the main flower entries in this guide also include a description of close relatives or look-alike species to help distinguish between them. As a result, over 700 species—native wildflowers and the more common weeds or exotic non-native species—are described. Photographs accompany most of the descriptions to illustrate the flowers, leaves, or other pertinent identification features of a given plant.

The next several pages of this introduction are key to using this guide successfully. These pages explain the system of icons and notations and how to use them in a process of elimination in order to identify a wildflower in the field. But before you get into the "how" of the book, it helps to understand some of the natural factors that influence where different types of wildflowers grow in New Brunswick.

The Big Picture

New Brunswick is a relatively small province, nearly square in outline, about 320 kilometres north to south and 240 kilometres east to west. The land area is about 73,000 square kilometres; this makes it the third smallest province in Canada after Prince Edward Island and Nova Scotia. Despite this, New Brunswick encompasses a wide variety of habitats and landscapes.

Plant distributions are affected by climate. The climate of New Brunswick varies significantly, depending on where you are in the province. The Fundy coast, for example, has the mildest winters, averaging about -8°C, and relatively cool summers, with an average temperature of about 17°C. The Fundy coast is also the wettest region, with about 1,400 millimetres of precipitation annually. The highlands of north-central New Brunswick have the coolest summers, averaging about 16°C, and the coldest winters, averaging about -13°C. The southern half of the province, away from the immediate influence of the coast, has warmer summers, with average temperatures near 20°C; the average winter temperature is -10°C. The south is also much drier, with about 1100 millimetres of precipitation annually. Despite the fact that nearly half of the province's border is along the Atlantic Ocean, the climate is generally more continental than that of the other Atlantic provinces (Nova Scotia, Prince Edward Island, and Newfoundland).

Elevation also influences plant life. Much of New Brunswick is located below an elevation of 150 metres. However, the province has two regions of highlands. In the south, near the Fundy coast, the Caledonian and St. Croix Highlands reach an elevation of over 400 metres. In the northern region of the province are the Miramichi Highlands, Chaleur Uplands, and the Notre Dame Mountains, the latter of which is home to the highest mountain in the province, Mount Carleton (817 metres). All of these highland regions are part of the Appalachian Mountains.

Despite boasting elevations higher than the highest points of land in Nova Scotia and Newfoundland, the New Brunswick "mountains" are not home to the Arctic-alpine species notable in the other provinces. The elevations of northern New Brunswick, combined with a relatively continental climate, results in predominately boreal forest dominated by balsam fir and white and black spruce. Floristically, northern New Brunswick has the lowest diversity of wildflowers.

The lower elevation central regions are generally mixed Acadian woodlands, a combination of hardwood and coniferous tree species. The southwestern region of the province, especially along the middle Saint John River valley, is dominated by hardwood forest and, consequently, is home to the richest assemblage of wildflowers, several species of which are not found in other parts of the province.

The nature of the soil is also an important factor in plant life. Most plants in New Brunswick have adapted to acidic soil derived from sandstone or granite, the most common rock types in the province. Others plants are calciphiles restricted to limestone-derived soil; these plants often have restricted distributions and, within New Brunswick, have Arctic-alpine affinity. Limestone outcrops are scattered primarily in the northern and western regions of New Brunswick, in the form of limestone ledges and gravels along the Restigouche River, along the upper Saint John River north of its confluence with the Keswick River, and, to a lesser degree, along the Hammond River. Gypsum outcrops are restricted to uplands in Albert County. Several highly restricted plants are found exclusively in these calcareous areas.

HOW TO USE THIS GUIDE

Wildflowers of New Brunswick organizes plants by their flowers, starting with flower colour, shape, and inflorescence (arrangement) and then working down to the finer details, including leaf shape and outline.

Examine the Flower / Colour

To use this guide, begin by noting the colour of the flower on the plant you wish to identify. For the purposes of this guide, the species have been divided into five main colour groups:

- Green / brown flowers (includes greenish-white and greenish-yellow)
- White flowers
- Yellow flowers (includes orange)
- Pink flowers (includes pale pink through to deep rose, as well as red)
- Blue flowers (includes pale blue to deep violet-blue to deep purple)

Use the coloured bars at the top of the pages to find the correct section for your flower. The process of describing colour can be subjective—some flowers may be considered pink by one person, for example, and purple by another. If you have a flower that may fall between two categories, please check both colour sections.

Examine the Flower / Shape

Within each colour section, flowers are next organized according to flower shape or outline. Take a close look at the flower itself, noting the number of petals and/or the outline of the flower. Ask yourself these three questions:

1. Is the flower shape unusual (lacking typical flower parts such as sepals and petals)?

Unusual

2. Is the flower shape irregular (having a bilateral symmetry such that you can only cut it in one plane to create halves—most iris or orchids have this shape, for example)?

Irregular

3. Is the flower shape regular (having radial or round symmetry)? If yes, count the number of petals. Are there 3, 4, 5, 6, or 7 or more?

One or more of the above flower shape icons will be in the colour bar at the top of each species page.

Examine the Flower / Inflorescence

Look closely at how the flowers are arranged on the stem—the inflorescence. Is the flower solitary or does it tend to grow in a pair or a cluster? Is it enclosed in a bract (spathe) or does the flower grow from the leaf axils? In this guide, flowers are categorized into one or more of the following types:

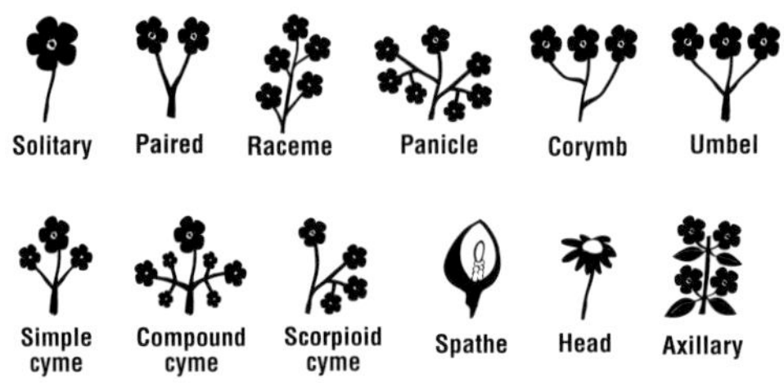

Examine the Leaf

Next, you'll need to note a few key leaf characteristics to narrow down the possibilities:

1. Are the leaves single-bladed (simple), or do multiple small leaflets combine to create a larger leaf (compound)?

2. Are the leaves in a basal rosette at the base of the plant or scattered along the stem? If along the stem, do they extend from either side of the stem in an alternating sequence ("alternate"), are they paired ("opposite"), or do three or more leaves grow from the same point on the stem ("whorled")? Are no leaves apparent?

3. What is the overall shape of the leaf? Leaves in this field guide are categorized as
   i. linear
   ii. elongate or lance-shaped

iii. elliptical
iv. round to egg-shaped
v. deltoid
vi. hand-shaped ("palmately lobed")
vii. oak leaf-shaped ("pinnately lobed")
viii. dissected ("pinnatifid")
ix. in multiple sections ("compound"—see next step)

Linear Lance Elliptical Egg/round Deltoid Palmately lobed Pinnately lobed Pinnatifid

4. If the leaf is compound, does it have three leaflets (making it "trifoliate" or "ternate"), five leaflets ("palmately compound"), or many leaflets ("pinnately compound")?

Trifoliate Palmately compound Pinnately compound

5. If the leaflets of a trifoliate or ternate leaf are themselves ternate, the leaf is "biternate"; if the leaflets of a biternate leaf are ternate, the leaf is "triternate"; if the leaflets of a pinnately compound leaf are themselves pinnate, the leaf is "bipinnate."

Biternate Triternate Bipinnate

6. Is the leaf edge smooth, toothed, or lobed?

Smooth Toothed Lobed

Icons on each page illustrate at a glance which of these features each plant has. The plant's status as either a native or an introduced species is also included.

Native Species Introduced Species

It is important to remember that plants do not strictly follow the rules in any of the above categories. For example, a plant may exhibit more than one flower type by producing individual and clustered blooms. Lower leaves may be compound, while upper leaves are single-bladed. In such circumstances, all the relevant icons for flower/leaf forms are included.

Details of each species are summarized in the text, and key identifying characteristics are illustrated in photographs. Your observations about flower colour and flower shape will lead you to the corresponding section of the guide, and the leaf shape and arrangement will help you to narrow down the possibilities. Finally, if you compare the plant you are looking at with the descriptions and photographs on the page, you should be able to identify, or come close to identifying, the flower.

Even with a System, Identifying Plants Can Be Tricky

About 350 species of herbaceous wildflowers which may be encountered in the wilds of New Brunswick have a dedicated page in this guide. Most entries also describe one or two close relatives. By using the information in each entry, you should be able to identify most species in the field.

No attempt to simplify nature is foolproof—nature is far too complex to fit into a tidy series of icons and colours. It is important, for example, to keep in mind that plants can show considerable variation in their flower colours and leaf shapes. While you are in the field, look around for similar plants, and compare the flowers and leaves on the same plant and on its neighbours. The more you practice and observe, the easier plant identification will become.

A Few Words about Plant Names and Terms

All known living organisms have scientific names. The naming process is known as taxonomy, and it is a science in itself. Taxonomic names are created in Latin, which is considered by scientists to be a "universal" language. Over time, as new information is learned about an organism (especially about its genetic makeup), its scientific name may be changed.

Plants are commonly affected by such name changes. For this reason, each plant in this book is listed by its most-accepted common name; the most current botanical (Latin) name and other common synonyms, including its most common name(s) in French, are also included. Both the common and taxonomic names applied generally follow VASCAN (the Database of Canadian Vascular Plants, data.canadensys.net/vascan/search/). Family names follow the system listed on the Angiosperm Phylogeny website (www.mobot.org/mobot/research/apweb). The listing of the plants within each colour and flower outline group follows *Flora of New Brunswick* by Harold R. Hinds (2000).

If you are keenly interested in following botanical name changes, you might want to look at the ongoing Flora of North America project which, when complete, will be a 30-volume online encyclopedia of the entire North American flora (floranorthamerica.org). As a new wildflower enthusiast you may be interested in joining the New Brunswick Botany Club, a group dedicated to expanding the knowledge of local New Brunswick flora through regular meetings and field trips (http://www.macbe.com/botanyclub/home.html).

Even though this guide is designed for the novice plant enthusiast—no plant science background is required!—some botanical terms are used. This is because they have precise meanings. Take this guide as your introduction to Botany and refer to the glossary and plant anatomy diagram at the back of the guide for explanations of terms that are new to you. You'll soon become familiar with them.

For those who are more botanically inclined, a list of the wildflowers included in this guide according to their taxonomic family relationships is found on page XX. You can also search for plants by either their (accepted) common name or their Latin name in these indexes.

Not All Plants Like the Same Places

Along the outer edge of each species listing page in this guide are habitat tabs, which indicate the major and minor habitat types favoured by the plant described. These habitat indicators provide general guidelines only—you should refer to the habitat description in the text for specific habitat details and locations. In some cases, reference is made to specific counties within New Brunswick, which are shown on the map on page 8.

Habitat Notes / Forests

Three major forest habitat tabs are used: coniferous forest, mixed forest, and deciduous forest.

New Brunswick's forests fall into two main groups: the North American boreal forest, dominated by coniferous trees, stretches across northern Canada from Newfoundland to the Yukon and into the State of Alaska; and the Acadian forest which, with the Great Lakes-St. Lawrence forest, forms the northern hardwood forest. The Acadian forest marks the transition between the boreal forest region to the north and the central hardwood forest region, dominated by deciduous trees, to the south.

The boreal forest of northern New Brunswick is dominated by trees such as balsam fir (*Abies balsamea*), black spruce (*Picea mariana*), and white spruce (*P. glauca*), along with deciduous white birch (*Betula papyrifera*) and mountain birch (*B. cordifolia*). Fire-prone areas are dominated by various pine species and trembling aspen (*Populus tremuloides*). Valleys often have significant patches of sugar maple (*Acer saccharum*), which become more predominant farther south in the province. The Acadian forest, which covers most of the rest of the province, contains a mixture of hardwood and coniferous trees. The southwestern region of New Brunswick has the greatest diversity of hardwood species and the least coverage by coniferous species.

For the purpose of this guide, if at least 75 per cent of a forest is made up of coniferous trees, then the forest type is considered coniferous. If a forest is 75 per cent deciduous, then it is considered a deciduous forest. Any other combination is considered a mixed forest.

Habitat Notes / Barrens

Barrens are often described as areas stripped of vegetation. Barrens, in the sense of

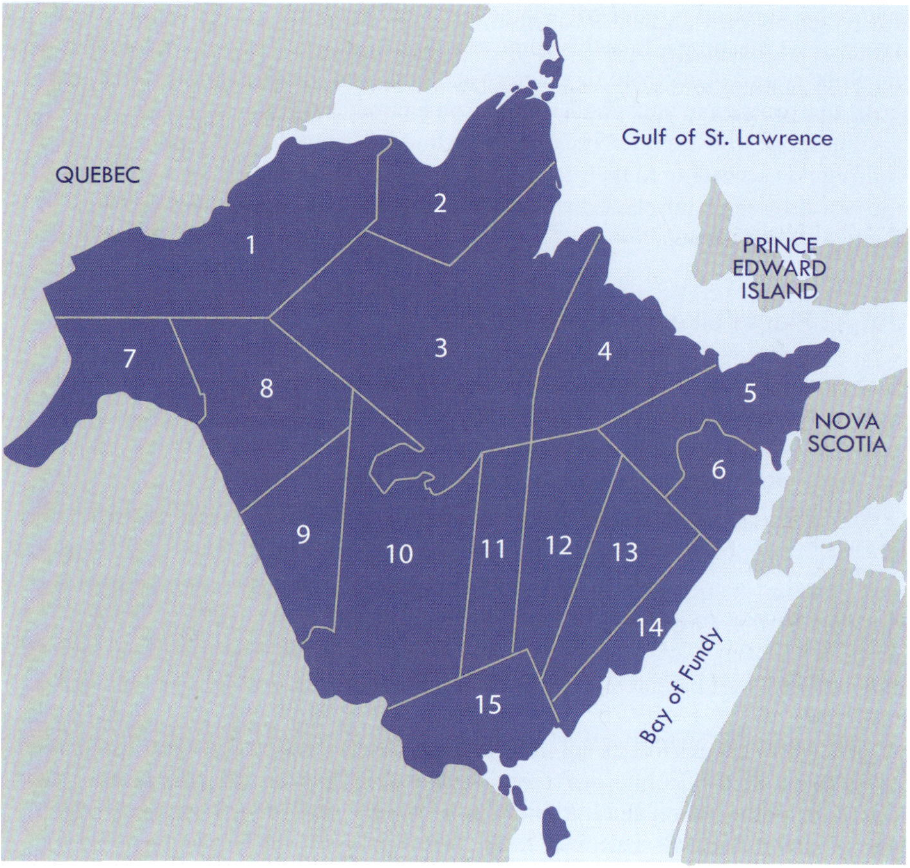

NEW BRUNSWICK COUNTIES

1. Restigouche
2. Gloucester
3. Northumberland
4. Kent
5. Westmoreland
6. Albert
7. Madawaska
8. Victoria
9. Carleton
10. York
11. Sunbury
12. Queens
13. Kings
14. St. John
15. Charlotte

those found in Nova Scotia or Newfoundland, are rare in New Brunswick. They are dominated by shrubs, particularly ericaceous shrubs (such as blueberry, sheep laurel, and huckleberry), and low, wind-stunted trees, as opposed to the taller trees typical of forests. Within the province, barrens are most often found close to the ocean on exposed headlands.

Habitat Notes / Coastal

New Brunswick borders the ocean on its southern and eastern margins, hence plants associated with the coast are a significant feature of the province's south and east coasts. For the purposes of this guide, coastal habitats include sand dune areas as well as gravelly and rocky beaches. Beaches are generally quite narrow, encompassing the land within a few metres of the high-tide line. Dune areas may be significantly wider. Under natural conditions—that is, undisturbed by human activity—sand dune coastlines would feature a series of dunes that mark the transition from outer sand beach to coastal forest vegetation. Today, many areas of sand dunes are severely degraded by human activity.

Not all dunes are created equal. Fore-dunes, closest to the sea, are held loosely in place by specialty grasses. Wind and tides cause them to move and shift over time; they are rarely static. Farther inland, secondary and tertiary dunes appear, the product of uninterrupted plant succession. Secondary dunes are nearly completely covered by vegetation, which is, again, mostly herbaceous with a few woody species. Tertiary dunes are farthest inland and feature more woody species, many of which are wind-stunted versions of the adjacent forest vegetation.

In this guide, salt marshes are also considered coastal habitat. These marshes are often inundated by salt water during the highest tides and, in all cases, are brackish. Salt marshes are common along both coasts of New Brunswick, especially around the estuaries of larger rivers.

Several herbaceous plant species are typical of coastal habitats and are rarely, if ever, found elsewhere. Some examples are Caroline sea lavender (*Limonium carolinianum*), beach-pea (*Lathyrus japonicus*), and sea rocket (*Cakile edentula*).

Habitat Notes / Wetlands

Another habitat tab used in this guide is wetlands. The term "wetlands" applies to several types of habitats in which water plays a key role. One major wetland group includes the margins of streams, rivers, and lakes, where the ground may be covered by water for at least a few weeks each year. In some of these places, water is present year-round except during the driest summer months. In either case, the soil is always quite moist.

A second major wetland type is peatlands. These areas remain wet year-round, which means that, because of a lack of oxygen in the waterlogged substrate, plant detritus is slow to decompose. It forms a thick layer of organic matter known as peat.

Bogs, the most prevalent category of wetlands in New Brunswick, are also the most nutrient-poor of the wetland types. Their nutrients come from rain and snow rather than from the mineral soils of surrounding forested areas. Bogs are dominated by sphagnum moss and dwarf ericaceous shrubs. Trees are generally absent, except for stunted eastern larch and black spruce. Pitcher plant (*Sarracenia purpurea*) is a common bog-indicator plant.

In New Brunswick, bogs are most prevalent in the eastern lowlands of Gloucester, Northumberland, and Kent counties, where many commercial peat harvesting farms are located. There are also many coastal bogs located along the Fundy coast, west of Saint John.

Fens are another type of wetland. Generally much smaller than bogs, they often occur in poorly drained areas next to larger streams and lakes or as patches inside forests. Because they receive nutrients from surrounding upland areas, they are more nutrient-rich than bogs and can support more plant life. Fens often resemble meadows because grasses and sedges dominate. Many wetland orchids make fens their home. Tall white bog orchid (*Platanthera dilatata*) is a good fen-indicator plant.

The terms "swamps" and "marshes" are often used interchangeably. Both are wetlands that are flooded on a regular basis; they are nutrient-rich wetlands and, hence, home to the greatest diversity of wetland plants. Showy lady's-slipper (*Cypripedium reginae*) is a typical marsh plant. Fens, marshes, and swamps dominate in southwestern New Brunswick and in the south-central counties of Queens and Sunbury, especially near Grand Lake and its watershed.

Habitat Notes / Disturbed Areas

In this guide, disturbed areas include roadsides and railway beds; urban areas such as scrublands, vacant lots, and city/town trails; pastures and meadows; and old or recent burn sites. All of these types of habitat have had their natural vegetation removed and underlying soil disturbed. Native wildflowers typical of disturbed habitats include fireweed (*Chamerion angustifolium*), New York aster (*Symphyotrichum novi-belgii*), and pearly everlasting (*Anaphalis margaritacea*).

Disturbed habitat is "new" habitat, and it is also the type of area most often occupied by introduced species, which are often considered weeds. Most frequently of European origin, introduced (or "alien") species are those that have arrived during the last five centuries. Some were brought as ornamentals, but many arrived accidentally, as seeds caught in ship ballast or packing materials. Nearly 20 per cent of all the plant species found in New Brunswick are not native to the province.

Some introduced plants have increased in population so much that they are now inhabiting natural areas and displacing native species. They are considered "invasive alien plants"—a phenomenon that is a concern worldwide. Plants such as purple loosestrife (*Lythrum salicaria*), coltsfoot (*Tussilago farafara*), and creeping buttercup (*Ranunculus repens*) are prime examples of invasive species in New Brunswick.

SAMPLE PAGE

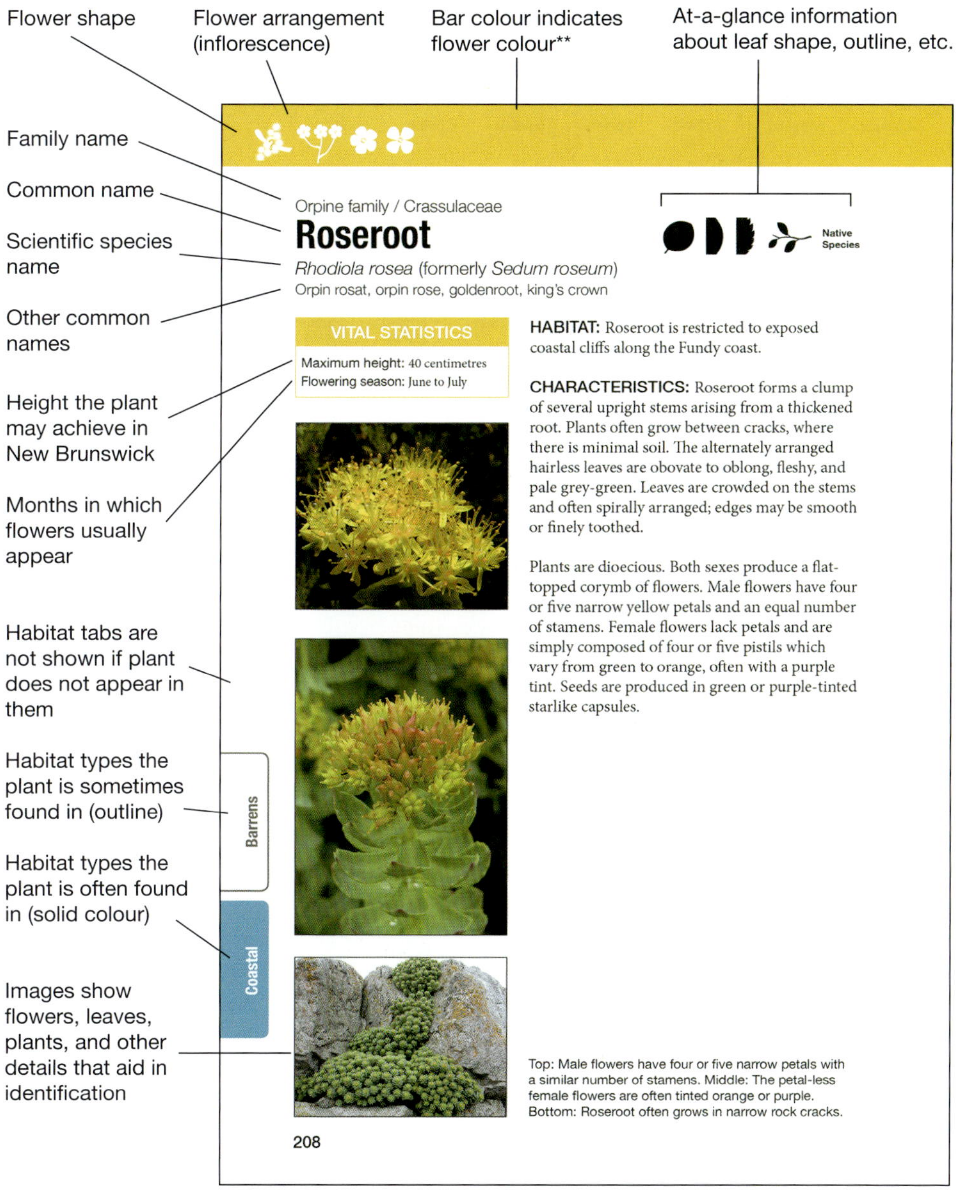

** Flowers have been divided into five colour groups:

Green / brown
Yellow
Blue
White
Pink

ICON LEGEND

Flower Shape

Unusual Irregular 3 petals 4 petals 5 petals 6 petals 7+ petals

Flower Arrangement / Inflorescence

Solitary Paired Raceme Panicle Corymb Umbel Simple cyme Compound cyme Scorpioid cyme Spathe Head Axillary

Simple Leaf Shape

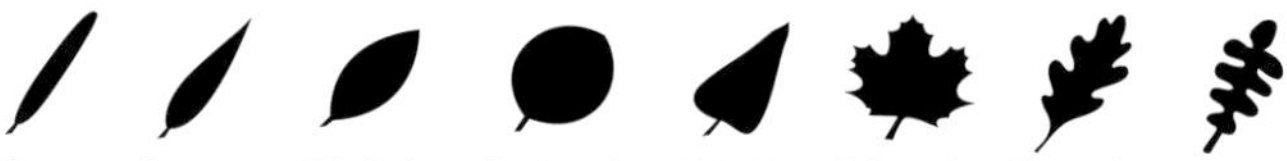

Linear Lance Elliptical Egg/round Deltoid Palmately lobed Pinnately lobed Pinnatifid

Compound Leaf Arrangement

Trifoliate Palmately compound Pinnately compound Biternate Triternate Bipinnate

Leaf Edge Outline

Smooth Toothed Lobed

Leaf Arrangement on Stem

No apparent leaves Opposite Alternate Whorled Basal

Additional Information

Native Species Introduced Species

Plant
PROFILES

Hemp family / Cannabaceae

Hops

Native Species Introduced Species

Humulus lupulus

Houblon, common hop

VITAL STATISTICS

Maximum height: 10 metres
Flowering season: July and August

HABITAT: Hops is occasionally found in waste places and abandoned homesteads throughout New Brunswick.

CHARACTERISTICS: Hops, a twisting vine, can reach a height of 10 metres. Opposite leaves are deeply tri-lobed or, less commonly, palmately lobed with toothed edges. Uppermost leaves are often simply heart-shaped. The undersides bear yellow aromatic granules and a hairy midrib. The petiole is nearly as long as the leaf. Stems are covered in short stiff backward-facing hairs. Despite its slightly woody stems, the plant is herbaceous.

Plants are dioecious. Male flowers are produced in small axillary panicles; individual flowers consist of five greenish-white sepals and five stamens. Female flowers are also axillary, with green catkin-like flowers that develop into green to brown globular cone-shaped fruit. This fruit is used in brewing beer.

Two varieties of hops occur in New Brunswick: native American hops, var. *lupuloides*; and introduced European hops, var. *lupulus*. The difference between the two is subtle.

Top: Details of the female flowers. Middle: Most leaves are palmately lobed. Bottom: Mature female flowers are cone-like.

Native Species Introduced Species

Nettle family / Urticaceae

Stinging nettle

Urtica dioica

Ortie dioïque

HABITAT: Stinging nettle is found in disturbed habitats, usually near settlements or farms, throughout New Brunswick. It prefers rich, organic soil.

CHARACTERISTICS: Stinging nettle quickly forms a large clump due to prolific rhizomes. New Brunswick has two subspecies: *dioica* from Europe, and the native *gracilis*. Often exhibiting branched stems, *dioica* is coarsely hairy on both stems and leaves. Its ovate, opposite leaves are sharply serrated with burning, stinging hairs on both surfaces. *Gracilis* typically has smooth unbranched stems and more slender elliptical leaves with stinging hairs only on the lower surface. Both forms have small stipules at the base of the leaves.

Dioica typically has dioecious flowers; *gracilis* is monoecious. Individual flowers of both are indistinguishable from each other: minute and green and produced in wiry, 5- to 15-centimetre-long clusters in the axils of the upper leaves. Close examination reveals four sepals but no petals.

Canada wood nettle, *Laportea canadensis*, is well distributed in rich, moist, mixed, and deciduous forests of New Brunswick. Superficially, it looks like stinging nettle but is less than 100 centimetres tall. Its stems and ovate leaves are also covered in stinging hairs, but they are alternate, not opposite. The minute green monoecious flowers are produced in a terminal rather than an axillary cyme.

VITAL STATISTICS
Maximum height: 150 centimetres
Flowering season: June to July

Top: Stinging nettle's minute flowers are in wiry panicles; the European form has cordate leaves. Middle: American stinging nettle's opposite leaves are coarsely toothed but more narrow than those of stinging nettle. Bottom: Canada wood nettle has alternate leaves.

Amaranth family / Amaranthaceae

Redroot amaranth

Introduced Species

Amaranthus retroflexus

Amarante à racine rouge, canne à pied rouge, green pigweed, redroot pigweed, green amaranth

VITAL STATISTICS
Maximum height: 2 metres
Flowering season: August to October

HABITAT: A European species, redroot amaranth is scattered in disturbed sites throughout New Brunswick.

CHARACTERISTICS: Redroot amaranth is a few-branched annual species. The alternate, prominently veined leaves are often 10 centimetres or longer; leaves are long petioled and ovate to elliptical in outline, with smooth but wavy edges. Leaves are hairless except for hairs located along the lower veins and upper stems. The short taproot is often bright red.

Inconspicuous monoecious flowers are produced in dense terminal panicles, with smaller clusters in the upper leaf axils. Close examination of the flowers reveals green to brown papery bracts, three green sepals, and no petals.

White amaranth or tumbleweed, *A. albus*, an introduced annual rare in the southwestern area of the province, reaches 1 metre in height and is densely branched, appearing almost bush-like. Its branches often arise at right angles to the main stem. Pale green leaves are up to 2.5 centimetres in length, and spatulate with smooth but wavy edges. Small clusters of inconspicuous monoecious flowers are produced among the upper leaf axils. In late fall, plants break at ground level and tumble in the wind, releasing seeds.

Top: Redroot amaranth's minute flowers are in dense panicles. Middle: Redroot amaranth panicles are terminal on the stems. Bottom: White amaranth has minute axillary flowers and spatulate leaves.

Native Species

Amaranth family / Amaranthaceae

Glabrous saltbush

Atriplex glabriuscula

Arroche glabriuscule, smooth orach, Babington's orach

HABITAT: Glabrous saltbush is encountered along cobble seashores, coastal dunes, and salt marshes throughout New Brunswick.

CHARACTERISTICS: Glabrous saltbush is an annual species with prostrate ridged stems and a mat-like habit. Leaf shapes are extremely variable. Lower leaves are usually opposite, triangular with two distinct basal lobes, and smooth-edged or with a few irregular teeth. Upper leaves are triangular, lance- to egg-shaped, and alternate or opposite. Leaves are fleshy; they may be green or, often, purple-tinted. Young leaves are often scurfy with silvery powder.

The minute green unisexual flowers (monoecious or dioecious) lack petals and sepals but have a pair of triangular bracteoles (tiny bracts) which enclose the developing fruit. Flowers are produced in small spikes among the upper leaf axils or terminating the stems. Small leafy bracts are scattered throughout the length of the spikes.

Common orach, A. *patula*, is similar to glabrous saltbush but is found in disturbed areas as well as along the coast, although it is not a halophyte species like *A. glabriuscula*. Its dense flower spikes lack the small leafy bracts indicative of glabrous saltbush.

The unisexual flowers of *Atriplex* distinguish them from those of the similar, but bisexual, *Chenopodium*.

VITAL STATISTICS
Maximum height: 100 centimetres
Flowering season: July to October

Top: Glabrous saltbush's unusual flowers are in small axillary spikes. Middle: Glabrous saltbush often has triangular leaves. Bottom: Common orach has dense axillary and terminal spikes.

Amaranth family / Amaranthaceae

Common lamb's-quarters

Chenopodium album

Introduced Species

Chénopode blanc, poulette grasse, chou gras, white pigweed, white goosefoot

VITAL STATISTICS

Maximum height: 100 centimetres
Flowering season: July to October

HABITAT: Common lamb's-quarters, a European species, is commonly found in disturbed areas throughout New Brunswick and is a pest in recently cultivated ground.

CHARACTERISTICS: Common lamb's-quarters is an annual with upright, branching, ridged stems which reach a height of 100 centimetres. Alternate leaves are ovate to diamond-shaped with a few irregular rounded teeth and are slightly fleshy. Young leaves are covered in a silvery powder that often remains on the undersides of mature leaves.

Close examination of the individual minute green flowers reveals five sepals, which enclose the developing seeds, five stamens, and two pistils. Flowers are produced in globular clusters scattered in spikes among the upper leaf axils and branch tips. A silvery powder covering the buds gives them a grey-green appearance.

Oak-leaved goosefoot, *C. glaucum*, is a similar introduced species distinguished by its spreading habit and elliptical, shallowly lobed leaves, which are green above and covered in white farina below. It has a localized distribution in the province.

Chenopodium is similar to *Atriplex* but it has mostly bisexual flowers, the latter unisexual.

Top: Common lamb's-quarters' minute flowers are in globular axillary and terminal clusters. Middle: Common lamb's-quarters leaves have irregularly rounded teeth. Bottom: Oak-leaved goosefoot has shallowly lobed leaves.

Native Species

Amaranth family / Amaranthaceae

Virginia glasswort

Salicornia depressa

Salicorne de Virginie, common glasswort, pickleweed, sea pickle

HABITAT: Virginia glasswort is found on salt marsh mudflats and tidal flats throughout New Brunswick. The plants are regularly inundated by water during high tides.

VITAL STATISTICS
Maximum height: 50 centimetres
Flowering season: August to October

CHARACTERISTICS: Virginia glasswort is an evergreen succulent plant with jointed and branched pencil-like stems. Overall, the plant resembles coral. Its green stems turn red in winter. Scale-like leaves, opposite on the stems, clasp the stems so tightly that the plants appear leafless. Inconspicuous flowers are produced on jointed pencil-like spikes that are usually red or purple-tinted.

Sea glasswort, S. *maritima*, is virtually identical to Virginia glasswort in appearance but has a lower stature—reaching 25 centimetres—and is commonly red-tinted even in summer.

Saltwort or tumbleweed, *Salsola kali*, is a multiple branching annual found along sandy shorelines of the province. Plants are superficially similar to glasswort when young but have small spiky linear leaves. Tiny inconspicuous flowers, surrounded by papery, often pink-tinted bractlets, are produced in the upper leaf axils. When seeds are mature, the plant breaks away at ground level and rolls away on the wind, dispersing its seeds.

Sea-blite, *Suaeda maritima*, is a common annual along coastal mudflats. It has fleshy alternate linear leaves on multi-branching stems up to 30 centimetres long. Tiny pale green flowers are solitary or in clusters of two or three among the leaf axils.

Top: Virginia glasswort has green coral-like stems. Middle: Saltwort has spiky linear leaves. Bottom: Sea-blite has fleshy linear leaves and tiny axillary flowers.

Buckwheat family / Polygonaceae

Sheep sorrel

Introduced Species

Rumex acetosella

Oseille, surette, sourweed, field sorrel

VITAL STATISTICS

Maximum height: 40 centimetres
Flowering season: June to October

HABITAT: Sheep sorrel is a European species commonly found along roadsides and in fields, pastures, and acidic barren soils throughout New Brunswick.

CHARACTERISTICS: Sheep sorrel has a mat-like habit and produces abundant underground rhizomes, allowing it to rapidly spread. Leaves are partially evergreen and form overwintering tufts. Lance-shaped with two diverging basal lobes, leaves are hairless, smooth-edged, and dark green, sometimes with a red tint. Throughout summer and early fall, wiry stems arise to 25 centimetres, rarely to 40 centimetres, high. Stem leaves are alternate.

Minute inconspicuous flowers are produced in narrow upright panicles. They are reddish- to yellowish-green with individual nodding flowers. Close examination reveals six sepals but no petals. Plants are monoecious. Seeds are produced within brown papery sepals.

Garden sorrel, *R. acetosa*, has similar, but larger, flowers, on stems reaching 100 centimetres in length. Plants are tap-rooted and produce a clump of long petioled, oblong, lance-shaped to elliptical basal leaves with heart-shaped bases. Erect stems are longitudinally ribbed. Stem leaves are alternate and clasp the stem. Flowers are reddish-green, and the developing heart-shaped papery fruit change from pink to brown. Both species have edible leaves with a zesty sour taste.

Top: Sheep sorrel's red-tinted flowers are in narrow upright panicles. Middle: The lance-shaped leaves of sheep sorrel have two diverging basal lobes. Bottom: Garden sorrel looks like a larger version of sheep sorrel.

Buckwheat family / Polygonaceae

Curled dock

Rumex crispus

Patience crépue, reguette, curly dock, yellow dock

Introduced Species

VITAL STATISTICS

Maximum height: 160 centimetres
Flowering season: June to September

HABITAT: Curled dock is a European species common along roadsides and in waste places and pastures throughout New Brunswick. Less commonly, it may be found along coastal beaches.

CHARACTERISTICS: Curled dock produces a clump of leaves that arises from a thick taproot. Alternate hairless leaves are lance-shaped with smooth but curly or waved edges. Summer foliage is green, often with a red to brown tint. Basal leaves are evergreen, often strongly tinted red in winter.

Stiff upright stems are ribbed, usually unbranched, and reach 90 to 160 centimetres in length. Flower stems consist of a dense panicle of upright racemes with numerous whorls of small yellowish- to reddish-green flowers. Flowers have three inner and three outer sepals and are either bisexual with three styles and six stamens, or female with just three styles. They have no petals. Seed capsules are dark brown, papery, smooth-edged, and ovate to triangular in outline. Each capsule encloses a single seed.

Blunt-leaved dock, *R. obtusifolius*, a common European weed, often co-occurs with curled dock. It is distinguished by its wider, flatter leaves whose bases are distinctly heart-shaped. Its flowering racemes are narrower and its seed capsule edges have ragged teeth.

Native greater water dock, *R. brittanica* (also known as *R. orbiculatus*), is distinguished by its preference for wet soils along ponds, swales, and swamps.

Top: Curled dock flowers are in a terminal panicle of narrow racemes. Middle: Blunt-leaved dock has heart-shaped leaf bases. Bottom: Blunt-leaved dock's seed capsule edges have ragged teeth.

Coastal

Disturbed

Buckwheat family / Polygonaceae

Seabeach dock

Native Species

Rumex pallidus

Patience pâle, seaside dock, pale willow dock, white dock

VITAL STATISTICS
Maximum height: 100 centimetres
Flowering season: June to September

HABITAT: Seabeach dock is found along coastal beaches, gravels, and brackish marshes throughout New Brunswick, primarily along the Northumberland coast.

CHARACTERISTICS: Seabeach dock is a clumping hairless plant with wide-spreading stems. Its alternate thick and leathery leaves are linear to lance-shaped, 10 to 20 centimetres long, with smooth or undulating edges. Plants tend to be prostrate along the ground.

Flowers, produced terminally or at the ends of axillary branches, are arranged in a loose panicle of racemes and in whorls of 10 to 20 along the racemes. Individual flowers are 0.6 to 0.8 centimetres wide, with six pale green sepals. The globular seed capsule, or valve, is commonly pale green to white. It has three wings and the tips of the wings barely exceed beyond the valve.

Willow-leaved dock, *R. triangulivalvis* (also known as *R. salicifolius*), may grow in coastal habitats but is most commonly found in waste places and disturbed sites with rich soil. Leaves are thin-textured and a paler yellow-green than those of seabeach dock. Flowers are similar to those of seabeach dock, but the valve is brown and the tips of the three wings extend well beyond the developing valve. Willow-leaved dock plants are usually more upright than seabeach dock.

Top: Seabeach dock has prostrate stems. Middle: Seabeach dock has smooth narrow leaves and terminal racemes with globular seed capsules. Bottom: Willow-leaved dock has narrow leaves but upright stems.

Coastal

Spurge family / Euphorbiaceae

Native Species

Wormseed spurge

Euphorbia vermiculata (formerly *Chamaesyce vermiculata*)

Euphorbe vermiculée, hairy-stemmed spurge, wormseed sandmat, hairy sandmat

VITAL STATISTICS

Maximum height: 40 centimetres

Flowering season: July to October

HABITAT: Wormseed spurge is widely scattered on gravelly shorelines, along dry sandy roadsides, and in waste places. It is most common along the Saint John River watershed.

CHARACTERISTICS: Wormseed spurge is a creeping matted plant. The red-tinted stems are covered in long white hairs. The 0.5- to 1.5-centimetre-long finely toothed opposite elliptical to ovate leaves have short petioles. The plant exudes white sap when cut.

The insignificant green flowers are solitary or in small cymes among the upper leaf axils. The pistil, which is the most noticeable portion of the flower, is globular with three forked styles.

Seaside spurge, *E. polygonifolia*, is extremely rare and usually confined to sand dunes and shorelines above the high-tide mark along the Northumberland coast. Its waxy blue- or grey-green leaves are lanceolate and smooth-edged. The hairless, often red-tinted stems are not as dark as wormseed spurge stems.

Spotted spurge, *E. maculata*, is also extremely rare and known only in Charlotte and York counties. Plants are generally larger than those of wormseed spurge and seaside spurge, with 3.5-centimetre-long oblong leaves. Young leaves are covered in fine pubescent hairs that are lost on older leaves. Generally, each leaf has a central purple blotch. Stems are hairy and often tinted red. The flowers, which are 0.3 centimetres in diameter, appear to have four dirty white petals (not true petals) and a central green globular pistil.

Top: Wormseed spurge's red-tinted stems are covered in long white hairs. Middle: Seaside spurge has blue- or grey-tinted lance-shaped foliage. Bottom: Spotted spurge leaves often have a distinct red blotch.

Parsley family / Apiaceae

Black snakeroot

Native Species

Sanicula marilandica

Sanicle de Maryland, Maryland sanicle

Mixed Forest

Deciduous Forest

VITAL STATISTICS

Maximum height: 120 centimetres

Flowering season: June to August

HABITAT: Black snakeroot grows throughout New Brunswick along shores and in thickets, meadows, and open woods.

CHARACTERISTICS: Black snakeroot is a clumping plant with mostly solitary stems which are 40 to 120 centimetres tall that arise from a thickened crown. Basal leaves are either palmately five- to seven-lobed or palmately compound, with long petioles. Farther up the stems, the petioles gradually shorten until they are nearly stemless. Individual leaflets are elliptical with toothed edges, alternate, and hairless.

Stems terminate in a panicle of small (1- to 2-centimetre-diameter) rounded umbels which are composed of 15 to 25 minute greenish-white flowers. Individual flowers are either staminate or perfect; the latter has two distinctive long styles. The dry fruit are in clusters of three to eight and are tiny and ovate and densely covered in short hooked bristles.

Yellow snakeroot, *S. odorata*, a very rare species found in rich hardwood and alluvial forests near the Maine border of Carleton county, is similar to black snakeroot but its plants are shorter, reaching 75 centimetres, with yellow-green flowers.

Top: Black snakeroot produces a terminal panicle of small rounded umbels. Middle: Black snakeroot's upper leaves are palmately compound and nearly stemless. Bottom: Yellow snakeroot has yellow-tinted flowers.

Plantain family / Plantaginaceae

Spring water-starwort

Native Species

Callitriche palustris

Callitriche des marais, marsh water-starwort, water chickweed

HABITAT: Spring water-starwort is an aquatic plant scattered in slow-moving streams, quiet waters, and wet shores throughout New Brunswick.

CHARACTERISTICS: Spring water-starwort is an aquatic floating plant that may rarely be terrestrial if water levels drop enough to strand the plant. Usually the delicate stems arch and float along the water's surface. The small pale green leaves, which are generally less than 1 centimetre in length, are opposite or whorled, hairless, and smooth-edged. Leaves are widely spaced but crowded at the stem tips.

The flowers are solitary or in clusters of two or three in the leaf axils. Plants are monoecious, but the minute green flowers are so small as to be inconspicuous.

Large water-starwort, *C. heterophylla*, is as common as spring water-starwort in the province, and only subtly different. Large water-starwort tends to have rounder leaves with longer petioles and a deeper green colour, but this difference is not always consistent. The only true difference between the two species is the seed capsules: those of large water-starwort are as wide as they are long and lack thin wings along the margins; those of spring water-starwort are slightly longer than wide, with thin wings along the margins.

VITAL STATISTICS
Maximum height: n/a
Flowering season: May to October

Top: Terminal leaves are often crowded. Bottom: Delicate stems usually float on the water's surface.

Plantain family / Plantaginaceae

Common mare's-tail

Native Species

Hippuris vulgaris

Hippuride vulgaire, queue de cheval

VITAL STATISTICS
Maximum height: 25 centimetres
Flowering season: June to September

HABITAT: Common mare's-tail, an aquatic species, grows in shallow, often brackish, coastal pools and along damp shores and, less commonly, along pond/stream shorelines. It is found throughout New Brunswick but is scattered and localized.

CHARACTERISTICS: Common mare's-tail produces erect unbranched hollow stems that arise from a creeping underwater rhizome. Narrow hairless leaves are produced in whorls of six to 12 and reach up to 3 centimetres in length. Leaves have smooth edges, lack a petiole, and are reduced in size toward the top.

Minute inconspicuous green to purple flowers are produced in the upper leaf axils throughout the summer months.

Top: Inconspicuous purple flowers are in the leaf axils. Bottom: Unbranched stems produce whorls of narrow smooth leaves.

Introduced Species

Plantain family / Plantaginaceae

Common plantain

Plantago major

Grand plantain, broad-leaved plantain, whiteman's-foot

HABITAT: Common plantain, a European introduction, is commonly found in disturbed areas throughout New Brunswick.

CHARACTERISTICS: Common plantain forms a low rosette of evergreen round to egg-shaped leaves which are 5 to 20 centimetres in diameter and have three to five distinct ribs and petioles. Leaves are covered in short stiff hairs that impart a rough texture. Leaf edges are smooth but often wavy.

Plants produce several leafless flower stems that arise to 50 centimetres. Flowers are minute and green-brown and arranged in a rattail-like spike.

Narrow-leaved plantain, *P. lanceolata*, another widespread European introduction found in waste places, has upright narrow 10- to 20-centimetre-long lance-shaped basal leaves with distinct ribs, scattered hairs, and smooth edges. Similar to common plantain, narrow-leaved plantain flower stems are leafless, but their minute flowers are clustered into an ovate-shaped, rather than long and narrow, spike.

VITAL STATISTICS
Maximum height: 50 centimetres
Flowering season: June to September

Top: Common plantain has rattail-like flower spikes and a flat rosette of round leaves. Middle: Narrow-leaved plantain has an ovate-shaped spike of flowers. Bottom: Narrow-leaved plantain has a low rosette of lance-shaped leaves.

Plantain family / Plantaginaceae

Seaside plantain

Native Species

Plantago maritima

Plantain maritime, perce-pierre, passé-pierre, sea plantain, goosetongue

VITAL STATISTICS
Maximum height: 30 centimetres
Flowering season: June to September

HABITAT: Seaside plantain is a conspicuous species found along rocky to sandy coastal shorelines, cliffs, and headlands throughout New Brunswick. More rarely, it may occur along roadsides in coastal communities.

CHARACTERISTICS: A tufted species, seaside plantain has basal upright smooth linear leaves that are succulent, evergreen, and salty when eaten. Younger plants often produce a flat rosette of leaves. Leaves range from deep green to almost brown.

The minute green-brown flowers appear on narrow leafless stems that reach 30 centimetres in height but are more commonly shorter. Flowers usually extend beyond the leaves. They are produced in a dense spike which resembles a rat's tail.

Top: The minute flowers are in rattail-like spikes.
Middle: Older plants often have a tufted appearance.
Bottom: Young plants often have a flat rosette of leaves.

Introduced Species

Aster family / Asteraceae

Common ragweed

Ambrosia artemisiifolia

Petite herbe à poux, ambroisie à feuilles d'armoise, annual ragweed, roman wormwood, hogweed, bitterweed

HABITAT: Common ragweed, an introduced European species, is encountered along disturbed roadsides, in meadows and waste places, and on cobble beaches throughout New Brunswick.

VITAL STATISTICS
Maximum height: 100 centimetres
Flowering season: August to September

CHARACTERISTICS: Common ragweed, a multiple branching annual species, produces rough-haired stems that reach 100 centimetres in height. Fern-like leaves are pinnately lobed to bipinnately compound, covered in fine hairs, and are opposite or alternate along the stem.

Individual small green flower heads are either male or female and the plants monoecious or dioecious. Female flowers are located in the upper leaf axils; male flowers are in terminal racemes.

Giant ragweed, *A. trifida*, a locally common European species found in waste places, it grows to 200 centimetres in height and has opposite, mostly tri-lobed leaves which are covered in short stiff hairs and have toothed edges. Small green flower heads are produced in terminal and axillary racemes. Both species cause hay fever.

Top: Common ragweed's male flower heads are in narrow racemes. Middle: Finely dissected common ragweed leaves are fern-like. Bottom: Giant ragweed has tri-lobed leaves.

Coniferous Forest | Mixed Forest | Barrens | Disturbed

Aster family / Asteraceae

Northern pussytoes

Native Species

Antennaria howellii subsp. *neodioica* (formerly *A. neodioica*)

Antennaire de Howell, Howell's pussytoes

VITAL STATISTICS

Maximum height: 25 centimetres
Flowering season: June to July

HABITAT: A common species, northern pussytoes is encountered in open woods and on dry meadows and rocky barrens throughout New Brunswick.

CHARACTERISTICS: Northern pussytoes forms a mat of rosettes. Flowering stems have alternate linear leaves. The basal leaves of trailing stems are 2 to 4 centimetres long and 1 to 2 centimetres wide and are ovate, spatulate to oblanceolate, and smooth-edged. Leaves are densely covered in white hairs, especially on the undersides, which impart a silvery hue to the foliage.

Wiry flower stems arise 10 to 25 centimetres and are topped by a corymb of several 0.5-centimetre-diameter flower heads. Individual flowers have a mass of tiny white or cream disc florets surrounded by cream, pale green, or light brown papery phyllaries.

Parlin's pussytoes, *A. parlinii*, is an extremely rare species found in a single site in each of Charlotte and Queens counties, most often in dry clearings, old pastures, and rocky embankments. Much larger than northern pussytoes, Parlin's pussytoes has low rosettes of grey-green basal leaves which are spatulate to obovate, 3 to 8 centimetres long, and up to 4 centimetres wide. Stem leaves are oblong to lanceolate.

Top: Flowers have brown-tinted papery-textured phyllaries. Bottom: The basal leaves are often spoon-shaped.

Introduced Species

Aster family / Asteraceae

Beach wormwood

Artemisia stelleriana

Armoise de stellar, dusty miller

HABITAT: Beach wormwood, a native of Japan and Russia, was introduced to New Brunswick as a garden ornamental. It is frequently seen along gravelly to sandy beaches and roadsides throughout the province.

CHARACTERISTICS: Beach wormwood forms a matted clump of leafy trailing stems. All parts are densely covered in white felted hairs, making the plant easy to identify. Alternate leaves have an obovate to spatulate outline and are pinnately divided with blunt lobes.

Flower stems are mostly upright and 20 to 70 centimetres in length, with a loose raceme of 0.6- to 0.9-centimetre-diameter flower heads.

Field wormwood, *A. campestris*, is more localized than beach wormwood. A low clumping plant, field wormwood is scattered along dry sandy and gravelly shores throughout New Brunswick. The pinnately divided, finely cut leaves are mostly basal and smooth or slightly hairy. In July and August, plants produce several reddish-purple stems, up to 25 centimetres in length and topped by a dense panicle of spike-like racemes. Individual flower heads are green and nodding.

VITAL STATISTICS

Maximum height: 70 centimetres
Flowering season: August to September

Top: Plants form clumps with trailing, leafy stems.
Middle: The pinnately lobed leaves are distinctly white and woolly; flowers are in loose narrow racemes.
Bottom: Field wormwood has finely cut basal leaves.

Coastal

Disturbed

Aster family / Asteraceae

Common wormwood

Artemisia vulgaris

Herbe Saint-Jean, armoise vulgaire, common mugwort

Introduced Species

VITAL STATISTICS

Maximum height: 150 centimetres

Flowering season: July to August

HABITAT: Common wormwood, a European introduction, is common in disturbed habitats throughout New Brunswick.

CHARACTERISTICS: Common wormwood has upright branched 50- to 150-centimetre-tall stems which are grooved and slightly woody at their base and often tinted reddish-purple. The ovate-outlined, pinnately lobed leaves are sparsely toothed along their edges. The upper leaf surface is smooth or has scattered white hairs; the lower is densely covered in fine white hairs.

Flowers are produced as a panicle of spikes. Individual flower heads, produced in small clusters along the spikes, are green and covered in grey-white hairs, lending them a distinct grey cast, which is especially noticeable before the flowers open.

Biennial wormwood, *A. biennis*, is a European biennial species found occasionally in waste places. In the first season, plants produce a low rosette of hairless pinnate to bipinnately lobed leaves. In the second season, an unbranched stem with alternate leaves arises to a height of 2 metres. Dense spikes or tight globular clusters of stemless small green flower heads are produced among the upper leaf axils.

Top: Common wormwood produces a panicle of narrow spikes. Middle: Common wormwood leaves are ovate in outline but pinnately lobed. Bottom: Biennial wormwood has unbranched stems and axillary flowers.

Aster family / Asteraceae

Native Species

Eastern burnweed

Erechtites hieraciifolius

Érechtite à feuilles d'épervière, American burnweed, pilewort

HABITAT: Eastern burnweed is fairly common in moist clearings and waste places, damp open woods, and old burn sites throughout New Brunswick.

VITAL STATISTICS
Maximum height: 70 centimetres
Flowering season: August to September

CHARACTERISTICS: Eastern burnweed is a rank-smelling bushy annual species. Stems are grooved and the sparsely hairy alternate leaves are lance-shaped to elliptical, and pinnately lobed with coarsely toothed edges.

Flowers are produced in open panicles, both terminal and from the upper leaf axils. Each flower head is cylindrical and up to 2 centimetres long with a central mass of small pale green disc florets. Ripe seeds have white plumes that are dispersed in the wind like those of dandelions.

Top: Individual flower heads are cylindrical with pale green disc florets. Bottom: Flowers are in open panicles.

Aster family / Asteraceae

Low cudweed

Gnaphalium uliginosum

Gnaphale des vases, marsh cudweed, mud cudweed

Introduced Species

VITAL STATISTICS

Maximum height: 20 centimetres
Flowering season: July to September

HABITAT: Low cudweed, a common European species, is found in disturbed areas, including gardens, throughout New Brunswick.

CHARACTERISTICS: An annual species, low cudweed forms a bushy, multiple branched plant which is 10 to 20 centimetres tall. Alternate leaves are linear and smooth-edged; both they and the stems are covered in white woolly hairs that give the plant a silvery appearance. Small clusters of light brown flower heads are produced in the upper leaf axils and at the branch tips.

Rabbit tobacco, *Pseudognaphalium obtusifolium* (formerly *G. obtusifolium*), is extremely rare and scattered in dry waste places in the southern half of the province. It is an annual that reaches 80 centimetres in height with non-branching stems, alternate lance-linear woolly leaves, and flat-topped corymbs of dirty white bracted flowers in August and September.

Woodland cudweed, *Omalotheca sylvatica* (formerly *G. sylvaticum*), is a native species scattered in disturbed areas and old meadows. Like low cudweed, woodland cudweed is a perennial species with linear silvery green woolly leaves. It grows 40 to 60 centimetres tall, is unbranched, has small pale brown flower heads in the upper leaf axils, and has a spike-like tip.

Top: Light brown flower heads are among the upper leaf axils and branch tips of low cudweed. Middle: Rabbit tobacco has flowers in flat-topped corymbs.
Bottom: Woodland cudweed is unbranched and produces a spike-like arrangement of flowers.

Aster family / Asteraceae

Native Species

Rough cockleburr

Xanthium strumarium

Lampourde glouteron, cockleburr, common cocklebur

HABITAT: Rough cockleburr, found along gravelly to sandy beaches above the high-tide line, is occasionally observed in cultivated fields or waste places. It is widely dispersed in New Brunswick, but can be locally common.

CHARACTERISTICS: Rough cockleburr is a sprawling annual with roughly hairy stems and leaves. The alternate long petioled leaves are up to 12 centimetres wide, maple leaf-shaped, and palmately lobed with sharp teeth.

Monoecious petal-less flowers are produced in compact axillary clusters and terminal spikes. Green seed capsules, which turn light brown with age, are burr-like, ovate with many hooked spines, with two stout teeth at the tip, and often have glandular hairs. They mature when they are 2 centimetres in length.

VITAL STATISTICS
Maximum height: 60 centimetres
Flowering season: August to September

Top: Small female flowers are in the leaf axils.
Middle: Leaves are maple-like in outline.
Bottom: Burr-like female fruit are covered in hooked spines.

Coastal

Disturbed

Pondweed family / Potamogetonaceae

Pondweed

Potamogeton species

Potamot

Native Species

VITAL STATISTICS
Maximum height: n/a
Flowering season: July to September

HABITAT: Pondweed, of which there are 20 species in New Brunswick, is an aquatic plant that grows in the shallow waters of streams, rivers, ponds, and lakes. Some species prefer flowing water; others prefer still water. Some require acidic water; others are restricted to alkaline water.

CHARACTERISTICS: Due to the large number of similar species of pondweed, they are described here as a group. Some species are entirely submerged, in which case their leaves are thin and translucent. Others have both submerged and floating leaves. The latter are more leathery, with smooth edges. The entire plant is hairless. Depending on the species, leaf shape can vary dramatically from ovate to linear. Leaves, alternate on thin rooting rhizomes, vary from bright green to purple-brown.

Minute flowers are produced on a short spike that rises just above the water's surface. Green to brown, they are composed of four sepals, four anthers, and a short thick style.

Top: Spike-like flowers are held just above the water's surface. Middle: Stems that reach the surface produce floating leaves. Bottom: Some species of pondweed have purple-brown-tinted leaves.

Arrowgrass family / Juncaginaceae

Seaside arrowgrass

Triglochin maritima

Troscart maritime, arrowgrass

Native Species

HABITAT: Seaside arrowgrass inhabits saltwater marshes and, rarely, inland freshwater calcareous marshes and shores throughout New Brunswick. It is often partially submerged.

CHARACTERISTICS: Seaside arrowgrass is a slender upright plant which forms grass-like clumps. The linear fleshy leaves arise directly from the base of non-stoloniferous plants. Leaves are smooth-edged and hairless. The leafless flower stalks produce blooms in a narrow dense spike. Individual flowers are tiny and green with six nondescript tepals. The seed capsules resemble rice grains.

The uncommon marsh arrowgrass, *T. palustris*, is essentially confined to coastal regions. This species is much like seaside arrowgrass in appearance but is stoloniferous with narrow seed capsules.

VITAL STATISTICS
Maximum height: 70 centimetres
Flowering season: June to July

Top: The tiny flowers are in narrow spikes. Middle: Seaside arrowgrass produces grass-like clumps. Bottom: Seed capsules resemble rice grains.

Wetlands

Coastal

Sweetflag family / Acoraceae

American sweetflag

Native Species

Acorus americanus

Acore d'Amérique, sweetflag

VITAL STATISTICS
Maximum height: 80 centimetres
Flowering season: June to August

HABITAT: American sweetflag is locally common in marshes and along slow-moving streams and pond margins throughout New Brunswick; it is uncommon in the north and northwestern regions of the province.

CHARACTERISTICS: American sweetflag is a grass-like aquatic plant with a thick rhizome. Bruised or cut stems and leaves emit a citrus-like fragrance. The hairless toothless leaves are basal and linear, overlapping at their base, and resemble iris leaves.

Flowers are minute and brownish-green and are spirally arranged on a finger-like spadix which is 3 to 7.5 centimetres long. The solitary spadix appears laterally on the sides of leaf-like stems. Close examination of individual flowers reveals six tepals (petals and sepals look alike), six stamens, and a single pistil. The fruiting spadix bears leathery tan-green berries when mature.

Top: Flowers are in a finger-like spadix.
Bottom: The linear leaves are similar to those of irises.

Native Species

Arum family / Araceae

Jack-in-the-pulpit

Arisaema triphyllum

Petit prêcheur, Indian turnip

HABITAT: Jack-in-the-pulpit inhabits shady rich damp woods and swamps throughout the province.

CHARACTERISTICS: Jack-in-the-pulpit has non-branching stems that arise from a turnip-shaped tuber. Each tuber produces one or two trifoliate or, rarely, palmate leaves whose petioles reach 30 to 100 centimetres in length. The hairless leaflets are ovate with smooth edges.

Plants produce a single spathe that arises between two leaves. The spathe is boldly striped in green, white, and purple-brown or just green and white in the variety *viride*. The hood of the spathe arches forward to partially hide the purple spadix within. The variety *stewartsonii* has a ridged hood that makes it more strongly reflexed than that of other varieties. In late summer, the spadix produces a cluster of orange-red berries. All parts of the plant are poisonous if ingested.

VITAL STATISTICS
Maximum height: 100 centimetres
Flowering season: Mid-May to early July

Top: The spathe is boldly striped white, green, and purple-brown. Middle: Leaves are usually trifoliate. Bottom: In late summer, the spadix produces a cluster of orange-red berries.

Arum family / Araceae

Eastern skunk cabbage

Native Species

Symplocarpus foetidus

Tabac du diable, chou puant, skunk cabbage, swamp cabbage

VITAL STATISTICS
Maximum height: 60 centimetres
Flowering season: April to May

HABITAT: Eastern skunk cabbage is very rare and primarily confined to southwestern New Brunswick. It is found in the swampy woods and wet alder thickets of Digby and Yarmouth counties.

CHARACTERISTICS: Eastern skunk cabbage is unmistakable: its large 30- to 60-centimetre-long heart-shaped leaves are basal, hairless, smooth-edged, and leathery.

This plant is among the earliest wildflowers to bloom in New Brunswick. In April to May, plants produce nearly stemless 10- to 15-centimetre-high green spathes heavily streaked with purple-brown. The spathes, which arise barely above the mud surface, emit a strong skunk-like odour. Within the spathe is a yellow-green or purple-tinted spadix, which later produces a rough, grey-brown fruit containing a cluster of pea-sized seeds. Plants flower several weeks before the leaves emerge. The flowers actually release heat, which allows them to literally melt through late-lying snow.

Eastern skunk cabbage's contracting roots push the plants deeper into the mud each season: they essentially grow down- rather than upward. All parts of the plant are poisonous if ingested.

Top: The nearly stemless spathes are heavily streaked purple-brown. Bottom: Eastern skunk cabbage produces large clumps of heart-shaped leaves.

Figwort family / Scrophulariaceae

Lance-leaved figwort

Scrophularia lanceolata

Scrofulaire lancéolée, American figwort

Native Species

HABITAT: Lance-leaved figwort, an uncommon native found in partly shaded thickets, open woodlands, and old meadows, is scattered along the Fundy coast and the western counties.

VITAL STATISTICS
Maximum height: 200 centimetres
Flowering season: June and July

CHARACTERISTICS: Lance-leaved figwort forms an upright clump of several unbranched stems. Lance-shaped to elliptical leaves, up to 20 centimetres in length, are opposite and sharply toothed. The main stem is square in cross-section and may be slightly hairy when young but becomes smooth with age. The leaves are also hairless. The entire plant is rank-smelling when bruised.

The flowers are produced in a cluster of loose cymes, which combine in a terminal open panicle. Individual flowers are distinctly tubular in outline with five rounded green to brown-tinted petals. The two upper petals are projected forward; the two lateral petals are short and round; and the lowermost petal is drooping and reflexed. The base of the flower is rounded and globular. Three of the four stamens are hidden within the flower; the fourth projects outward. This fourth stamen is sterile and yellow-green. Seed capsules are teardrop-shaped and often brown-tinted.

Knotty figwort, *S. nodosa*, is a European introduction distinguished from lance-leaved figwort by a projecting chocolate brown sterile stamen and its leaf edges, whose teeth are more rounded than those of lance-leaved figwort. It is rare and found in disturbed areas primarily in Saint John and Kings counties.

Top: Tubular flowers are produced in open panicles. Middle: Leaf edges are sharply toothed. Bottom: Knotty figwort has leaves with more rounded teeth.

Broomrape family / Orobanchaceae

Beechdrops

Native Species

Epifagus virginiana
Épifage de Virginie

VITAL STATISTICS

Maximum height: 45 centimetres
Flowering season: August to October

HABITAT: Beechdrops is restricted to beech forests throughout New Brunswick.

CHARACTERISTICS: Beechdrops parasitizes the roots of American beech, *Fagus americana*. The plant lives for years underground, but, when conditions are optimal, it sends up branched brown to maroon stems that contain many narrow spikes of flowers.

The flowers are in two forms: the lower flowers on each spike are fertile, tiny, and bud-like in shape; the upper 1-centimetre-long tubelike flowers are sterile. The tubes end in four lobes and appear light tan to maroon-brown, but closer examination reveals them to be cream with maroon-purple stripes. The overall brown appearance of the plants causes them to be easily overlooked.

American cankerroot, *Conopholis americana*, is another parasitic relative that is rare in the oak forests of southern Nova Scotia. Overall, this plant is yellow-brown and its shape is similar to that of a cone of an eastern white pine, *Pinus strobus*. American cankerroot has stout fleshy stems which are 10 to 25 centimetres long and covered in brown scales. From April through June a cream-coloured tubular 1.5-centimetre-long flower emerges from the axils of each scale.

Top: Beechdrops' tubelike upper flowers are white with maroon-purple stripes. Middle: Beechdrops' brown stems are leafless and easily overlooked. Bottom: American cancerroot plants are cone-like.

Native Species

Orchid family / Orchidaceae

Early coralroot

Corallorhiza trifida

Corallorhize trifide, pale coralroot, northern coralroot

HABITAT: Early coralroot inhabits moist shady woodlands throughout New Brunswick.

CHARACTERISTICS: Early coralroot is a leafless saprophytic species. The smooth yellow to green stem arises 10 to 20 centimetres in height, exceptionally to 30 centimetres.

Flowers are produced in a loose raceme containing three to 15 flowers. Individual flowers are green, sometimes tipped in brown, and are up to 1 centimetre in diameter. The dorsal sepal and lateral petals are angled upward and outward; the lateral sepals are arched downward. The lip is white, variously spotted with purple at its base.

Spotted coralroot, *C. maculata*, which prefers dry old-growth forests, may reach 50 centimetres in height and has reddish-purple stems. Up to 35 brownish-red flowers are produced per stem, and bloom in July. Like early coralroot, the lip of spotted coralroot is also white but more distinctly spotted purple-red. It is less common than early coralroot but still widely distributed in the province.

VITAL STATISTICS
Maximum height: 20 centimetres
Flowering season: May to June

Top: The green flowers of early coralroot have white lips with a few fine spots. Middle: Spotted coralroot has brownish-red flowers whose lips are white with purple-red spots. Bottom: Spotted coralroot has red-tinted leafless stems.

Orchid family / Orchidaceae

Frog orchid

Native Species

Dactylorhiza viridis (formerly *Coeloglossum viride*)

Orchis à longues bractées, orchis grenouille, bracted green orchid

VITAL STATISTICS
Maximum height: 35 centimetres
Flowering season: July to August

HABITAT: Frog orchid is rare and localized in New Brunswick. It inhabits open woodlands, turfy shores, and damp meadows, usually in calcareous areas.

CHARACTERISTICS: Frog orchid is a narrow upright plant with up to six lance-shaped to elliptical leaves, which are hairless with smooth edges. The alternately arranged leaves are reduced in size up the stem until they become conspicuous 2-centimetre-long bracts at the base of each flower.

Flowers are produced in a loose cylindrical spike. The 1- to 1.5-centimetre-wide flowers are green. The tongue-like lip is up to 1 centimetre long and often suffused red or brown. The lip ends in three lobes—two larger outer lobes and a smaller middle lobe. The sepals and lateral petals form a hood-like structure above the lip. The nectar spur is short and indistinct.

Top: Flowers have a tongue-like lip.
Bottom: The narrow upright plants have slender smooth leaves that become reduced in size up the stem.

Orchid family / Orchidaceae

Broad-leaved helleborine

Epipactis helleborine

Epipactis petit-hellébore, eastern helleborine, common helleborine

Introduced Species

HABITAT: Broad-leaved helleborine, a European orchid, has been naturalized in isolated areas across New Brunswick. It grows in deciduous and mixed forests as well as in open meadows, especially in calcareous areas.

VITAL STATISTICS
Maximum height: 80 centimetres
Flowering season: July to August

CHARACTERISTICS: Broad-leaved helleborine is a narrow upright leafy orchid with three to 10 ovate, elliptical, or lance-shaped leaves. Leaves, which have distinct parallel veins and smooth edges, are covered in soft downy hairs. Leaves clasp the stem and are alternate along its length.

Fifteen to 30 flowers are produced in a loose one-sided raceme; each flower is subtended by a narrow leafy bract which is 2 to 6 centimetres in length. Individual flowers are green, often suffused with purple, and are about 2 centimetres in diameter. The lip is commonly white, variously tinted pink, and its inside base is dark purple-brown. Unlike similar orchids in New Brunswick, this species has no nectar spur.

Top: The lip's inside base is distinctly darkened.
Bottom: Flowers are in loose one-sided racemes.

Orchid family / Orchidaceae

Loesel's twayblade

Native Species

Liparis loeselii

Liparis de Loesel, bog twayblade

VITAL STATISTICS
Maximum height: 15 centimetres
Flowering season: July

HABITAT: Loesel's twayblade is rare in bogs, peaty meadows, calcareous fens, and along freshwater sandy shorelines throughout New Brunswick.

CHARACTERISTICS: Loesel's twayblade has greenish-yellow ridged stems. Plants produce two alternate leaves, which are lance-shaped to elliptical, smooth-edged, and shiny and clasp the stems.

Flowers are produced in a loose raceme of two to 25 flowers. Individual flowers are translucent and about 1 centimetre wide and vary from green to yellowish- or whitish-green. The unlobed lip is the most significant part of the flower's appearance: it is keeled like a boat. The sepals and lateral petals are narrow, and the sepals are typically curled under along their length. Flowers are often held horizontally. Overall, flowers have a ragged appearance.

Top: The translucent flowers have a keel-like lip.
Bottom: Each plant produces two alternate leaves.

Orchid family / Orchidaceae

Broad-leaved twayblade

Native Species

Neottia convallarioides (formerly *Listera convallarioides*)
Listère faux-muguet, broad-lip twayblade

HABITAT: Broad-leaved twayblade is an uncommon to rare orchid found in cool mossy glades, old-growth woodlands, and swampy shorelines, especially in calcareous areas. It is scattered throughout New Brunswick.

VITAL STATISTICS
Maximum height: 30 centimetres
Flowering season: June to August

CHARACTERISTICS: Broad-leaved twayblade commonly reaches 10 to 20 centimetres in height and, exceptionally, 30 centimetres. Each plant produces a pair of stemless, hairless leaves which are round to elliptical in outline. Smooth-edged leaves are held near the middle of the stem.

Flowers are produced in a loose raceme. Individual flowers are translucent, yellowish-green, and about 1 centimetre wide. Lateral petals and sepals are strongly reflexed. The lip, which is nearly 1 centimetre long, is projected forward and resembles an elongated upside-down heart. It lacks a nectar spur. The flower stem is covered in fine sticky hairs.

Auricled twayblade, *N. auriculata*, is also uncommon to rare in the province. It is distinguished from broad-leaved twayblade by its lip, which is more rectangular in outline with a cleft tip. The habitat of auricled twayblade is also very specific; it grows in mossy patches overlying calcareous sand among streamside alder beds.

Top: The lip is projected forward. Middle: Each plant produces a pair of leaves. Bottom: Auricled twayblade has a rectangular lip with a cleft tip.

Coniferous Forest

Mixed Forest

Wetlands

Orchid family / Orchidaceae

Heart-leaved twayblade

Native Species

Neottia cordata (formerly *Listera cordata*)

Listère cordée

VITAL STATISTICS
Maximum height: 20 centimetres Flowering season: June to August

HABITAT: An fairly common orchid in New Brunswick, heart-leaved twayblade inhabits shady, cool, mossy, swamps, bogs, and coniferous woodlands.

CHARACTERISTICS: Despite being the most common *Listera* species in the province, heart-leaved twayblade is often overlooked. Stems reach a length of 10 to 20 centimetres. A pair of 1- to 3-centimetre-long round to heart-shaped stemless leaves is located about halfway along the length of the stem. Leaves are hairless and smooth-edged.

Translucent flowers, produced in a loose to dense raceme, are each about 0.5 centimetres wide and pale green to purplish-brown. The distinct lip is widely forked like a snake's tongue. Flowers have no nectar spur, but the flower stem often has a few sticky hairs.

Southern twayblade, *N. australis* (fomerly *L. australis*), is extremely rare and has only been found in two locations in New Brunswick—Kents and York counties. The forked lobes of this species' longer lip hang down or cross rather than being wide-spreading as they are on *N. cordata*. Southern twayblade usually grows on mossy hummocks in black spruce bogs.

Top: Heart-leaved twayblade's distinct lip is forked like a snake's tongue. Middle: Heart-leaved twayblade produces a pair of round leaves. Bottom: The forked lobes of southern twayblade's longer lip hang down, rather than being wide-spreading.

Orchid family / Orchidaceae

Green adder's-mouth orchid

Malaxis unifolia

Malaxis unifolié, green malaxis

Native Species

VITAL STATISTICS

Maximum height: 30 centimetres

Flowering season: July to August

HABITAT: Green adder's-mouth orchid is found in wet habitats throughout New Brunswick, including bogs, swamps, alder thickets, and forest edges. Less commonly, it grows in coniferous woodlands. It is easily overlooked due to its small size.

CHARACTERISTICS: Green adder's-mouth orchid is a delicate hairless plant with a single ovate leaf located near the middle of the stem. Rarely, a second leaf clasps the stem.

The crowded flowers appear umbel-like when they first open but later extend to create a spike-like raceme. The earliest flowers are often held horizontally; later ones are more vertical. The flowers, each 0.3 to 0.5 centimetres in diameter, are green. The lip is distinctly three-lobed with two large rounded outer lobes and a smaller, pointed middle lobe. The threadlike petals are strongly recurved. Plants on exposed gravels are very compact, often less than 10 centimetres high, and are yellow-green.

White adder's-mouth orchid, *M. monophyllos* var. *brachypoda*, is extremely rare, currently only known to grow in one site in Gloucester county. It inhabits rotting logs in calcareous cedar swamps. The stem-clasping single elliptical to ovate leaf is held close to the base of the plant. The 0.3- to 0.5-centimetre-long yellow-green flowers are on a slender raceme. The widely spaced sepals and petals create a starlike effect. The lip, often pointing upward, does not have lobes as green adder's-mouth orchid does; rather, it is rounded at the base, tapering to an elongate central lobe.

Top: The crowded flowers of green adder's-mouth orchid appear umbel-like when they open. Middle: Each plant produces a single ovate leaf. Bottom: White adder's-mouth orchid has starlike flowers on narrow racemes.

Orchid family / Orchidaceae

Tall northern green orchid

Native Species

Platanthera aquilonis (formerly *P. hyperborea*)

Platanthère du nord, northern green bog orchid, leafy northern green orchid

VITAL STATISTICS

Maximum height: 60 centimetres
Flowering season: June to August

HABITAT: Tall northern green orchid, fairly common in New Brunswick, grows along roadsides and in open bogs, fens, damp woodlands, open seepages, and peaty barrens.

CHARACTERISTICS: Tall northern green orchid is a narrow erect plant with hollow stems that arise 10 to 60 centimetres from a thickened tuberous root. Leaves are alternate along the stem; the lowermost leaf may reach 20 centimetres in length, and the upper leaves gradually become smaller as they ascend the stem. Leaves are stemless, lance-shaped, hairless, and smooth-edged.

Individual flowers are small, each about 1 to 1.5 centimetres long, yellowish-green, and fragrance-free. Each flower is subtended by a distinct narrow green bract. The lateral petals and dorsal sepal form a hoodlike structure. The lip is elliptical to lance-shaped in outline. The nectar spur is narrow and 0.5 centimetres in length. Flowers are arranged in a dense cylindrical spike.

The similar Lake Huron or fragrant green orchid, *P. huronensis*, was once included with tall northern green orchid as *Platanthera hyperborea*. It often co-occurs with *P. aquilonis* but is distinguished by its whitish-green strongly clove-scented flowers. Robust plants may reach 100 centimetres in height.

Top: The lateral petals and dorsal sepal form a hoodlike structure over the narrow lip. Middle: Flowers are in dense cylindrical spikes. Bottom: Lake Huron green orchid is often more robust than tall northern green orchid.

Native Species

Orchid family / Orchidaceae

Club-spur orchid

Platanthera clavellata

Platanthère claviforme, green woodland orchid

HABITAT: Club-spur orchid is found among wet meadows, seepages, low woodlands, and peatlands throughout New Brunswick.

CHARACTERISTICS: Club-spur orchid is often overlooked but surprisingly common. Each plant generally produces a single elliptical hairless smooth-edged basal leaf which is 5 to 15 centimetres in length. Stem leaves are much reduced and alternate.

The flower stem is hollow and may reach 40 centimetres in height, although 10 to 20 centimetres is more common. Individual flowers are about 1 centimetre in length and pale green to yellowish-green. The nectar spur is club-shaped and about 1 centimetre in length. The lateral petals and the dorsal sepal form a hoodlike structure. The lip terminates in three lobes. Flowers are held in a moderately dense terminal spike.

Tubercled orchid, *P. flava*, has two or three smooth alternate lance-shaped to elliptical leaves. The largest leaf may reach 15 centimetres in length. Ten to 40 0.6-centimetre-wide yellow-green flowers are produced in a loose to dense terminal spike. Lateral petals and a dorsal sepal form an upper hood. Lateral sepals are wide-spreading, often arching backward, while the lip is tongue-like with two small lobes at its base and a distinct bump (tubercle) near the centre. A short 0.5- to 0.8-centimetre-long spur extends behind the lip. Flowers are sweetly fragrant. A narrow leafy bract is located at the base of each flower. This orchid is extremely rare, known only to grow in Sunbury County.

VITAL STATISTICS
Maximum height: 40 centimetres
Flowering season: June to August

Top: The nectar spur is club-shaped. Middle: Each plant produces a single basal leaf. Bottom: Flowers of tubercled orchid are in moderately dense narrow spikes.

Orchid family / Orchidaceae

Hooker's orchid

Native Species

Platanthera hookeri

Platanthère de Hooker

VITAL STATISTICS
Maximum height: 40 centimetres
Flowering season: June to August

HABITAT: Hooker's orchid is an uncommon orchid restricted to dry open mixed deciduous forests, preferably overlying limestone. It is widely distributed throughout New Brunswick.

CHARACTERISTICS: Hooker's orchid produces a pair of ground-hugging round to elliptical leaves, which are up to 15 centimetres long and hairless with smooth edges.

The flower stem arises between the leaves and reaches 30 centimetres in height. Flowers are produced in a loose raceme. Individual flowers are green to yellowish-green and about 2 centimetres wide. These fragrant flowers have a jaw-like appearance. The pointed dorsal sepal and narrow strongly decurved petals form the "upper jaw." The narrow lip is arched forward and upward to form the "lower jaw." Lateral sepals are strongly reflexed; the 1.5- to 2.5-centimetre-long nectar spurs point backward to downward.

Top: Flowers have a jaw-like appearance. Bottom: Each plant produces a pair of ground-hugging round leaves.

Orchid family / Orchidaceae

Native Species

Ragged fringed orchid

Platanthera lacera

Platanthère lacérée, green fringed orchid

HABITAT: Ragged fringed orchid appears in acidic moist meadows, clearings, open damp woodlands, and peat bogs in the southern and eastern regions of New Brunswick.

VITAL STATISTICS
Maximum height: 70 centimetres
Flowering season: July to August

CHARACTERISTICS: Ragged fringed orchid produces a smooth hollow stem that may arise to 70 centimetres, although 30 to 50 centimetres is more common. Plants have two to six alternate elliptical to lance-shaped leaves that become smaller as they ascend the stem. The lowermost leaf may reach 18 centimetres in length. The stemless leaves are hairless with smooth edges.

Plants produce a loose to dense cylindrical spike-like raceme of flowers throughout July and into August. The fragrant flowers are yellowish- to whitish-green and measure 1 to 1.5 centimetres in diameter. Each flower is subtended by a distinct narrow bract. The lip is divided into three deep lobes, each heavily fringed. The downward-curving nectar spur is 1 to 2 centimetres in length.

Top: The flower's lip has three heavily fringed lobes.
Bottom: Flowers are held in cylindrical spike-like racemes.

Orchid family / Orchidaceae

Blunt-leaved orchid

Native Species

Platanthera obtusata

Platanthère à feuille obtuse, small northern bog orchid, one-leaved rein orchid

VITAL STATISTICS
Maximum height: 30 centimetres
Flowering season: June to August

HABITAT: Blunt-leaved orchid is found in cool moist mossy coniferous woodlands and white cedar bogs throughout New Brunswick.

CHARACTERISTICS: Blunt-leaved orchid generally has a single 5- to 12-centimetre-long leaf near the base of the flower stem. This leaf is hairless and oblanceolate to spatulate in outline, with a smooth edge.

Flower stems are slender and may arise to 30 centimetres, although they are more commonly less than 20 centimetres in length. The stem is terminated by a loose spike of whitish- or yellowish-green flowers. Flowers are about 1 centimetre in length. Lateral petals and a dorsal sepal form a hook-like structure. The lip is narrow and 0.4 to 0.8 centimetres in length; the narrow nectar spur reaches similar lengths.

Top: The flower's lip is very narrow.
Bottom: Each plant has a single leaf near its base.

Coniferous Forest | Mixed Forest | Deciduous Forest

Orchid family / Orchidaceae

Lesser round-leaved orchid

Native Species

Platanthera orbiculata

Platanthère à feuilles orbiculaires, small round-leaved orchid

HABITAT: Lesser round-leaved orchid is an uncommon orchid scattered in moist shady mossy woodlands throughout New Brunswick.

CHARACTERISTICS: Lesser round-leaved orchid produces a pair of round basal leaves which may reach 10 centimetres in diameter. Leaves are relatively shiny, hairless, and smooth-edged.

Flowering stems, which arise between the two leaves, may reach 40 centimetres in height. Greenish-white flowers are produced in a loose raceme. Individual flowers are up to 2 centimetres wide. Sepals are rounded; lateral petals are more pointed and arch upward. The downward-pointing lip is narrow and up to 1.5 centimetres long. The nectar spur is commonly 2 to 2.5 centimetres long.

Large round-leaved orchid, *P. macrophylla*, is extremely rare and localized in New Brunswick. Its individual parts are slightly larger than the analogous parts of lesser round-leaved orchid; the distinguishing feature is the longer nectar spur, which reaches 3 to 4.5 centimetres in length.

VITAL STATISTICS
Maximum height: 50 centimetres
Flowering season: July

Top: Lesser round-leaved orchid flowers have rounded sepals and narrow lips. Middle: Each plant has a pair of round basal leaves. Bottom: Large round-leaved orchid flowers have very long nectar spurs.

Birthwort family / Aristolochiaceae

Canada wild ginger

Native Species

Asarum canadense

Gingembre sauvage, wild ginger, Canadian snakeroot

VITAL STATISTICS
Maximum height: 20 centimetres
Flowering season: May to June

HABITAT: Canada wild ginger grows in the shady calcareous deciduous forests of western and northwestern New Brunswick near the Maine and Quebec borders.

CHARACTERISTICS: Canada wild ginger forms a spreading groundcover with creeping rhizomes. When bruised, the rhizome has a ginger-like fragrance. Solitary or paired smooth-edged heart- to kidney-shaped basal leaves arise directly from the rhizome and may reach 15 centimetres in diameter. Leaves and their long petioles are covered in fine soft hairs.

Solitary flowers have three distinct triangular maroon petal-like sepals that often curl backwards. Flowers, up to 3 centimetres in diameter, are hidden beneath the leaves and generally lie on the ground. The rounded ovary at the base of the sepals is covered in white hairs. Flowers bloom in spring just after the leaves unfurl.

Top: Petioles are covered in long silky hairs; flowers have three maroon petals. Bottom: Plants are produced in low clumps with heart-shaped leaves.

Pink family / Caryophyllaceae

Procumbent pearlwort

Sagina procumbens

Sagine couchée, bird's-eye pearlwort, matted pearlwort

Native Species

HABITAT: Procumbent pearlwort inhabits moist, often shady, seepages, cliffs, fresh or brackish shorelines, and damp fields throughout New Brunswick. Abundant across the province, it can be a weed in damp garden soils.

CHARACTERISTICS: Procumbent pearlwort forms a low bright green evergreen mat. Plants are composed of both multiple rosettes and thin trailing stems up to 15 centimetres in length. Threadlike leaves on the trailing stems are opposite or whorled.

Axillary or terminal flowers are solitary and produced on thin 0.5- to 2-centimetre-long stems. The four or, rarely, five white short-lived petals are each 0.1 to 0.2 centimetres long, half the size of the green rounded sepals. The flowers. which are only 0.3 to 0.5 centimetres wide, appear green.

Knotty pearlwort, *S. nodosa*, is very rare in the province, found only in Charlotte and Gloucester counties. It has similar leaves but a less matted appearance than procumbent pearlwort. Stems and leaves are dark green or purple-tinted. Leaf axils often have minute rosettes that root into new plantlets. Flowers are 0.5 to 1 centimetre wide, slightly larger than those of procumbent pearlwort, and have five white petals which are twice the size of the pointed sepals. Knotty pearlwort inhabits coastal cliffs and gravelly to sandy shores, often overlying limestone. It flowers from July to September.

VITAL STATISTICS
Maximum height: 5 centimetres
Flowering season: June to October

Top: The green sepals of procumbent pearlwort are like petals. Middle: Procumbent pearlwort plants produce evergreen mats. Bottom: Knotty pearlwort looks similar to procumbent pearlwort but its flowers have five distinct white petals.

Saxifrage family / Saxifragaceae

American golden-saxifrage

Chrysosplenium americanum

Dorine d'Amérique, American watermat, water carpet

Native Species

Wetlands

VITAL STATISTICS
Maximum height: 15 centimetres
Flowering season: May to July

HABITAT: American golden-saxifrage is encountered in low-lying wet areas throughout New Brunswick.

CHARACTERISTICS: American golden-saxifrage is a semi-aquatic plant that forms a mat-like growth. Lower stems root as they creep over muddy surfaces. Succulent leaves are mostly opposite, less commonly alternate, and less than 2 centimetres long. They are generally stemless, round, and ovate or fan-shaped with shallowly toothed edges. The entire plant is hairless.

The tiny 0.3-centimetre-wide flowers are solitary at the ends of the upper branches. They are flat and a yellow- or purple-tinted green. The distinguishing features of the flowers are the four green sepals and the eight purple anthers. Each flower has a leaf held below it. The fruit is a tiny two-horned capsule.

Top: Flowers are distinguished by four green sepals and eight purple anthers. Bottom: Plants have trailing stems and usually opposite round leaves.

Rose family / Rosaceae

Native Species | Introduced Species

Thin-stemmed lady's mantle

Alchemilla filicaulis

Alchémille filicaulis, dew-cup, hairy lady's-mantle

HABITAT: Thin-stemmed lady's mantle is a European species found in old meadows of New Brunswick, primarily along the coasts of Charlotte, Saint John, and Restigouche counties.

VITAL STATISTICS

Maximum height: 50 centimetres
Flowering season: June to July

CHARACTERISTICS: Thin-stemmed lady's mantle is a mounding, leafy plant with long petioled basal leaves. Flowering stems produce alternately arranged short petioled to sessile leaves with paired stipules. Leaves are toothed, round in outline, and palmately lobed, commonly with nine lobes. Overall, lady's mantle has a plaited fan-like appearance. Leaves and stems are covered with silky hairs.

Flowers are tiny, less than 0.5 centimetres in diameter, and greenish-yellow with four sepals, four green bracts, and no petals. They grow in panicles at the ends of weak stems.

Top: Individual flowers have four green sepals and four narrow green bracts. Bottom: Leaves have a plaited fan-like appearance.

Evening primrose family / Onagraceae

Marsh seedbox

Native Species

Ludwigia palustris

Ludwigie palustre, marsh purslane, water purslane, common water-primrose

VITAL STATISTICS

Maximum height: 30 centimetres
Flowering season: Late June to September

HABITAT: Marsh seedbox is an aquatic plant found in shallow and clear but muddy-bottomed pools, lakes, and stream edges. It is most common in southern New Brunswick.

CHARACTERISTICS: Marsh seedbox has mostly non-branching stems rooted in the muddy bottoms of shallow pools. Stems are upright when under water but sprawl across the water's surface when they extend above the water. The leaves, each up to 4 centimetres long, are opposite, lance-shaped to ovate, and fleshy. They are hairless with smooth edges and often strongly tinted red, especially if growing in full sun.

The solitary flowers are sessile and produced in the upper leaf axils on stems held above the water. Each tiny flower is composed of four green triangular sepals. Petals are extremely small or absent.

Top: Solitary axillary flowers have four green sepals. Bottom: Red-tinted stems sprawl across the water's surface.

Gentian family / Gentianaceae

Native Species

Branched bartonia

Bartonia paniculata

Bartonie paniculée, twining screwstem, panicled screwstem

HABITAT: Branched bartonia, which occurs on wet acidic, peaty, or sandy soils, in very rare in New Brunswick and restricted to Charlotte, Kings, and Saint John counties.

VITAL STATISTICS

Maximum height: 40 centimetres

Flowering season: August to October

CHARACTERISTICS: Branched bartonia is a slender, often overlooked, annual. Plants are usually upright but at times are almost twining in nature. Tiny 0.1- to 0.25-centimetre-long scale-like leaves are yellow-green or purple-tinted, widely spaced, and alternate. They are linear to lanceolate but appear scale-like. The entire plant is hairless.

Flowers are produced in racemes. Individual flowers, which are up to 0.5 centimetres long, have four cream-coloured lance-shaped petals, often with purple tips. Flowers have four yellow or purple anthers and a 0.08- to 0.15-centimetre-long stigma.

Top: Branched bartonia flowers, each with four tiny cream petals, are in racemes. Bottom: Yellow bartonia is stiffly upright; flowers are yellow-green.

Buckwheat family / Polygonaceae

Fowler's knotweed

Polygonum fowleri

Renouée de Fowler

Native Species

Wetlands

VITAL STATISTICS	
Maximum height:	50 centimetres
Flowering season:	Mid-July to September

HABITAT: Fowler's knotweed is scattered but locally common along gravelly to sandy coasts of New Brunswick.

CHARACTERISTICS: Fowler's knotweed is a bushy native species that has mostly creeping, often zigzagging, stems. Leaves and stems are succulent and blue- to grey-green or purple-tinted. Leaves are alternate and elliptical to obovate, with smooth edges. They measure 1 to 3 centimetres in length and are two to three times as long as they are wide. All leaves are essentially the same size.

Produced in axillary clusters, flowers are tiny, just 0.3 to 0.6 centimetres wide, with five green petal-like sepals which have thin white to pink edges. Its coastal habitat preference distinguishes this species from others in the province.

Perhaps the most common introduced species found along roadsides and in waste places of the province is the annual common knotweed, *P. aviculare*. It is similar in appearance to Fowler's knotweed, but the leaves on its side branches are significantly smaller than those on the main stems.

Top: Tiny axillary flowers of Fowler's knotweed have five green sepals with white or pink-tinted edges. Middle: Fowler's knotweed's trailing stems often have a zigzag pattern. Bottom: Common knotweed flowers have deep pink sepals.

Native Species

Heath family / Ericaceae

One-sided wintergreen

Orthilia secunda (formerly *Pyrola secunda*)
Pyrole unilatérale, one-sided pyrola

HABITAT: One-sided wintergreen grows in woodlands throughout New Brunswick.

CHARACTERISTICS: One-sided wintergreen's creeping rhizomes form a groundcover in both shaded and sunny woodland areas. The leathery shiny evergreen leaves are hairless and elliptical to round in outline, have finely toothed or wavy edges, and reach 2 to 6 centimetres in length. Most leaves are basal and rosette-like but some may be found on the lower flower stems.

Flowering stems arise 7 to 20 centimetres and have a few small 0.2- to 0.4-centimetre-long alternate bracts. Flowers are produced in a strongly one-sided raceme of six to 20 greenish-white flowers. Each bell-like flower has five petals; the central style is straight and extends beyond the petals. Flowers rarely open fully.

Green-flowered pyrola, *Pyrola chlorantha*, also produces basal rosettes of leathery evergreen leaves from a creeping rhizome. It prefers coniferous forests. Round hairless leaves are 1.5 to 3.5 centimetres wide with long petioles; their edges may be smooth or have a few slightly rounded teeth. Flower stems arise to 7 to 20 centimetres in height and produce a loose cylindrical raceme of two to 13 flowers. Individual bell-like flowers have five waxy greenish-white petals. The style extends beyond the petals and appears hook-shaped: it curves downward and has an upward-turning tip.

VITAL STATISTICS

Maximum height: 20 centimetres
Flowering season: July

Top: One-sided wintergreen flowers are held in one-sided racemes. Middle: The round basal leaves of one-sided wintergreen are shiny and smooth. Bottom: Green-flowered pyrola has bell-like flowers with five waxy greenish-white petals.

Ditch stonecrop family / Penthoraceae

Ditch-stonecrop

Penthorum sedoides

Penthorum faux-orpin, Virginia stonecrop

Native Species

VITAL STATISTICS

Maximum height: 60 centimetres
Flowering season: July to August

HABITAT: Ditch-stonecrop grows along muddy and gravelly shorelines. Uncommon, it is found mainly in western and northern New Brunswick.

CHARACTERISTICS: Ditch-stonecrop is a clumping plant with many, usually unbranched, stems. Stems are often tinted red and may have longitudinal ridges as well as scattered hairs. The alternate leaves, up to 10 centimetres in length, are elliptical to lanceolate with finely toothed edges.

Flowers grow in a cluster of cymes; individual flowers are upward-facing along one side of the stem. Each flower, which is about 0.6 centimetres wide, is composed of five green sepals, 10 yellow-green to pale yellow stamens and five styles, but no petals. Developing seed capsules are five-angled, five-beaked, starlike, and usually red-tinted.

Top: Green-sepaled flowers are upward-facing along the upper side of the stems. Middle: Leaves are lance-shaped and the stems are often red-tinted. Bottom: Seed capsules are star-like and often red-tinted.

Native Species

Saxifrage family / Saxifragaceae

Naked mitrewort

Mitella nuda

Mitrelle nue, naked bishop's-cap, bare-stemmed bishop's-cap

HABITAT: Naked mitrewort inhabits mostly cool mossy coniferous forests but is occasionally found in mixed or hardwood forests. It occurs throughout New Brunswick.

CHARACTERISTICS: Naked mitrewort forms small clumps of evergreen basal rosettes that arise from threadlike rhizomes. The 2- to 5-centimetre-wide leaves are heart-shaped with rounded teeth and scattered stiff hairs. This plant is often overlooked as it is mixed among other woodland wildflowers.

Thin wiry flower stems, each 3 to 20 centimetres long, produce a loose raceme of two to 13 minute flowers. Each flower is only 0.4 centimetres wide and has five rounded green sepals. Petals are unmistakable and deeply divided into four pairs of threadlike lobes, which gives them an antennae-like appearance.

VITAL STATISTICS
Maximum height: 20 centimetres
Flowering season: June to July

Top: The unmistakable petals are deeply divided into four threadlike lobes. Middle: Flowers are produced in loose racemes. Bottom: Round leaves have rounded teeth.

Sandalwood family / Santalaceae

Northern comandra

Geocaulon lividum

Comandre livide, false toadflax

Native Species

VITAL STATISTICS

Maximum height: 25 centimetres
Flowering season: June to July

HABITAT: Northern comandra inhabits sterile acidic sites in open coniferous woodlands, barrens, or, more rarely, sphagnum bogs. It is uncommon and found mostly in the northern half of New Brunswick.

CHARACTERISTICS: Northern comandra produces several upright unbranched stems which are 10 to 25 centimetres in length. Thin-textured oblong leaves are bright green and alternate along the stem; they are often purple-tinted when they first emerge, turning purple by late summer. Leaves measure 1 to 3 centimetres in length, are hairless and smooth-edged, and have a short petiole.

Plants are usually monoecious. From the leaf axils partway up the stems, plants produce small clusters of two to four flowers on 1- to 3-centimetre-long stems. Individual flowers are 0.4 to 0.5 centimetres wide, green or tinted purple-brown, and star-shaped with five pointed sepals. Petals are small and undistinguished. The middle flowers of the cluster are usually female; the outer, male. Female flowers develop into dull orange-red berry-like fruit which is 0.5 to 0.8 centimetres in diameter. Remnants of the calyx create a crown-like projection at the end of each fruit. Although the fruit is juicy, it is not considered edible.

Northern comandra, a hemiparasitic plant, obtains some nutrients from neighbouring plants.

Top: The axillary starlike flowers have five green sepals.
Bottom: Female flowers develop into dull orange-red berry-like fruit.

Ginseng family / Araliaceae

Native Species

Bristly sarsaparilla

Aralia hispida

Salsepareille, aralie hispide, bristly spikenard, dwarf elder

HABITAT: Common throughout New Brunswick, bristly sarsaparilla occurs in open dry sandy barren areas and forest areas disturbed by clearing or burning.

CHARACTERISTICS: Bristly sarsaparilla is a shrub-like wildflower that grows up to 90 centimetres tall. Lower stems are slightly woody and covered in sharp bristles. Upper stems are branching, lack bristles, and are often red-tinted. Relatively large leaves are alternate, and bipinnate with ovate to elliptical sharply toothed leaflets.

Flowers are produced on long-stalked globular umbels which arise from the upper leaf axils and branch tips. Individual flowers are tiny, 0.3 to 0.5 centimetres wide, with five backward-curling greenish-white petals. These later develop into purple-black berries whose calyx remains as a crown-like tip. Although they are juicy, the berries are not considered edible.

American spikenard, *A. racemosa*, can reach 2 metres in height. It is found in calcareous rich hardwood forests. This species lacks bristles on its stems. Leaves are similar to those of bristly sarsaparilla, but the leaflets are more heart-shaped. Flowers are also produced in globular umbels but are terminal on the stems in the form of an elongate panicle. The large clusters of reddish-black berries are conspicuous in the autumn.

VITAL STATISTICS
Maximum height: 90 centimetres
Flowering season: Late June to August

Top: Bristly sarsaparilla flowers are in globular umbels. Middle: Flowers later develop into rounded clusters of black berries. Bottom: American spikenard has rounded umbels arranged in an elongate panicle.

Ginseng family / Araliaceae

Wild sarsaparilla

Native Species

Aralia nudicaulis

Salsepareille, aralie à tige nue, small spikenard

VITAL STATISTICS

Maximum height: 40 centimetres
Flowering season: May to June

HABITAT: Wild sarsaparilla occurs primarily in shady woodlands or, less commonly, on barrens throughout New Brunswick.

CHARACTERISTICS: Wild sarsaparilla grows on the forest floor. Each plant produces a single compound leaf. Although technically a basal leaf, it has a long stem that arises to 20 to 40 centimetres in height. The leaf is divided into three groups of three to five elliptical to ovate toothed hairless leaflets. Leaves are shiny and purple-brown when they emerge.

The leafless flower stem is solitary and arises directly from the base of the leaf. The flower stem is shorter than the leaf stalk, resulting in its being partly hidden; it is branched generally into three globular umbels, which are 3 to 5 centimetres in diameter. Individual flowers are only 0.3 to 0.5 centimetres wide with five strongly recurved greenish-white petals. Flowers later develop into blue-black berries whose calyx remains as a crown-like tip. Even though they are juicy, the berries are not considered edible.

Top: Flowers are in globular umbels. Middle: Leaves are shiny and purple-brown when they emerge. Bottom: Flowers later develop into rounded clusters of blue-black berries.

Parsley family / Apiaceae

American water pennywort

Native Species

Hydrocotyle americana

Hydrocotyle d'Amérique, marsh pennywort

HABITAT: American water pennywort is found in wet forest depressions and ditches and along the edges of streams, usually in partly shaded locations, throughout New Brunswick.

CHARACTERISTICS: American water pennywort forms creeping mats with thin trailing stems and rooting internodes. Leaves are alternate and round in outline, with six to 10 broad, rounded teeth or shallow, rounded lobes. Leaves measure up to 5 centimetres in width. All parts of the plant are hairless.

The five-petalled greenish-white flowers are inconspicuous. Two to seven flowers are arranged in small sessile umbels in the axils of the leaves. Individual flowers are only 0.2 centimetres in diameter.

VITAL STATISTICS
Maximum height: 20 centimetres
Flowering season: July to August

Top: American water pennywort produces tiny stemless umbels of green flowers in the leaf axils.
Bottom: American water pennywort's round leaves have shallow rounded teeth and lobes.

Parsley family / Apiaceae

Purple-stemmed angelica

Angelica atropurpurea

Angélique noire-pourprée, purple alexanders, great angelica

Native Species

VITAL STATISTICS
Maximum height: 3 metres
Flowering season: June to September

HABITAT: Purple-stemmed angelica is found along wet meadows, thickets, and streamsides primarily in the central and northern regions of New Brunswick.

CHARACTERISTICS: Purple-stemmed angelica is among the largest wildflowers in New Brunswick with plants reaching to 3 metres in height. The unbranched stems are smooth, hollow, and typically purple with a waxy appearance. The hairless alternate leaves are large—up to 60 centimetres wide—triangular in outline, and bi- or triternately compound. Leaflets are elliptical to ovate and coarsely toothed. Emerging upper leaves and flowers are enclosed in distinctly veined inflated basal sheaths.

Plants produce large spherical umbels of many small spherical umbellets, creating a starburst effect. Individual flowers have five green petals and are about 0.6 centimetres in diameter. These flowers produce brown rolled-oat-like fruit in late summer.

Very localized introductions of woodland angelica, *A. sylvestris*, occur along the Saint John River valley. This species also has purple stems, but the main umbel is hemispherical, the leaves less coarse and shinier than those of purple-stemmed angelica, and the flowers white or pale pink. The stems of the umbellets are finely pubescent.

Top: Purple-stemmed angelica plants produce large spherical umbels with many smaller umbellets. Bottom: Woodland angelica produces flowers in hemispherical umbels.

Deciduous Forest

Native Species

Barberry family / Berberidaceae

Blue cohosh

Caulophyllum thalictroides

Caulophylle faux-pigamon, grains à chapelet, papoose-root, squaw-root

HABITAT: Blue cohosh is uncommon to rare in rich deciduous and riverside forests, primarily in the western half of New Brunswick.

VITAL STATISTICS
Maximum height: 90 centimetres
Flowering season: April to early June

CHARACTERISTICS: Blue cohosh is a clumping plant with several upright non-branching stems. Emerging stems and leaves are smoky purple but turn blue-green as they mature. Stems and leaves are hairless. Non-flowering stems terminate in a single triternately compound leaf with nine long-stemmed ovate leaflets whose edges are smooth but have two to five rounded cleft lobes at their ends. Flowering stems have two compound leaves. The entire lower "leaf" is composed of a whorl of three triternately compound leaves, each essentially looking like a single leaf of a non-flowering plant. From the centre of this whorl arises the second "leaf," which is a single biternately compound leaf.

A loose panicle of five to 30 flowers arises from the base of the leaflets on the second leaf. Individual flowers are about 0.8 centimetres wide and composed of six thick petaloid sepals which vary from yellow- to brown- to purple-green. The six true petals are tiny and insignificant. Flowers also have six stamens and a single beak-like pistil. Each flower develops into a single seed, which is covered in a bright blue seed coat. The plant is toxic if ingested.

Top: Each flower has six petal-like sepals. Middle: Mature leaves have a blue-green tint. Bottom: Each flower develops into a single seed, which has a blue seed coat.

Asparagus family / Asparagaceae

Garden asparagus

Asparagus officinalis

Asperge commun, asparagus fern

Introduced Species

VITAL STATISTICS

Maximum height: 150 centimetres
Flowering season: June and July

HABITAT: Garden asparagus, a garden escape uncommon along roadsides and sandy meadows, is scattered throughout New Brunswick.

CHARACTERISTICS: Garden asparagus forms a clump of upright stems that arise from a thick rootstock. Smooth hairless stems are freely branching. Lower leaves are alternate and scale-like; upper leaves are linear, soft, and needle-shaped and are produced in whorls of three to six. The plant has a wispy shrub-like appearance.

Plants may be male, female, or bisexual. Individual flowers are about 0.5 centimetres in diameter, nodding, and bell-like with six tepals. Flowers may be green-white to yellow-green and solitary or in pairs among the upper leaf axils. Female and bisexual flowers develop into an orange 0.6- to 1-centimetre-diameter berry.

Top: Tiny flowers are bell-like. Middle: Flowers are in the upper leaf axils; leaves are tiny and needle-like. Bottom: In autumn, the flowers become red berries.

Native Species

Asparagus family / Asparagaceae

Indian cucumber-root

Medeola virginiana

Concombre sauvage, jarnotte

HABITAT: Indian cucumber-root is widespread but uncommon in open acidic hardwood forests throughout much of New Brunswick.

CHARACTERISTICS: Indian cucumber-root's non-branching stems arise from an underground white tuber that tastes like cucumber. Stems reach 60 centimetres in height and are covered in white woolly hairs when young; these often erode as the season progresses. If flowering, plants will produce two whorls of leaves: the lower with five to nine leaves; the upper, three to five smaller leaves. Non-flowering stems produce only a single whorl of leaves. Leaves are elliptical to ovate in outline, hairless, and smooth-edged, with three to five parallel veins. They lack petioles and attach directly to the main stem.

Flowers are produced in a stemless umbel of three to nine blossoms immediately above the upper whorl of leaves. The greenish-yellow lily-like flowers are 1 centimetre in diameter and have six green recurved tepals. Each flower has six stamens and three rather long purple recurved stigmas. Flowers are nodding at or just below the level of the upper leaf whorl and later develop into globular dark purple berries. Leaves in the upper whorl are often tinted wine red at their bases as the fruit develop.

VITAL STATISTICS

Maximum height: 60 centimetres
Flowering season: June to July

Top: Individual nodding flowers have six green recurved tepals. Middle: Leaves are produced in whorls. Bottom: Flowers develop into dark purple berries.

Asparagus family / Asparagaceae

Hairy Solomon's-seal

Native Species

Polygonatum pubescens

Sceau-de-Salomon pubescent, downy Solomon's-seal

Mixed Forest

Deciduous Forest

VITAL STATISTICS
Maximum height: 100 centimetres
Flowering season: June

HABITAT: Hairy Solomon's-seal is occasionally encountered in rich deciduous woodlands and shaded ravines and along riversides throughout most of New Brunswick except along the Northumberland Coast, where it is rare.

CHARACTERISTICS: Hairy Solomon's-seal produces non-branching stems that arise from a thick underground rhizome. Stems are smooth and arching. Alternate leaves are produced along the upper half of the stems. Leaves are waxy, smooth-edged, and lance-shaped to elliptical in outline and have several distinct parallel veins. On the underside of the leaves, fine soft hairs run along the veins. Leaves lack a petiole and attach directly to the main stem.

One or two, rarely three or four, tubular green or yellowish-green flowers are each 1 centimetre long and hang from the leaf axils on a forked flower stem. Each flower ends in six lobes. The six stamens are attached halfway down on the inside tube of the flower. In autumn, flowers develop into globular, fleshy blue-black berries, which may be mildly toxic.

Top: Tubular flowers hang from leaf axils. Middle: Leaves are produced on the upper sides of the arching stems. Bottom: In autumn, flowers develop into blue-black berries.

Bunchflower family / Melanthiaceae

Native Species

Green false hellebore

Veratrum viride

Tabac du diable, American false hellebore, Indian hellebore, Indian poke, white hellebore

HABITAT: Green false hellebore grows along rich low wet woodlands and damp riverside meadows in central and western New Brunswick.

CHARACTERISTICS: Green false hellebore produces a non-branching stout leafy stem that grows up to 2 metres in height. The stem may have long fine white hairs or be smooth. Leaves, which clasp the main stem, are elliptical to ovate in outline with smooth edges, parallel veins, and a pleated appearance. Leaves are usually hairless on the upper surface or may be covered in white hairs; undersides are pale with dense soft hairs. Leaves are strongly pleated and overlapping when they emerge in spring. When mature, they may reach 30 centimetres in length and 20 centimetres in width.

Flowers are produced in a series of spike-like racemes and, together, they form a terminal pyramidal panicle. Individual flowers are green to yellowish-green with six tepals and six distinct globular yellow stamens and a three-lobed stigma. Flower stems and tepal undersides are covered in soft hairs.

All parts of the plant are highly toxic.

VITAL STATISTICS
Maximum height: 2 metres
Flowering season: June to July

Top: Each flower has six green tepals whose backs are covered in soft hairs. Middle: Flowers are in spike-like racemes. Bottom: The pleated leaves clasp the unbranched stems.

Aster family / Asteraceae

Three-leaved rattlesnakeroot

Nabalus trifoliolata

Prenanthe trifoliolée, pattes d'oie, gall-of-the-earth

Native Species

VITAL STATISTICS
Maximum height: 120 centimetres
Flowering season: August to September

HABITAT: Three-leaved rattlesnakeroot is common throughout New Brunswick along roadsides and in open woods, barrens, and forested areas disturbed by clear-cutting or burning.

CHARACTERISTICS: Three-leaved rattlesnakeroot has upright non-branching green or purple-tinted stems. Plants are monocarpic, growing as a basal rosette for several years before flowering. After flowering, the plant dies. Long petioled basal leaves are deltoid, tri-lobed, or palmately lobed; lobes may be so deep that the leaves appear compound and may have a few large teeth. Lower leaves of blooming plants have similarly variable leaves; upper leaves are deltoid or elliptical and smooth-edged. The entire plant is hairless and, if cut, exudes a milky sap.

Nodding flowers are produced in an open panicle. Individual flower heads have seven to 10 phyllaries and a similar number of greenish-white or -yellow ray florets. Ripe seed heads resemble small cotton balls.

Tall rattlesnakeroot, *N. altissima*, can reach 2 metres in height and has tri-lobed to palmately lobed deltoid or ovate sharply toothed leaves. Each nodding flower head is composed of five phyllaries and five ray florets. It inhabits hardwood forests and is common throughout the province.

Purple rattlesnakeroot, *N. racemosa*, is uncommon, and primarily found in the Saint John River valley. Leaves are lance-shaped and coarsely toothed. Flowers are pink; phyllaries are covered in stiff hairs. Plants reach 150 centimetres in height.

Top: Three-leaved rattlesnakeroot has nodding flowers in open panicles. Middle: Tall rattlesnakeroot flowers have five ray florets. Bottom: Purple rattlesnakeroot has pink flowers and hairy phyllaries.

Native Species

Buttercup family / Ranunculaceae

Red baneberry

Actaea rubra

Pain de couleuvre

HABITAT: Red baneberry occurs in open mixed and deciduous woodlands. It is common throughout New Brunswick.

CHARACTERISTICS: Red baneberry is a clumping wildflower with several non-branching stems that reach 60 to 90 centimetres in length. Alternate leaves are bi- or triternate with ovate, sharply toothed, or lobed leaflets. Leaves have scattered hairs.

Flowers are produced in a dense conical terminal raceme. Individual flowers are white and about 0.5 centimetres wide and consist of three to five sepals, five to 10 petals, and a mass of stamens, lending them a fluffy look. Flowers later become glossy red berries that sit at the ends of narrow green pedicles. White-fruited forms, which occur occasionally, belong to the variety *neglectum*.

Doll's-eyes, *A. pachypoda*, prefers rich deciduous forests and river valleys. Although not as common as red baneberry, doll's-eyes is distributed throughout the province. Doll's-eyes and red baneberry are similar in appearance, but doll's-eyes' leaves are generally smooth. White berries with a black eye sit atop a thickened red pedicle.

The fruit of both species is mildly poisonous.

VITAL STATISTICS
Maximum height: 90 centimetres
Flowering season: Mid-May to June

Top: Flowers are in a dense conical terminal raceme. Middle: Red baneberry produces red berries later in the season. Bottom: Doll's-eyes produces white berries with a central black spot.

Coniferous Forest
Mixed Forest
Wetlands
Disturbed

Buttercup family / Ranunculaceae

Tall meadow-rue

Native Species

Thalictrum pubescens

Grand pigamonate, meadow-rue, king-of-the-meadow, muskrat-weed

VITAL STATISTICS
Maximum height: 250 centimetres Flowering season: July to August

HABITAT: Tall meadow-rue is found along river and pond shorelines and in damp thickets, wet woods, ditches, swamps, fens, and damp meadows throughout New Brunswick.

CHARACTERISTICS: Tall meadow-rue is among the tallest wildflowers in the province. Clumping plants produce both basal and stem leaves. Basal leaves have long petioles and each compound leaf is multi-divided into 15 to 27 stalked leaflets. Each leaflet is round with smooth edges and one to three rounded lobes. They are grey-green and smooth on top but may be finely pubescent on the lower surface. Leaves on the flower stalks are smaller than the basal leaves, sessile, and alternately arranged.

Plants are dioecious. Individual flowers lack petals but have four to five sepals that fall soon after the flowers open. The most noticeable part of the flower is the starburst of stamens (male) or pistils (female). Flowers are produced in a large panicle. Female flowers produce small spiky green to brown capsules.

Northern meadow-rue, *T. confine*, is uncommon along calcareous shores and mainly confined to the Saint John River system. It may reach 100 centimetres in height. Leaflets generally have five to seven lobes; the leaves below the flowers are short-petioled, not sessile. Northern meadow-rue flowers in late May to early June, much earlier in the season than tall meadow-rue does.

Top: Male flowers' starburst effect is created by many stamens; leaflets have one to three lobes. Middle: Close-up of female flowers. Bottom: Northern meadow-rue is distinguished by having leaflets with five to seven rounded lobes.

Rose family / Rosaceae

Canada burnet

Sanguisorba canadensis

Native Species

Sanguisorbe du Canada, herbe à pisser, bottlebrush, wild burnet

VITAL STATISTICS
Maximum height: 120 centimetres
Flowering season: July to September

HABITAT: Canada burnet is found in peaty or boggy soils, generally near the ocean. It is uncommon in New Brunswick, confined to Gloucester County and near the border between Saint John and Albert Counties.

CHARACTERISTICS: Canada burnet is a relatively large leafy wildflower that arises from a thick rootstock. Stems are generally non-branching. Alternate leaves are hairless, pinnately compound with seven to 15 leaflets, and up to 45 centimetres in length. Leaflets are elliptical, coarsely toothed, and 3 to 6 centimetres long. Leaf tips are rounded and the base heart-shaped. Leaves are often waxy, imparting a blue- to grey-green colour.

Flowers are produced in multiple long-stemmed white-flowered cylindrical spikes which vary from 5 to 20 centimetres in length. Individual flowers are small, lack petals, and are essentially a mass of stamens and pistils.

Top: Flowers are in dense cylindrical spikes.
Bottom: Plants produce large clumps with pinnate leaves.

Aster family / Asteraceae

Common boneset

Native Species

Eupatorium perfoliatum

Herbe à souder, boneset, thoroughwort

VITAL STATISTICS
Maximum height: 150 centimetres
Flowering season: August to September

HABITAT: Common boneset occurs on the margins of streams and wetlands and in ditches throughout much of New Brunswick.

CHARACTERISTICS: Common boneset is a stout wildflower with non-branching stems which reach 150 centimetres in length. The entire plant is covered in white hairs, particularly along the stems. Leaves are opposite and lance-shaped with finely scalloped edges and may reach 20 centimetres in length. The rugose pale green or yellow-green leaves are joined at the base; the stem passes through the centre.

Flat-topped loosely separated but dense corymbs of flowers are 5 to 20 centimetres wide. Corymbs have long stems and are produced both terminally and from the upper leaf axils. Each corymb is composed of multiple flower heads containing 10 to 40 tightly packed disc florets. They lack ray florets. Individual flowers are about 0.4 centimetres wide, with five small pointed petals and several elongate stamens. White or pink-tinted flower heads appear fluffy and are pleasantly fragrant.

Uncommon throughout the province, white snakeroot, *Ageratina altissima* (formerly *Eupatorium rugosum*), grows in cool moist woods and thickets. It may reach 150 centimetres in height and has opposite long petioled ovate leaves with sharp teeth and fine hairs. Minute white flowers, in a loose terminal panicle, bloom in August and September.

Top: Common boneset flowers are in flat-topped loosely separated but dense corymbs. Bottom: White snakeroot has paired ovate leaves with distinct petioles; flower panicles are smaller and looser than the boneset flower arrangements.

Aster family / Asteraceae

Arctic sweet coltsfoot

Native Species

Petasites frigidus

Pétasite palmé, Arctic butterbur, northern sweet coltsfoot

HABITAT: Arctic sweet coltsfoot is found in cool moist woodlands and clearings throughout New Brunswick.

VITAL STATISTICS
Maximum height: 60 centimetres
Flowering season: May to early June

CHARACTERISTICS: Arctic sweet coltsfoot is a perennial that spreads by creeping underground rhizomes, resulting in loose patches of colonies of plants. Leaves are basal and solitary. Each leaf is round in outline but palmately divided into five to seven deep lobes with coarsely toothed edges. When leaves emerge, they are covered in long white hairs; as leaves age, the upper surface becomes smooth, but the underside retains hairs. Leaves may reach 40 centimetres in diameter.

Flowers are produced before leaves emerge. Flower stems are leafless but have numerous green leafy bracts. When the flower first blooms, the stout stems are 10 to 20 centimetres high; they may elongate to 60 centimetres over time. Flowers are produced in globular clusters that elongate into a loose raceme. Fragrant flower heads are white or pale pink; each head is composed of many disc florets, which impart a fluffy look. Flowers are dioecious. Male flowers rapidly shrivel after blooming; females eventually produce numerous round seed heads that look like a miniature dandelion.

Top: Early flowers are in globular racemes. Middle: Less commonly, flowers may be pink. Bottom: The solitary flowers are palmately lobed with five to seven deep lobes.

Eriocaulaceae

Seven-angled pipewort

Native Species

Eriocaulon aquaticum

Ériocaulon, white buttons, common pipewort, duckgrass

VITAL STATISTICS	
Maximum height:	20 centimetres
Flowering season:	Mid-July to September

HABITAT: Seven-angled pipewort is an aquatic species found throughout New Brunswick growing in still, clear water to a depth of 100 centimetres.

CHARACTERISTICS: Seven-angled pipewort is an aquatic species with tufted grass-like foliage. The only portion typically seen above water is the upper stem and flower. Leaves, which vary from 2 to 12 centimetres in length, are linear, blade-like, and translucent. Each leaf has three to seven distinct parallel veins.

Each rosette sends up a hollow angled stem that extends above the water's surface by 5 to 20 centimetres. Flowers are produced at the terminus of this stem. Individual flowers, stigma, and anthers are grey-black but tepal tips are covered by white cottony hairs. The overall effect is a pale grey-white button-like flower cluster which is 0.5 to 1 centimetres in diameter.

Top: Flowers are in a button-like head. Bottom: Generally only the upper flower stem and flower are above the water.

Native Species

Arum family / Araceae

Wild calla

Calla palustris

Calla des marais, choucalle des marais, water arum

HABITAT: Wild calla is found in bogs and swamps and along marshy shorelines throughout New Brunswick.

CHARACTERISTICS: A colonial plant, wild calla has alternate smooth heart-shaped leaves arising from a thick rhizome that creeps at or near the water's surface. Petioles may be 30 centimetres in length; the leaf, up to 15 centimetres. Leaves have smooth edges, parallel veins, and a waxy texture.

Plants produce solitary white ovate pointed spathes which are 3 to 6 centimetres in length. Within the spathe is a cylindrical, thick 2-centimetre-long spadix which, later in the season, produces a dense cluster of red joined berries.

All parts of the plant are poisonous.

VITAL STATISTICS
Maximum height: 45 centimetres
Flowering season: June to July

Top: Wild calla produces its flowers in a solitary white spathe. Bottom: Plants produce smooth heart-shaped leaves.

Poppy family / Papaveraceae

Dutchman's breeches

Native Species

Dicentra cucullaria

Dicentre à capuchon

VITAL STATISTICS
Maximum height: 25 centimetres
Flowering season: May to early June

HABITAT: Dutchman's breeches, found in the shade of rich, often calcareous, deciduous woodlands, is widely distributed throughout New Brunswick.

CHARACTERISTICS: Dutchman's breeches is a spring ephemeral. Plants arise in early spring but become dormant by early summer. Their hairless blue-green fern-like leaves are ternately compound and arise directly from a corm-like underground tuber. Leaf petioles are often brown-tinted. Leaflet edges are smooth but deeply lobed.

Up to 12 nodding dainty flowers are produced along a slender arching raceme. Flower stems are leafless. Individual flowers, each about 2 centimetres wide, are distinctive in shape, appearing, as the name suggests, like a pair of Dutchman's breeches or the wings of a butterfly. The "breeches" or "wings" are bright white; the spurs at the bottom of the flower are yellow.

All parts of this plant are poisonous if ingested.

Top: Individual flowers are shaped like butterfly wings.
Bottom: The finely divided leaves are smooth and fern-like.

Introduced Species

Violet family / Violaceae

European field pansy

Viola arvensis

Pansée des champs, petite pansée, heart's ease, small wild pansy

HABITAT: European field pansy is a European species that is rare and scattered in recently disturbed areas of New Brunswick.

CHARACTERISTICS: European field pansy is a low matted leafy annual. Stems are prostrate to weakly ascending and multiple branching. Alternate leaves are elliptical to lanceolate with rounded teeth. Leafy stipules at the base of leaves are pinnately divided; the largest divisions have rounded teeth. Leaves and stems are hairless.

The long-stalked flowers are solitary from the upper leaf axils. Flowers are 1 to 1.5 centimetres wide with five creamy white (most common) to pale yellow or light purple petals. Two petals are held erect and two are lateral with long hairs on their inside bases. The lower petal is widest, with a short spur and a deep yellow, purple-striped patch at its base. The five narrow pointed sepals are almost as long as the petals. The seed capsule is globular with three longitudinal ridges.

Less common, and probably a garden escape, is Johnny-jump-up, *V. tricolor*. It looks much like European field pansy, but its leaves are larger and its flowers are 1.5 to 2.5 centimetres in diameter and more intensely coloured: upper petals are deeper shades of blue-violet, lateral petals lighter blue-violet, and the lower petal often entirely yellow. Lower and lateral petals may have purple stripes.

VITAL STATISTICS

Maximum height: 40 centimetres
Flowering season:

Top: Flowers have two erect petals, two lateral petals with hairy bases, and a lower lip with a deep yellow, purple-striped patch. Middle: Flowers arise individually from the upper leaf axils. Bottom: Johnny-jump-up has larger flowers with usually blue or purple upper petals.

Violet family / Violaceae

Lance-leaved violet

Native Species

Viola lanceolata

Violette lancéolée, bog white violet

VITAL STATISTICS
Maximum height: 12 centimetres Flowering season: May to July

HABITAT: Lance-leaved violet grows on boggy ground along damp roadsides and shorelines and in moist open woodlands and meadows. It is generally confined to the southwestern region of New Brunswick.

CHARACTERISTICS: Lance-leaved violet spreads by leafy mat-forming stolons. The 6- to 12-centimetre-long alternately arranged leaves are lance-shaped to elliptical, unlike any other violet in the province. Leaves are hairless on top but may have scattered hairs on the bottom. Leaf edges have a few rounded teeth.

Solitary flowers are 1.5 centimetres wide and usually held at or above the level of the leaves. Lateral petals are usually beardless; the lowest petal has purple veins and is often narrower and more pointed than the other petals. Flowers lack any fragrance. In areas where their distribution overlaps with that of *V. macloskeyi*, the hybrid *V. X sublanceolata* may be found. It is similar to *V. lanceolata* but its leaves are more elliptical or arrowhead-shaped.

Top: The lateral petals lack hairs and the lower petal is longer than the other petals. Bottom: The lance-shaped leaves are unique among native violets.

Native Species

Violet family / Violaceae

Small white violet

Viola macloskeyi (formerly *V. pallens*)

Violette de Macloskey, violette pâle, northern white violet

VITAL STATISTICS
Maximum height: 10 centimetres
Flowering season: May to July

HABITAT: Small white violet, common in various wetland habitats, usually in full sun, is found throughout New Brunswick.

CHARACTERISTICS: Small white violet is the first of the white-flowered violets to bloom in the province and also the only one to prefer moist to wet sites. Tufted plants have alternate leaves that arise from slender stolons. Leaves are heart-shaped to round and hairless; leaf stalks may have a few hairs. Leaf edges have a few rounded teeth.

Flowers usually arise higher than the leaves. They are solitary, highly fragrant, and about 1 centimetre wide. Petals are white with distinct purple veins toward the centre. Lateral petals are beardless (lack hairs at their base).

Sweet white violet, *V. blanda*, grows in dry shady deciduous woodlands. Young leaves are pubescent but may retain hairs only on their undersides when older. Flowers are up to 1.5 centimetres wide and slightly fragrant, if at all. Lateral petals are heavily bearded. The plants are reasonably common.

Kidney-leaved violet, *V. renifolia*, another woodlander with pubescent young leaves, has beardless lateral petals and scentless flowers. The key distinguishing feature is its lack of stolons. It prefers coniferous and mixed forests and is well distributed in the province.

Top: Small white violet flowers are held just above the height of the leaves. Middle: Sweet white violet grows in lightly shaded woodlands. Bottom: Kidney-leaved violet leaves are wider than long.

Pea family / Fabaceae

White sweet-clover

Introduced Species

Melilotus albus (also known as *M. officinalis*)

Mélilot blanc, honey clover, Bokhara clover, white melilot

VITAL STATISTICS
Maximum height: 150 centimetres
Flowering season: June to August

HABITAT: White sweet-clover, a European species, was probably introduced to New Brunswick as a fodder crop. It is found in disturbed areas throughout the province, particularly in the calcareous central regions.

CHARACTERISTICS: White sweet-clover is a large bushy annual or biennial plant. Alternately arranged leaves are trifoliate with sharply toothed, oblong to obovate leaflets. Leaves are smooth or sparsely hairy. A pair of rounded stipules is at the base of each leaf.

Numerous white flowers are produced in 4- to 12-centimetre-long racemes located in the upper leaf axils. Flowers are sweetly fragrant. Individual flowers are 0.4 to 0.6 centimetres in length and pea-like in shape.

Botanists are undecided whether *M. albus* is simply a white-flowered version of *M. officinalis*. The latter species, commonly known as yellow sweet-clover, is also found throughout New Brunswick, often side by side with *M. albus*. It looks almost identical except for its yellow flowers. Tall yellow sweet-clover, *M. altissimus*, occasionally seen in New Brunswick, is distinguished by seed pods with fine hairs.

Top: Flowers are in narrow racemes. Middle: Leaves are trifoliate with finely toothed margins. Bottom: Yellow sweet-clover looks like white sweet-clover but has yellow flowers.

Introduced Species

Pea family / Fabaceae

White clover

Trifolium repens

Trèfle blanc, Dutch clover, creeping white clover

HABITAT: A European introduction, white clover was cultivated initially in the province as a fodder crop and then as a lawn species. It is now a common species along roadsides and on lawns, meadows, and other disturbed areas throughout New Brunswick.

CHARACTERISTICS: White clover is a low mat-forming plant with long creeping stems. The hairless leaves have long petioles and are alternate along the stems. Each leaf is trifoliate with heart-shaped tooth-edged leaflets, which end in a notch and usually have a pale green crescent in their middles.

Fragrant flowers are held just above the leaves at the ends of long flower stalks. They are produced in a globular 2-centimetre-long head of many small pea-like flowers. When flowers open, they are a creamy white but as they age they may develop a pink tint. Individual flowers are 0.5 to 0.9 centimetres long, narrow, and almost tubular.

Alsike clover, *T. hybridum*, is similar but its leaves are plain green and the flowers are two-toned pink and white. Alsike clover grows taller than white clover and is more clumping than creeping. It is found throughout New Brunswick and is often grown as a fodder crop.

VITAL STATISTICS
Maximum height: 20 centimetres
Flowering season: June to September

Top: White clover produces a globular head of many tiny pea-like flowers. Middle: The trifoliate leaves have a pale central crescent. Bottom: Alsike clover has pink and white flowers and green leaves.

Mint family / Lamiaceae

Northern water-horehound

Lycopus uniflorus

Lycope à une fleur, northern bugleweed, tuberous water-horehound

Native Species

Wetlands

VITAL STATISTICS	
Maximum height:	60 centimetres
Flowering season:	Late June to September

HABITAT: Northern water-horehound prefers wet seepages, woods, meadows, and shorelines, often growing into the water. It occurs throughout the province.

CHARACTERISTICS: Northern water-horehound has non-branching square stems that arise from a tuberous-like root. Light green or purple-tinted leaves are opposite and elliptical to lance-shaped and usually have coarsely toothed edges, although plants in the shade may have smooth-edged leaves. Leaves vary from 2 to 11 centimetres in length and have short leaf stalks. Both stems and leaves are hairless. Plants are fragrant when bruised.

Tiny 0.3-centimetre-long flowers are produced in clusters along the upper leaf axils. Usually only a few flowers in each cluster are open at the same time. Each flower has a two-lipped appearance with two upper and three lower petals. The lowermost petals often have a few fine purple spots.

American water-horehound, *L. americanus*, is almost as common as northern water-horehound and grows in similar habitats. It reaches 90 centimetres tall and its leaves are deeply lobed or dissected at their bases while sharply toothed toward their tips. Leaves are generally hairless but have a few fine hairs along their lower leaf veins. Plants are not fragrant when bruised. Unlike *L. uniflorus*, which has five petals, this species has four petals.

Top: The tiny five-petalled flowers of northern water-horehound are in axillary clusters. Middle: Plants produce coarsely toothed paired lanceolate leaves. Bottom: American water-horehound flowers have four rather than five petals.

Plantain family / Plantaginaceae

Native Species

White turtlehead

Chelone glabra

Tête de tortue, galane glabre, smooth balmony

HABITAT: White turtlehead is found in swamps, wet meadows, and ditches and along streamsides throughout the province.

VITAL STATISTICS
Maximum height: 90 centimetres
Flowering season: Mid-July to August

CHARACTERISTICS: White turtlehead has non-branching 60- to 90-centimetre-tall stems, which are square in cross-section. Opposite leaves are lance-shaped to elliptical, with toothed edges and short petioles. Each set of leaves is often at right angles to the next set. Stems and leaves are hairless.

Pleasantly fragrant flowers are held in a dense terminal spike. Individual flowers are creamy white, less commonly tinted pink, and two-lipped and measure 2.5 to 3.5 centimetres in length. The upper lip has two fused petals which form a hoodlike structure; the lower lip is made of three fused petals. The interior of the lower lip is hairy.

Top: The two-lipped flowers are in dense terminal spikes. Bottom: The paired leaves are lanceolate to elliptical and finely toothed.

Broomrape family / Orobanchaceae

Northeastern paintbrush

Castilleja septentrionalis

Castilléjie pale, northern paintbrush, Labrador Indian paintbrush

Native Species

VITAL STATISTICS
Maximum height: 50 centimetres
Flowering season: June and July

HABITAT: Northeastern paintbrush grows in calcareous gravels and ledges and peaty soils over limestone. It is very rare and primarily confined to the northwestern regions of New Brunswick.

CHARACTERISTICS: Northeastern paintbrush is a clumping plant with several upright non-branching stems. Leaves are alternate, linear to lance-shaped, smooth-edged, and sessile; leaves and stems are often purple-tinted.

Flowers are produced in a terminal spike. The white floral bract is green-, pink-, or purple-tinted, hairy on the outer surface, and often three-lobed at the end. The flower, hidden beneath the floral bract, is bilobed with five fused petals. The thick green horn-like pistil extends beyond the flower. This hemi-parasitic plant partially parasitizes neighbouring grasses.

Top: Flowers are in a terminal spike; floral bracts are white with green bases. Bottom: Alternate leaves are sessile and narrow; stems are unbranched.

Broomrape family / Orobanchaceae

Native Species

Common eyebright

Euphrasia nemorosa

Euphraise des bois, euphraise des forêts, hairy eyebright

HABITAT: Common eyebright is a common species found in disturbed habitats and barren rocky areas throughout the province.

CHARACTERISTICS: Common eyebright is an annual with stiffly upright finely hairy stems which are 10 to 20 centimetres or, rarely, to 30 centimetres tall. Hairless glossy deep green opposite leaves are densely arranged along the stems. Leaves are 0.6 to 2.2 centimetres long and ovate with sharply toothed edges.

Flowers are arranged in terminal spikes. Individual flowers are about 1 centimetre wide. White or pale lavender flowers have five petals arranged in a two-lipped fashion. The upper two petals curl slightly backward; the lower three petals are more wide-spreading and are notched. Each petal has three purple veins; the lowermost also has a yellow patch in the middle. Each flower has a green bristle-tipped bract at its base.

Stiff eyebright, *E. stricta*, appears throughout New Brunswick in similar habitats as common eyebright. Stiff eyebright is distinguished by its floral bracts, which generally arch upwards.

Extremely rare on Grand Manan Island and the neighbouring mainland is Rand's eyebright, *E. randii*. Usually less than 10 centimetres tall, it has rounded teeth, hairy leaves, and 0.3- to 0.4-centimetre-long white, pink, or purple flowers.

Hemiparasitic, eyebrights obtain nutrients by parasitizing neighbouring plants.

VITAL STATISTICS
Maximum height: 30 centimetres
Flowering season: July to September

Top: The striped flowers have a two-lipped appearance. Middle: Flowers are in terminal spikes and the opposite round leaves are coarsely toothed. Bottom: Rand's eyebright leaves have rounded teeth; flowers are often pink-tinted.

Broomrape family / Orobanchaceae

American cow-wheat

Native Species

Melampyrum lineare

Mélampyre linéaire, cow-wheat

VITAL STATISTICS
Maximum height: 40 centimetres
Flowering season: July to August

HABITAT: American cow-wheat is found on barrens and bogs and in open coniferous forests throughout the province.

CHARACTERISTICS: An annual, American cow-wheat has single stems or it may be multiple branching. The stem is square in cross-section with fine, often glandular, hairs. Linear to lance-shaped leaves are opposite and have short petioles. Leaves may be purple-tinted, hairless or slightly hairy, and slightly sticky on their upper surfaces. Leaf edges are mostly smooth but upper leaves have a few bristle-tipped teeth at their bases.

Flowers, solitary and produced in the upper leaf axils, are approximately 1 centimetre long and tubular with a two-lipped opening, reminiscent of a snake's head. The upper lip is shorter than the lower and curls back to reveal a hairy-fringed edge. The tube is white and the opening has a yellow patch.

Plants are hemiparasitic and obtain nutrients by tapping into the root systems of neighbouring plants.

Top: Each two-lipped flower is shaped like a snake's head. Bottom: Flowers are in the upper leaf axils.

Broomrape family / Orobanchaceae

Native Species

One-flowered broomrape

Orobanche uniflora

Orobanche uniflore, naked broomrape, one-flowered cancerroot

HABITAT: One-flowered broomrape is very rare and scattered in thickets, meadows, and open woodlands throughout the province.

CHARACTERISTICS: One-flowered broomrape is a parasitic plant that feeds off various plants. In New Brunswick, goldenrods, *Solidago*, are a common host. Plants live for years as underground tuberous-like roots. When the conditions are right, plants will send up several leafless pale brown fleshy stalks topped by a single flower. Stalks and flowers are covered in fine sticky hairs.

Flowers have long curved tubes which are up to 2.5 centimetres long and which end in five petals: two upper and three lower. Flowers are typically white with pale lavender veins, but they may be entirely lilac. The middle of the three lower petals has two raised yellow beards that extend into the back of the flower. Flowers are delicately fragrant.

VITAL STATISTICS
Maximum height: 25 centimetres
Flowering season: June to July

Top: The middle of the three lower petals has two raised yellow beards. Middle: Less commonly, flowers are entirely lavender. Bottom: Plants are leafless and the flower stems covered in sticky hairs.

Orchid family / Orchidaceae

Showy lady's-slipper

Native Species

Cypripedium reginae

Cypripède royal, pink and white lady's-slipper

VITAL STATISTICS
Maximum height: 80 centimetres
Flowering season: June to July

HABITAT: Showy lady's-slipper is restricted to calcareous wetlands and cedar swamps. It is localized in its distribution within New Brunswick.

CHARACTERISTICS: Showy lady's-slipper is unmistakable: It produces clumps of non-branching stems that arise to 80 centimetres. Stems and leaves are fuzzy with short hairs. Plants produce three to five alternate overlapping leaves that are ovate in outline and clasp the stem. Leaves are smooth-edged and distinctly ribbed with parallel veins. The lowest leaves may reach up to 25 centimetres in length, but upper leaves are smaller.

Stems terminate in one, two, or, rarely, three large showy flowers measuring about 8 centimetres by 12 centimetres. Each flower is backed by a distinct green bract. Sepals and lateral petals are white. The dorsal sepal often leans forward; lateral petals arch slightly backward. The rounded pouch-like lip is in variable shades of pink or, rarely, white, and measures 3 to 5 centimetres in diameter.

Touching this orchid can cause dermatitis in people with sensitive skin.

Top: Flowers are white with a distinctive pink slipper-like pouch. MIddle: Its overlapping leaves clasp the stem. Bottom: Plants form clumps of non-branching stems.

Native Species

Orchid family / Orchidaceae

Rattlesnake-plantain

Goodyera species

Goodyérie

HABITAT: Rattlesnake-plantain may be found in mossy shady areas in coniferous and mixed forest or cedar swamps. There are three species in New Brunswick: dwarf and checkered rattlesnake-plantain, *G. repens* and *G. tesselata*, are widespread throughout the province; Menzie's rattlesnake-plantain, *G. oblongifolia*, is very rare and restricted to the northern regions.

CHARACTERISTICS: New Brunswick's rattlesnake-plantains produce a basal rosette of alternate egg-shaped to elliptical succulent evergreen leaves. Leaves are marked with silver-white veins.

Flowers of all species are pubescent and held on narrow leafless spikes. Individual flowers are white and about 0.3 centimetres wide. The dorsal sepal and lateral petals form a hood over the tiny pointed lip. Lateral sepals are usually strongly reflexed.

These features help distinguish among the three species:

- *G. repens*: milk-white flowers on a loose one-sided raceme; dark green leaves, 1 to 3 centimetres in length, with large silver-white veins.
- *G. tesselata*: milk-white flowers spirally arranged; dull blue-green leaves, 2 to 7 centimetres in length, with pale green veins.
- *G. oblongifolia*: off-white flowers on a loose one-sided spike; dull green leaves, each 4 to 10 centimetres long with a central silver-white stripe, with or without finer veins.

VITAL STATISTICS
Maximum height: 30 centimetres
Flowering season: July to August

Top: Flowers are in narrow spikes. Middle: All rattlesnake-plantains produce a basal rosette of leaves. Bottom: *Goodyera repens* has striking silver-veined leaves.

Orchid family / Orchidaceae

White fringed orchid

Native Species

Platanthera blephariglottis

Platanthère à gorge frangée

VITAL STATISTICS
Maximum height: 60 centimetres
Flowering season: July to August

HABITAT: White fringed orchid is very rare on wet meadows, fens, and bogs. It is widely scattered and localized in New Brunswick.

CHARACTERISTICS: White fringed orchid produces stems which are 20 to 60 centimetres in length. Plants have two to four alternate lance-shaped leaves that clasp the stem; leaves are hairless and smooth-edged and become smaller as they ascend the stem.

Flowers are produced in a dense cylindrical spike. Individual flowers are bright white and about 2 centimetres in diameter. Dorsal sepals and lateral petals form a hood over the lip. Lateral sepals are ovate and often reflexed. The lip is narrow with heavily fringed edges. The nectar spur is 1.5 to 2 centimetres long.

Top: The narrow lip has heavily fringed edges.
Middle: Flowers are in a dense cylindrical spike.
Bottom: Plants commonly inhabit grassy fens.

Orchid family / Orchidaceae

Tall white bog orchid

Native Species

Platanthera dilatata

Platanthère dilatée, bog candles, scent-bottle, leafy white orchid

HABITAT: Tall white bog orchid, a fairly common orchid throughout New Brunswick, grows in wetland habitats.

CHARACTERISTICS: Tall white bog orchid is a tall narrow plant with three to 12 alternate hairless smooth-edged lance-shaped leaves. Leaves become smaller farther up the stem.

Clove-scented snow-white flowers are produced in a dense narrow spike. Each flower has a narrow 2-centimetre-long leaf-like bract at its base. Individual flowers are about 2 centimetres wide. Dorsal sepal and lateral petals form a hood over the lip. Lateral sepals are wide-spreading and slightly reflexed, appearing like a tern in flight. The lip, rounded at the base, narrows toward the tip. The nectar spur is about the same length as the lip.

VITAL STATISTICS
Maximum height: 100 centimetres
Flowering season: Late June to August

Top: The dorsal sepal and lateral petals form a hood over the lip. Bottom: Flowers are in dense cylindrical spikes.

Orchid family / Orchidaceae

Nodding ladies'-tresses

Native Species

Spiranthes cernua

Spiranthe penchée, screw-auger, white nodding ladies'-tresses, drooping ladies'-tresses

VITAL STATISTICS
Maximum height: 60 centimetres Flowering season: July to August

HABITAT: Nodding ladies'-tresses grows in wetland habitats such as seepages, wet meadows, and moist sandy freshwater shorelines. It is very rare in New Brunswick, and found mainly in the southwestern regions.

CHARACTERISTICS: A slender plant, nodding ladies'-tresses produces several lanceolate hairless leaves near the base of the plant. Stem leaves are reduced to small bracts.

Flowers are held in three rows along a dense spike. The flower rows are slightly spiralled, but, less commonly, they may be parallel. Each flower has a short green bract at the base. Sepals and lateral petals are united to form an upward-arching hood. The lip arches downward. Individual flowers are about 1 centimetre wide and covered in fine hairs. Flowers have a slight vanilla scent.

Yellow ladies'-tresses, *S. ochroleuca*, is extremely rare in New Brunswick; it has only been found on Grand Manan Island, where it grows on lawns and gravel roadsides. Flowers are pubescent and similar to nodding ladies'-tresses, but they are creamy yellow, especially in the throat, and have a strong fragrance.

Top: Flowers are covered in pubescent hairs. Middle: Nodding ladies'-tresses produces flowers in three parallel rows along a dense spike. Bottom: Yellow ladies'-tresses has creamy yellow flowers.

Orchid family / Orchidaceae

Northern slender ladies'-tresses

Native Species

Spiranthes lacera

Spiranthe découpée

HABITAT: Uncommon in New Brunswick, northern slender ladies'-tresses grows in sandy to gravelly clearings along the edges of coniferous forests and in peaty meadows and old burn sites.

VITAL STATISTICS
Maximum height: 35 centimetres
Flowering season: Mid-July to August

CHARACTERISTICS: Northern slender ladies'-tresses has slender leafless stems arising from one to four basal elliptical to oblong leaves that lie flat on the ground. Smooth-edged hairless leaves may be shrivelled at the time of blooming.

White flowers, produced in a dense spike, are strongly one-sided or widely spiralled along the stem. Individual flowers are about 0.5 centimetres in diameter. The lip, together with the dorsal sepal and lateral petals, has a tubelike appearance and an inside green patch. Lateral sepals are narrow and separated from the rest of the flower. The flower base is often sparsely pubescent.

Case's ladies'-tresses, *S. casei*, is extremely rare and has only been found on Currie Mountain in York County, where it grows on an open slope. Densely pubescent flowers are creamy white and their lips lack a central green patch. Basal leaves are held erect and are green at flowering during mid-August to September. It is an Atlantic Coastal Plain species.

Shining ladies'-tresses, *S. lucida*, is very rare along the flood plains of the larger rivers of the province. White flowers bloom in late June and July and have a yellow lip on a three-rowed spiralled spike. Oblong to oblanceolate leaves are not fully basal.

Top: Northern slender ladies'-tresses flowers often spiral along the slender spike and have a distinct green patch at the lip base. Middle: Case's ladies'-tresses flowers also spiral along the stem but the lip does not have a green patch. Bottom: Shining ladies'-tresses has a yellow lip.

Orchid family / Orchidaceae

Hooded ladies'-tresses

Native Species

Spiranthes romanzoffiana

Spiranthe de Romanzoff

VITAL STATISTICS
Maximum height: 35 centimetres
Flowering season: Mid-July to September

HABITAT: Hooded ladies'-tresses is common throughout the province, growing along shorelines and in damp meadows, clearings, seepages, fens, and thickets.

CHARACTERISTICS: Hooded ladies'-tresses is a stout orchid which is 15 to 35 centimetres tall, with three to six alternate lance-shaped leaves that decrease in size up the stem. Leaves are hairless with smooth edges.

Flowers are held in three rows along a dense spike. Normally, flower rows are parallel, but they are sometimes spiralled. Each flower has a narrow green bract at the base that is nearly as long as, or longer than, the flower. Sepals and lateral petals unite to form an upward-arching hood. The lip arches downward. Individual flowers are about 1 centimetre wide and have a strong vanilla fragrance.

Top: Flowers are in three parallel rows along the dense cylindrical spike. Bottom: The narrow lance-shaped leaves decrease in size up the stem.

Evening primrose family / Onagraceae

Small enchanter's nightshade

Circaea alpina

Circée alpine, dwarf enchanter's nightshade

Native Species

HABITAT: Small enchanter's nightshade inhabits cool moist shady woodlands, ravines, slopes, and wetland-forest borders in New Brunswick.

VITAL STATISTICS
Maximum height: 30 centimetres
Flowering season: June to September

CHARACTERISTICS: A common plant, small enchanter's nightshade is often overlooked due to its small size and tiny flowers. While plants may reach 30 centimetres, they are more commonly 10 to 20 centimetres in height. Plants form large colonies, but individual stems are non-branching. Pale green succulent 2- to 5-centimetre-long leaves are opposite and heart-shaped. Leaves have coarsely toothed edges and hairs along their lower veins.

Flowers are held on slender racemes. Flower stems are covered in tiny sticky hairs. The flowers are only 0.2 centimetres wide, with two deeply lobed white petals (resembling four petals) that point forward, two petaloid white sepals that curl backward, one exerted style, and two exerted stamens. The base of the flower is covered in hooked hairs.

Large or broad-leaved enchanter's nightshade, *C. canadensis* (formerly *C. lutetiana*), is common in the southern half of the province and grows in rich moist deciduous forests. Plants are generally over 30 centimetres tall with ovate leaves which grow up to 10 centimetres in length, twice as long as they are wide. Their petaloid sepals are generally green rather than white.

Top: Individual flowers have two white sepals and two deeply lobed petals. Middle: Opposite heart-shaped leaves have coarsely toothed edges. Bottom: Large enchanter's nightshade has green rather than white sepals.

Water-plantain family / Alismataceae

Northern water-plantain

Alisma triviale

Alisma commun

Native Species

VITAL STATISTICS
Maximum height: 80 centimetres
Flowering season: June to September

HABITAT: Northern water-plantain grows in muddy-bottomed shallow waters such as pond shorelines, streamsides, and ditches, and it is especially fond of calcareous muds. It is common throughout much of New Brunswick.

CHARACTERISTICS: Northern water-plantain usually grows in shallow water. Leaves are basal but arise on long petioles. They are ovate to elliptical in outline, with parallel veins, smooth edges, and a slightly wrinkled appearance. Leaves on robust specimens may reach 18 centimetres in length. The entire plant is hairless.

Flowers are held in a large panicle. Branchlets arise in whorls well above the foliage. Individual flowers are about 1 centimetre in diameter with three white petals, three significantly smaller green sepals, six stamens, and a globular green centre. A small yellow patch can be seen at the base of each petal. Seed heads look like small green buttons.

Southern water-plantain, *A. subcordatum*, is extremely rare in Carleton and York counties. Its petals are about the same size as its sepals. Flowers are often less than 0.5 centimetre in diameter.

Top: A small yellow patch is visible at the base of the three white petals. Middle: Plants produce a basal rosette of long petioled ovate leaves; flowers are in large sprays Bottom: Petals and sepals of southern water-plantain flowers are the same size.

Water-plantain family / Alismataceae

Native Species

Broad-leaved arrowhead

Sagittaria latifolia

Sagittaire à larges feuilles, common arrowhead, duck-potato, swamp potato, wapato

HABITAT: Broad-leaved arrowhead grows in muddy-bottomed shallow water and is common throughout the province.

CHARACTERISTICS: Broad-leaved arrowhead grows immersed in shallow water. Roots are tuberous and potato-like. Basal leaves arise on long petioles and measure 10 to 25 centimetres in length. Leaves are triangular ("sagittate") with three lobes: one large broad lobe and two narrower, downward-pointing lobes. Leaves are hairless with smooth edges and parallel veins. Stems and leaves exude a milky sap when cut.

Flowers are in whorls along the flower stems, which are held at the same level as the leaves or slightly above. Plants are monoecious; the lower flowers are female, the upper male. Four-centimetre-wide flowers are satiny white with three rounded petals and three smaller green sepals. Male flowers have a cluster of golden stamens in the centre; female centres are green and burr-like.

Giant arrowhead, *S. montevidensis*, is extremely rare in Northumberland and Kent counties. White flowers, hidden by overtopping leaves, have purple patches and short stalks.

Northern arrowhead, *S. cuneata*, has 5- to 15-centimetre-long leaves and 2.5-centimetre-diameter flowers. It prefers calcareous muds.

Grass-leaved arrowhead, *S. graminea*, is uncommon in southern New Brunswick along silty and sandy pond margins. It is 20 to 50 centimetres in height and has narrow linear to lance-shaped leaves.

VITAL STATISTICS
Maximum height: 90 centimetres
Flowering season: July to September

Top: Individual flowers have three rounded white petals.
Middle: Leaves are distinctly arrowhead-shaped.
Bottom: Grass-leaved arrowhead has narrow linear to lance-shaped leaves.

Bunchflower family / Melantheaceae

Nodding trillium

Trillium cernuum

Trille penché, birthroot, nodding wakerobin

Native Species

VITAL STATISTICS
Maximum height: 30 centimetres
Flowering season: Mid-May to late June

HABITAT: Nodding trillium is common in New Brunswick; it grows in mature deciduous forests and on the flood plains of larger rivers.

CHARACTERISTICS: Nodding trillium forms loose colonies in the shade of deciduous trees. From an underground rhizome arises a single stem of 15 to 30 centimetres, topped with a whorl of three ovate leaves. The smooth-edged hairless leaves have obscure petioles.

A solitary 3- to 5-centimetre-diameter flower arises from the junction of three leaves. The flower stem is bent downward such that the flower is nodding below the leaves. The flower is composed of three elliptical white petals, three lance-shaped green sepals, six anthers, and a three-lobed stigma. Petals and sepals have recurving tips. Flowers develop into 3-centimetre-diameter fleshy red berries later in the season. The fruit is poisonous.

Top: Each flower has three white petals and three green sepals. Middle: The nodding flowers are held below the whorl of leaves. Bottom: Leaves are in a whorl of three.

Native Species

Bunchflower family / Melanthiaceae

Painted trillium

Trillium undulatum

Trille ondulé, painted lady, painted wakerobin

HABITAT: Painted trillium is found mostly in dry coniferous woods but may occur in any woodland location, including cutover areas. It is common throughout New Brunswick.

CHARACTERISTICS: Painted trillium forms a loose colony of solitary stems that arise from an underground rhizome. Stems are often purple-tinted early in the season. Elliptical to ovate leaves have long pointed tips and are produced in a whorl of three; they have short but obvious petioles and are also often purple-tinted, especially early in the season. Leaves are hairless and smooth-edged.

A solitary flower arises from the junction of the three leaves. Each flower is 5 to 7 centimetres in diameter and composed of three white tongue-shaped petals, three green lance-shaped sepals, six stamens, and a three-lobed stigma. Each petal has a pink-stained base, giving a pink centre to each flower. Later in the season, flowers develop into 1- to 2-centimetre-diameter poisonous red berries.

VITAL STATISTICS
Maximum height: 40 centimetres
Flowering season: Late May to June

Top: Each petal has a pink-stained base. Middle: Plants produce a whorl of three leaves. Bottom: Flowers develop into a red berry.

Mustard family / Brassicaceae

Garlic mustard

Alliaria petiolata

Alliaire, hedge garlic

Introduced Species

VITAL STATISTICS
Maximum height: 100 centimetres Flowering season: May to July

HABITAT: Garlic mustard is a European species found in disturbed habitats and on moist riversides. It is currently confined to the Saint John River valley of New Brunswick but is spreading rapidly.

CHARACTERISTICS: Garlic mustard is a biennial plant. In the first season, it produces an evergreen rosette of long-petioled round to kidney-shaped leaves with scalloped edges. These leaves may be up to 10 centimetres wide. In the second season, the plant sends up an unbranched stem with alternately arranged leaves. Lower leaves resemble the rosette leaves; upper leaves are more triangular with sharply toothed edges. Petioles are finely pubescent but the leaves are hairless. Young leaves emit a garlic-like fragrance when cut or bruised.

The stem terminates in a compact raceme of white flowers which elongates as the season progresses. Individual flowers measure 6 to 8 millimetres wide and have four white petals, six stamens, and a single pistil. The thin seed capsule may be up to 6 centimetres long.

Considered a very invasive species, garlic mustard is still restricted in its distribution in much of the region, but populations are slowly spreading.

Top: Four-petalled flowers are at the stem ends.
Bottom: Triangular-shaped upper leaves have sharply toothed edges.

Mustard family / Brassicaceae

Horseradish

Armoracia rusticana

Raifort

Introduced Species

HABITAT: Horseradish, a European species, is a garden escape occasionally seen along roadsides and in fields along the Saint John River Valley.

CHARACTERISTICS: Horseradish is a leafy plant with large floppy elliptical basal leaves up to 60 centimetres in length. Basal leaves are hairless with finely toothed, often undulating, edges; petioles are almost as long as the leaf blade. Alternately arranged lance-shaped stem leaves are smaller than the basal leaves, often less than 15 centimetres in length, and may have short or no petioles. The edges of stem leaves are much more deeply toothed than basal leaves. The undersides of all leaves are paler than their upper surfaces. Plants arise from a stout taproot and form thick rhizomes that result in a colonial habit.

Numerous flowers are produced in either racemes or panicles at the ends of the main stem and its side branches. Individual flowers are about 0.8 centimetres in diameter and have four broad white petals which are about twice the length of the narrow green sepals. Narrow seed capsules are up to 0.6 centimetres in length.

VITAL STATISTICS
Maximum height: 120 centimetres
Flowering season: May to July

Top: Numerous flowers are produced in sprays at the ends of the branches. Bottom: Plants produce large, elliptical basal leaves.

Mustard family / Brassicaceae

Drummond's rockcress

Native Species

Boechera stricta (formerly *Arabis drummondii*)

Arabette de Drummond

VITAL STATISTICS
Maximum height: 80 centimetres
Flowering season: May to July

HABITAT: Drummond's rockcress is a widely distributed but very rare calciphile in New Brunswick, generally confined to rocky calcareous shores and thickets.

CHARACTERISTICS: Drummond's rockcress, a slender plant with non-branching stems, is a biennial or a short-lived perennial. The rosette leaves are oblanceolate, usually hairless, and smooth-edged. The numerous stem leaves are alternate and lance-shaped but widest at their bases. Two backward-pointed lobes are found at the base of each stem leaf.

Flowers are produced in strongly erect racemes which are up to 80 centimetres tall. Opening flowers, each 1 to 2 centimetres wide, have four white petals that age to lavender. The narrow seed capsules, or siliques, are held stiffly erect and are up to 10 centimetres long.

Top: White four-petalled flowers age to lavender.
Bottom: Basal and stem leaves are narrow, hairless, and smooth-edged.

Mustard family / Brassicaceae

Native Species

Shepherd's purse

Capsella bursa-pastoris

Tabouret

VITAL STATISTICS
Maximum height: 60 centimetres
Flowering season: May to November

HABITAT: Shepherd's purse, a European introduction, is commonly found in disturbed habitats throughout the province.

CHARACTERISTICS: Shepherd's purse is an annual that often overwinters as an evergreen rosette. Basal leaves are elliptical to lance-shaped, have a petiole, and are pinnately lobed. The alternately arranged stem leaves are scattered and elliptical to lance-shaped with smooth or slightly toothed edges. These leaves are sessile and clasp the stem, often with a pair of ear-like lobes at their base. The entire plant may be hairless or have scattered stiff hairs.

Flowers are produced in a raceme. Individual flowers are about 0.5 centimetres wide with four white petals. Flower stems significantly elongate as they set seed. Seed pods are heart-shaped and flattened.

Field pennycress, *Thlaspi arvense*, which often grows with shepherd's purse, is an annual with a few petioled basal leaves that are elliptical and widest at their tip. Flower stems are ribbed. The numerous stem leaves are elliptical to lance-shaped with sparingly toothed edges. They are alternately arranged and sessile, either clasping the stem or with a pair of ear-like lobes at its base. The entire plant is hairless. Its flowering habit is virtually identical to that of shepherd's purse, but its seed pods, although flattened, are rounded with a notch at the top.

Top: Seed pods of shepherd's purse are heart-shaped and flattened. Middle: Narrow leaves clasp the stem. Bottom: Field pennycress has rounded flattened seed pods with a notch at their ends.

Mustard family / Brassicaceae

Two-leaved toothwort

Native Species

Cardamine diphylla

Snicroûte, broad-leaved toothwort, crinkleroot

VITAL STATISTICS
Maximum height: 40 centimetres
Flowering season: April to early June

HABITAT: Two-leaved toothwort occurs primarily in rich deciduous forest. It is locally common in the province.

CHARACTERISTICS: Two-leaved toothwort is a spring ephemeral that disappears by mid-summer. Leaves are trifoliate with elliptical to ovate leaflets that are hairless and coarsely toothed. Non-flowering plants have a single basal leaf on a long petiole. Flowering stems have a pair of opposite or sub-opposite leaves with shorter petioles. Each leaflet has a short petiole.

Flowers are produced in a loose raceme. Individual flowers have four white, sometimes lilac, petals and are 2 to 3 centimetres in diameter. They develop into long thin siliques.

Cut-leaved toothwort, *C. concatenata*, is extremely rare and isolated in deciduous forests of York, Victoria, and Carleton counties. Its basal leaves are trifoliate; lance-shaped leaflets are pinnatifid with deep lobes. Smaller than the basal leaves but similar in shape, stem leaves are in whorls of three. Flowers resemble those of two-leaved toothwort.

Top: Flowering plants have trifoliate leaves and a loose raceme of flowers. Middle: Each flowering plant produces a pair of trifoliate leaves. Bottom: Each flowering stems of cut-leaved toothwort has a whorl of three narrow deeply lobed leaves.

Mustard family / Brassicaceae

Native Species

Pennsylvania bittercress

Cardamine pensylvanica

Cardamine de Pennsylvanie

HABITAT: Pennsylvania bittercress, which grows along muddy pond and stream shorelines as well as in ditches and swamps, is common throughout New Brunswick.

VITAL STATISTICS
Maximum height: 45 centimetres
Flowering season: May to July

CHARACTERISTICS: Pennsylvania bittercress is a biennial species. Plants overwinter as an evergreen rosette and bloom early in the second year. The base of the stem has stiff hairs but the rest of the plant is hairless. Leaves are pinnately compound. Basal and lower stem leaves have rounded leaflets; leaves farther up the stem have more linear leaflets. The terminal leaflet is usually the largest. Leaflet edges may be shallowly lobed or have a few rounded teeth.

Flowers are produced in racemes. Individual flowers are 0.3 to 0.8 centimetres in diameter with four white petals and six stamens. The fruit is an elongate narrow silique up to 3.5 centimetres long.

Small-leaved watercress, *Nasturtium microphyllum*, a similar-looking introduced species found along slow-moving streams, is a perennial with stems that root in the water or mud. The fleshy, pinnately compound leaves have round leaflets with a few rounded teeth. Flowers are larger than those of Pennsylvania bittercress. Watercress is rare and often overlooked.

Top: Pennsylvania bittercress flowers develop into long slender siliques. Middle: The upper stem leaves of Pennsylvania bittercress have pinnate leaves with narrow leaflets. Bottom: The pinnate leaves of small-leaved watercress have round leaflets.

Wetlands

Mustard family / Brassicaceae

Rock draba

Draba arabisans

Drave arabette, rockcress whitlowgrass

Native Species

VITAL STATISTICS

Maximum height: 40 centimetres
Flowering season: May to July

HABITAT: Rock draba, an extremely rare calciphile, is found on the limestone gravels and cliffs of southern and northern New Brunswick.

CHARACTERISTICS: Rock draba grows a loose mat of evergreen rosettes. Oblanceolate to spatulate leaves have toothed edges. Slender flower stems have alternate, ovate to oblong leaves.

Flowers are in a branched raceme. Individual flowers are 0.5 to 1 centimetre in diameter with four white petals and six anthers. Sepals, flower stems, and stalks are densely pubescent. Seed capsules are narrow and teardrop-shaped, and distinctly flattened but twisted.

Twisted draba, *D. incana*, is also extremely rare and is restricted to the northeastern tip of Gloucester County. It is biennial with a single evergreen rosette in the first year and a stout leafy flower stem in the second. White four-petalled 0.5- to 1-centimetre-diameter flowers are in a raceme.

Extremely rare, Norway draba, *D. norvegica*, is confined to one calcareous site near Grande-Anse, Gloucester County. It has small, pubescent evergreen rosettes and a much-tufted appearance. Norway draba has fewer flowers than the other species, on shorter, up to 15 centimetres long, stems. Seed capsules are oval.

Spring whitlow-grass, *D. verna*, is an introduction found on compacted gravels around campsites. It has a small tight basal rosette of hairy purple-tinted leaves and wiry 5- to 10-centimetre-long stems with a few tiny white flowers in April-May.

Top: Rock draba often has flowers in branched racemes.
Middle: Twisted draba has stout, leafy flower stems.
Bottom: Spring whitlow-grass has a small purple-tinted basal rosette and wiry stems with a few white flowers.

Mustard family / Brassicaceae

Introduced Species

Field peppergrass

Lepidium campestre

Cresson des champs, cow cress, field cress

HABITAT: Field peppergrass, a European introduction, is found in disturbed habitats, such as roadsides, gardens, and waste places, throughout New Brunswick.

VITAL STATISTICS
Maximum height: 60 centimetres
Flowering season: May to September

CHARACTERISTICS: Field peppergrass is a winter annual or biennial plant that overwinters as an evergreen rosette. Leaves are elliptical but widest at their tips. They have petioles; leaf edges are smooth toward the tip but undulating and sharply toothed or lobed toward their base. The alternately arranged stem leaves are sessile and numerous. The slightly triangular leaves clasp the stem with two ear-like lobes; leaves are often toothed or undulating at the base but become smooth-edged toward the tip. The entire plant is covered in fine hairs.

Flowers are produced in dense branching racemes. Individual flowers are 0.3 centimetres wide with four white petals. Seed pods are flattened, concave, and ovate in outline with a small notch at the tip.

Common peppergrass, *L. densiflorum*, is also found in waste areas throughout the province. It is more common than field peppergrass. Common peppergrass has pinnatifid basal leaves but linear to lance-shaped stem leaves. It is essentially hairless. Flowers are in dense branching racemes, but the petals are minute, each only about 0.1 centimetre long, or may be missing; flowers appear green due to the presence of sepals.

Top: Field peppergrass flowers are in dense branching racemes. Bottom: Common peppergrass has lobed leaves and nearly non-existent petals.

Heath family / Ericaceae

Creeping snowberry

Gaultheria hispidula

Petit thé, oeufs de perdrix, moxieplum

Native Species

VITAL STATISTICS
Maximum height: 5 centimetres Flowering season: June

HABITAT: Creeping snowberry, scattered throughout New Brunswick, grows in shady mossy coniferous to mixed forests or, less commonly, on open barrens, bogs, and headlands.

CHARACTERISTICS: This plant is a broad-leaved trailing evergreen sub-shrub. Thin stems of creeping snowberry are brown with short stiff hairs. Its ovate leaves are alternate and stiff with smooth revolute edges. The upper surfaces of the leaves are glossy, bright green, and hairless; the undersides are pale with a few short stiff hairs.

Plants produce tiny bell-shaped white or almost transparent solitary flowers with four petals. Blossoms are usually hidden under the foliage. In August and September, solitary white egg-shaped berries are produced. These edible winter-green-flavoured berries have a few short brown hairs.

Creeping snowberry is sometimes confused with twinflower (*Linnaea borealis*)—but twinflower's leaves are opposite (not alternate) on the stem, and twinflower lacks a wintergreen fragrance when its leaves are crushed.

Top: Tiny bell-like flowers are hidden under the leaves.
Middle: Plants form evergreen mats of round leaves.
Bottom: Later in the season, flowers become white egg-shaped berries.

Native Species

Dogwood family / Cornaceae

Bunchberry

Cornus canadensis

Quatre-temps, rougets, crackerberry, creeping dogwood, dwarf cornel

HABITAT: Bunchberry, common throughout New Brunswick, occurs in many habitats including forests, barrens, and wetlands.

CHARACTERISTICS: This sub-shrub often forms large colonies that grow from semi-woody subterranean rhizomes. Bunchberry stems (10 to 25 centimetres tall) are topped by three pairs of closely spaced leaves that initially appear whorled; the lowest pair is largest. Leaves are mostly ovate to obovate, less commonly elliptical with untoothed edges. They are often evergreen through winter, replaced by new shoots in spring.

What appear to be white flowers are sets of four white petal-like leaves (bracts). The actual flowers are tiny with four creamy white petals, four anthers, and a single style. They are produced in a cluster at the bract's centre. By August, flowers develop into a dense cluster of orange-red drupes. The fruit is edible but has little taste.

VITAL STATISTICS
Maximum height: 25 centimetres
Flowering season: June

Top: "Flowers" are four white bracts surrounding a central head of tiny central flowers. Middle: Flowers develop into a raspberry-like cluster of orange-red berries. Bottom: Swedish bunchberry's true flowers are purple.

Madder family / Rubiaceae

Bedstraw

Galium species

Gaillet, cleavers

Native Species Introduced Species

VITAL STATISTICS
Maximum height: 50 centimetres
Flowering season: June to September

HABITAT: Thirteen species of bedstraw occur throughout New Brunswick in disturbed habitats, woodlands, wetlands, or barrens (depending on the species).

CHARACTERISTICS: All *Galium* produce thin trailing stems which are square in cross-section. Small leaves grow in whorls of four to eight. Flowers, less than 0.5 centimetres wide, have four, less often three, white petals and are usually in cymes. Here the similarities end. Plants may be smooth or have short stiff hairs, leaves lance-shaped to round, and flowers in threes or large panicles.

The six most frequently encountered species are

- Rough bedstraw, *G. asprellum*: six elliptical leaves per whorl; stems with stiff backward-facing hairs; flowers in loose open panicle; wetlands.
- Smooth bedstraw, *G. mollugo*: introduced species with six to eight lance-linear leaves per whorl; greenish-white flowers in large dense panicles; disturbed areas.
- Marsh bedstraw, *G. palustre*: four to six elliptical to spatulate leaves per whorl; flowers in large open panicles; wetlands.
- Dyer's bedstraw, *G. tinctorium*: five or six oblanceolate to spatulate leaves per whorl; flowers solitary or in groups of threes; wetlands.
- Three-petalled bedstraw, *G. trifidum*: four lance-linear leaves per whorl; flowers solitary or in groups of three; three-petalled flowers; wetlands.
- Three-flowered bedstraw, *G. triflorum*: six lance-elliptical leaves per whorl; greenish-white flowers in threes; mixed or deciduous woodlands.

Top: Smooth bedstraw has large panicles. Middle: Smooth bedstraw's leaves are in whorls of six to eight. Bottom: Three-petalled bedstraw has leaves in whorls of four.

Madder family / Rubiaceae

Partridgeberry

Mitchella repens

Native Species

Pain-de-perdrix, mitchella rampant, running box, two-eyed berry

HABITAT: Partridgeberry favours coniferous and mixed forests throughout New Brunswick.

CHARACTERISTICS: A prostrate evergreen sub-shrub, partridgeberry may grow 1 to 2 centimetres tall. Opposite, round leaves are shiny green, leathery in texture, and hairless. Only about 1 centimetre wide, leaves have smooth or wavy edges and pale central veins. Stems are smooth.

Small white hairy four-petalled flowers are produced in pairs at the ends of the stems. Each flower has four stamens and a single style with four stigmas. Some flowers have exerted stamens; others have exerted stigmas. This irregularity is botanically referred to as having dimorphous flowers. Distinctively, each pair of flowers shares a single ovary. The paired flowers develop into conjoined red berries in September; berries persist through winter.

VITAL STATISTICS
Maximum height: 2 centimetres
Flowering season: July

Top: The four-petalled flowers are in pairs. Bottom: Later in the season, flowers become red berries with two eyes.

Asparagus family / Asparagacae

Wild lily-of-the-valley

Native Species

Maianthemum canadense

Muguet, Canada mayflower, false lily-of-the-valley

VITAL STATISTICS
Maximum height: 15 centimetres
Flowering season: Mid-May to June

HABITAT: Wild lily-of-the-valley, which grows in both sun and shade in a variety of habitats, including forests, barrens, dry wetland hummocks, clearings, old burn sites, and dunes, is common throughout New Brunswick.

CHARACTERISTICS: Wild lily-of-the-valley forms large colonies which spread by thin underground rhizomes. Plants produce two types of leaves. Non-flowering plants produce a single basal heart-shaped leaf with a distinct petiole; flowering plants produce two or three alternate leaves that are heart-shaped and clasp the stem. Leaves are shiny, bright green, hairless, and smooth-edged. Veins are parallel.

Flowers are produced in a dense raceme which is 2 to 3 centimetres long. The tiny 0.4-centimetre-diameter flowers have four white petals and four stamens and are sweetly fragrant. Flowers develop into brown-speckled 0.4-centimetre-diameter berries that turn shiny red when fully ripe. Berries are poisonous.

Top: Individual flowers have four petals and four exerted stamens. Middle: Flowers are in short dense racemes. Bottom: Later in the season, plants produce speckled berries, which eventually turn red.

Buttercup family / Ranunculaceae

Native Species

Canada anemone

Anemone canadensis

Anémone du Canada, Canada windflower, meadow anemone

VITAL STATISTICS
Maximum height: 60 centimetres
Flowering season: May to July

HABITAT: Canada anemone grows along streamsides and in moist meadows, woodland borders, and the flood plains of large rivers. It is rare, primarily confined to calcareous soil in the western half of the province.

CHARACTERISTICS: Canada anemone forms large colonies; plants spread rapidly from underground rhizomes. Basal leaves have long hairy petioles, which reach 20 centimetres in length; stem leaves are opposite and have no petioles. The palmately lobed leaves have scattered hairs and are deeply cut into five to seven parts; each segment is also deeply cut or toothed.

Each stem produces one to three 3- to 4-centimetre-diameter flowers with five rounded petaloid sepals and a mass of yellow stamens and green pistils. Seed heads are globular and spiky.

Virginia anemone, *A. virginiana* (also known as *A. riparia*), is stout with palmately, deeply lobed leaves. Stem leaves are paired or in whorls of three; each leaf has a petiole. Plants produce a few 2-centimetre-diameter flowers with five white petaloid sepals. Seed heads are thimble-shaped and woolly. This species is seen mostly along calcareous shorelines.

The rare cut-leaved anemone, *A. multifida*, grows among calcareous gravels along the upper Saint John River and the Restigouche River. It is tufted, reaches 30 centimetres in height, and has bi- to triternate, deeply divided, almost feathery leaves. The entire plant is densely pubescent. Its off-white flowers are 1 to 2 centimetres wide.

Top: Canada anemone has palmately lobed, deeply cut leaves; flowers have five rounded white petaloid sepals. Middle: Virginia anemone flowers have globular spiky centres. Bottom: Cut-leaved anemone is densely pubescent, including its flowers.

Mixed Forest

Deciduous Forest

Wetlands

Buttercup family / Ranunculaceae

Woodland anemone

Native Species

Anemone quinquefolia

Anemone à cinq folioles, wood anemone

VITAL STATISTICS
Maximum height: 20 centimetres
Flowering season: Late May to early June

HABITAT: Woodland anemone grows in wooded ravines, most thickets and along riverbanks. Is is often encountered in the southern half of the province.

CHARACTERISTICS: Woodland anemone is a spring ephemeral, germinating and flowering early in the spring, then becoming dormant and disappearing by early summer. The slender flowering stem has a whorl of three petioled trifoliate leaves. Outer leaflets are so deeply divided that the leaves appear palmate. Leaflets have toothed edges and are hairless. Immature shoots produce a single basal leaf, similar in shape to the stem leaves.

A solitary 2.5-centimetre-diameter white flower with five to nine white petaloid sepals is produced at the junction of the stem leaves. Sepal undersides may be tinted pink or lilac. The flower stem is generally hairless.

Small-flowered anemone, *A. parviflora*, is a tufted 10- to 20-centimetre-diameter calciphile. It is extremely rare, found only along the Restigouche River and a single site near Albert Mines. Basal leaves are trifoliate with round leaflets, dark green, and shiny. Leaflets are lobed or have rounded teeth at their tips. Stem leaves are in a whorl of three with each leaf nearly stemless and deeply tri-lobed. Leaves are smooth or have varying amounts of fine hairs. Flowers are solitary, 2 centimetres in diameter, with five to seven rounded white petaloid sepals. Sepal undersides are hairy and may be tinted blue.

Top: Woodland anemone has a whorl of three trifoliate leaves; each deeply lobed leaflet appears to have five leaflets. Bottom: Small-flowered anemone has dark green shiny foliage; stem leaves are a whorl of three tri-lobed leaves.

Mixed Forest
Deciduous Forest

Buttercup family / Ranunculaceae

Native Species

Goldthread

Coptis trifolia (formerly *C. groenlandica*)

Savoyane, coptide trifoliolée, canker-root, goldenroot

HABITAT: Goldthread is common in mossy coniferous forests but it also occurs in mixed or deciduous forests as well as on open barrens, bogs, cutovers, and recent burn sites. It is well distributed throughout New Brunswick.

VITAL STATISTICS	
Maximum height:	13 centimetres
Flowering season:	Mid-May to mid-June

CHARACTERISTICS: Goldthread forms small colonies that spread by golden yellow threadlike rhizomes: hence the common name. Leaves are basal and trifoliate with round leaflets; each leaflet has three obscure lobes and several teeth. Leaves are evergreen, leathery, shiny, and hairless, arising on a 5- to 10-centimetre-long petiole.

Flowers arise from the ground on thin leafless stems that are up to 13 centimetres long. The solitary starlike flowers have five (most common) to seven white petaloid sepals and a central cluster of stamens and pistils. Each flower is about 1 centimetre in diameter.

Top: Goldthread produces solitary starlike flowers.
Bottom: The basal leaves are shiny, hairless, and trifoliate with round leaflets.

Buttercup family / Ranunculus

White water buttercup

Native Species

Ranunculus aquatilis

Herbes aux écrevisses, white water-crowfoot, common water-crowfoot

VITAL STATISTICS
Maximum height: 5 centimetres
Flowering season: July to August

HABITAT: White water buttercup grows in shallow muddy-bottomed acidic pools in fresh or brackish water or along slow-moving streams. It is well distributed throughout New Brunswick.

CHARACTERISTICS: White water buttercup forms floating mats. Plants have two types of leaves, both of which are alternately arranged and hairless. Submerged leaves are finely dissected and feather-like, promptly collapsing when removed from the water. Floating leaves, if present, are stiffer and kidney-shaped with three main lobes and several minor lobes, with or without additional rounded teeth. Overall the leaves appear tri-lobed to palmately lobed.

Solitary flowers, which are 1 to 1.5 centimetres in diameter, arise from the leaf axils and extend a few centimetres above the water's surface. They have five shiny white petals, each with a yellow base and a cluster of yellow stamens in the middle.

Small yellow water buttercup, *R. gmelinii*, is also aquatic with a similar mat-like habit and submerged and emergent leaves. It has 1- to 1.5-centimetre-diameter flowers, which may be solitary or in a cluster of up to four flowers. The number of yellow petals varies from four to 14. This species is very rare in the province and restricted to wet calcareous meadows and streams. It is isolated in a few localities mostly in the southern counties and in Gloucester County.

Top: The shiny white flowers have a yellow patch at the base of each petal. Bottom: Small yellow water buttercup is also aquatic but has yellow flowers.

Introduced Species

Carpetweed family / Molluginaceae

Green carpetweed

Mollugo verticillata

Mollugine, Indian carpetweed, carpetweed

HABITAT: Green carpetweed, native to the southern areas of North America, has been introduced to New Brunswick, where it grows along moist sandy roadsides and riverbanks as well as in gardens.

CHARACTERISTICS: Green carpetweed is a low creeping matted annual with multiple branching stems. Young plants have a basal rosette, but plants quickly begin to branch, and the basal leaves then fade. Sessile leaves are linear, lanceolate, elliptical, or spatulate and are held in whorls of three to eight. Leaf edges are smooth; the plant is hairless. Plants are superficially similar to bedstraw or *Galium*.

Flowers are produced in axillary umbels with two to six 0.3- to 0.4-centimetre-diameter blossoms. Each flower has five petaloid white sepals, and three (rarely four) stamens, which meet at the top of the green globular ovary.

VITAL STATISTICS
Maximum height: 5 centimetres
Flowering season: June to October

Top: Stamens meet at the top of the globular ovary.
Bottom: Leaves are whorled but in variable shapes.

Pink family / Caryophyllaceae

Field chickweed

Native Species

Cerastium arvense

Mouron d'alouette, meadow chickweed, field-mouse-ear chickweed

VITAL STATISTICS
Maximum height: 30 centimetres Flowering season: June to July

HABITAT: Field chickweed is scattered along roadsides and in gravelly or turfy barrens, headlands, and old pastures throughout New Brunswick. It prefers calcareous soils.

CHARACTERISTICS: Field chickweed's trailing stems grow to 30 centimetres in length, but plants form a matted clump about 10 to 15 centimetres tall. The opposite sessile leaves vary in shape from linear to elliptical and have smooth edges. The entire plant is covered in soft pubescent hairs. Tufts of small leaves are often present in the lower leaf axils.

Two to 20 flowers are produced in a loose cyme at the ends of wiry stems. The 2-centimetre-diameter flowers have five white petals with two-lobed tips, 10 stamens, and five styles. Petals are two to three times longer than the narrow green sepals.

Snow-in-summer, *C. tomentosum*, an occasional garden escape in the province, resembles field chickweed but has distinctive silver-white foliage due to the long white silky hairs which cover the plant.

Top: Flowers have five notched petals. Middle: Plants form matted clumps. Bottom: Snow-in-summer has silver hairy foliage.

Pink family / Caryophyllaceae

Common mouse-ear chickweed

Introduced Species

Cerastium fontanum subsp. *vulgare* (formerly *C. vulgatum*)

Mouron à oreille de souris, mouse-ear chickweed

VITAL STATISTICS

Maximum height: 45 centimetres

Flowering season: June to September

HABITAT: Common mouse-ear chickweed is an introduced European species found on moist disturbed areas and in meadows throughout New Brunswick.

CHARACTERISTICS: Common mouse-ear chickweed has trailing matted stems that reach 45 centimetres in length. The entire plant is covered in fine, occasionally sticky, pubescent hairs. The opposite sessile leaves are elliptical to ovate in outline with smooth edges.

Flowers are produced in a loose cluster or cyme. Each blossom is 1 to 1.5 centimetres in diameter and has five white cleft petals, 10 stamens, and five styles. Petals are the same length as or slightly longer than the green elliptical sepals.

Five-stamen mouse-ear chickweed, *C. semidecandrum*, is another European introduction recently found in several campgrounds throughout New Brunswick. It is more compact than common mouse-ear chickweed and the entire plant is covered in glandular hairs. Flowers, which are 0.5 to 0.7 centimetres in diameter, have five rather than 10 stamens and the petals are a little shorter than the sepals.

Top: Common mouse-ear chickweed's white petals are only slightly longer than the green sepals. Bottom: Five-stamen mouse-ear chickweed's white petals are a little shorter than the green sepals.

Pink family / Caryophyllaceae

Seabeach sandwort

Native Species

Honckenya peploides

Sabline faux-péplus, seaside sandwort, sea chickweed, sea purslane

VITAL STATISTICS
Maximum height: 30 centimetres
Flowering season: May to September

HABITAT: Seabeach sandwort is restricted to sandy and fine gravelly beaches along the Gulf coast of New Brunswick, along with a single site on Grand Manan Island.

CHARACTERISTICS: Seabeach sandwort forms clumps or mats with multiple branching trailing stems. The base of the stems may be considerably buried in sand. Leaves are sessile, opposite, and egg-shaped to elliptical with a pointed tip. They are fleshy, shiny, and hairless and have crenate edges. Each pair of leaves is often at right angles to the next.

Honey-scented flowers are produced terminally and are axillary, solitary, or in small cymes. Sepals and petals are about the same length but the egg-shaped sharp-pointed sepals are broader than the rounded petals. Individual flowers measure 1 to 1.5 centimetres in diameter. Each flower has 10 stamens and three styles. The globular yellow-green seed capsule resembles a berry.

Top: Petals and sepals are about the same length.
Bottom: Plants form mats of opposite egg-shaped pointed leaves.

Pink family / Caryophyllaceae

Native Species

Grove sandwort

Moehringia lateriflora (formerly *Arenaria lateriflora*)

Sabline latériflore, blunt-leaved sandwort

HABITAT: Grove sandwort is found along gravelly or turfy shores and in damp thickets and meadows, dry heaths, and open woodlands throughout New Brunswick.

CHARACTERISTICS: Grove sandwort has weak stems and commonly rambles through surrounding vegetation. Stems have backward-facing hairs that impart a roughness when the stem is rubbed. Leaves are opposite, sessile or with a very short pedicle, elliptical, and smooth-edged; they are hairless on the top surface but may have a few fine hairs on the underside.

Flowers may be solitary or in a loose cyme with two to five blossoms from the leaf axils. Individual flowers have five rounded white petals, which are twice as long as the sepals. Flowers are each about 1 centimetre in diameter with 10 stamens and three styles.

VITAL STATISTICS
Maximum height: 30 centimetres
Flowering season: June to September

Top: Individual flowers have five rounded petals, 10 stamens, and three styles. Bottom: Grove sandwort's weak stems ramble through neighbouring vegetation.

Mixed Forest | Deciduous Forest | Barrens | Coastal

Pink family / Caryophyllaceae

Bladder campion

Introduced Species

Silene vulgaris (formerly *S. cucubalus*)

Pétards, péteux, maiden's-tears

VITAL STATISTICS

Maximum height: 60 centimetres
Flowering season: June to August

HABITAT: Bladder campion, a European introduction, is found in fields and waste places, generally near larger towns and cities, throughout New Brunswick.

CHARACTERISTICS: Bladder campion is a clumping plant with multiple branched stems. Smooth-edged fleshy leaves are opposite and sessile to almost clasping the stem; the waxiness of the grey-green leaves imparts a dull texture. Leaves are oblong, oblanceolate to lanceolate in outline, and can reach 8 centimetres in length.

Flowers are produced in a loose panicle. Individual flowers are about 2.5 centimetres wide and composed of five deeply cleft white petals, which give the appearance of 10 petals. Each flower has 10 stamens and three pistils. The calyx is bladder-like and pale green to pink-tinted, with noticeable net-veins. Flowers are mostly nodding.

Night-flowering catchfly, *S. noctiflora*, another European introduction occasionally found in the province, is an annual covered in sticky glandular hairs. Lower leaves are oblanceolate but upper leaves are elliptical to lanceolate. White flowers, which only open at night, are in small cymes. The calyx is more ellipsoid and not as inflated as that of bladder campion.

The uncommon white campion, *S. latifolia*, is similar to *S. noctiflora* but its flowers are dioecious. Male flowers have 10 stamens; female flowers have five styles. All flowers are fragrant.

Top: The five petals of each bladder campion flower are so deeply cleft they appear to be 10 petals. Middle: Night-flowering catchfly's stems have fine glandular hairs. Bottom: White campion's flowers are similar to those of night-flowering catchfly but close examination reveals stamens or styles, not both.

Introduced Species

Pink family / Caryophyllaceae

Corn spurrey

Spergula arvensis

Spargoute des champs, grippe, stickwort, starwort

HABITAT: Corn spurrey is a European species commonly found in newly disturbed sites throughout the province.

CHARACTERISTICS: Corn spurrey is a low bushy branching annual. Leaves, which are up to 5 centimetres long, are linear and in whorls and have a narrow channel at their base. Leaves and stems are smooth or, less commonly, stems have glandular hairs.

Flowers are produced in loose terminal cymes. Individual flowers, each about 0.3 centimetres wide, consist of five green sepals, five white petals, five or 10 stamens, and five pistils. Sepals and petals are about the same length. Flower stems are often purple-tinted and covered in glandular hairs. Flower stems angle downward as the seed capsules develop.

VITAL STATISTICS
Maximum height: 40 centimetres
Flowering season: June to October

Top: Petals and sepals are the same length.
Bottom: The linear leaves are whorled.

Pink family / Caryophyllaceae

Grass-leaved starwort

Introduced Species

Stellaria graminea

Mouron des champs, grass-leaved stitchwort, common stitchwort

VITAL STATISTICS

Maximum height: 45 centimetres

Flowering season: May to October

HABITAT: Grass-leaved starwort is a European introduction and a weedy species in disturbed areas throughout New Brunswick.

CHARACTERISTICS: Grass-leaved starwort is a delicate species which forms mats or rambles through surrounding vegetation. Stems are square in cross-section. The plant is nearly hairless except for a few hairs located near the base of each leaf. Smooth-edges sessile opposite leaves are s lance to linear-shaped with pointed tips.

Flowers are produced in loose terminal cymes. Individual flowers are 0.5 to 1 centimetre in diameter; petals are slightly longer than the sepals. Each has 10 stamens and three styles.

Long-leaved starwort, *S. longifolia*, and bog stitchwort, *S. alsine*, are native species uncommon in seepages and damp meadows and along shorelines. The former's lance- to linear-shaped leaves are widest at the tip and narrow to the base; flowers are in small loose clusters from the upper leaf axils and petals are longer than sepals. Bog stitchwort has fleshy elliptical leaves. Its flowers, held in small axillary clusters, have petals that are shorter than the sepals. Similar to bog stitchwort, but more common, is northern starwort, *S. calycina*, distinguished by solitary flowers in the leaf axils.

Long-stalked starwort, *S. longipes*, is extremely rare and confined to coastal gravels of Restigouche and Gloucester counties. Its fleshy, linear to lance-shaped leaves are distinctly blue-grey. The flower clusters are mostly terminal and the stamens are often pink.

Top: Grass-leaved starwort flowers are in loose cymes; narrow leaves have pointed tips. Middle: Northern starwort's solitary flowers have petals that are shorter than the sepals. Bottom: Long-stalked starwort has blue-tinted leaves.

Pink family / Caryophyllaceae

Introduced Species

Common chickweed

Stellaria media

Mouron des oiseaux, chickweed, common starwort

HABITAT: A European introduction, common chickweed is found in disturbed habitats throughout New Brunswick. It can be a pest in agricultural regions.

VITAL STATISTICS
Maximum height: 50 centimetres
Flowering season: April to November

CHARACTERISTICS: Common chickweed, an annual plant, has trailing stems which reach 50 centimetres in length, resulting in a clumping or matted habit. Leaves are opposite, round to elliptical in outline, and smooth-edged. Lower leaves have petioles; upper leaves are sessile. One or two rows of hairs grow along the stem; sometimes hairs also grow along leaf edges.

Flowers are produced in cymes, both terminal and from the upper leaf axils. Flower stems and sepals have short hairs. Individual flowers, each about 1 centimetre in diameter, have five white petals that are so deeply lobed that they appear to be 10 petals. These petals are shorter than the green sepals. Flowers generally have five stamens and always three styles, which separates common chickweed flowers from those of the similar genus *Cerastium*, which have five styles.

Top: The flower stems have short hairs. Middle: The deeply cleft petals are shorter than the sepals. Bottom: The ovate leaves are opposite and the stems have scattered long hairs.

Knotweed family / Polygonaceae

Eurasian black bindweed

Fallopia convolvulus

Renouée liseron, chevrier, black bindweed, climbing buckwheat, wild buckwheat

Introduced Species

VITAL STATISTICS
Maximum height: 150 centimetres
Flowering season: June to October

HABITAT: Eurasian black bindweed is a European introduction often found in waste areas and, less commonly, on gravelly beaches throughout New Brunswick.

CHARACTERISTICS: Eurasian black bindweed is a twining annual vine. Thin stems are light green or tinted red. Alternate leaves are widely spaced and long petioled. Leaves are heart- or arrowhead-shaped with smooth edges. Stems may be finely pubescent; leaves are hairless. The largest leaves are up to 7 centimetres long. The base of each leaf has a membranous sheath (ocrea), which is also hairless.

Tiny 0.3- to 0.5-centimetre-wide flowers are produced in thin 2- to 10-centimetre-long axillary spikes. Individual flowers have five petaloid sepals, which are white, less commonly tinted pink, with a green central stripe. Sepals are keeled when in fruit.

Fringed black bindweed, *F. cilinodis*, is perennial, native to New Brunswick, and grows to 5 metres. The distinguishing feature is the ocrea, which has a ring of fringed hairs. Leaves have slightly hairy undersides. Axillary flowers are in open spiked panicles. Fringed black bindweed inhabits waste areas, rocky slopes, and clearings; it is more scattered than Eurasian black bindweed.

Climbing false buckweed, *F. scandens*, is a locally common native species found in wet streamside meadows. Sepals are strongly winged when in fruit.

Top: The tiny flowers are in narrow racemes. Middle: Eurasian black bindweed's twining stems produce arrowhead-shaped leaves. Bottom: Climbing false buckweed has winged sepals.

Buckwheat family / Polygonaceae

Introduced Species

Japanese knotweed

Fallopia japonica (formerly *Polygonum cuspidatum* or *Reynoutria japonica*)

Renouée du Japon, canne de Saint-Joseph, fleeceflower, mile-a-minute

VITAL STATISTICS
Maximum height: 2.5 metres
Flowering season: August to September

HABITAT: Japanese knotweed, an invasive species found throughout New Brunswick, occurs in disturbed areas such as roadsides, waste areas, and neglected gardens.

CHARACTERISTICS: Japanese knotweed is unmistakable simply because of its size. Spring foliage is red-tinted. Stout stems are hollow, smooth, and often mottled red. They are swollen at the joints where leaves or branches arise. Plants are multiple branching; overall, the plant is shrub-like. The alternately arranged leaves are round to triangular, hairless, and smooth-edged with a distinct narrow tip. They may reach up to 15 centimetres in diameter.

During late summer, flowers are produced in upright spray-like forking panicles among the upper leaf axils. Individual flowers are minute, each 0.2 to 0.3 centimetres wide, with five white tepals. Plants are dioecious with male and female parts. Male flowers are distinguished by their eight stamens.

Giant knotweed, *F. sachalinensis*, is far less common than Japanese knotweed but also found throughout New Brunswick. It is similar but overall larger, reaching to 4 metres in height. The plant is sparingly branched. Leaves are heart-shaped and up to 30 centimetres in length, with hairs along the main veins on the undersides. Panicles are bushier than those of Japanese knotweed. A hybrid between these two species, *F. X bohemica*, has intermediate characteristics.

Top: Flowers are in axillary narrow panicles. Middle: Plants have a shrub-like habit. Bottom: Giant knotweed has larger heart-shaped leaves and bushier panicles than Japanese knotweed.

Sundew family / Droseraceae

Round-leaved sundew

Native Species

Drosera rotundifolia

Rossolis à feuilles rondes

VITAL STATISTICS
Maximum height: 15 centimetres
Flowering season: July to August

HABITAT: Round-leaved sundew, common throughout New Brunswick, grows in damp to wet habitats.

CHARACTERISTICS: An insectivorous plant, round-leaved sundew produces a rosette of ground-hugging round leaves which have long hairy petioles. Leaves are covered in red hairs with distinctive glandular tips; these glands exude a clear glutinous fluid that appears like dewdrops. Insects are attracted to, and become trapped by, the sticky fluid and are gradually digested by the plant, providing an essential source of nitrogen. Leaves partially enfold larger insect prey.

Flowers are produced on a one-sided raceme upon a wiry erect leafless stalk; each flower has five white petals and is about 0.5 to 0.8 centimetres in diameter.

Spoon-leaved sundew, *D. intermedia*, has spatulate leaves and hairless petioles. It is nearly as common as round-leaved sundew.

English sundew, *D. anglica,* is extremely rare and only known from Restigouche County. It has lance-shaped leaves and hairless petioles.

Top: Flowers are on a leafless one-sided raceme.
Middle: Round leaves are covered in sticky red hairs.
Bottom: Spoon-leaved sundew has narrow leaves and hairless petioles.

Native Species

Heath family / Ericaceae

One-flowered wintergreen

Moneses uniflora

Monésès uniflore, one-flowered pyrola, one-flowered shinleaf

VITAL STATISTICS
Maximum height: 10 centimetres
Flowering season: Mid-June to July

HABITAT: One-flowered wintergreen inhabits mossy shady forest floors throughout New Brunswick.

CHARACTERISTICS: One-flowered wintergreen is a delicate forest-floor wildflower which forms small colonies or mats from underground rhizomes. Leaves, either paired or in a whorl of three, are located at ground level—thus appearing basal. The round to egg-shaped leaf is evergreen and veiny, with fine teeth along its edges.

Flowers are solitary and nod at the end of 5- to 10-centimetre-long leafless stems. Fragrant flowers are 1.5 to 2.5 centimetres in diameter with five waxy wavy-edged white petals, 10 stamens, and a relatively large five-lobed stigma. The flower is held parallel to the ground.

Top: The solitary flowers have a relatively large five-lobed stigma. Middle: Flowers are distinctly nodding. Bottom: Leaves are often in a whorl of three.

Heath family / Ericaceae

Indian pipe

Native Species

Monotropa uniflora

Monotrope uniflore, ghostflower, ghost pipe, corpse plant

VITAL STATISTICS
Maximum height: 30 centimetres
Flowering season: July to September

HABITAT: Indian pipe grows in mossy shady woodlands throughout New Brunswick.

CHARACTERISTICS: Indian pipe is a non-photosynthetic plant that survives by parasitizing mushrooms from the genus *Russula*. The plant has no green leaves and appears more like a fungus than a plant. Indian pipe may live for years underground but, when conditions are optimal, several waxy hairless stems appear above ground. Although leafless, the plants do have white or translucent alternately arranged 1-centimetre-long fleshy flaps along the stems—their answer to leaves.

Flowers are solitary, nodding, and bell-shaped, measuring 1.5 to 2.5 centimetres in length. They have five fleshy white or pink-tinted petals. The flowers become erect once they set seed.

Pinesap, *Hypopitys monotropa* (formerly *Monotropa hypopitys*), is less common than Indian pipe. It, too, is a parasitic plant. It is similar to Indian pipe but flowers are smaller, up to 1 centimetre in diameter, and are in a nodding or upright raceme with two to 11 flowers. Summer flowers are cream or yellow-tinted with a slight pubescence; fall flowers are tinted red-pink and densely pubescent. It is partial to coniferous forests.

The extremely rare pine-drops, *Pterospora andromedea*, is another parasitic plant. It is confined to white pine forests in Restigouche and York counties. Leafless stems arise to 80 centimetres with a spike of nodding urn-shaped flowers. The stems are pink and covered in glandular hairs while the flowers are cream-white.

Top: Indian pipe has white or translucent stems and solitary nodding flowers. Middle: Pinesap has yellow-tinted stems and produces clusters of flowers. Bottom: Pine-drops produces a spike of nodding urn-shaped flowers.

Heath family / Ericaceae

Shinleaf

Pyrola elliptica

Native Species

Pyrole elliptique, wax-flowered pyrola, white-flowered pyrola, wax-flowered wintergreen

HABITAT: Shinleaf prefers open mixed woodlands but is occasionally seen along roadsides and in pastures, bogs, and fens. It is well distributed throughout the province.

VITAL STATISTICS
Maximum height: 25 centimetres
Flowering season: July to August

CHARACTERISTICS: Shinleaf has a basal rosette of evergreen thin-textured and elliptical, oblong, or obovate leaves. Leaves, commonly 5 to 8 centimetres long, are dull green with a few shallow teeth along their edges. The leaf tip is rounded and the base tapers into the petiole, which is generally shorter than the length of the blade.

Flowers are produced in a cylindrical raceme on a leafless stem. Up to 15 nodding 1-centimetre-wide flowers are produced; each flower has five ovate waxy white petals and a curved style reminiscent of an elephant's trunk. Sepals are triangular in shape and about as long as they are wide.

The uncommon but widespread round-leaved pyrola, *P. americana*, occurs in both wetlands and woodlands. It has round leathery evergreen leaves which are fairly shiny. The 1.5-centimetre-diameter flowers are highly fragrant and milky white. The style is arched down and out like an elephant's trunk. The egg-shaped sepals are twice as long as they are wide.

Top: Shinleaf produces a cylindrical raceme of flowers on a leafless stem. Middle: Shinleaf's curved style is reminiscent of an elephant's trunk. Bottom: Round-leaved pyrola has a long raceme of flowers and leathery round leaves.

Bittersweet family / Celastraceae

Fen grass-of-Parnassus

Parnassia glauca

Parnassie à feuilles glauques

Native Species

VITAL STATISTICS
Maximum height: 30 centimetres
Flowering season: July

HABITAT: Fen grass-of-Parnassus prefers wet calcareous soil. It is uncommon and restricted to western and northern regions of the province.

CHARACTERISTICS: Fen grass-of-Parnassus produces a basal rosette of ovate to oblong hairless thick fleshy smooth-edged leaves. Plants produce several flower stems; each stem is topped with a solitary flower. The flowering stem may be leafless or have a single small leaf attached just above its base. A single sessile leaf is produced near or below the middle of the flower stem.

Flowers have five white petals with distinct green veins and measure about 2.5 centimetres in diameter. The petals are nearly three times the length of the green sepals. Flowers have five stamens, which alternate with the petals, and four stigmas. They also have three false stamens, called staminodia, which are glandular-tipped, green-yellow and shiny.

Top: The solitary flowers have white petals with distinct green veins. Bottom: Plants produce a basal rosette of leaves from which arise several solitary flowers.

Native Species

Saxifrage family / Saxifragaceae

White mountain saxifrage

Saxifraga paniculata

Alpine saxifrage, encrusted saxifrage, livelong saxifrage

HABITAT: White mountain saxifrage, a calciphile restricted to calcareous gravels, ledges, and cliffs, is extremely rare and confined to Albert, Kings, and Saint John counties.

VITAL STATISTICS
Maximum height: 15 centimetres
Flowering season: June to July

CHARACTERISTICS: White mountain saxifrage is a tufted evergreen plant with basal rosettes of stiff leathery oblong to spatulate leaves. Silvery green leaves have white lime-encrusted finely toothed edges. Flower stems have alternately arranged leaves.

Flowers are produced in a small panicle. Individual flowers, each up to 1 centimetre wide, are white, often with fine red spotting. They have five petals, 10 stamens, and two pistils.

Also extremely rare and confined to rocky cliffs on the southern end of Keswick Ridge, York County, is early saxifrage, *Micranthes virginiensis* (formeraly *S. virginiensis).* It produces a flat rosette of 1- to 7-centimetre-long oval leathery leaves with toothed edges. Glandular-sticky leafless stems arise 5 to 30 centimetres and end in a dense panicle of white flowers. Early saxifrage blooms in May and June.

Top: Flowers are in small panicles. Middle: Plants produce rosettes of silvery green leaves with lime-encrusted white edges. Bottom: Early saxifrage has a basal rosette of leathery leaves and a dense panicle of white flowers.

Saxifrage family / Saxifragaceae

Heart-leaved foamflower

Tiarella cordifolia

Tiarelle cordifoliée, creeping foamflower, false mitrewort

Native Species

Deciduous Forest

VITAL STATISTICS
Maximum height: 30 centimetres
Flowering season:

HABITAT: Heart-leaved foamflower is found in lush, primarily deciduous, woods and river bottoms. It is common in the southern-central-western regions but mostly absent in the north and east.

CHARACTERISTICS: Heart-leaved foamflower has a tufted to mat-forming habit. Leaves are basal and also alternately arranged along the length of running stolons; leaves are heart- to egg-shaped, sparsely hairy on their upper surfaces, and pubescent on their undersides. Their petioles are densely pubescent. Leaves are palmately lobed and their edges have sharp teeth.

Plants produce several leafless 10- to 30-centimetre-high flower stalks. Flowers are produced in a cylindrical raceme which is up to 15 centimetres in length. Individual white or pale pink starlike flowers are tiny, just 0.25 to 0.5 centimetres wide. They have five petals and five petaloid sepals, which give the impression that the flowers have 10 petals. They also have 10 stamens and two styles.

Top: Flowers are in cylindrical racemes. Bottom: The heart-shaped leaves are palmately lobed and toothed along their margins.

Introduced Species

Rose family / Rosaceae

Queen-of-the-meadow

Filipendula ulmaria

Reine-des-près, meadowsweet

HABITAT: Queen-of-the-meadow, a European species introduced as a garden ornamental, has become naturalized along roadsides and thickets, albeit locally, throughout the province.

VITAL STATISTICS
Maximum height: 150 centimetres
Flowering season: July to August

CHARACTERISTICS: Queen-of-the-meadow is a clumping plant with many non-branching stems that arise from a thick rhizome. Stems, often tinted purple or red, are stiff, erect, and furrowed. The basal and alternate stem leaves are pinnately compound with alternating large and small leaflets. The terminal leaflet is the largest and is often tri-lobed. Leaflets are sharply and coarsely toothed. The upper leaf surface is dark green; the lower is whitened with dense, soft pubescent hairs. Basal leaves have long petioles; upper stem leaves are short petioled but have a pair of kidney-shaped toothed stipules at their base.

The fragrant flowers are produced in irregularly branched cymes, creating a fluffy panicle of blooms. Individual flowers are about 0.5 centimetres wide with five creamy white petals and 20 or more stamens. Rarely, a double-flowered form is encountered.

Queen-of-the-prairie, *F. rubra*, is another occasional garden escape found in southern counties. It may reach 2 metres in height with unbranched stems. Its large leaves resemble those of queen-of-the-meadow, except their undersides are green. Fluffy panicles of minute flowers are various shades of pink.

Top: Queen-of-the-meadow flowers are in fluffy irregular panicles. Bottom: Queen-of-the-prairie also produces fluffy panicles of bloom but in shades of pink.

Rose family / Rosaceae

Wild strawberry

Fragaria virginiana

Fraisier des champs, common strawberry

Native Species

VITAL STATISTICS
Maximum height: 15 centimetres
Flowering season: May to June

HABITAT: Wild strawberry grows along roadsides and trailsides and in old meadows and pastures throughout New Brunswick.

CHARACTERISTICS: Wild strawberry is a mat-forming plant that spreads by stolons. Leaves, often evergreen with a bluish tint, are basal and trifoliate with ovate sharply toothed leaflets. Leaf top surfaces are hairless; undersides may have silky hairs. The terminal tooth of the middle leaflet is shorter than the adjacent teeth.

Flowers are produced in clusters on leafless stems. Individual flowers have five white petals and are 1.5 to 2 centimetres wide. Flower stems are generally shorter than the leaf petioles. Seeds of the ovate fruit are embedded within pits on the fruit surface. The fruit is fleshy and sweet-tasting.

The less common woodland strawberry, *F. vesca*, is usually found in slightly shadier locations than wild strawberry, such as open woodlands, slopes, and ravines. It prefers calcareous soils. Plants have long petioled leaves and the terminal tooth of the middle leaflet is longer than the adjacent teeth. The flower stem is longer than the leaf petioles. One- to 1.5-centimetre-wide flowers are smaller than those of wild strawberry and are produced on a raceme. Seeds on the fruit are not embedded in a pit. It is most common along the Saint John River watershed and the Restigouche River.

Top: Flowers have five petals and a central cluster of stamens and styles. Middle: Seeds are embedded in pits on the ovate fruit's surface. Bottom: Woodland strawberry's long flower stems result in flowers being held above the leaves.

Rose family / Rosaceae

Native Species

White avens

Geum canadense

Benoîte du Canada, Canada avens

HABITAT: White avens is found in rich woodlands, thickets, and intervales throughout New Brunswick.

CHARACTERISTICS: White avens is a leafy plant with slender coarsely hairy stems. Plants have both basal leaves and alternately arranged stem leaves. Basal leaves, often evergreen over the winter, vary in shape from round with three to five shallow lobes to trifoliate or pinnately compound with five, rarely seven, leaflets, always with sharply toothed edges. Basal leaves may be smooth or have a few hairs, especially along the lower veins. Lower stem leaves are often trifoliate with short petioles; the upper are deeply tri-lobed and sessile. At the base of all stem leaves is a pair of stipules.

Flowers are solitary or in a loose cluster of up to three; each flower has five white petals and is 1 to 1.5 centimetres in diameter. Flower stems are finely pubescent. Seeds are produced in a spiky rounded head.

Less common than white avens, rough avens, *G. laciniatum*, prefers similar, but wetter, habitats; it is coarser and stouter, with rough hairy leaves. Basal leaves are commonly pinnate with five leaflets; stem leaves are trifoliate or tri-lobed. White petals are only half the length of the sepals; flower stems have long hairs. Seeds are produced in a spiky globular head. Rough avens is mostly found along the Saint John River watershed.

VITAL STATISTICS
Maximum height: 80 centimetres
Flowering season: July

Top: Flowers have five white petals and finely pubescent stems. Middle: Lower leaves are commonly trifoliate with sharply toothed edges. Bottom: Rough avens' small petals are shorter than the sepals.

Rose family / Rosaceae

Cloudberry

Native Species

Rubus chamaemorus

Chicouté, mûres blanches, ronce petit-mûrier, bakeapple, salmonberry

VITAL STATISTICS
Maximum height: 25 centimetres
Flowering season: June to early July

HABITAT: Cloudberry grows in acidic bogs and, less commonly, on rocky coastal headlands. Uncommon in New Brunswick, it is encountered in the extreme southwest and northeast of the province.

CHARACTERISTICS: This plant is a low deciduous sub-shrub with unbranched stems arising from subterranean and semi-woody rhizomes. Non-flowering stems often have a solitary leaf; flowering stems may have two or three alternate leaves. The leaves—palmate with five lobes and sharply toothed edges—resemble a cloak in shape. Leathery and rugose, leaves are slightly glossy, often bronzy green (especially in exposed locations), and turn bronzy purple in autumn.

Plants are dioecious. Separate male and female plants bloom in June and early July. Solitary white flowers (2 to 4 centimetres in diameter) have four to seven petals and many stamens. The calyx tightly encloses developing fruit. On ripening (August and September), it curls back to reveal the solitary orange to amber raspberry-like fruit, which is edible and highly prized for jams and jellies.

Top: Male flowers have a central cluster of many stamens. Middle: Leaves are cloak-like in shape. Bottom: Flowers develop into an orange raspberry-like fruit.

Native Species

Rose family / Rosaceae

Dewberry

Rubus pubescens

Ronce pubescente, dwarf raspberry

VITAL STATISTICS
Maximum height: 25 centimetres
Flowering season: June

HABITAT: Dewberry prefers damp forests but also grows on damp rocky slopes, at wetland edges, and along shorelines. It is well distributed throughout the province.

CHARACTERISTICS: A sub-shrub with short slender stems, dewberry can be either flowering or vegetative. It appears to be herbaceous, but look closer: the loosely upright flowering stems (10 to 25 centimetres long) are somewhat woody at the base. Trailing vegetative stems can grow to 100 centimetres or more in length; their tips often root to create new plants. Both stem types are softly hairy. The alternate thin leaves are trifoliate or palmately compound with double-toothed edges. Trifoliate leaves often have lower leaflets that are lobed as well as toothed. Leaves may have a few hairs and, in full sun, a bronze tint.

Dewberry produces five-petalled flowers that are white or pale pink. The petals, held at right angles to the calyx, meet at the tips or can be recurved; flowers appear singly or in a loose cluster of two to five blossoms. They develop into small sweet-tasting translucent shiny red raspberry-like fruit.

Top: Petals often meet at the top of the flower; leaves are often bronzy when exposed to full sun. Middle: Leaves are either trifoliate or palmately compound. Bottom: Flowers develop into shiny raspberry-like fruit.

Rose family / Rosaceae

Dewdrop

Native Species

Rubus repens (formerly *Dalibarda repens*)

Dalibarde rampante, robin-run-away, false violet, star violet

VITAL STATISTICS
Maximum height: 10 centimetres
Flowering season: August

HABITAT: Dewdrop, found in moist deciduous or mixed woodlands, is distributed mostly in the southern half of New Brunswick.

CHARACTERISTICS: Dewdrop is a low tufted to creeping plant. Leaves are basal as well as alternate along the creeping rhizomes. Individual leaves, which are 3 to 5 centimetres wide, are round to heart-shaped with scalloped edges. Petioles are densely hairy; leaves are less hairy than the petioles.

Flowers are solitary and of two types. Typical flowers, which are 0.8 to 1.6 centimetres in diameter, are produced on thin hairy stems and held just above the leaves. Although they have five white petals and numerous stamens, they are sterile. Fertile flowers lack petals and are held on curving stems hidden beneath the leaves. Although now classified as a *Rubus*, this plant does not produce a fleshy raspberry-like fruit.

Top: Held above the leaves, sterile flowers have five petals and a central cluster of stamens. Bottom: Leaves are round with scalloped edges.

Rose family / Rosaceae

Three-toothed cinquefoil

Sibbaldia tridentata (formerly *Potentilla tridentata*)

Potentille tridentée

Native Species

HABITAT: Three-toothed cinquefoil occurs primarily on exposed rocky barrens, mountains, and coastal headlands. Less commonly, it may be encountered in open coniferous woodlands, along roadsides, or on mature meadows and sand dunes. It is found throughout New Brunswick but more frequently along the coast.

CHARACTERISTICS: Three-toothed cinquefoil is a tufted or mat-forming plant with leathery evergreen basal leaves and alternately arranged stem leaves along creeping stems. Each leaf is trifoliate with elliptical leaflets and a pair of stipules at the base of the petiole. Edges are smooth except for three terminal teeth. The upper surface is glossy and generally hairless, but the underside has fine hairs. Winter foliage is often tinted red.

Flowers are produced in loose clusters of up to 25 flowers. Individual flowers have five white petals, are 1 to 1.5 centimetres wide, and have 20 to 30 stamens, which form a central pincushion effect. Flower stems are pubescent and often tinted red.

VITAL STATISTICS
Maximum height: 25 centimetres
Flowering season: June to July

Top: A central cluster of stamens create a pincushion effect. Middle: Plants produce loose clusters of flowers. Bottom: The trifoliate leaves have three terminal teeth.

Sandalwood family / Santalaceae

Bastard toadflax

Comandra umbellata

Comandre à ombelle, common comandra

Native Species

VITAL STATISTICS
Maximum height: 30 centimetres Flowering season: June to July

HABITAT: Bastard toadflax grows in dry sandy soils on dunes and exposed headlands and in open coniferous forests. Uncommon in New Brunswick, it is found primarily along the east coast.

CHARACTERISTICS: Bastard toadflax is a smooth leafy plant with branched or unbranched stems. Hemiparasitic, it obtains nutrients from neighbouring plants. The alternately arranged leaves are elliptical to spatulate, thick-textured, hairless, and smooth-edged. They are pale green but sometimes tinted olive-brown. They are either sessile or have short petioles.

Flowers are produced in a terminal corymb. Individual flowers are about 0.6 centimetres wide and have five or, rarely, six white or pale pink pointed petaloid sepals which impart a starlike appearance. Plants commonly have non-flowering branches located immediately below the flower clusters.

Top: Small starlike flowers are in a terminal corymb.
Bottom: The unbranched stems have pale green leaves.

Aralia family / Araliaceae

Dwarf ginseng

Panax trifolius

Petit ginseng, groundnut, fairy spuds

Native Species

HABITAT: Dwarf ginseng is found in rich deciduous forests and intervales. It is uncommon and widely scattered in New Brunswick.

CHARACTERISTICS: Dwarf ginseng is a spring ephemeral that forms loose colonies. Plants produce tuberous roots and go dormant, disappearing by mid-summer. Plants send up a single stem that ends in a whorl of three to five long petioled, trifoliate, or palmately compound leaves. Each compound leaf has three to five lance-shaped to elliptical toothed leaflets, which are sessile and 2 to 4 centimetres in length. All parts of the plant are hairless.

Flower stems arise from the top of the whorl of leaves. Flowers are produced in a rounded umbel. Individual flowers are about 0.3 centimetres wide with five white petals. Flowers may be male or bisexual; the former has five stamens and a single non-functional pistil. Bisexual flowers have five stamens and three pistils. The sex of the plants can change from year to year. Flower stems are often white. Bisexual flowers develop berries that change colour from green to yellow. Berries are dry and contain three seeds.

VITAL STATISTICS
Maximum height: 20 centimetres
Flowering season: June

Top: Flowers are held in a round umbel.
Bottom: Compound leaves (trifoliate shown) have toothed elliptical leaflets.

Parsley family / Apiaceae

Goutweed

Introduced Species

Aegopodium podagraria

Égopode podagraire, herbe aux goutteux, bishop's goutweed, ground elder

VITAL STATISTICS

Maximum height: 100 centimetres
Flowering season: June to August

HABITAT: Goutweed, a European plant, is now a troublesome weed in many gardens, especially if the soil is moist and shaded. It grows in waste areas throughout the province.

CHARACTERISTICS: Goutweed, an aggressive groundcover plant, spreads rapidly by underground rhizomes. Most leaves are basal and solitary, arising directly from the rhizome. Leaves have long petioles, which are 30 centimetres or more in length. Each leaf is biternate; the short-stemmed leaflets are ovate and sharply toothed or lobed. Flowering stems have alternately arranged leaves. Lower stem leaves are similar to the basal leaves, but upper stem leaves are smaller and may be simply trifoliate. Stems and leaves are hairless.

The lower portion of flowering stems is generally unbranched, but the upper portion may branch to produce several leafless hemispherical compound umbels. Individual flowers, each about 0.3 centimetres wide, have five white petals, five stamens, and two pistils.

Occasionally, the variegated ornamental form is encountered as a garden escape.

Top: Flowers are in hemispherical umbels.
Bottom: Leaves are biternately compound with ovate toothed leaflets.

Introduced Species

Parsley family / Apiaceae

Wild caraway

Carum carvi

Anis canadien, caraway, common caraway

VITAL STATISTICS
Maximum height: 60 centimetres
Flowering season: June

HABITAT: A European introduction, wild caraway is found in waste places and neglected lawns and pastures throughout New Brunswick.

CHARACTERISTICS: Wild caraway is a biennial plant. In the first season, plants produce a basal rosette of finely dissected bi- to tripinnately compound leaves. In the second season, plants produce multiple branches with alternately arranged carrot-like leaves. Stems and leaves are hairless.

Branches terminate in flat-topped compound umbels. Individual flowers, about 0.3 centimetres in diameter, have five white or pale pink petals, five stamens, and two pistils. The crescent-shaped ribbed caraway seeds are commonly used as a spice in cooking.

Burnet saxifrage, *Pimpinella saxifraga*, is uncommon in New Brunswick, found mostly near Fredericton and along the coast of Restigouche and Gloucester counties. This introduced perennial, which reaches to 60 centimetres in height, has coarse basal leaves that are pinnately compound with sessile oblong to obovate toothed leaflets. The upper stem leaves are smaller than those of wild caraway, with narrow leaflets which may have deep narrow lobes. The compound umbels of flowers are like those of wild caraway but they do not bloom until August to September.

Top: Wild caraway flowers are held in flat-topped compound umbels. Middle: The finely dissected leaves of wild caraway are similar to carrot leaves. Bottom: Burnet saxifrage has pinnate leaves with rounded toothed leaflets.

Carrot family / Apiaceae

Bulbous water-hemlock

Native Species

Cicuta bulbifera

Cicutaire bulbifère

VITAL STATISTICS
Maximum height: 100 centimetres
Flowering season: August

HABITAT: Bulbous water-hemlock grows in shallow water along streams, ponds, and cattail marshes throughout New Brunswick.

CHARACTERISTICS: Bulbous water-hemlock is a tall, slender member of wetland communities. Alternately arranged leaves are finely dissected. Lower leaves have long petioles and are bipinnately compound; linear leaflets are narrowly lobed and/or sharply toothed. Upper leaves are short petioled to sessile and pinnately compound. The plant is hairless. Upper leaf axils produce bulblets in late summer.

Terminal flowers are in compound umbels, often consisting of eight flat umbellets of about 16 tiny flowers. Each 0.3-centimetre-diameter blossom has five white petals, five stamens, and two styles.

Widely distributed and growing in similar habitats is the biennial spotted water-hemlock, *C. maculata*. It has basal leaves in the first year and flowering stems in the second. The stout stems often have purple mottling. Leaves are bipinnate with lance-shaped to elliptical leaflets. Their compound umbels each consist of 10 to 20 slightly domed umbellets. Both water-hemlocks are poisonous if ingested.

Another wetland plant found throughout New Brunswick, common water-parsnip, *Sium suave,* has ribbed stems and pinnate leaves with seven to 17 lance-shaped to elliptical sharp-toothed leaflets. Their compound umbels consist of 10 to 25 umbellets. The base of the main umbel has six to 10 narrow downward-curving bracts.

Top: Flowers are in compound umbels. Middle: The bipinnate leaflets of spotted water-hemlock are lanceolate to elliptical. Bottom: Common water-parsnip has pinnate leaves with elliptical leaflets.

Native Species

Parsley family / Apiaceae

Hemlock-parsley

Conioselinum chinense

Coniosélinum de Genesee

HABITAT: Hemlock-parsley inhabits cool wet coniferous forests, shady ravines, and wet peaty slopes. Scattered in New Brunswick, it is most common in the northwestern and southern areas.

VITAL STATISTICS
Maximum height: 100 centimetres
Flowering season: August to October

CHARACTERISTICS: Hemlock-parsley is a slender upright plant with basal and alternately arranged stem leaves that are finely dissected and carrot-like. Stems and leaves are hairless but hairs are usually present on the flower stems.

Flowers are terminal, in compound umbels. Individual flowers are 0.3 to 0.5 centimetres in diameter with five white notched petals, five stamens, and two pistils. The round but flattened seeds have two distinct wings.

Top: Flowers are in flattened compound umbels.
Bottom: The finely dissected leaves are similar to those of carrots.

Parsley family / Apiaceae

Queen Anne's lace

Introduced Species

Daucus carota

Carotte sauvage, wild carrot

VITAL STATISTICS
Maximum height: 100 centimetres
Flowering season: July to September

HABITAT: Queen Anne's lace, a European species, is uncommon along roadsides and fields in the southwestern counties. It prefers calcareous soil.

CHARACTERISTICS: Queen Anne's lace is a biennial. In the first season, plants produce a basal rosette of bi- to tripinnately compound leaves whose toothed leaflets are narrow and threadlike; they resemble carrot leaves. In the second season, plants produce one to several upright stems with alternately arranged leaves. Stems, petioles, and the veins on leaf undersides are covered in soft hairs.

Flowers are produced in a terminal flat-topped compound umbel. The base of the primary umbel has a skirt of threadlike divided bracts. Individual flowers are 0.3 to 0.5 centimetres wide with five white, rarely pink, petals (two smaller and three larger). Umbellet stems arch inward as ovate bristly seeds develop, creating what looks like a bird's nest.

The European wild chervil, *Anthriscus sylvestris*, is rare and localized. It blooms much earlier than Queen Anne's lace, from late May through June. Plants are biennial or short-lived perennials and hairless except for some pubescent hairs at the base of the strongly ribbed stems. Primary umbels have no leafy bracts; the bases of umbellets have a small ring of green bracts. Umbellet stems do not curl in on themselves as the narrow ribbed seeds develop. Wild chervil is most often encountered in Saint John and Kings counties.

Top: Flowers are in flat-topped compound umbels. Middle: Because Queen Anne's lace umbellets curl inward as seeds develop, the seed heads appear like a bird's nest. Bottom: Wild chervil resembles Queen Anne's lace but blooms in late spring-early summer.

Parsley family / Apiaceae

American cow parsnip

Heracleum maximum

Berce très grande, cow parsnip

Native Species

VITAL STATISTICS
Maximum height: 2.8 metres
Flowering season: June to August

HABITAT: American cow parsnip grows along streams and roadsides and in wet meadows and river bottoms throughout New Brunswick.

CHARACTERISTICS: American cow parsnip forms a large clump. Stems are hairy, grooved, and hollow. Leaves are basal on non-flowering plants but alternately arranged along flowering stems. Leaves are trifoliate with palmately lobed, coarsely toothed leaflets. Leaves, often 60 centimetres long, are covered in short hairs, especially on the undersides. Stem leaves, enlarged at the base, sheathe the stem.

Several hemispherical umbels of flowers may reach 30 centimetres in diameter; each is composed of many umbellets. Each 1-centimetre-wide flower has five white petals, one or two of which are twice as large as the others and deeply cleft. Seed capsules are ovate to round and flat.

Common hogweed, *H. sphondylium*, a rare introduction, is distinguished by pinnately compound blunt-toothed lobed hairy leaves and confined to the Saint Andrew's area.

Giant hogweed, *H. mantegazzianum*, is another rare introduction and is found in the Sackville area. It can grow to over 3 metres in height. Smooth stems have hairs at the leaf nodes; leaves are smooth, shiny, and toothed. Purple blotches and warts differentiate this species.

The sap of these three species can cause severe blistering on skin exposed to sun.

Top: American cow parsnip's large trifoliate leaves have palmately lobed leaflets; flowers are in large hemispherical umbels. Middle: Common hogweed leaves are pinnate with blunt-toothed and lobed leaflets.
Bottom: Giant hogweed has large flat-topped umbels, shiny deeply cut leaves, and stems with purple blotches.

Parsley family / Apiaceae

Scotch lovage

Ligusticum scoticum

Livèche écossaise, persil de mer, beach lovage, sea lovage

Native Species

VITAL STATISTICS
Maximum height: 60 centimetres
Flowering season: July to August

HABITAT: Scotch lovage is found along the Fundy and east coasts of New Brunswick, growing along rocky or peaty headlands, saline marshes, and gravelly beaches.

CHARACTERISTICS: Scotch lovage is a clumping plant with many upright non-branching stems. Both the basal and alternately arranged stem leaves are biternate and celery-like, with ovate leaflets which grow to 5 centimetres in length. The leaflets are coarsely toothed along the outer three quarters, sometimes lobed, shiny, and fleshy. The stems and leaf petioles are often tinted red, especially at the base of the petiole. The entire plant is hairless.

Flowers are produced in terminal compound umbels and have five stamens and two pistils. Individual flowers, each 0.3 to 0.5 centimetres wide, have five white petals that curl inward at the tip, showing a green stripe on the underside. The seeds are ovate with strong ribs.

Seacoast angelica, *Angelica lucida*, often co-occurs with Scotch lovage. Seacoast angelica can reach 150 centimetres in height and has dense umbels of greenish-white flowers. It has globose seeds with ribs and broader, more distinctly veined leaves than Scotch lovage. Leaves are often triternate and the leaflets are toothed along their entire length.

Top: Flowers are in flat-topped compound umbels and stems are often tinted red. Middle: The biternate leaves of Scotch lovage are smooth and celery-like. Bottom: Seacoast angelica has green-tinted flowers and veiny leaves.

Carrot family / Apiaceae

Native Species

Hairy sweet cicely

Osmorhiza claytonii

Osmorhize de Clayton, Clayton's sweetroot

HABITAT: Hairy sweet cicely grows in semi-shady sites in moist rich deciduous or mixed woodlands throughout New Brunswick. It is uncommon along the east coast.

VITAL STATISTICS
Maximum height: 90 centimetres
Flowering season: May to June

CHARACTERISTICS: Hairy sweet cicely has slender stems and basal and alternately arranged stem leaves. Leaves are hairy and biternately compound with ovate toothed and lobed leaflets. The petioles have long hairs. Plants may reach 90 centimetres but generally grow 40 to 60 centimetres in height.

Compound umbels of flowers have four to seven umbellets; each umbellet base has a ring of narrow hairy-fringed bracts. Each 0.3- to 0.5-centimetre-wide flower has five notched petals, five white stamens, and two pistils. Bristly seed pods are narrow, up to 1 centimetre in length, and split in two when ripe.

Smooth sweet cicely, *O. longistylis*, is uncommon, found primarily in deciduous forests along the upper Saint John and Restigouche rivers. It may reach 120 centimetres in height, with smooth stems and petioles; leaf axils may have scattered hairs and leaves may be pubescent. A distinct sweet anise fragrance is produced by the foliage when bruised.

Mountain sweet cicely, *O. berteroi*, resembles hairy sweet cicely; mountain sweet cicely's flowers are more greenish-white, its umbels are wider-spreading, and its narrow seed capsules are longer, reaching 2 centimetres in length. Plants may reach 100 centimetres in height. It is scattered across the province.

Top: Hairy sweet cicely stems are finely pubescent; umbels have four to seven umbellets. Middle: Smooth sweet cicely usually has smooth stems. Bottom: Mountain sweet cicely has green-tinted flowers in wide-spreading umbels.

Nightshade family / Solancaeae

Eastern black nightshade

Solanum ptychanthum

Tuechien, morelle noir, crève-chien, American black nightshade

Introduced Species

VITAL STATISTICS
Maximum height: 100 centimetres
Flowering season: June to September

HABITAT: Eastern black nightshade, while native to North America, has been introduced into waste areas in scattered localities in New Brunswick.

CHARACTERISTICS: Eastern black nightshade is a busy, coarse annual. Alternate dark green leaves are oval, up to 8 centimetres long, with irregular rounded teeth or smooth edges. Leaves and stems are hairless.

Flowers are produced in axillary umbels of five to 10. Individual 1- to 1.5-centimetre-wide flowers have five recurved white pointed petals and five erect, conical yellow anthers surrounding the single style. Flowers develop into shiny black berries, each 0.7 to 0.9 centimetres in diameter.

An introduced species, ground-cherry, *S. physalifolium*, is often considered a weed. This branching annual may reach 60 centimetres in height. Smooth-edged leaves are ovate to triangular. Leaves and stems are covered in soft, dense greyish hairs. White starlike flowers are in axillary umbels. Green to yellow berries are half-covered by the calyx.

Top: Individual eastern black nightshade flowers have five recurved white petals and conical anthers that surround a single style. Middle: Eastern black nightshade has glossy black fruit. Bottom: Ground-cherry fruit are partly covered by the large softly hairy calyx.

Morning-glory family / Convolvulaceae

Introduced Species

Hedge bindweed

Calystegia sepium (formerly *Convolvulus sepium*)

Gloire du matin, wild morning-glory, larger bindweed

HABITAT: Hedge bindweed has two forms in New Brunswick: the European form grows primarily in waste areas; the native form grows along fresh- and saltwater marshes. The native form is more common in the province.

VITAL STATISTICS
Maximum height: 3 metres
Flowering season: July to September

CHARACTERISTICS: Hedge bindweed is a twining plant that clambers over its neighbours. Plants many be hairless or finely pubescent. The smooth-edged leaves are alternate, 5 to 10 centimetres long, and arrowhead, triangular, heart-shaped, or egg-shaped, often with incised bases. Leaves have long petioles.

Solitary funnel-shaped flowers, each 6 to 7.5 centimetres in diameter, are produced from the upper leaf axils. Each flower has five shallow lobes—evidence of five fused petals—and a pair of green bracts. The introduced European form has white flowers; the native variation *americana* has pink flowers. Flowers open in the morning and close by late afternoon.

Field bindweed, *Convolvulus arvensis*, is a rare European introduction localized in disturbed areas near Saint John. It is also a vine, but it more often grows along the ground, with stems reaching 100 centimetres in length. Leaves are similar to those of hedge bindweed but are smaller; flowers may also be white or pale pink but are less than 2.5 centimetres wide and lack the pair of green bracts present at the base of hedge bindweed flowers.

Top: Hedge bindweed's unmistakable funnel-shaped white flowers. Middle: The native variety *americana* has pink-tinted flowers. Bottom: Field bindweed flowers are smaller than those of hedge bindweed and plants ramble along the ground.

Wetlands

Disturbed

Morning-glory family / Convolvulaceae

Swamp dodder

Native Species

Cuscuta gronovii

Cuscute de Gronovius

VITAL STATISTICS
Maximum height: 200 centimetres
Flowering season: Late July to August

HABITAT: Swamp dodder is found in swamps, marshes, and wet thickets and along lakeshores in the southern half of the province.

CHARACTERISTICS: Swamp dodder is an annual parasitic vining plant that lacks leaves, although small scale-like bracts may be present. The tangled stems are smooth and gold, orange, or pink-tinted. The most frequent hosts include *Impatiens*, *Salix*, *Cephalanthus*, *Decodon*, and *Eupatorium*.

Flowers are produced in small dense panicles scattered along the upper stems. Individual flowers are 0.2 to 0.4 centimetres in diameter with five white triangular petals. Flowers, and especially the developing seed capsules, are covered in sticky glandular hairs.

Buttonbush dodder, *C. cephalanthi*, is an extremely rare species which has been found in Northumberland, Victoria, and Gloucester counties, where it occurs along low-lying coastal regions. It is distinguished by its flowers, which have four rather than five translucent white petals. It commonly parasitizes asters.

Top: Flowers are in small dense panicles.
Bottom: Dodder lacks leaves and forms a tangle of yellow or orange-tinted twining stems.

Bog buckbean family / Menyanthaceae

Bog buckbean

Menyanthes trifoliata

Herbe à canards, bogbean, buckbean

Native Species

HABITAT: Bog buckbean grows in the shallow water of various wetland habitats throughout New Brunswick.

CHARACTERISTICS: Bog buckbean forms floating mats. Plants spread by a thick creeping rhizome located at or just below the water's surface. At the end of the rhizome arise a few long petioled trifoliate leaves whose bases sheathe the rhizome. Each leaf has three hairless ovate leaflets whose edges are smooth or have a few rounded teeth. Leaves are held 10 to 30 centimetres above the water's surface.

The cylindrical raceme of flowers arises to 30 centimetres on leafless stems. Individual flowers are intricate. From pink buds open 1.5-centimetre-diameter star-shaped flowers with five, rarely six or seven, white or pale pink petals. The upper surface of the petals is covered with long white hairs. The golden style in the centre is noticeable. Seeds are produced in globular capsules.

VITAL STATISTICS
Maximum height: 30 centimetres
Flowering season: June

Top: The long hairy blossoms of bog buckbean.
Bottom: Bog buckbean forms large colonies.

Buckbean family / Menyanthaceae

Little floatingheart

Nymphoides cordata

Faux-nymphéa à feuilles cordées, floating hearts

Native Species

VITAL STATISTICS	
Maximum height:	2 metres (water depth)
Flowering season:	July to September

HABITAT: Little floatingheart is found along the shores of shallow mud-bottomed ponds and slow-moving streams. The species is locally common in the southern regions of the province.

CHARACTERISTICS: Little floatingheart is an aquatic plant with long thin stems that arise from rhizomes growing in muddy-bottomed streams and ponds. A single floating leaf is produced on each stem. Leaves are heart-shaped, often purple-mottled, and 2 to 5 centimetres in length. They are smooth-edged and hairless and look like a smaller version of a water-lily leaf.

Flowers, held just above the water surface, are solitary but arise from an umbel. The flower stem arises where the leaf petiole joins the stem, usually a few centimetres below the water's surface. A cluster of fleshy spur-like roots often arise at this junction later in the season. Each 1-centimetre-diameter flower has five sepals, five petals, five stamens, and a single pistil. Sepals and petals are united at their base. Petals are white and hairy and have a yellow gland at their bases.

Top: The white petals have a yellow gland at their base. Bottom: The small waterlily-like leaves are often mottled purple.

Native Species | Introduced Species

Aster family / Asteraceae

Common yarrow

Achillea millefolium

Herbe à dindes, milfoil, yarrow

HABITAT: Common yarrow, both European and native forms, is found in disturbed habitats and, less often, in barrens throughout New Brunswick.

CHARACTERISTICS: Common yarrow is a mat-like or clumping plant with several non-branching stems and both basal and stem leaves. The alternately arranged narrow fern-like leaves are bipinnately compound with fine narrow leaflets which may be toothed or smooth-edged. Leaves are usually covered in fine white hairs. Basal leaves are larger with a petiole; upper stem leaves are smaller and sessile. The entire plant is aromatic when bruised.

Flowers are produced in dense flat-topped compound corymbs. Individual flower heads are about 0.5 centimetres wide and are composed of five white ray florets and 15 to 20 white disc florets. Each ray floret ends in three teeth. Less commonly, the ray and disc florets may be pink to rose-purple.

Woolly yarrow, *A. millefolium* var. *lanulosa*, is the native version of yarrow. Difficult to distinguish from the European form, it has more round-topped corymbs and densely white woolly stems and leaves.

Sneezeweed, *A. ptarmica*, a garden escape occasionally found along roadsides and shorelines and in fields throughout the province, has lance-shaped to linear leaves with finely toothed edges along non-branching upright stems. It is commonly hairless. Blooms are produced in a loose corymb; each flower head has eight to 12 white ray florets.

VITAL STATISTICS
Maximum height: 100 centimetres
Flowering season: July to September

Top: Flowers are in flat-topped clusters. Middle: Common yarrow foliage is finely dissected. Bottom: Sneezeweed flowers have eight to 12 ray florets in loose flat-topped corymbs.

Aster family / Asteraceae

Hairy galinsoga

Introduced Species

Galinsoga quadriradiata

Galinsoga cilié, shaggy galinsoga, quicksilver, shaggy soldier

VITAL STATISTICS	
Maximum height:	60 centimetres
Flowering season:	August to September

HABITAT: Hairy galinsoga, a Mexican species, is scattered as a garden weed in isolated areas throughout New Brunswick.

CHARACTERISTICS: Hairy galinsoga is a loosely branched annual with sticky glandular hairs over almost the entire plant. The opposite oval to elliptical leaves are up to 7 centimetres long and have three distinct veins radiating from the base. Leaves are hairy and have coarsely serrated teeth. Lower leaves have petioles; the upper are often sessile.

Flowers are held on open few-flowered cymes among the upper leaf axils and at the ends of the upper branches. Individual flower heads, each about 0.6 to 0.8 centimetres wide, are usually composed of five small white three-toothed ray florets surrounding a cluster of yellow disc florets.

Top: Individual flowers have five small white petals with three terminal teeth. Bottom: Flowers are in open few-flowered cymes among the upper leaf axils.

Native Species

Gourd family / Cucurbitaceae

Wild cucumber

Echinocystis lobata

Concombre grimpant, prickly cucumber, wild balsam apple

HABITAT: Wild cucumber appears on flood plains and in wet meadows, thickets, and waste places throughout New Brunswick.

CHARACTERISTICS: Wild cucumber is an annual vine that climbs by twisting tendrils. Stems are smooth. Tendrils have three forks and are located opposite the leaves. Alternate leaves, which are up to 15 centimetres wide, are palmately lobed and similar in shape to those of a maple. They are finely toothed or smooth along their edges and generally hairless.

Plants are monoecious. Male flowers are produced in a loose 30- to 40-centimetre-long raceme along the upper leaf axils of the vine. Each blossom is about 1.5 to 2 centimetres wide with six narrow pubescent greenish-white petals. Solitary female flowers are located at the base of the male flower cluster. Female fruit is a 5-centimetre-long globular green gourd covered in soft spines. Superficially the fruit looks like a small spiny watermelon.

VITAL STATISTICS
Maximum height: 3 metres
Flowering season: July to September

Top: Male flowers are in elongate racemes.
Middle: Plants produce maple-like leaves.
Bottom: Mature female fruit resemble a small spiny watermelon.

Asparagus family / Asparagaceae

Large false Solomon's-seal

Maianthemum racemosum (formerly *Smilacina racemosa*)

Faux sceau-de-Salomon, false spikenard, false Solomon's-seal

Native Species

Mixed Forest

Deciduous Forest

VITAL STATISTICS
Maximum height: 90 centimetres
Flowering season: June

HABITAT: Large false Solomon's-seal is found in rich deciduous or mixed forests and clearings. It is more common in the southern half of New Brunswick than the north.

CHARACTERISTICS: Large false Solomon's-seal has non-branching slightly zigzagging stems that often lean to one side. Parallel-veined, alternately arranged leaves are elliptical with smooth but undulating edges. Reaching up to 15 centimetres in length, leaves are usually sessile, although lower leaves may have a short petiole. The upper leaf surface is smooth; the lower, finely pubescent.

Flowers are produced in plume-like branching panicles which are up to 15 centimetres long. Individual flowers are only about 0.5 centimetres in diameter with six narrow white tepals, six stamens, and one style. Stamens are a little longer than tepals. Later in summer, flowers develop into smooth globular red-speckled berries that ripen to bright red. Berries are inedible.

Top: Flowers are held in plume-like panicles. Middle: The alternately arranged elliptical leaves have distinct parallel veins. Bottom: Flowers become small red berries in autumn.

Native Species

Asparagus family / Asparagaceae

Star-flowered false Solomon's-seal

Maianthemum stellatum (formerly *Smilacina stellata*)

Smilacine étoilée, starry false Solomon's-seal, starry false lily-of-the-valley

HABITAT: Star-flowered false Solomon's-seal is found along coastal headlands and swales, and, less commonly, in inland wet meadows and marshes. It is locally common along the coasts and the upper Saint John River but rare in central New Brunswick.

CHARACTERISTICS: Star-flowered false Solomon's-seal is a colonial species which spreads by thin underground rhizomes. The alternate leaves, which are up to 12 centimetres long, are elliptical and sessile and clasp the stem. The smooth-edged leaves have prominent parallel veins and finely pubescent undersides. The upper surface is dull and waxy. The unbranched stem slightly zigzags between the leaves and has a tendency to lean to one side.

Flowers are a terminal raceme with three to 20 flowers. Each flower is about 1 centimetre wide with six white tepals, six stamens, and a single three-parted style. They later develop into maroon-striped berries that turn bright red when ripe. Berries are inedible.

VITAL STATISTICS
Maximum height: 40 centimetres
Flowering season: June to July

Top: Flowers are held in a few-flowered terminal raceme. Middle: The alternately arranged elliptical leaves clasp the stem. Bottom: In late summer, plants produce maroon-striped berries.

Wetlands

Coastal

Asparagus family / Asparagaceae

Three-leaved false Solomon's-seal

Native Species

Maianthemum trifolium (formerly *Smilacina trifolia*)

Smilacine trifoliée, three-leaved false lily-of-the-valley, three-leaved Solomon's plume

VITAL STATISTICS
Maximum height: 20 centimetres Flowering season: June

HABITAT: Three-leaved false Solomon's-seal is found in bogs and wet meadows across the province.

CHARACTERISTICS: Three-leaved false Solomon's-seal is a colonial plant which spreads by thin underground rhizomes. Leaves are elliptical and sessile and clasp the stem. Non-blooming plants often have just one or two leaves; flowering plants produce three alternate leaves. Leaves, which may reach 10 centimetres in length, are usually held erect. They are hairless and shiny with smooth edges and parallel veins.

Five to 15 flowers are produced on a terminal raceme. Individual flowers have six white tepals, six stamens, and a single three-parted style. Flowers are about 0.5 to 0.7 centimetres in diameter; they become green berries with fine red spots which fully ripen into bright red berries.

Top: Flowers are in a few-flowered terminal raceme. Middle: Flowering plants typically produce three alternately arranged elliptical leaves. Bottom: In late summer, plants produce green berries, which later turn red.

Wetlands

Lily family / Liliaceae

Clasping-leaved twisted-stalk

Native Species

Streptopus amplexifolius

Streptope amplexicaule, white mandarin, clasping twisted-stalk, liverberry

HABITAT: Clasping-leaved twisted-stalk, uncommon in New Brunswick, grows in damp woodlands and river bottoms.

CHARACTERISTICS: Clasping-leaved twisted-stalk has a stout stem with a few zigzagged stemmed branches. The elliptical to ovate leaves are alternate and sessile and clasp the stem. The 5- to 12-centimetre-long leaves have parallel veins and are hairless and smooth-edged; leaf undersides are often waxy grey-green.

One-centimetre-long flowers are solitary and hang from the upper leaf axils on thin kinked stems. Each flower has six white strongly reflexed tepals that have a few fine purple speckles at their base. Flowers become bright red elliptical juicy berries that taste like cucumber.

VITAL STATISTICS
Maximum height: 90 centimetres
Flowering season: Late May to July

Top: Individual flowers have six tepals, which are variously spotted purple at their base. Middle: Plants produce a stout stem with a few zigzagging branches. Bottom: In late summer, flowers become elliptical red berries; note the kinked pedicle.

Lily family / Liliaceae

Sticky tofieldia

Native Species

Triantha glutinosa (formerly *Tofieldia glutinosa*)

Tofieldie glutineuse, sticky false asphodel

VITAL STATISTICS
Maximum height: 35 centimetres
Flowering season: July

HABITAT: Sticky tofieldia grows in calcareous marshes and wet meadows. It is very rare and widely scattered in western and northern New Brunswick.

CHARACTERISTICS: Sticky tofieldia forms grass-like clumps with erect basal linear leaves which are one-half to two-thirds of the length of the flower stem. The stem is heavily glandular, very sticky, and red-tinted.

Flowers are produced in a cylindrical raceme which is 2 to 6 centimetres long and 1 to 2 centimetres wide. Individual flowers have six white tepals and six dark stamens and are about 1 centimetre in diameter. They are produced in groups of two or three along the raceme. The developing seed capsules are commonly red.

Top: Individual flowers have six white tepals and six dark red stamens. Middle: Flowers are in a cylindrical raceme; stems are sticky-glandular. Bottom: Leaves are grass-like.

Wetlands

Waterlily family / Nymphaceae

Fragrant water-lily

Nymphaea odorata

Nénuphar blanc, fragrant white water-lily

Native Species

HABITAT: Fragrant water-lily prefers still clear acidic water with a muddy bottom. It occurs around the margins of ponds or in wetland pools, primarily in southwestern New Brunswick.

CHARACTERISTICS: Fragrant water-lily is an aquatic plant which produces floating leaves from a thick, horizontal rhizome. Leaf petioles can extend up to 3 metres to accommodate the water depth. The 10- to 30-centimetre-diameter leaves are smooth, leathery, and round, with a cleft from the middle on one side. The top surfaces of the leaves are deep green; their undersides are mottled purple.

Solitary floating flowers are produced at the ends of long stalks. Flowers are 8 to 15 centimetres in diameter with 20 to 30 pointed upward-curving white petals. The centre of the flower has multiple yellow stamens and a single large pistil. The fragrant flowers open in the morning and close by late afternoon. The globular seed capsule bends down under the water, where it matures and releases floating seeds.

VITAL STATISTICS

Maximum height: 3 metres
Flowering season: June to September

Top: Solitary floating flowers have multiple petals and a central cluster of yellow stamens. Bottom: The floating leaves are round with a cleft at one end.

Mixed Forest

Deciduous Forest

Poppy family / Papaveraceae

Bloodroot

Sanguinaria canadensis

Sanguinaire du Canada, sanguinaire, pucoon-root

Native Species

VITAL STATISTICS
Maximum height: 30 centimetres
Flowering season: May

HABITAT: Bloodroot grows in rich deciduous or mixed forests, especially along river bottoms. It is scattered throughout New Brunswick.

CHARACTERISTICS: Bloodroot is among the earliest of wildflowers to bloom in New Brunswick. Plants form colonies with solitary basal leaves arising from a thick rhizome. The rhizome oozes red sap when broken, giving the plant its common name. The single leaf is round, hairless, and palmately lobed with five to seven rounded lobes. The divisions are also shallowly lobed or have a few rounded teeth. The base of the leaf is heart-shaped; its underside has raised veins and a waxy appearance. The leaf curls around the developing flower and unfurls after the bloom has opened.

The solitary flower arises on a leafless stalk to a height just above the level of the leaf, usually around 15 centimetres at blooming time, although the stem may elongate to 30 centimetres as seeds develop. The 2.5- to 3.5-centimetre-diameter flower is composed of eight to 12 elliptical to lance-shaped white tepals and a mass of golden yellow stamens. The flower lives only a few days and then develops into an elliptical to lance-shaped seed capsule.

Top: Solitary flowers with eight to 12 petals are held just above the leaves; note how the leaves curl around the flower. Bottom: The round leaves are palmately lobed.

Primrose family / Primulaceae

Northern starflower

Native Species

Trientalis borealis

Trientale boréale, starflower, American starflower

HABITAT: A common plant, northern starflower grows in woodland settings and on barrens throughout New Brunswick.

CHARACTERISTICS: Northern starflower forms loose colonies as plants spread by slender underground rhizomes. Each stem is solitary with a terminal whorl of five to nine (usually seven) lance-shaped hairless leaves. Leaf edges may be smooth or faintly toothed.

Just above where the leaves join together, plants produce a solitary star-shaped flower or an umbel of two or three flowers at the end of thin stems. Individual flowers are about 1 centimetre in diameter with five to nine (usually seven) petals and an equal number of stamens.

VITAL STATISTICS
Maximum height: 20 centimetres
Flowering season: May to July

Top: The starlike flowers typically have seven petals.
Bottom: Plants produce a whorl of lance-shaped leaves.

Aster family / Asteraceae

Pearly everlasting

Anaphalis margaritacea

Immortelle

Native Species

VITAL STATISTICS
Maximum height: 80 centimetres
Flowering season: August to October

HABITAT: Pearly everlasting grows in disturbed habitats such as roadsides, forest clearings, meadows, open barrens, and open woodlands throughout New Brunswick.

CHARACTERISTICS: Pearly everlasting forms bushy clumps of pale grey-green foliage. Stems are mostly non-branching and covered in dense soft white hairs. The lance-shaped to linear leaves are densely woolly on the undersides but less so on the upper surfaces. Leaves are alternate on the stem and lack petioles. They have smooth edges that are often rolled under.

Flowers are produced in flat-topped panicles. Individual flower heads are about 1 centimetre wide; they have no petals but the many white papery phyllaries are petal-like. The central disc florets are yellow.

Top: Flowers are in flat-topped panicles. Bottom: Plants form bushy clumps with narrow silvery green foliage.

Aster family / Asteraceae

Native Species

Flat-top white aster

Doellingeria umbellata (formerly *Aster umbellatus*)

Aster à ombelles, tall white aster

HABITAT: Flat-top white aster grows in damp habitats, including the edges of ponds and streams, ditches, swamps, marshes, meadows, and damp woodlands. It is common throughout the province.

CHARACTERISTICS: Flat-top white aster is a tall wildflower with many non-branching stout stems that are mostly smooth and often tinted purple. The elliptical to lance-shaped leaves are alternate along the stem and smooth or stiffly hairy, with distinct veins. Leaf edges are also smooth but fringed in fine hairs. Leaves are either sessile or have a short petiole.

Flowers are produced in a series of corymbs which, together, form a flat-topped panicle up to 30 centimetres in diameter. Individual flower heads are about 2 centimetres wide, consisting of five to 15 white ray florets and 12 to 35 yellow disc florets; the latter turn off-white after blooming. Flower stems and base are covered in fine grey-white hairs.

VITAL STATISTICS
Maximum height: 2 metres
Flowering season: August to September

Top: Daisy-like flowers are in flat-topped clusters.
Bottom: Stems are unbranched with alternately arranged narrow leaves and purple-tinted stems.

Aster family / Asteraceae

Hyssop-leaved fleabane

Native Species

Erigeron hyssopifolius

Erigeron à feuilles d'hysope

VITAL STATISTICS

Maximum height: 25 centimetres
Flowering season: June to July

HABITAT: Hyssop-leaved fleabane, a calciphile restricted to limestone and gypsum cliffs, outcrops, and shores, is locally common but scattered in the southern, western, and northern regions of New Brunswick; it is rare or absent along the east coast and central areas.

CHARACTERISTICS: Hyssop-leaved fleabane forms a tufted plant with numerous thin non-branching stems. The linear to lance-shaped leaves are alternately arranged and crowded along the stems. They are smooth-edged and hairless or may have a few scattered hairs.

Flower heads are usually solitary and terminal. Individual heads are about 2 centimetres wide with 20 to 30 white ray florets, which often turn pink as they age, and numerous yellow disc florets.

Top: Plants produce solitary daisy-like flowers.
Bottom: Plants form tufted clumps with crowded narrow leaves on unbranched stems.

Native Species

Aster family / Asteraceae

Rough fleabane

Erigeron strigosus

Vergerette rude, whitetop fleabane, rough daisy fleabane

VITAL STATISTICS
Maximum height: 100 centimetres
Flowering season: July to September

HABITAT: Rough fleabane is commonly found in disturbed areas throughout New Brunswick.

CHARACTERISTICS: Rough fleabane is an annual or, less commonly, a biennial species. Plants produce several non-branching stems that arise to 100 centimetres and have scattered white hairs. The alternately arranged leaves are oblanceolate, oblong, or spatulate. They are minutely hairy and mostly smooth-edged, although larger basal leaves have a few coarse teeth along their outer edges.

Flowers are produced in a loose corymb. Individual daisy-like flowers are 1 to 2 centimetres wide with 40 to 100 white or pale lavender ray florets and numerous yellow disc florets. Flowers are mildly fragrant.

Annual fleabane, *E. annuus*, is found in similar habitats as rough fleabane but differs in having stouter, leafier stems and leaves which are more regularly coarsely toothed.

Horseweed, *Erigeron (Conyza) canadensis*, an annual species reaching to 200 centimetres, has crowded linear leaves, conspicuously hairy stems, and small white flowers in many-branched terminal clusters. Its ray florets are very short, held erect, and often inconspicuous.

Top: Rough fleabane produces a loose corymb of flowers; each flower head has numerous narrow petals. Middle: Annual fleabane has leafy stems with coarsely toothed leaves. Bottom: Horseweed's numerous small flower heads' ray florets are very short.

Aster family / Asteraceae

Oxeye daisy

Introduced Species

Leucanthemum vulgare (formerly *Chrysanthemum leucanthemum*)
Marguerite, marguerite daisy, field daisy

VITAL STATISTICS
Maximum height: 80 centimetres Flowering season: June to July

HABITAT: Oxeye daisy is a European species commonly found along roadsides and on pastures, meadows, and other disturbed areas across the province.

CHARACTERISTICS: Oxeye daisy is a clumping plant with numerous non-branching stems. Plants have both evergreen basal leaves and alternately arranged stem leaves. The oblanceolate basal leaves have distinct petioles and may reach 12 centimetres in length; they become smaller and oblong up the stem, where they are sessile or may even clasp the stem. They are coarsely toothed, fleshy, and generally hairless. The furrowed stem may have scattered hairs.

The 4- to 5-centimetre-diameter flower heads are solitary, with 15 to 35 white ray florets and numerous yellow disc florets.

Feverfew, *Tanacetum parthenium* (formerly *Chrysanthemum parthenium*), is a widespread European garden escape widely scattered in the province. It is a short-lived bushy perennial with light green pinnate leaves whose leaflets are coarsely toothed and lobed. Plants reach 80 centimetres in height and have a loose leafy corymb of flowers. Individual flower heads are about 1 centimetre in diameter with many white ray florets and yellow disc florets. The plant has a rank smell when bruised.

Top: Oxeye daisy's unmistakable white flowers have many flat white ray florets surrounding a button of yellow disc florets. Middle: Oxeye daisy forms a clump of many unbranched stems; each stem is topped by a single flower. Bottom: Feverfew has pale green pinnate leaves; flowers are in loose corymbs.

Aster family / Asteraceae

Native Species

White goldenrod

Solidago bicolor

Verge d'or bicolore, silverrod

VITAL STATISTICS	
Maximum height:	100 centimetres
Flowering season:	August and September

HABITAT: White goldenrod occurs in disturbed areas such as roadsides, old fields, and recent burn sites, as well as in open woodlands and on open barrens and seaside cliffs. It is common throughout New Brunswick.

CHARACTERISTICS: White goldenrod plants produce solitary or a few generally non-branching erect stems ranging from 30 to 50 centimetres, exceptionally to 100 centimetres, in height. Stems and leaves are covered in soft hairs which impart a grey-green appearance. Plants produce both basal and stem leaves. Basal leaves are relatively large, thick, oblanceolate to spatulate, and pubescent with finely toothed edges. They gradually taper into elongate petioles. Stem leaves are elliptical, smooth-edged, and without petioles; they rapidly become smaller up the length of the stem.

Flowers are produced in one or more wand-like panicles which are 10 to 15 centimetres in length. Flower stems are covered in fine hairs. Individual flower heads are only 0.4 centimetres wide and have seven to nine white to cream ray florets and nine to 12 yellow disc florets.

Hairy goldenrod, *S. hispida*, is virtually identical to white goldenrod in form and habitat, except for its yellow flowers and preference for calcareous substrates. It is uncommon and localized in the western and northern areas of the province.

Top: Individual flowers have seven to nine narrow ray florets and nine to 12 disc florets. Middle: White goldenrod flowers are in narrow wand-like panicles. Bottom: Hairy goldenrod resembles white goldenrod but has yellow flowers.

Aster family / Asteraceae

Rush aster

Native Species

Symphyotrichum boreale (formerly *Aster borealis*)
Aster boréal, northern bog aster

VITAL STATISTICS	
Maximum height:	100 centimetres
Flowering season:	August to September

HABITAT: Rush aster prefers calcareous gravelly shorelines of lakes and rivers as well as cedar swamps. It is a rare species localized in the southwestern, western, and northern regions of New Brunswick.

CHARACTERISTICS: Rush aster is a slender plant with non-branching stems which are 40 to 60 centimetres, rarely to 100 centimetres, in length. The lance-shaped to linear leaves are hairless with smooth edges that are rolled under. They are alternately arranged and lack petioles.

Flowers are produced in a loose panicle or may be solitary. Individual flower heads are 1.5 to 2 centimetres in diameter and have 25 to 35 white ray florets and a similar number of disc florets which change from pale yellow to purple-brown as they age.

Tradescant's aster or shore aster, *S. tradescanti*, has a similar habit as rush aster, but is often more bushy and commonly 20 to 40 centimetres in height. It also grows along gravelly shorelines. Leaves are lance-shaped to elliptical with smooth or slightly toothed edges. Flowers are produced in narrow loose panicles but are rarely solitary; individual flower heads have 15 to 25 ray florets and a similar number of disc florets. This species, uncommon across the province, is confined to the southwestern region.

Top: Rush aster often produces solitary flower heads. Middle: Rush aster is a slender plant with narrow hairless sessile leaves. Bottom: Tradescant's aster is often bushy with loose panicles of flower heads.

Native Species

Aster family / Asteraceae

Calico aster

Symphyotrichum lateriflorum (formerly *Aster lateriflorus*)

Aster latériflore, white woodland aster, one-sided aster, farewell to summer

HABITAT: Calico aster is found along roadsides and in old fields, woodland borders, and barrens throughout New Brunswick.

VITAL STATISTICS
Maximum height: 80 centimetres
Flowering season: July to October

CHARACTERISTICS: Calico aster is a clumping plant with many slender multiple branching stems. Stems, and the veins on the undersides of the leaves, are hairy; toothed leaves are otherwise smooth. Leaves are lance-shaped to spatulate. Plants produce overwintering basal leaves which shrivel by the time the plants bloom. Stem leaves are alternate and 5 to 15 centimetres in length.

Flowers are produced in an open panicle of one-sided racemes. Individual flower heads are 1 to 1.5 centimetres in diameter and have eight to 15 white ray florets and a similar number of mauve to purple disc florets.

White panicled aster, *S. lanceolatum*, grows in damp woodlands, intervales, and thickets and along roadsides and river bottoms. Plants reach 150 centimetres in height. Lance-shaped leaves are 10 to 20 centimetres long, smooth, and with or without toothed edges. Flowers are in a leafy pyramidal panicle. Flower heads are 1.5 to 2 centimetres in diameter with 20 to 40 white ray florets and a similar number of yellow disc florets.

Smooth white oldfield aster, *S. racemosum*, is very rare and confined to York, Sunbury, and Queens counties, where it grows in open woodlands and fields and along shorelines. It reaches to 150 centimetres with very rough-hairy, ridged stems, and leaves that are soft-hairy on both surfaces.

Top: Calico aster flower heads have white ray florets and purple disc florets. Middle: The narrow smooth-edged leaves are alternate along the stem. Bottom: White panicled aster flower heads have white ray florets and yellow disc florets.

Aster family / Asteraceae

Scentless chamomile

Introduced Species

Tripleurospermum inodorum (formerly *Matricaria maritima*)
Matricaire inodore, false chamomile, scentless mayweed

VITAL STATISTICS	
Maximum height:	60 centimetres
Flowering season:	June to September

HABITAT: Scentless chamomile, a European introduction which grows in disturbed areas, usually near the coast, is scattered throughout New Brunswick.

CHARACTERISTICS: Scentless chamomile is a bushy annual or biennial with wide-spreading upright branches and fine feathery leaves. The entire plant is essentially hairless and lacks any scent when bruised. The alternately arranged leaves are bipinnately dissected with linear lobes. They are not particularly fleshy.

Solitary flower heads are produced at the ends of the many branches. Each flower head is 3 to 4 centimetres in diameter with 10 to 25 white ray florets and numerous yellow disc florets. The flower head becomes conical as the flower ages.

Stinking chamomile, *Anthemis cotula*, a European species, is found in waste places in the southern and eastern regions of the province. It appears similar to scentless chamomile but stinking chamomile is rank-smelling when bruised. It often has fine hairs on its stems.

Top: Scentless chamomile produces solitary white daisies at the ends of its many branches. Middle: Scentless chamomile has finely dissected foliage. Bottom: Stinking chamomile also has solitary white daisies and finely dissected leaves.

Aster family / Asteraceae

Introduced Species

Devil's beggarticks

Bidens frondosa

Bident feuillu, common beggarticks, leafy beggarticks, large-leaved beggarticks

HABITAT: Devil's beggarticks inhabits damp waste places throughout New Brunswick.

CHARACTERISTICS: Devil's beggarticks is an erect annual with branched smooth stems, which are often tinted purple. Its opposite leaves are trifoliate or pinnately compound with five lance-shaped sharply toothed leaflets. Leaflets, each 5 to 10 centimetres long, have distinct stalks; the terminal leaflet is larger than the other leaflets. Leaves are smooth, with fine hairs on their undersides. Uppermost leaves are often simple and lance-shaped.

The long-stalked 1- to 2-centimetre-wide flower heads are solitary or in groups of three at the ends of the branches. Flowers, composed of many orange-yellow disc florets, generally lack ray florets. Below the flowers is a whorl of six to 10 unequal-sized green leafy bracts with hairy edges. Two barbed awns on the seeds allow them to stick to fur and clothing.

Tall beggarticks, *B. vulgata*, is less common than devil's beggarticks but it is found in similar habitats. These robust plants reach 150 centimetres in height; their stems and petioles are finely hairy. Leaflets from the trifoliate or pinnately compound leaves are almost sessile and flower heads lack ray florets. The base of the flower heads has a whorl of 11 to 20 green leafy bracts with hairy edges.

VITAL STATISTICS	
Maximum height:	100 centimetres
Flowering season:	Late July to September

Top: Below the petal-less flower heads of devil's beggarticks is a whorl of six to 10 irregular green bracts. Middle: Plants commonly have trifoliate leaves with sharply toothed leaflets. Bottom: The base of the rayless tall beggarticks flowers has a whorl of 11 or more hairy-edged green bracts.

Aster family / Asteraceae

Grass-leaved goldenrod

Native Species

Euthamia graminifolia (formerly *Solidago graminifolia*)

Verge d'or à feuilles de graminée, lance-leaved goldenrod, flat-topped goldentop

VITAL STATISTICS	
Maximum height:	150 centimetres
Flowering season:	August to September

HABITAT: Grass-leaved goldenrod commonly grows in disturbed sites such as clearings, roadsides, ditches, and old meadows throughout New Brunswick.

CHARACTERISTICS: Grass-leaved goldenrod is a clump-forming plant with upright, slender leafy stems. Stems are mostly non-branching except near the top, where they branch into many flowering corymbs; stems may be hairless but often have lines of fine hairs along their length. Leaves, which are up to 10 centimetres long, are alternately arranged and linear to lance-shaped with smooth edges. The upper surface is often smooth, while the underside has short fine hairs along the one to three main veins.

Numerous flowers are produced in many corymbs, which may be densely or loosely arranged or more open. Overall, flower clusters have a flat-topped appearance. Individual flowers are about 0.5 centimetres wide with 20 to 35 disc and ray florets. This species does not have recognizable "petals" as do other goldenrods.

Top: Flowers are in a cluster of flat-topped corymbs.
Bottom: The linear to lance-shaped leaves of grass-leaved goldenrod have smooth edges.

Aster family / Asteraceae

Introduced Species

Pineappleweed

Matricaria discoidea (formerly *M. matricarioides*)

Matricaire suave, herbe à crapaud, disc mayweed, rayless chamomile

HABITAT: Pineappleweed is an introduced European plant now common in disturbed areas throughout New Brunswick.

CHARACTERISTICS: An annual species, robust pineappleweed plants are multiple branching and appear bush-like; those growing in less than perfect locations are non-branching and only a few centimetres in height. Plants are hairless. The alternately arranged 5-centimetre-long fern-like dissected foliage is bipinnate to tripinnate, like small carrot leaves. The entire plant has a pineapple-like fragrance when bruised.

Solitary flower heads are formed from the axils of the upper leaves. Each head is about 0.8 centimetres wide, consisting of numerous yellow disc florets but no ray florets; hence, the flowers appear petal-less. The base of the flower head has several overlapping green phyllaries that have light brown papery upper edges.

VITAL STATISTICS

Maximum height: 20 centimetres
Flowering season: July to September

Top: The solitary flower heads appear petal-less.
Bottom: The fern-like foliage is finely dissected.

Aster family / Asteraceae

Common tansy

Introduced Species

Tanacetum vulgare

Tanaisie commune, herbe de Saint-Marc, golden buttons

VITAL STATISTICS

Maximum height: 150 centimetres
Flowering season: July to August

HABITAT: Common tansy, a European introduction originally grown as an ornamental or medicinal plant, is occasionally seen along roadsides and in waste areas in New Brunswick.

CHARACTERISTICS: A clumping plant, common tansy has many hairless leafy stems and a strong, rank odour when bruised. The hairless alternate leaves have an elliptical outline but are bipinnately divided and appear fern-like.

Flowers are produced in terminal flat-topped corymbs. Each flower head is 0.5 to 1 centimetre in diameter and contains many yellow disc florets but lacks ray florets; this gives the flowers a button-like appearance.

Native along gravelly riversides of the Restigouche and Saint John rivers is the Lake Huron tansy, *T. huronense*. Plants may reach 40 centimetres in height. Stems are usually non-branching, and bipinately divided leaves are covered in hairs. Plants produce up to six 1.5- to 2-centimetre-diameter flower heads composed of yellow disc florets but no ray florets. This plant is rank-smelling when bruised.

Top: The petal-less flower heads look like yellow buttons. Middle: The finely dissected bipinnate leaves are fern-like. Bottom: Lake Huron tansy has larger flowers than common tansy, in small corymbs.

Violet family / Violaceae

Native Species

Downy yellow violet

Viola pubescens

Violette pubescente, common yellow violet, smooth yellow violet

HABITAT: Downy yellow violet occurs in cool, damp, mostly deciduous forests and shady rocky slopes. It is common throughout New Brunswick.

CHARACTERISTICS: Downy yellow violet forms a small clump with several thin, leafy, and softly hairy stems. Some leaves may be basal but most are alternate along the stems. The leaves, which are up to 7 centimetres long, are broadly cordate with toothed or scalloped edges. The leaf stalk is also softly hairy. The base of each leaf has a pair of ovate stipules. Emerging leaves have fine hairs but are less obviously hairy as they mature.

The 2-centimetre-diameter flowers are solitary and arise on thin stems from the upper leaf axils. They have five yellow petals with fine purple-brown lines at their bases, especially on the lowermost lip-like petals. The fruit is an egg-shaped capsule that, when mature, shoots seeds several feet from the parent plant.

VITAL STATISTICS

Maximum height: 45 centimetres
Flowering season: April to May

Top: Flowers are solitary; the lowest petals have distinctive purple stripes at their bases. Bottom: Heart-shaped leaves have scalloped edges.

Pea family / Fabaceae

Meadow pea

Lathyrus pratensis

Gesse des prés, meadow vetchling, yellow vetchling

Introduced Species

VITAL STATISTICS

Maximum height: 80 centimetres
Flowering season: July

HABITAT: Meadow pea, a European species, is widely scattered and occasionally found along the edges of fields or roadsides in the province.

CHARACTERISTICS: Meadow pea is a slender vine with multiple branches and ridged stems. The alternate leaves are compound with a pair of lance-shaped smooth-edged leaflets. The tip of the leaf has a single or a forked tendril; the base has a pair of arrow-shaped stipules. The entire plant is hairless.

Flowers are produced in axillary, usually one-sided, racemes with four to 10 yellow pea-like flowers measuring 1.5 to 2 centimetres in length. Seeds are produced in a 4-centimetre-long narrow pod.

Top: Flowers are held on one-sided racemes.
Middle: Leaves terminate in a twining tendril.
Bottom: Each leaf has a single pair of narrow leaflets and a pair of narrow stipules at its base, giving the appearance of four leaflets.

Introduced Species

Pea family / Fabaceae

Bird's-foot trefoil

Lotus corniculatus

Lotier corniculé, garden bird's-foot trefoil

HABITAT: A European species, bird's-foot trefoil is now naturalized along roadsides and in waste areas throughout New Brunswick.

CHARACTERISTICS: Bird's-foot trefoil, a clumping plant with many prostrate stems, often occurs in large colonies. Its stems may be smooth or hairy. The alternately arranged leaves are pinnately compound with three to five elliptical to oblong leaflets. The lowest pair of leaflets is basal, giving the appearance of stipules; the upper three leaflets resemble a trifoliate leaf. Leaflet edges are finely toothed and often fringed with hair.

Flowers are produced in a long-stemmed umbel among the upper leaf axils. Each umbel is composed of three to 15 yellow pea-like flowers. Flower buds, and sometimes the flowers themselves, have a red tint. Individual flowers are 0.8 to 1.5 centimetres long. The fruit is a small pea pod containing up to 25 brown-black seeds.

VITAL STATISTICS

Maximum height: 60 centimetres
Flowering season: July to September

Top: The pea-like flowers are held in a rounded umbel.
Bottom: Plants appear clumped with trailing stems; its flowers are among the upper leaf axils.

Pea family / Fabaceae

Yellow clover

Introduced Species

Trifolium aureum (formerly *T. agrarium*)

Trèfle jaune, yellow hop clover, large hop clover

VITAL STATISTICS

Maximum height: 45 centimetres
Flowering season: June to September

HABITAT: Yellow clover, a European species, grows in disturbed habitats such as roadsides, waste places, and gardens throughout New Brunswick.

CHARACTERISTICS: An annual or biennial, yellow clover forms a low mat-like growth with wide-spreading lateral branches. Stems may be smooth or have short flattened hairs. Alternately arranged leaves are trifoliate with ovate stemless leaflets. Leaflets have toothed edges except at their bases. Each leaf has a pair of stipules which are almost as long as its petiole.

Axillary flowers are in rounded head-like clusters, each about 2 centimetres wide, sitting atop 2- to 5-centimetre-long stems. Each flower cluster is composed of many small yellow pea-like flowers that change to cream and then rusty brown as they set seed.

Low hop clover, *T. campestre*, a similar species found throughout the province, is generally shorter than yellow clover and is distinguished by its terminal stalked leaflet.

Small hop clover, *T. dubium*, is the smallest of the three yellow clovers, with three to 15 flowers per flower cluster. Its terminal leaflet has a short stalk. The upper petal is barely striated, whereas it is clearly striated on low hop clover. It is rare and mostly found in the Saint John area.

Black medick, *Medicago lupulina*, is a province-wide yellow clover look-alike. It has small 1-centimetre-diameter flower heads, prostrate hairy stems, and trifoliate leaves with hairy undersides. The terminal leaflet is stalked. Its curled seed pods distinguish black medick from the yellow clovers, whose seed pods are straight.

Top: Yellow clover flowers turn rusty brown as they age. Middle: The terminal leaflet of low hop clover has a distinct short petiole. Bottom: Black medick has tiny rounded heads of pea-like flowers.

Balsam family / Balsaminaceae

Spotted jewelweed

Native Species

Impatiens capensis

Chou sauvage, impatiente du Cap, orange jewelweed, spotted touch-me-not

HABITAT: Common throughout New Brunswick, spotted jewelweed prefers damp locations such as streamsides, wet thickets, and ditches.

CHARACTERISTICS: Spotted jewelweed is an upright annual with single stems and scattered branches. It often grows in self-seeding colonies. The entire plant is smooth, fleshy, and brittle. Stems are shiny and may be tinted red. The alternate leaves are ovate, thin-textured, and dull, pale green. Leaves have low broad teeth.

Flowers are produced among the upper leaf axils, usually solitary but sometimes in clusters of two or three. The conical flowers, located at the ends of thin drooping stems, are held horizontal. Flowers are about 2.5 centimetres long and orange with yellow and red markings and composed of three sepals and three petals. Two of the sepals are small; the third is modified to form a backward-projecting nectar spur with a curled tip. The uppermost petal and the lower two petals are larger than the two lateral petals, giving an upper and lower lipped appearance. Flowers produce an ovate seed capsule that explodes when ripe, shooting seeds several feet.

Pale jewelweed, *I. pallida*, is extremely rare, with a preference for calcareous substrates. It is confined to the northwestern region of the province. It is distinguished by its yellow flowers, which are finely spotted with red in the throat, its elliptical blue-tinted leaves, and its preference for alkaline substrates.

VITAL STATISTICS

Maximum height: 120 centimetres
Flowering season: July to August

Top: The conical orange flowers are mostly solitary among the upper leaf axils. Middle: The flower's side-profile reveals the backward-pointing but curl-tipped nectar spur. Bottom: Pale jewelweed has yellow flowers.

Lopseed family / Phrymaceae

Musk monkeyflower

Introduced Species

Erythranthe moschata (formerly *Mimulus moschatus*)
Mimule musqué, muskflower

VITAL STATISTICS

Maximum height: 30 centimetres
Flowering season: July to August

HABITAT: A western North American species now naturalized in southern and eastern New Brunswick, musk monkeyflower occasionally grows in stream margins, damp ditches, and areas which have natural springs.

CHARACTERISTICS: A creeping plant, musk monkeyflower has weakly upright stems; its stems and leaves are covered in sticky hairs. Stems that extend along the ground often root at their nodes. The opposite leaves are ovate to oblong and may have smooth or toothed edges.

The funnel-shaped bright yellow flowers are solitary and produced on a thin pedicle from the upper leaf axils. Up to 2-centimetre-long flowers have two petals that form an upper lip and three petals that form a lower lip. The throat of the lower lip is finely veined in red and has two densely hairy lines. The flower may or may not have a musky scent.

Top: The flower's throat has fine red spots and two hairy lines. Bottom: The solitary flowers are among the upper leaf axils.

Plantain family / Plantaginaceae

Golden hedge-hyssop

Gratiola aurea

Gratiole dorée, golden pert

Native Species

HABITAT: Golden hedge-hyssop is extremely rare and confined to gravelly or muddy lakeshores west of Saint John. It is often partially submerged in water up to 15 centimetres deep.

VITAL STATISTICS

Maximum height: 40 centimetres
Flowering season: July to August

CHARACTERISTICS: Golden hedge-hyssop is a semi-aquatic low bushy plant with several upright mostly unbranched stems arising from fleshy rhizomes. Stems are square in cross-section. The opposite leaves, which are up to 3 centimetres long, vary from linear to ovate and are stem-clasping with smooth or slightly toothed edges. The entire plant is hairless, but leaves have glandular spots, which impart a slightly sticky feel. Plants produce purple-tinted stolons.

Flowers are solitary among the upper leaf axils. They are about 1.5 centimetres in diameter with five yellow petals, two of which are fused to form a cleft upper lip; the other three are partly fused and form a three-lobed lower lip. The inside base of the upper lip has a cluster of hairs.

Clammy hedge-hyssop, *G. neglecta*, is extremely rare and found in only a few muddy locations along the Saint John River watershed within Sunbury, York, and Carleton counties. Leaves are lanceolate, opposite, and sessile; leaves and stems are clammy and sticky. The solitary flowers are smaller than those of the golden hedge-hyssop. The upper lip may be a single lobe or two-lobed; the lower lip has three distinct lobes. The upper lobe has an interior yellow beard. Flowers are white with yellow bases and floral tubes.

Top: The flower's notched upper lip has hairs at its base.
Middle: Flowers are solitary among the upper leaf axils.
Bottom: Clammy hedge-hyssop's solitary flowers have four white yellow-throated petals.

Plantago family / Plantaginaceae

Butter-and-eggs

Introduced Species

Linaria vulgaris

Gueule de lion, common toadflax, yellow toadflax

VITAL STATISTICS

Maximum height: 80 centimetres
Flowering season: July to August

HABITAT: Butter-and-eggs, a European introduction, is common in disturbed habitats throughout New Brunswick.

CHARACTERISTICS: A suckering plant, butter-and-eggs has non-branching upright stems and often forms extensive colonies. The entire plant is essentially hairless. Its smooth-edged leaves are numerous, linear, and a waxy pale green. Leaves are mostly alternate, although, due to denseness, some may appear opposite or whorled.

Flowers are produced in a dense raceme. The pale to deep yellow tubular flowers are about 2.5 centimetres long and composed of an upper and lower lip, both of which are two-lobed. The palette between the two lips is orange-yellow. The flowers look like snapdragon flowers. A narrow nectar spur extends behind each flower.

Dalmatian toadflax, *L. dalmatica*, another European introduction, is rarely found in disturbed areas. Dalmatian toadflax is distinguished by its waxy blue-tinted ovate to oblong clasping leaves and large (to 4 centimetres wide) deep yellow flowers.

Top: Butter and eggs' snapdragon-like flowers are in dense racemes. Middle: Some butter-and-eggs plants produce pale yellow flowers. Bottom: Dalmatian toadflax has ovate blue-tinted foliage and large flowers.

Broomrape family / Orobanchaceae

Native Species

Little yellow rattle

Rhinanthus minor (formerly *R. crista-galli*)

Claquette, sonnette, common yellow rattle, rattlebox, yellow rattle

HABITAT: Little yellow rattle occurs on old meadows, roadsides, barrens, and coastal headlands. It is well distributed throughout New Brunswick.

VITAL STATISTICS

Maximum height: 60 centimetres
Flowering season: June to July

CHARACTERISTICS: Little yellow rattle is a single-stemmed upright loosely branched annual. It is hemiparasitic, parasitizing nearby grasses. The plant is mostly hairless; its stems are often tinted or streaked with red or brown. The opposite, sessile leaves are dark green, often tinted bronze. They are lance-shaped with sharp bristle-tipped teeth and distinct veins.

Flowers are arranged in a leafy one-sided raceme. The inflated calyx is rounded with flat sides; initially green, it becomes brown and papery when mature. Each tubelike flower has five yellow petals: the upper two are fused, forming a hood; the lower three form a three-toothed lip. Seeds are produced inside a flattened capsule within the inflated calyx. When mature and dry, the plants "rattle," giving them their common name.

Top: Plants have a flattened inflated calyx behind the tubular flowers. Bottom: The opposite narrow leaves have sharp teeth, distinctive veins, and often a bronzy tint.

Bladderwort family / Lentibulariaceae

Horned bladderwort

Native Species

Utricularia cornuta

Utriculaire

Wetlands

VITAL STATISTICS

Maximum height: 25 centimetres

Flowering season: June to September

HABITAT: Horned bladderwort is an aquatic species found in shallow muddy bogs and fen pools throughout New Brunswick.

CHARACTERISTICS: An aquatic plant, horned bladderwort has fine threadlike leaves which are generally concealed by the muddy bottoms of the pools they inhabit. Leaf tips have minute bladders which trap and digest planktonic organisms.

The fragrant flowers are held just above the water's surface at the tips of wiry stems. These stems may reach 30 centimetres from the base of the plant to the water's surface. The bright yellow flowers are solitary or produced in a raceme of up to six flowers (two or three flowers are most common). Individual flowers are about 2 centimetres long and have an upper and lower lip, reminiscent of a snapdragon flower. The lower lip is relatively large and helmet-shaped; the upper lip is small and held more erect. A 0.7- to 1.2-centimetre-long spur extends downward below the flower.

Common bladderwort, *U. macrorhiza*, has similar flowers as horned bladderwort, but have a shorter, hooked spur and a brown strip on the base of the lower lip. Six to 20 flowers are produced per raceme. Its feathery foliage floats on the water's surface.

Intermediate bladderwort, *U. intermedia*, also has floating feathery foliage. Its flowers are similar to those of common bladderwort but only have 2 to 5 flowers per raceme and lack a spur. Both common and intermediate bladderwort are found throughout New Brunswick.

Top: Horned bladderwort flowers are reminiscent of a snapdragon's. Middle: Flowers are held atop leafless wiry stems. Bottom: Intermediate bladderwort has brown markings at the base of the lip and lacks a spur.

Orchid family / Orchidaceae

Native Species

Yellow lady's-slipper

Cypripedium parviflorum

Cypripède jaune, American yellow lady's-slipper, small yellow lady's-slipper

HABITAT: Yellow lady's-slipper grows in cedar swamps and rich deciduous woodlands, less commonly on gravelly limesone shorelines. It is uncommon but well distributed in New Brunswick.

VITAL STATISTICS
Maximum height: 60 centimetres
Flowering season: June to July

CHARACTERISTICS: Yellow lady's-slipper forms a low clump with non-branching stems. The alternate leaves are ovate to lance-shaped with pointed tips and distinct parallel ribs. Up to six smooth-edged leaves are produced; each leaf is smaller than the one below it. Leaves are covered in fine hairs on the variety *pubescens* (the most common form in the province) but nearly smooth on the very rare variety *makasin*.

Flowers are usually solitary but rarely up to three are produced per stem. Sepals vary from yellow to green to mahogany and may be variously spotted purple-brown. Lateral petals, also variable in colour, are usually twisted. The lip is yellow and distinctly pouched or slipper-like. The variety *makasin* has a 2- to 3-centimetre-long lip and is sweetly fragrant; *pubescens* has a larger lip, is 2.5 to 5 centimetres in length, and is only slightly fragrant.

Top: The sepals and twisted lateral petals are commonly mahogany with a distinct yellow slipper-like lip. Middle: Plants form clumps with alternate ribbed leaves. Bottom: Sepals and lateral petals are sometimes greenish-yellow.

Iris family / Iridaceae

Yellow iris

Native Species

Iris pseudacorus

Iris faux-acore, iris jaune, iris des marais, yellow flag iris, yellow flag

VITAL STATISTICS

Maximum height: 100 centimetres
Flowering season: Late June to July

HABITAT: Yellow iris, a European species, was originally grown in New Brunswick as a garden ornamental. It is now widely scattered and naturalized throughout the province in marshes, along streams and ponds, and in roadside ditches.

CHARACTERISTICS: Yellow iris is a clumping grass-like plant. Leaves are strap- or sword-like and all basal; central median ridges help differentiate yellow iris from other "wild" irises in the province. Leaves are hairless with smooth edges and their bases are often pink-tinted.

Flowers are produced on stout leafless stems. These stems may be single or have two to three branches, each producing one to three flowers. The bright yellow flowers are showy and about 8 centimetres wide. Flowers have three downward-arching, broad sepals (the falls) and three small, erect, narrow petals (the standards). Sepals and petals are bright yellow. The base of the falls has a brown ring as well as brown veins. The falls are 5 to 7.5 centimetres long; standards are 2 to 3 centimetres long. The thick cylindroid seed capsule is three-angled and 4 to 7 centimetres long, with a nipple-like beak at its terminus.

Top: The three broad downward-arching sepals are the flower's most significant feature. Bottom: Plants produce sword-like foliage.

Poppy family / Papaveraceae

Introduced Species

Greater celandine

Chelidonium majus

Grand éclaire, herbe aux verrues, swallowwort, rock poppy, celandine

HABITAT: Greater celandine is a European plant originally introduced in New Brunswick as a garden ornamental. It is now naturalized and widely scattered in disturbed areas, thickets, and roadsides near communities.

CHARACTERISTICS: Greater celandine is an upright bushy plant with ribbed stems. Plants have basal leaves in winter and early spring, then alternate leaves on the flowering stems. Leaves, which are up to 20 centimetres long, are pinnately compound, with five to nine oval leaflets which are variously lobed with round-toothed edges. Although most leaves are hairless, they are often covered in a blue-green wax. Petioles and stems have long white hairs, especially near the base. When cut, the plant exudes orange-coloured sap.

The long-stemmed flowers are produced in axillary umbels of three to eight flowers. Individual flowers, each about 2 centimetres wide, have four yellow petals, numerous stamens, and a single stout green style. Black seeds are produced in slender cylindrical capsules that are 3 to 5 centimetres long.

VITAL STATISTICS

Maximum height: 100 centimetres
Flowering season: July to August

Top: Individual flowers have four yellow petals, a cluster of stamens, and a single stout green style.
Bottom: Leaves are pinnate with variously lobed and round-toothed oval leaflets.

Mustard family / Brassicaceae

Bitter wintercress

Barbarea vulgaris

Cresson d'hiver, herbe de Saint-Barbe, common wintercress, yellow rocket, garden yellow rocket

Introduced Species

VITAL STATISTICS
Maximum height: 60 centimetres
Flowering season: Late May to June

HABITAT: Bitter wintercress is a European introduction commonly seen in disturbed habitats, including roadsides, waste areas, and cultivated grounds, throughout New Brunswick.

CHARACTERISTICS: Bitter wintercress is a biennial plant. In the first season, plants produce a basal rosette of evergreen dark green leaves. These leaves are elliptical in outline and lyrate: deeply lobed with a large rounded lobe at the end and one to four pairs of small rounded lobes toward the base. Shiny hairless leaves may reach 15 centimetres in length. Leaf edges may be smooth, coarsely toothed, or wavy. In its second season, the plant produces several upright leafy stems with alternately arranged leaves. Stems are ridged and often tinted purple. Stem leaves are similar to basal leaves, but smaller. The uppermost stem leaves may be simply rounded with coarse teeth.

Flowers are produced in multiple racemes, which are globular when they first bloom but elongate as the flowering season progresses. One-centimetre-wide flowers have four golden yellow petals and six stamens. Their seed capsules are narrow, upwardly curved, and up to 3 centimetres long.

Erect-fruited wintercress, *B. orthoceras*, is an uncommon native biennial found along gravelly shorelines, mostly in Restigouche, Charlotte, and Victoria counties. Pale yellow flowers are about 0.5 centimetres in diameter. Narrow seed capsules are helf stiffly erect. Basal leaves are elliptic and may have two or four small basal lobes. Lower stem leaves are often purple-tinted.

Top: In their second season, plants produce multiple racemes on upright leafy stems. Middle: First-season plants produce a low rosette of deeply lobed smooth leaves. Bottom: Erect-fruited wintercress has smaller flowers and seed capsules that are held more erect.

Introduced Species

Mustard family / Brassicaceae

Black mustard

Brassica nigra

Moutarde noire

HABITAT: A European introduction, black mustard is found in disturbed habitats, usually near towns and farms, throughout New Brunswick.

CHARACTERISTICS: Black mustard is a tall, slender to bushy annual. Its alternate leaves are covered in short bristly hairs; leaves are up to 20 centimetres long at the stem base but smaller toward the summit. Lower leaves are oblanceolate to spatulate, pinnately lobed with a large terminal lobe and smaller lateral lobes, and coarsely toothed. Upper leaves are lance-shaped to elliptical and coarsely toothed, with or without lobes. All leaves have slender petioles. Stems have a few stiff hairs at their base. Plants often wilt during the day but stiffen at night.

Flowers are produced in multiple narrow elongate racemes up to 60 centimetres long. Each 2-centimetre-wide flower has four yellow petals, four yellow-green sepals, six stamens (four long and two short), and a single pistil. The seed capsules are narrow, cylindrical, stiffly upright, and often overlapping. The flower pedicles are short and thick, 0.3 to 0.5 centimetres long.

Field mustard, *B. rapa*, is similar to black mustard in appearance but its upper stem leaves clasp the stem. Wild mustard, *Sinapsis arvensis*, has stiffly hairy sessile leaves. Lower leaves are lyrate to pinnatifid; upper are diamond-shaped and toothed.

The leaves of wild radish, *Raphanus raphanastrum*, are covered in stiff hairs; its branched stems are sprawling. Emerging flowers are pale yellow then turn dirty white with violet veins. It is found province-wide.

VITAL STATISTICS

Maximum height: 2.5 metres
Flowering season: June to October

Top: Robust black mustard plants can produce multiple racemes. Middle: Field mustard has clasping upper leaves that are often tinted blue. Bottom: Wild radish has pale yellow flowers and a sprawling habit.

Mustard family / Brassicaceae

Flixweed

Introduced Species

Descurainia sophia

Sagesse-des-chirurgiens, common tansy mustard, herb Sophia

VITAL STATISTICS

Maximum height: 100 centimetres
Flowering season: June to August

HABITAT: A European species, flixweed is uncommon and widely dispersed in waste areas throughout New Brunswick.

CHARACTERISTICS: Flixweed is a leafy branching annual. The alternate leaves are lance-shaped in outline but dissected with bipinnate lobes which have narrow divisions. Overall, they appear fern-like or similar to real tansy, *Tanacetum*; however, the foliage is not rank-smelling like tansy's. Under a magnifying glass, the hairs on stems and leaves are star-shaped; to the naked eye, hairs appear pubescent and greyish.

Flowers are produced in narrow racemes. Unlike the petals of most yellow "mustards," flixweed petals are narrow and held erect, not wide-spreading. Individual flowers are about 0.5 centimetres in diameter. The greenish-yellow petals are shorter than the green sepals and the exerted stamens and style. The narrow seed capsules are 2 to 3 centimetres long and upward-arching.

Top: Flixweed's small narrow petals are held erect. Middle: Plants produce many narrow racemes. Bottom: The narrow leaves are bipinnate, finely dissected, and fern-like.

Mustard family / Brassicaceae

Introduced Species

Wormseed mustard

Erysimum cheiranthoides

Herbe au chantre, wormseed wallflower, treacle mustard, treacle wallflower

HABITAT: Wormseed mustard is a European introduction common in waste areas throughout New Brunswick.

CHARACTERISTICS: Wormseed mustard is an upright annual or biennial with a single leafy stem or a few branches in the upper portion of the plant. Overwintering plants produce an evergreen rosette. The elliptical to lance-shaped leaves have slight teeth and often wavy edges and are alternately arranged along the stem. Both stems and leaves are finely pubescent. The stem is rough-textured and longitudinally ridged.

Flowers are produced in narrow racemes. Individual flowers are 0.6 to 0.8 centimetres wide with four bright yellow petals, four green sepals, six stamens, and one central style. The seed capsules are 1 to 2 centimetres long, narrow, and cylindrical.

VITAL STATISTICS

Maximum height: 100 centimetres
Flowering season: June to September

Top: Flowers, with four wide-spreading yellow petals, are typical of the mustards. Bottom: Plants have simple lance-shaped to elliptical leaves and flowers in terminal racemes.

Mustard family / Brassicaceae

Marsh yellowcress

Rorippa palustris

Cresson palustre, bog yellowcress

Native Species

VITAL STATISTICS

Maximum height: 60 centimetres

Flowering season: July to September

HABITAT: Marsh yellowcress grows along wet shorelines and in damp waste areas throughout New Brunswick.

CHARACTERISTICS: Marsh yellowcress is a tap-rooted upright annual or biennial. If germination occurs late in the season, plants overwinter as an evergreen rosette. Stems are furrowed and may appear zigzagged. The alternate leaves are up to 15 centimetres long, becoming smaller as they ascend the stem. Smooth or hairy leaves are lance-shaped to spatulate and usually pinnately lobed with rounded teeth. One or two pairs of moderately deep lobes may be found near the base of each leaf; elsewhere, lobes are shallow. Some of the lowermost leaves may be pinnatifid. Lower leaves have petioles; upper leaves are mostly sessile.

Upper stems terminate in several 10- to 20-centimetre-long racemes of flowers. Racemes are at first globular, but elongate as the season progresses. Each 0.3-centimetre-wide flower consists of four yellow petals, four greenish-yellow sepals, six stamens, and a single stout style. Seed capsules are 0.5 to 1 centimetre long, elliptical, and often curved.

Creeping yellowcress, *R. sylvestris*, scattered throughout New Brunswick, is a European introduction that inhabits damp waste areas and shorelines. A perennial, its wide-spreading or ascending stems may reach 50 centimetres in length. Hairless lanceolate pinnatifid leaves have seven to 11 lobes; the terminal lobe is the largest. Branch ends have a raceme of bright yellow flowers up to 0.8 centimetres wide.

Top: Marsh yellowcress has globular racemes of flowers early in the season. Middle: Creeping yellowcress racemes are not as globular as those of marsh yellowcress. Bottom: Creeping yellowcress is bushy with deeply lobed pinnatifid leaves.

Mustard family / Brassicaceae

Introduced Species

Tall tumble mustard

Sisymbrium altissimum

Sisymbre des hautes, sisymbre élevé, tumble mustard, tall hedge mustard, tall rocket

HABITAT: Tall tumble mustard has been naturalized in disturbed areas throughout New Brunswick, particularly along the east coast and in the southwest.

VITAL STATISTICS

Maximum height: 100 centimetres
Flowering season: July to August

CHARACTERISTICS: Tall tumble mustard is a tall, slender branched annual. The lower stem and lower petioles are densely hairy; hairs are scattered higher up the plant. Alternate lance-shaped leaves are deeply pinnately lobed to pinnatifid, with toothed edges. The lower leaves have broad lobes; the upper are linear and threadlike.

Flowers are produced on slender branching racemes. Individual 1-centimetre-wide flowers have four pale yellow petals, six stamens (four long and two short), and a two-lobed stigma. Cylindrical slender seed capsules, up to 10 centimetres long, are held outward from the main stem and often curve.

Common tumble mustard, *S. officinale*, reaches 60 centimetres in height and is more hairy than tall tumble mustard. Its lance-shaped pinnatifid leaves are toothed; the terminal lobe is large and triangular. Upper leaves are often simply lanceolate or elliptical. Flowers are about 0.5 centimetres wide; seed capsules are just 1 to 2 centimetres long and held erect, parallel to the main stem. It is found province-wide.

Common dog mustard, *Erucastrum gallicum*, occasional in the province, is usually confined to railway yards. Its toothed lance-shaped leaves are pinnatifid with round-lobed divisions. Stems are pubescent. Flowers are pale yellow and about 1 centimetre in diameter. Seed capsules are 2.5 to 3.5 centimetres long and angle away from the main stem.

Top: Tall tumble mustard produces flowers in narrow branched racemes. Middle: Common tumble mustard has simple lanceolate leaves near its flowers. Bottom: Dog mustard has pale yellow flowers and pinnatifid leaves with round-lobed divisions.

Orpine family / Crassulaceae

Roseroot

Native Species

Rhodiola rosea (formerly *Sedum roseum*)

Orpin rosat, orpin rose, goldenroot, king's crown

VITAL STATISTICS

Maximum height: 40 centimetres
Flowering season: June to July

HABITAT: Roseroot is restricted to exposed coastal cliffs along the Fundy coast.

CHARACTERISTICS: Roseroot forms a clump of several upright stems arising from a thickened root. Plants often grow between cracks, where there is minimal soil. The alternately arranged hairless leaves are obovate to oblong, fleshy, and pale grey-green. Leaves are crowded on the stems and often spirally arranged; edges may be smooth or finely toothed.

Plants are dioecious. Both sexes produce a flat-topped corymb of flowers. Male flowers have four or five narrow yellow petals and an equal number of stamens. Female flowers lack petals and are simply composed of four or five pistils which vary from green to orange, often with a purple tint. Seeds are produced in green or purple-tinted starlike capsules.

Top: Male flowers have four or five narrow petals with a similar number of stamens. Middle: The petal-less female flowers are often tinted orange or purple. Bottom: Roseroot often grows in narrow rock cracks.

Barrens

Coastal

Evening primrose family / Onagraceae

Common evening primrose

Native Species

Oenothera biennis

Onagre bisannuelle, king's cureall, yellow evening primrose

HABITAT: Common evening primrose grows throughout the province in disturbed areas and on sandy and gravelly shorelines of both fresh and salt water.

VITAL STATISTICS

Maximum height: 150 centimetres
Flowering season: June to October

CHARACTERISTICS: Common evening primrose is a biennial. During the first season, plants form a flat rosette of leaves from a fleshy taproot. Each long tapered leaf is lance-shaped and up to 20 centimetres in length with finely hairy undersides and smooth or slightly toothed edges. Leaves are often tinted red, especially in winter. In the second year, plants produce a stout stem that may be unbranched or branched to become bush-like. The stem is green or tinted red and covered in white hairs. Densely arranged stem leaves are alternate and willow-like.

Flowers are in terminal leafy-bracted racemes. Each 3- to 5-centimetre-wide lightly fragrant flower has four shallow-notched lemon yellow petals that often overlap, four backward-facing narrow green sepals, eight stamens, and a distinct cross-shaped stigma. Flowers generally open in the evening and close by late morning.

Small-flowered evening primrose, *O. parviflora*, has less upright unbranched stems and fleshier leaves than common-evening primrose; the petals of its 2- to 2.5-centimetre-wide flowers rarely overlap. Flowers are covered in sticky hairs when in bud. It is common throughout the province.

Perennial evening primrose, *O. perennis*, is widespread. Often less than 30 centimetres tall, it has several non-branching thin stems with small linear to lanceolate smooth-edged leaves and spikes of 1-centimetre-wide flowers.

Top: Common evening primrose flowers are held on leafy-bracted racemes. Middle: Small-flowered evening primrose's petals rarely overlap. Bottom: Perennial evening primrose has narrow leaves and a terminal spike of four-petalled flowers.

Buttercup family / Ranunculaceae

Marsh marigold

Native Species

Caltha palustris

Souci d'eau, populage des marais, yellow marsh marigold, kingcup

VITAL STATISTICS

Maximum height: 60 centimetres
Flowering season: Late May to early July

HABITAT: Marsh marigold grows in swamps, wet meadows, ditches, and wet woodlands. It is distributed throughout New Brunswick.

CHARACTERISTICS: Common marsh marigold forms a clump of several upright or partly sprawling stems. Stems are hollow and furrowed. Plants produce both basal and alternately arranged stem leaves. The long-stalked leaves are round, heart-, or kidney-shaped with a rounded tip and deeply cleft base. Leaves are glossy, fleshy, and hairless with smooth or finely toothed edges.

Flowers are produced in an open corymb. Individual flowers are composed of five (rarely to nine) rounded shiny yellow petal-like sepals. Three to 5 centimetres in diameter, the flowers have a dense cluster of stamens and pistils at their centres. Flowers are reminiscent of a large buttercup, to which marsh marigold is related. This plant is toxic if eaten raw.

Top: The five-petalled flowers have a dense cluster of stamens and styles in their centre. Bottom: Plants form clumps with round leaves.

Buttercup family / Ranunculaceae

Kidney-leaved buttercup

Ranunculus abortivus

Renoncule abortive, small-flowered buttercup

Native Species

HABITAT: Kidney-leaved buttercup is frequently found in partly shaded rich deciduous or mixed forest hillsides on river bottomlands throughout New Brunswick.

VITAL STATISTICS

Maximum height: 60 centimetres
Flowering season: May to June

CHARACTERISTICS: Kidney-leaved buttercup is a slender forking biennial or short-lived perennial. Fleshy basal leaves are 4 to 9 centimetres wide, long petioled, and round to kidney-shaped with rounded teeth. Lower stem leaves are alternate and shorter petioled and are deeply divided into three rounded lobes. Upper stem leaves are sessile and lance-shaped to elliptical with smooth, rarely lobed or toothed, edges. Stems and leaves are hairless and slightly waxy.

Stems terminate into one to three flowers. Individual flowers, each about 0.6 centimetres wide, have five pale yellow triangular petals which are smaller than the five green sepals.

Hooked buttercup, *R. recurvatus*, grows in similar habitats and blooms at a similar time as kidney-leaved buttercup. It is locally common, especially in the southern and western regions of the province. Basal leaves have long hairy petioles and are tri-lobed or palmately cleft with five lobes, which are often divided again into smaller lobes and teeth. Main stems are softly hairy. Alternate stem leaves are smaller than the basal leaves, with shorter petioles and fewer, deeper lobes. Flowers are in a loose cyme. Individual flowers have five pale yellow petals, which are smaller than the green sepals. Seeds have a hooked beak.

All buttercups are toxic if ingested.

Top: Kidney-leaved buttercup leaves vary dramatically; the small pale yellow flowers have short triangular petals. Bottom: Hooked buttercup leaves are often broad and tri-lobed; flowers have five tiny pointed petals.

Buttercup family / Ranunculaceae

Tall buttercup

Introduced Species

Ranunculus acris

Bouton d'or, common buttercup, meadow buttercup

VITAL STATISTICS

Maximum height: 100 centimetres
Flowering season: June to August

HABITAT: Tall buttercup, a European species commonly found in pasturelands and gardens and along roadsides, especially in moist sites, is common throughout New Brunswick.

CHARACTERISTICS: Tall buttercup is a clumping plant with upright branching stems. Plants have both basal and alternately arranged stem leaves. Basal leaves have long petioles; upper stem leaves are nearly sessile. Leaves are palmately lobed with five to seven divisions and coarsely toothed. Stems and leaves are covered in hairs and are a solid green; this colouring helps differentiate tall buttercup from creeping buttercup, which generally has pale mottling on its leaves.

Flowers are produced in a loose panicle. Individual flowers are 2.5 centimetres wide with five overlapping rounded petals. The centre of each flower has a globular mass of stamens and pistils; five small green sepals are covered in hairs.

All buttercups are toxic if ingested.

Top: Flowers have five, often overlapping, petals.
Middle: Flowers are in loose panicles.
Bottom: Leaves are palmately lobed and green.

Buttercup family / Ranunculaceae

Native Species

Lesser spearwort

Ranunculus flammula var. *flammula*

Renoncule rampante, creeping spearwort

HABITAT: Lesser spearwort is scattered along damp shores and in shallow water throughout New Brunswick.

CHARACTERISTICS: Lesser spearwort is a creeping plant with stoloniferous stems that root as they grow over muddy surfaces. Elliptical basal leaves are up to 5 centimetres long with petioles that are up to 7 centimetres long. Leaves are fine-toothed or have smooth, undulate edges. Stem leaves are alternate, linear to lanceolate, toothless, and sessile or nearly so. Most plants are hairless.

Flower stems are erect or upward-arching and often purple-tinted, especially at their base. Flowers are produced in loose cymes with individual flowers that are about 1.5 centimetres wide with five yellow petals.

Ranunculus flammula var. *reptans* (formerly *R. reptans*) is more aquatic than lesser spearwort and prostrate, with linear grass-like foliage and solitary 0.5- to 1-centimetre-wide flowers in the leaf axils along the wiry stolons.

Seaside buttercup, *Halerpestes cymbalaria* (formerly *R. cymbalaria*), is scattered along the coast in saline marshes and muds. This species is tufted, with creeping stolons. Long petioled basal leaves are round to kidney-shaped, up to 3 centimetres wide, and fleshy, with rounded teeth. Flower stems are erect to 25 centimetres in height with a solitary flower or a loose cluster of 0.5- to 1-centimetre-wide five-petalled yellow flowers. The seed head is thimble-shaped rather than globose as typically found on *Ranunculus*.

All buttercups are toxic if ingested.

VITAL STATISTICS

Maximum height: 40 centimetres

Flowering season: July to September

Top: Lesser spearwort has flowers in loose cymes. Middle: The variety *reptans* has solitary long-stemmed flowers. Bottom: Seaside buttercup appears tufted with round basal leaves and a few rounded teeth.

Buttercup family / Ranunculaceae

Pennsylvania buttercup

Ranunculus pensylvanicus

Renoncule de Pennsylvanie, bristly buttercup, bristly crowfoot

Native Species

VITAL STATISTICS

Maximum height: 90 centimetres
Flowering season: July to August

HABITAT: Scattered throughout New Brunswick, Pennsylvania buttercup may be encountered in damp to wet locations in open woodlands, seepages, wet meadows, ditches, and marshes and along stream and pond shorelines.

CHARACTERISTICS: Pennsylvania buttercup is a clumping plant with several upright unbranched stems. Stems are hollow and covered in dense stiff white hairs. Basal and alternate stem leaves are rounded in outline but ternately divided. Each leaflet, deeply trilobed and with each division also lobed and/or toothed, is covered in stiff hairs.

The long-stalked flowers are produced in loose open cymes from the upper leaf axils. Individual flowers are small, 0.3-0.6 centimetres wide, with five shiny round pale yellow petals. The sepals are shorter than the petals. Seed heads are thimble-shaped and each seed has a bristle-tip.

All buttercups are toxic if ingested.

Top: The small flowers have five shiny petals; seed heads are thimble-like and bristly. Bottom: Leaves are round in outline but ternately divided and deeply lobed.

Buttercup family / Ranunculaceae

Introduced Species

Creeping buttercup

Ranunculus repens

Bassinet, creeping crowfoot

HABITAT: Creeping buttercup is a European introduction common in damp disturbed areas, lawns, and gardens throughout New Brunswick. Considered invasive, this species has infiltrated wetlands and open woodlands.

CHARACTERISTICS: Creeping buttercup is a mat-forming plant with trailing hairy stems that root along their length. The long petioled leaves are basal but alternately arranged along any trailing stems. Leaves are up to 6 centimetres long, trifoliate, and dark green, often with pale mottling. The obovate to elliptical leaflets are deeply lobed and coarsely toothed and covered with stiff hairs, especially on their undersides. The lower pair of leaflets is often sessile; the middle leaflet has a distinct petiole.

Solitary or loose cymed flowers are produced from the axils of the leaves on the trailing stems. They are about 2 centimetres wide with five (rarely to nine) shiny rounded yellow petals that often overlap. The centre of each flower has a globular mass of stamens and pistils. The five small green sepals are covered in hairs.

All buttercups are toxic if ingested.

VITAL STATISTICS

Maximum height: 10 centimetres

Flowering season: May to September

Top: Flowers are held in loose cymes with petals that often overlap. Middle: Creeping buttercup can form large mats. Bottom: The trifoliate leaves have deeply lobed leaflets; lateral leaflets are nearly sessile and the terminal leaflet has a distinct stem.

Purslane family / Portulacaceae

Common purslane

Introduced Species

Portulaca oleracea

Pourpier potager, poupier gras, purslane, little hogweed

VITAL STATISTICS

Maximum height: 50 centimetres
Flowering season: June to October

HABITAT: A European species, common purslane is becoming a weed in disturbed areas and gardens, primarily in the southern regions of New Brunswick.

CHARACTERISTICS: Common purslane is a low creeping many-branched annual with fleshy leaves and stems. Stems, which are often tinted red, radiate from a central taproot. The alternate or opposite leaves are up to 3 centimetres long, smooth-edged, and spatulate to oval with a short petiole. The entire plant is hairless.

Flowers are solitary at the ends of short branches. A whorl-like cluster of three to six leaves is at the base of each flower. Flowers are 0.5 to 0.8 centimetres wide with five yellow notched petals, six to 12 stamens, and three to six stigmas. Each flower lasts a single day and is open only for a few hours in the morning.

Top: The solitary flowers have five notched yellow petals. Bottom: The trailing stems have spoon-shaped fleshy leaves.

St. John's-wort family / Hypericaceae

Native Species

Canada St. John's-wort

Hypericum canadense

Millepertuis du Canada

HABITAT: Canada St. John's-wort is found in damp to wet areas throughout New Brunswick.

CHARACTERISTICS: Canada St. John's-wort is a slender upright annual plant with one to several smooth stems. The hairless opposite leaves are linear, stemless, and smooth-edged. Leaves have one to three main veins and taper toward their bases. Although plants can reach 70 centimetres in height, they are more commonly less than 20 centimetres high.

Flowers are produced in a few-flowered cyme. Individual flowers are about 0.5 centimetres wide with five yellow petals that are nearly the same length as the sepals. Flowers have fewer than 20 stamens each; their red seed capsules are pointed.

Pale St. John's-wort, *H. ellipticum*, is common throughout the province. Unlike dwarf St. John's-wort, pale St. John's-wort has elliptical leaves and three to five flowers which have more than 20 stamens each. It is a perennial with creeping underground stolons.

Dwarf St. John's-wort, *H. mutilum* (also known as *H. boreale*), is uncommon in wet open areas in the southern half of the province. Its oblong to ovate-shaped leaves have five main veins and clasp the stem at its base, differentiating it from Canada St. John's-wort. Seed capsules are rounded at the tips.

VITAL STATISTICS

Maximum height: 70 centimetres
Flowering season: July to August

Top: Canada St. John's-wort has small narrow leaves and loose clusters of small flowers. Middle: Pale St. John's-wort has terminal flowers in small clusters of only three to five flowers. Bottom: Dwarf St. John's-wort has round leaves and more than five flowers per terminal cluster.

St. John's-wort family / Hypericaceae

Common St. John's-wort

Introduced Species

Hypericum perforatum

Millepertuis commun

VITAL STATISTICS

Maximum height: 90 centimetres
Flowering season: July to August

HABITAT: Common St. John's-wort, a European introduction, is now widespread and common in disturbed habitats throughout New Brunswick.

CHARACTERISTICS: Common St. John's-wort is an upright shrub-like plant with many branches. Plants form subterranean stolons that give rise to more plants, resulting in a colonial, invasive habit. The smooth stems are often red-tinted and the base of the plant is somewhat woody. The hairless opposite stemless leaves are elliptical to oblong with smooth edges. When the leaves are held up to the light, they show minute transparent dots.

Flowers are produced in flat-topped many-flowered cymes. Individual flowers are about 2.5 centimetres wide with five pointed yellow petals which occasionally have fine black dots along their edges. The flower has three pistils; numerous tufted stamens give the plant a starburst appearance. Developing seed capsules are red-brown and covered in fine sticky hairs.

Top: Individual common St. John's-wort flowers have five pointed petals and a starburst of central stamens. Bottom: Flowers are in flat-topped cymes.

Myrsine family / Myrsinaceae

Native Species

Swamp yellow loosestrife

Lysimachia terrestris

Lysimaque terrestre, bog loosestrife, swamp loosestrife, bog candles

HABITAT: Swamp yellow loosestrife is common in wet habitats such as ditches, wet thickets, marshes, and stream and lake shorelines throughout New Brunswick.

VITAL STATISTICS

Maximum height: 80 centimetres
Flowering season: July

CHARACTERISTICS: Swamp yellow loosestrife produces slender upright sparsely branching smooth stems that arise from a creeping stoloniferous root. Opposite lance-shaped leaves reach 10 centimetres in length; they are hairless and smooth-edged, often with minute dots. Leaves taper to the base but have no petiole. Late in the season, reddish bulblets, resembling caterpillars, can form in the leaf axils. These drop to produce new plants.

Starlike flowers, produced in long narrow terminal spike-like racemes, are 1.5 to 2 centimetres wide; the five yellow petals have red dots at their bases and fine red veins in their centres.

Tufted yellow loosestrife, *L. thyrsiflora*, is uncommon in similar habitats as swamp yellow loosestrife. It has non-branching smooth stems and narrow lance-shaped to elliptical smooth-edged leaves. Nearly hairless leaves increase in size up the stem. Dense 2.5- to 4-centimetre-long racemes are produced from the leaf axils of the middle stem leaves. Flowers are about 0.8 centimetres wide with narrow yellow petals.

Fringed yellow loosestrife, *L. ciliata*, is common in wet thickets and meadows, and along shores. Smooth-edged elliptical to egg-shaped leaves have finely hairy petioles. The 1.5- to 3-centimetre-wide yellow flowers are solitary or in loose clusters among the upper leaf axils. It is not restricted to wet soils.

Top: Swamp yellow loosestrife has terminal racemes of starlike flowers. Middle: Tufted yellow loosestrife has axillary flowers in dense conical racemes. Bottom: Fringed yellow loosestrife has fewer but larger flowers than other native loosestrifes.

Myrsine family / Myrsinaceae

Creeping yellow loosestrife

Lysimachia nummularia

Lysimaque nummulaire, monnayère, creeping jenny, moneywort

Introduced Species

VITAL STATISTICS

Maximum height: 5 centimetres
Flowering season: July

HABITAT: Creeping yellow loosestrife, a European species introduced to New Brunswick as an ornamental plant, is occasionally seen along roadsides, trails, and moist lawns.

CHARACTERISTICS: Creeping yellow loosestrife is a prostrate plant with stems that root as they creep over the soil surface. The paired leaves are rounded and 1.5 to 3 centimetres long with short petioles. Leaf edges are smooth and the plants hairless.

Individual 2- to 3-centimetre-diameter flowers are axillary, with short pedicles. Each flower is star-shaped with five yellow petals.

Garden yellow loosestrife, *L. vulgaris*, is another garden escape occasionally seen near settlements. A clumping upright plant, it may grow to 120 centimetres. Eight- to 13-centimetre-long lance-shaped to elliptical leaves are opposite or whorled and covered in soft hairs. Stems end in several branched panicles of 1.5- to 2.5-centimetre-diameter yellow flowers.

Spotted yellow loosestrife, *L. punctata*, resembles garden yellow loosestrife but is leafier, with ovate leaves and stems that end in an elongate leafy raceme of whorled flowers. The base of the petals is often orange-flushed.

Top: Creeping yellow loosestrife is a prostrate plant with solitary, axillary flowers. Middle: Garden yellow loosestrife has whorled leaves with stiff hairs; flowers are in terminal racemes. Bottom: Spotted yellow loosestrife produces flowers in leafy whorls.

Native Species

Rose family / Rosaceae

Woodland agrimony

Agrimonia striata

Aigremoine striée, grooved agrimony, roadside agrimony

HABITAT: Woodland agrimony usually grows along the borders of woodlands and thickets and, less commonly, in disturbed areas. It is found throughout most of New Brunswick.

VITAL STATISTICS

Maximum height: 150 centimetres
Flowering season: July to August

CHARACTERISTICS: Woodland agrimony is a clumping plant with multiple arching leafy stems. The alternately arranged leaves are pinnately compound with five to nine large coarsely toothed veiny lance-shaped leaflets. Smaller leaflets are scattered between the larger leaflets. Uppermost leaves are often trifoliate. A pair of small deeply cleft leafy stipules are at the base of each leaf. Leaf undersides are finely hairy and slightly sticky, and stems are covered in hairs.

Flowers are produced in terminal and axillary narrow wand-like racemes. The main flower stem is covered in fine glandular hairs. Individual flowers are about 0.6 centimetres wide with five, rarely six, ovate yellow petals. Below the sepals is a flange of ascending hooked bristles. The minute fruit are bell-shaped and burr-like, which enables them to stick to fur and clothing.

Hooked or common agrimony, *A. gryposepala*, is uncommon and found mostly in the west-central regions of New Brunswick. It resembles woodland agrimony but its leaves have a thinner texture and are less veiny. Hairs on the undersides of leaves are restricted to the veins. Stems have scattered hairs and the flower stem has scattered long, but non-glandular, hairs. The flange of hooked bristles are wide-spreading rather than ascending.

Top: Flowers are in narrow wand-like racemes; the hooked bristles at their base point upward. Middle: The pinnate leaves have large leaflets interspersed with the smaller. Bottom: The bases of hooked agrimony flowers have wide-spreading hooked bristles.

Rose family / Rosaceae

Large-leaved avens

Native Species

Geum macrophyllum

Benoîte à grandes feuilles, big-leaved avens

Mixed Forest | Deciduous Forest | Wetlands

VITAL STATISTICS

Maximum height: 50 centimetres
Flowering season: June

HABITAT: Large-leaved avens grows in damp sites such as streamsides, wet thickets, swamps, and damp meadows. It is found throughout New Brunswick but is uncommon along the east coast.

CHARACTERISTICS: Large-leaved avens is a leafy clumping plant with short thick rhizomes. Basal leaves have long petioles; alternate stem leaves are nearly sessile. The basal leaves, up to 30 centimetres in length, are pinnately compound with five to nine toothed leaflets. The rounded terminal leaflet is much larger than the ovate to elliptical lateral leaflets. Upper stem leaves are often tri-lobed and pointy with leafy stipules at their bases. All parts of the plant are hairy.

Flowers, produced in loose cymes, are 1 to 1.5 centimetres in diameter with five widely spaced rounded yellow petals and five broadly triangular sepals. Spiky seed heads are slightly sticky.

Yellow avens, *G. aleppicum*, grows in similar habitats as large-leaved avens. It may reach 100 centimetres in height. Its large terminal leaflet is wedge-shaped and often deeply tri-lobed; flowers are 1.5 to 2 centimetres in diameter; spiky seed heads are not sticky.

Wood avens, *G. urbanum*, is a European introduction occasionally seen in southwestern New Brunswick. It is similar to yellow avens but the stem leaves are ternately compound with large toothed stipules. The leaf edges have rounded teeth and the 1- to 1.5-centimetre-diameter flowers have paler yellow petals and narrow, not broadly triangular, sepals.

Top: Large-leaved avens has small flowers with widely spaced petals in open cymes. Middle: Large-leaved avens has a rounded terminal leaflet. Bottom: Yellow avens has larger flowers than large-leaved avens.

Rose family / Rosaceae

Native Species

Common silverweed

Potentilla anserina

Argentine, richette, silverweed

HABITAT: Common silverweed is found along gravelly and sandy shorelines along the coast of New Brunswick. It is also found inland on disturbed areas such as roadsides.

VITAL STATISTICS

Maximum height: 20 centimetres
Flowering season: June to August

CHARACTERISTICS: A rosetted plant, common silverweed forms dense mats and multiplies quickly through stolons that are often tinted red. All parts of the plant are densely covered in fine hairs. Ten- to 20-centimetre-long basal leaves are pinnately compound with up to 23 oblong sharply toothed leaflets. The lower leaflets are much smaller than those farther along the leaf. The top leaf surface is usually shiny, while the underside is silver-white with a dense coating of fine hairs. The variety *sericea* has silver hairs on both leaf surfaces.

Flowers, solitary at the ends of slender stems, are produced from the leaf axils of the stolons or basal rosettes. Individual flowers are 1.5 to 2.5 centimetres in diameter with five rounded yellow petals and a central cluster of many stamens and pistils.

Top: Each flower has five rounded yellow petals and a central cluster of stamens and pistils. Middle: Pinnate leaves with sharply toothed leaflets. Bottom: Plants produce many red-stemmed stolons.

Rose family / Rosaceae

Rough cinquefoil

Introduced Species

Potentilla norvegica

Potentille de Montpellier, potentille de Norvège, Norwegian cinquefoil

VITAL STATISTICS

Maximum height: 50 centimetres

Flowering season: July to August

HABITAT: Rough cinquefoil is scattered in disturbed habitats throughout New Brunswick.

CHARACTERISTICS: Rough cinquefoil is an upright annual, biennial, or short-lived perennial. In the first season, plants produce a flat basal rosette of long petioled evergreen trifoliate leaves, similar to those of strawberries. Each leaflet is ovate, up to 5 centimetres long, and lightly hairy with coarsely toothed edges. The petiole is covered in long hairs. In subsequent seasons, plants produce upright hairy, often red-tinted, stems. The stem leaves are similar to basal leaves but are alternately arranged with shorter petioles. The uppermost leaves are often simple, not trifoliate.

Flowers are produced in open leafy cymes. Individual flowers are about 1.5 centimetres in diameter with five heart-shaped yellow petals which are a little shorter than the five green sepals. Below the sepals are five green bracts that give the flowers the appearance of having 10 sepals.

The introduced downy cinquefoil, *P. intermedia*, is uncommon in disturbed areas. It resembles rough cinquefoil but has palmately divided leaves with five leaflets covered in fine grey hairs. Downy cinquefoil petals are more rounded than those of rough cinquefoil, and a little longer than the green sepals below them.

Top: Rough cinquefoil petals are shorter than the sepals. Middle: Rough cinquefoil has mostly trifoliate leaves; its flowers are in leafy cymes. Bottom: Tall cinquefoil has creamy white petals with yellow bases.

Introduced Species

Rose family / Rosaceae

Sulphur cinquefoil

Potentilla recta

Potentille dressée, sulphur five-fingers, rough-fruit cinquefoil

HABITAT: Sulphur cinquefoil, a European introduction, is occasionally found on dry fields and other disturbed areas throughout New Brunswick.

VITAL STATISTICS

Maximum height: 60 centimetres
Flowering season: July

CHARACTERISTICS: An upright plant with non-branching stems, sulphur cinquefoil has long petioled basal leaves and alternate shorter petioled to sessile stem leaves. The palmately compound leaves have five to seven oblanceolate toothed leaflets, each up to 5 centimetres long. The base of each leaf has a pair of deeply cut stipules. Stems and leaves are covered in hairs. Leaflet undersides are paler than their upper surfaces.

Flowers are produced in a cyme. Individual flowers are up to 2.5 centimetres in diameter with five pale yellow, rarely deep yellow, slightly notched petals. The base of each petal is often a deeper yellow than the rest of the petal. At the centre of the flower is a mass of about 30 stamens and pistils. Petals are nearly twice as long as the hairy sepals below them.

Tall or white cinquefoil, *Drymocallis arguta* (formerly *Potentilla arguta*), is native in New Brunswick where it grows on rocky embankments. It has a similar habit as sulphur cinquefoil but its leaves are pinnately compound with seven to 11 ovate toothed leaflets which are covered in sticky glandular hairs. Flowers are creamy white, often with yellow bases. It is locally common, primarily in the western half of the province.

Top: Flowers are typically pale yellow with deeper yellow centres. Middle: Leaves are palmately compound with five or seven toothed leaflets. Bottom: Less commonly, flowers may be deep yellow.

Rose family / Rosaceae

Old field cinquefoil

Potentilla simplex

Potentille simple, common cinquefoil

Introduced Species

Mixed Forest

Deciduous Forest

Barrens

Disturbed

VITAL STATISTICS

Maximum height: 20 centimetres

Flowering season: June to July

HABITAT: Old field cinquefoil, a European introduction, is found on old meadows and barrens, in open woodlands, and along roadsides throughout New Brunswick.

CHARACTERISTICS: Old field cinquefoil is a low spreading plant with trailing, often red-tinted stems and stolons. The leaves, up to 7.5 centimetres long, are alternate and palmately compound with five ovate to elliptical leaflets. The outer three-quarters of the leaflet edge is toothed; the lower quarter, smooth. Young leaves often have upwardly curled edges. The upper leaf surfaces are smooth; stems and undersides may have hairs. Lower leaves have long petioles; the upper are nearly sessile.

The long-stemmed flowers are solitary in the upper leaf axils; they are about 2 centimetres wide with five rounded yellow petals. The five green sepals are shorter than the petals.

Silvery cinquefoil, *P. argentea*, another introduced trailing cinquefoil commonly found in disturbed areas, has palmately compound leaves with five narrow leaflets. Leaf undersides are white and hairy; upper surfaces have scattered hairs and are deep green. Leaves have a few sharp teeth at their tips. The 1- to 1.5-centimetre-wide flowers, in open cymes, have five yellow petals and five near-equal-length green sepals. Lower leaves are long petioled; the upper, nearly sessile.

Top: Old field cinquefoil has palmately compound leaves and solitary flowers. Middle: Silvery cinquefoil's palmately compound dark green leaves have narrow, deeply toothed leaflets.

Shamrock family / Oxalidaceae

Introduced Species

European wood-sorrel

Oxalis stricta

Pain d'oiseau, surette, common yellow wood-sorrel

HABITAT: European wood-sorrel, an introduced species, is locally naturalized in disturbed areas, primarily near settlements, throughout New Brunswick.

VITAL STATISTICS

Maximum height: 40 centimetres
Flowering season: May to October

CHARACTERISTICS: European wood-sorrel is a tufted plant with upright or reclining stems. Leaves are often in whorls of three or four but may also be alternately arranged. Each leaf is trifoliate with three folded heart-shaped leaflets. Each leaflet is 1 to 2 centimetres wide and smooth-edged. The main stems have fine scattered hairs.

Flowers are solitary or produced in umbels of up to four flowers from the leaf axils. Each flower has 10 stamens and five styles. Flower stems usually overtop the leaves. The sepals are finely hairy. Flowers are about 1 centimetre wide with five yellow petals; flower stems become reflexed as seeds develop. Cylindrical ridged seed capsules, which are 1.5 to 2.5 centimetres in length, explode when ripe to shoot seeds from the parent plant.

Fairly similar in appearance to European wood-sorrel is slender wood-sorrel, *O. dillenii*, but it is much less common, found mostly near plant nurseries. Leaves have a small stipule at their bases, the flowers are paired, and the hairs on the stems are held close to the stem rather than spreading. Cylindrical seed capsules explode when ripe.

Top: Each five-petalled flower has 10 stamens and five styles. Middle: The green trifoliate leaves have folded heart-shaped leaflets. Bottom: Slender wood-sorrel has paired flowers.

Parsley family / Apiaceae

Wild parsnip

Pastinaca sativa

Panais sauvage, panais

Introduced Species

VITAL STATISTICS

Maximum height: 150 centimetres
Flowering season: July

HABITAT: Wild parsnip, a European introduction, is scattered but locally common in New Brunswick. It is found in disturbed areas such as roadsides, old meadows, and waste areas.

CHARACTERISTICS: Wild parsnip is a biennial plant with a stout taproot, a rosette of leaves in the first season, and sparsely branching stems with alternately arranged leaves in the second season. Plants are hairless with furrowed stems. Long petioled basal and lower stem leaves, each up to 45 centimetres long, are pinnately compound with seven to 11 leaflets. Leaflets are elliptical to ovate, with cleft lobes and sharp teeth.

Flowers are produced in terminal flat-topped umbels. Each umbel is composed of 15 to 25 umbellets; each umbellet, 12 to 35 flowers. Individual flowers are about 0.7 centimetres in diameter with five tiny yellow inwardly curling petals. Flowers later develop into flattened winged seeds.

Golden alexanders, *Zizia aurea*, is a native perennial occasionally encountered along damp roadsides and in old meadows and damp thickets of western New Brunswick. Its smooth shiny stems can reach 80 centimetres in length. Long petioled leaves are trifoliate to biternately compound. Leaflets are thin, hairless, and toothed; the lowest leaflets often have one or two cleft lobes. Each flat-topped umbel is composed of up to 12 umbellets; each umbellet, 20 0.7-centimetre-wide five-petalled yellow flowers. Petals curve inward. Their flattened seeds are not winged.

Top: Wild parsnip flowers have inwardly curling petals. Middle: Flowers are in multiple flat-topped umbels, and their large leaves are pinnate. Bottom: Golden alexanders' trifoliate or biternately compound leaves have sharply toothed edges.

Figwort family / Scrophulariaceae

Introduced Species

Common mullein

Verbascum thapsus

Tabac du diable, bouillon blanc, great mullein, flannel mullein, flannel plant

HABITAT: Common mullein, a European species, is naturalized in disturbed habitats throughout New Brunswick.

CHARACTERISTICS: Common mullein is a tap-rooted biennial. In the first year, plants produce a large rosette of white woolly felted leaves. Finely toothed leaves are oblong to lance-shaped and may reach 50 centimetres in length. In the second year, plants produce a leafy stout white woolly stem that can reach 2 metres in length. Alternate leaves reduce in size up the stem. Plants are non-branching but may have several smaller flower spikes at the base of the main flower spike.

The stem terminates in a dense cylindrical spike of nearly stemless yellow flowers. Flowers are 1.5 to 3 centimetres in diameter and consist of five petals which are fused at their base. Flowers are unequal in outline, with two petals on top and three on the bottom. They have five stamens: three on the top and two larger and longer ones on the bottom. Sepals are white and woolly. The old stems are woody and often persist through the winter to release seeds over the fall and winter.

Moth mullein, *V. blattaria*, is a rare introduction occasionally encountered in waste areas in Charlotte and Carleton counties. It may reach to 150 centimetres, but has a more slender habit than common mullein and smaller, smooth or only slightly hairy leaves with coarsely toothed edges. The spike of flowers is not dense and each flower has a short 1.5 centimetre stem. Yellow, rarely white, 2.5 centimetre diameter flowers have anther filaments that are covered in distinct purple hairs.

VITAL STATISTICS

Maximum height: 2 metres

Flowering season: Late June to September

Top: Flowers are in dense spikes. Middle: First-year plants produce a basal rosette of elliptical felted leaves. Bottom: Moth mullein has a looser raceme of flowers; pictured here is the less common white form.

Waterlily family / Nymphaceae

Yellow pond-lily

Native Species

Nuphar variegata

Pied-de-cheval, bullhead lily, spatterdock, variegated pond-lily

VITAL STATISTICS

Maximum height: 2 metres (water depth)

Flowering season: July to August

HABITAT: Yellow pond-lily grows in shallow ponds or slow-moving streams throughout New Brunswick.

CHARACTERISTICS: An aquatic plant, yellow pond-lily has a thick rhizome that embeds in the mud and gravel of ponds, usually in water less than 2 metres deep. Leaves float on the water's surface and are essentially basal, arising individually from the rhizome. Ten- to 25-centimetre-long leaves are ovate to heart-shaped with a rounded tip and deeply cleft base; they are deep green, waxy, hairless, and smooth-edged.

Solitary globular flowers are held on a thick stalk above the water's surface. Each 5-centimetre-wide blossom consists of six thick waxy yellow sepals (three outside, three inside). The outside base of the sepals may be green; the inside base, red. Petals are small and indistinct. At the flower's centre is a round disc surrounded by a dense ring of stamens. Seeds are produced in a flat-topped globular ribbed capsule.

Small yellow pond-lily, *N. microphylla*, is smaller than yellow pond-lily, with 10-centimetre-long leaves and 1.5- to 3-centimetre-wide flowers with five yellow sepals. Very rare and widely dispersed, this species is most likely to be seen in calcareous areas. A natural hybrid of the two species, *N. X rubrodisca*, also exists.

Yellow pond-lily often cohabits with white waterlily, *Nymphaea odorata*. When not in bloom, the latter can be distinguished by its purple-red leaf undersides.

Top: The centres of the solitary flowers have a rounded disc of stamens. Bottom: Plants produce round floating leaves with a deeply cleft base.

Native Species

Lily family / Liliaceae

Corn lily

Clintonia borealis

Lis-boréale, bluebead lily, yellow clintonia

VITAL STATISTICS

Maximum height: 30 centimetres
Flowering season: June

HABITAT: Corn lily is a woodland plant common across the province in shady coniferous or mixed forests and, less commonly, on open barrens and in deciduous forests.

CHARACTERISTICS: A low plant, corn lily forms colonies through thin underground rhizomes. Each plant produces two to four elliptical to narrow egg-shaped basal leaves. These leaves are light green and glossy and have smooth but finely hairy edges.

A loose umbel of two to eight flowers is produced at the end of a leafless stem. The 2.5-centimetre-diameter flowers are outward-facing or pendant. They have six yellow to yellow-green tepals—three sepals and three petals that look alike. The six stamens are slightly longer than the tepals. By August, each flowering stem may produce one to a few berries on stiff erect stalks. Berries are mildly poisonous, about 1 centimetre in diameter, bright to deep blue, and often shiny. Berry flesh is firm and white, with many seeds.

European lily-of-the-valley, *Convallaria majalis*, is a European garden plant which is occasionally naturalized in moist woods, thickets, and waste places, primarily in the southern half of the province. Its flowers are held on leafless racemes. The white sweetly fragrant flowers are nodding with recurved petal tips. Plants produce red berries in late summer.

Corn lily and European lily-of-the-valley are both toxic if ingested.

Top: The yellow flowers are lily-like with six narrow tepals; the basal leaves have smooth edges. Middle: Flowers develop into blue berries. Bottom: European lily-of-the-valley produces racemes of nodding white bell-shaped flowers.

Lily family / Liliaceae

Yellow trout lily

Native Species

Erythronium americanum

Ail doux, mulehpon, American trout lily, yellow dog's-tooth violet, yellow adder's-tongue

VITAL STATISTICS

Maximum height: 20 centimetres
Flowering season: May

HABITAT: In New Brunswick, yellow trout lily is primarily found in hardwood forests of the southern and western regions.

CHARACTERISTICS: Yellow trout lily is a small stature plant that arises from a tooth-shaped bulb. The plant is ephemeral, arising early in spring but going dormant and then disappearing by late June to early July. Non-flowering plants produce a single basal elliptical to lance-shaped leaf. Flowering plants produce a pair of basal leaves, which are smooth-edged, fleshy, hairless, grey-green, and usually mottled purple-brown. Leaves are 7 to 20 centimetres long.

A single nodding flower is produced on a 10- to 15-centimetre-long leafless stalk that arises between the pair of basal leaves. The flower is 2 to 4 centimetres in diameter with six reflexed tepals; the three petals and three sepals look alike. Tepals are yellow, often with fine brown spots at their bases, and have six stamens with brown anthers and a single pistil. The globular seed capsule matures as the plants go dormant.

Top: The solitary nodding flowers have six yellow tepals.
Bottom: Leaves are mottled purple-brown.

Native Species

Lily family / Liliaceae

Canada lily

Lilium canadense

Lis du Canada, yellow Canada lily, meadow lily

HABITAT: Canada lily is uncommon in New Brunswick. It grows in riverside meadows and moist open deciduous forests.

CHARACTERISTICS: Canada lily is a tall slender non-branching plant that arises from a scaly bulb. Plants produce whorls of three to eight sessile, lance-shaped, smooth-edged leaves with parallel veins. The upper leaf surface is hairless and waxy; veins on the leaf underside have fine hairs.

Stems terminate in a single flower or an umbel-like cluster of several flowers. Flower stems are long and curve at the ends so that the flowers are nodding. Individual flowers are 6 to 7 centimetres wide with six tip-reflexed tepals; the three petals and three sepals look alike. Tepals are thick-textured and yellow to orange, with copious brown spots on the inside surface. The seed capsule is up to 5 centimetres long, cylindrical, and longitudinally ribbed.

Orange lily, *L. bulbiferum*, is a rare garden escape occasionally seen in Carleton and Westmorland counties. Lance-shaped leaves are alternate but closely spaced along the stem. Upward-facing flowers are orange with fine maroon spots.

VITAL STATISTICS

Maximum height: 150 centimetres
Flowering season: July

Top: Flowers are in umbels; the tepals have reflexed tips. Middle: The sessile lance-shaped leaves are in whorls. Bottom: Orange lily has cup-shaped flowers with narrow alternate leaves.

Daylily family / Hemerocallidaceae

Orange daylily

Hemerocallis fulva

Hémérocalle fauve, lis d'un jour

Introduced Species

VITAL STATISTICS

Maximum height: 200 centimetres
Flowering season: July to August

HABITAT: Orange daylily, introduced to New Brunswick as a garden ornamental, is occasionally seen in areas where homesteads once existed, as well as in waste areas.

CHARACTERISTICS: Orange daylily forms large clumps of narrow grass-like leaves. The elongate basal leaves are 1 to 2 centimetres wide. Leaf edges are smooth and the entire plant is hairless.

Flower stems are leafless, reaching up to 200 centimetres in height and ending in a cluster of three to 16 flowers. Individual flowers are about 10 centimetres in diameter with three recurved petals and three recurved petaloid sepals, which gives the appearance of six petals. The tawny orange petals become darker toward the centre but are yellow in the centre. Each flower only lasts a single day.

Less common in the province, also as an occasional garden escape, is the yellow daylily, *H. lilioasphodelus*. It is smaller in stature, with leafless flower stems reaching 120 centimetres in height. Blooming in June, it has fragrant yellow flowers, each outward-facing and about 6 centimetres in diameter.

Top: Individual flowers are large with six recurved orange tepals. Middle: Plants form large clumps with grass-like foliage. Bottom: Yellow daylily flowers are more outward-facing than those of orange daylily.

Autumn-crocus family / Colchicaceae

Native Species

Sessile-leaved bellwort

Uvularia sessilifolia

Uvulaire à feuilles sessiles, sessile bellwort, straw-lily, wild-oats

HABITAT: Sessile-leaved bellwort occurs in lightly shaded locations in rich hardwood forests and moist meadows. It is locally common in most areas but rare in the far north of the province.

VITAL STATISTICS

Maximum height: 30 centimetres
Flowering season: May

CHARACTERISTICS: Sessile-leaved bellwort produces loose colonies of plants that spread by thin underground rhizomes. Their smooth stems commonly fork at their upper ends. Bright green elliptical leaves are alternately arranged and sessile. Leaves, which may reach 7.5 centimetres in length, are hairless, waxy on both surfaces, and smooth-edged.

The 2.5-centimetre-long narrow bell-shaped flowers are strongly pendent on a thin stalk. They bloom before leaves are fully expanded. Individual flowers have six pale yellow to cream-coloured tepals which curve slightly outward at their tips. Hidden inside the flower are six stamens and a single three-lobed stigma. Most plants produce just a single flower but, less commonly, they produce a pair; flowers are often hidden under the leaves. The 2.5-centimetre-diameter globular seed capsule has three distinct winged edges.

Top: Less commonly, plants produce a pair of narrow bell-shaped straw yellow flowers. Bottom: The sessile elliptical leaves alternate along the stem.

Aster family / Asteraceae

Lance-leaved arnica

Arnica lanceolata

Arnica soyeux, New England arnica

Native Species

VITAL STATISTICS

Maximum height: 50 centimetres

Flowering season: June and July

HABITAT: Lance-leaved arnica is uncommon; it is found along wet shores and in ditches and moist meadows, primarily in northern New Brunswick.

CHARACTERISTICS: Lance-leaved arnica forms clumps of several unbranched stems. Each stem has three to eight pairs of sessile lanceolate to elliptical opposite leaves; leaves have hairs and slightly toothed edges.

Flowers are terminal and solitary or produced in a terminal corymb with three to 10 flowers. Individual flower heads, 4 to 6 centimetres in diameter, have seven to 17 yellow ray florets surrounding many disc florets. Ray florets tend to droop. Each seed has tawny plumes that allow it to be carried on the wind.

Long-leaved arnica, *A. lonchophylla*, is an extremely rare calciphile growing on limestone cliffs along the Upsalquitch River in Restigouche County. Plants are often solitary rather than in clumps like lance-leaved arnica. Opposite leaves vary from lance-shaped to ovate and have coarsely toothed edges. Stems have two to seven pairs of leaves, most located near the base of the plant. Lower stem leaves have a petiole; upper leaves are nearly sessile. Leaves and stems have scattered long hairs. Basal leaves are often withered by the time the plant flowers. Flowers are terminal, either solitary or in a corymb with up to seven 4- to 6-centimetre-wide flowers.

Top: Plants form clumps and flowers may be in small clusters. Bottom: Long-leaved arnica often has solitary stems.

Aster family / Asteraceae

Native Species

Nodding beggarticks

Bidens cernua

Bident penché, fourchettes, pitchfork, sticktight, nodding burr marigold

HABITAT: Nodding beggarticks grows in swamps and wet thickets and along streams throughout New Brunswick.

CHARACTERISTICS: Nodding beggarticks is a colonial annual plant whose lower stems root if they come in contact with soil. Opposite linear to lance-shaped leaves are finely toothed and hairless and may reach 12 centimetres in length. Leaf bases usually clasp the stem. Leaves often become purple-tinted in the autumn.

Long-stalked flowers are solitary or in small clusters from the upper leaf axils. Individual flowers are 2 to 4 centimetres wide and usually have eight yellow ray florets, if present, and numerous yellow disc florets. The base of each flower has six to 10 narrow leaf-like bracts which curl backward. Flower heads nod as seeds develop. Four barbed awns allow seeds to stick to fur and clothing.

Purple-stemmed beggarticks, *B. connata*, is uncommon and widely scatterd along shorelines and in wet ditches. Stout bushy plants grow to 150 centimetres in height and typically have purple stems. Narrow leaves have petioles and coarse teeth. Loosely clustered flowers usually lack ray florets; large green bracts at the flower base are held horizontal. Flower heads remain erect as seeds mature.

VITAL STATISTICS
Maximum height: 100 centimetres
Flowering season: July to September

Top: The flower heads of nodding beggarticks typically have eight ray florets. Middle: Plants form clumps and often have purple stems. Bottom: Purple-stemmed beggarticks flowers have horizontally held bracts and lack ray florets.

Aster family / Asteraceae

Estuary beggarticks

Native Species

Bidens hyperborea

Bident hyperboréal, coastal beggarticks, northern beggarticks

VITAL STATISTICS

Maximum height: 45 centimetres
Flowering season: August to September

HABITAT: As the name suggests, estuary beggarticks grows in muddy tidal river estuaries, especially in brackish areas. Locally frequent, it is confined to the eastern coastal regions of Restigouche County south to Kent County.

CHARACTERISTICS: Estuary beggarticks forms open colonies of several upright or arching stems that are often freely branching. Stems may be smooth or slightly hairy with stiff hairs. Linear to lanceolate toothed leaves clasp the stem and are usually opposite and hairless.

Flowers are in an open leafy panicle. Individual flowers are 2 to 3 centimetres wide and usually have eight yellow ray florets, if present, and numerous yellow disc florets. Some plants lack ray florets and have button-like flowers. Each disc floret has four lobes; this differentiates it from the other wetland beggarticks whose disc flowers have five lobes. The base of each flower has four to eight narrow leaf-like bracts. Unlike nodding beggarticks, seed-developing flowers remain erect and their four-awned seeds are barbless.

Water beggarticks, *B. beckii*, a very rare aquatic species found in slow-moving streams or ponds, is widely dispersed in the province. Submersed leaves are dissected and threadlike. Emergent leaves are lance-shaped and finely toothed. Solitary 2- to 3-centimetre-wide flowers have eight ray florets and are positioned a few centimetres above the water's surface.

Top: The linear leaves clasp the stem; some plants lack petals. Middle: Leaves are opposite with toothed edges. Bottom: Water beggarticks' flowers are held just above the water's surface.

Aster family / Asteraceae

Jerusalem artichoke

Helianthus tuberosus

Topinambour

Introduced Species

HABITAT: A species native to areas south and west of New Brunswick, Jerusalem artichoke was introduced to the province as a garden ornamental. It is becoming naturalized and widely dispersed along shorelines and in moist meadows.

VITAL STATISTICS

Maximum height: 3 metres
Flowering season: August to September

CHARACTERISTICS: A tall colonial plant, Jerusalem artichoke is generally unbranched with rough and hairy stems and leaves. Leaves are opposite on the lower portion of the plant but alternate on the upper. Slightly toothed leaves are elliptical to ovate. Lower leaves have petioles; upper are sessile. Lower leaves reach 25 centimetres in length and become smaller toward the flowers. Plants produce an irregularly shaped edible tuber.

Flowers are produced in open corymbs. Individual flower heads are 5 to 10 centimetres wide with 10 to 20 bright yellow ray florets and numerous yellow disc florets.

Another introduced species also widely scattered is beautiful sunflower, *H. X laetiflorus*, a hybrid of *H. tuberosus* and *H. pauciflorus*. This naturalized ornamental looks like a smaller version of Jerusalem artichoke but does not produce swollen tubers. It may reach 2 metres but is usually 100 to 150 centimetres high. Most leaves are elliptical and opposite, except those close to the flowers.

Giant sunflower, *H. giganteus*, is another garden ornamental rarely naturalized in York and Albert counties. It can reach over 2 metres with coarsely toothed leaves and thick, purple, hairy stems. Flowers resemble those of beautiful sunflower.

Top: Jerusalem artichoke flowers have 10 to 20 yellow ray florets surrounding a mass of yellow disc florets. Middle: Stems are rough-hairy and the upper leaves alternate on the stem. Bottom: Beautiful sunflower is similar to Jerusalem artichoke but has smaller flowers.

Mixed Forest

Deciduous Forest

Disturbed

Aster family / Asteraceae

Narrow-leaved hawkweed

Native Species

Hieracium umbellatum

Épervière en ombelle, northern hawkweed, umbellate hawkweed, Canada hawkweed

VITAL STATISTICS

Maximum height: 100 centimetres
Flowering season: July to August

HABITAT: Narrow-leaved hawkweed occurs along roadsides and in clearings, waste places, thickets, and open woods throughout New Brunswick.

CHARACTERISTICS: Narrow-leaved hawkweed is a slender often clumping plant with leafy non-branching stems. Alternate leaves, up to 12 centimetres in length, are lanceolate, sessile, and pointed at their tips; they have scattered large teeth or tooth-like projections. Leaves and stems are covered in fine stiff hairs, which impart a rough texture. All parts of the plant ooze a milky sap when cut.

Loose nearly flat-topped panicles are composed of up to 25 flower heads. Individual flower heads, 2 to 2.5 centimetres wide, have many yellow ray florets but no disc florets. The phyllaries below the flower are green and curl back—this feature distinguishes this species from the introduced hawkweeds. Seed heads look like small dandelion seed heads.

The species *H. canadense*, *H. scabriusculum*, and *H. kalmii*, sometimes listed in older wildflower reference books, are now all included under *H. umbellatum*.

Rough hawkweed, *H. scabrum*, another native hawkweed, is found in thickets and forest borders, especially on sandy soils. It has leafy stems and dull-tipped oval to elliptical hairy leaves with smooth or slightly toothed edges. Leaves near the base have short petioles and are larger than the sessile upper leaves. Stems are hairy and glandular near the flowers. Flowers are in a loose panicle but their phyllaries are covered in sticky hairs.

Top: The narrow leaves have scattered teeth; the phyllaries curl back. Middle: Rough hawkweed phyllaries are covered in sticky hairs. Bottom: Rough hawkweed has broad leaves with smooth edges; the lower leaves are much larger than the upper.

Introduced Species

Aster family / Asteraceae

Common hawkweed

Hieracium vulgatum

Épervière vulgaire, English hawkweed, showy hawkweed

HABITAT: Common hawkweed is a European species commonly found throughout New Brunswick on old disturbed sites such as roadsides, thickets, and pasturelands and also in open woodlands.

CHARACTERISTICS: Common hawkweed, an upright non-branching plant, often forms colonies. Plants have both basal and alternately arranged stem leaves; the elliptical to lance-shaped leaves are up to 15 centimetres long with tapered bases. The shallow teeth along leaf edges may be larger toward the base of the leaf. Leaves may be mottled purple or bronze. Both stems and leaves are covered in hairs. All parts of the plant exude a milky sap when cut.

Flowers are produced in a loose panicle. Flower stems have two to 12 scattered leaves. Individual flower heads are dandelion-like and up to 4 centimetres wide with bright yellow ray florets but no disc florets. Ray florets are rectangular in outline with comb-like tips. Phyllaries are hairy, with glandular dark tips. Seed heads are like those of dandelion, but smaller. *Hieracium lachenalii*, listed in older wildflower reference literature, is now considered the same species as *H. vulgatum*.

Wall hawkweed, *H. murorum*, is uncommon and most often found the southern half of the province. It is similar in appearance to common hawkweed but distinguished by its heart-shaped to rounded leaf bases; it may have no, or up to two, leaves on the flower stems.

VITAL STATISTICS

Maximum height: 100 centimetres
Flowering season: July to August

Top: The dandelion-like flowers, composed of all ray florets, are in loose panicles. Middle: Common hawkweed stems are leafy and their toothed leaves taper at the base. Bottom: Wall hawkweed leaves are often mottled and its leaf bases lobed; flower stems may be leafless or have one or two leaves.

Aster family / Asteraceae

Elecampane

Inula helenium

Inule aulnée, inula, elf dock

Introduced Species

VITAL STATISTICS

Maximum height: 150 centimetres
Flowering season: August

HABITAT: Elecampane, a European species introduced as a garden ornamental, is occasionally found in fields or along damp roadsides or shorelines, especially in southern and eastern New Brunswick.

CHARACTERISTICS: Elecampane, a stout leafy plant arising from a thick rootstock, produces stout non-branching stems. Large alternate leaves, which are up to 50 centimetres long, are ovate with finely toothed edges; the hairs are rough on the upper surface and soft on the underside. Lower leaves have petioles; upper leaves clasp the stem. Young plants produce basal leaves only until they are old enough to bloom.

The 5-centimetre-diameter flower heads are solitary or in a loose terminal cluster. Individual flower heads have numerous narrow yellow ray florets surrounding orange-yellow disc florets. Green bract-like phyllaries are usually wide-spreading. Seeds have a tuft of hairs at one end.

Top: The ray florets are narrow. Bottom: Plants have large broad leaves and loose terminal clusters of flowers.

Aster family / Asteraceae

Introduced Species

Tansy ragwort

Jacobaea vulgaris (formerly *Senecio jacobaea*)

Séneçon jacobée, herbe-de-Jacob, stinking Willie

HABITAT: Tansy ragwort is a European introduction common in disturbed habitats and waste places throughout New Brunswick.

CHARACTERISTICS: Tansy ragwort is a bush-like biennial or, rarely, short-lived perennial. In the first year, plants produce a low but leafy rosette of evergreen bi- to tripinnatifid oblanceolate leaves. Lobes and teeth are rounded. These petioled basal leaves reach 20 centimetres in length and have a ruffled appearance; upper leaf surfaces are hairless, and leaf undersides are whitened with dense fine hairs. Alternately arranged stem leaves are sessile and smaller and more finely lobed than the basal leaves. The stout stems can also be white-haired when young, but the hair often wears away later in the growing season. The plant has a rank smell when bruised.

Flowers are produced in large flat-topped compound corymbs. Individual flower heads are 2 to 2.5 centimetres wide with 10 to 15 yellow ray florets and numerous yellow disc florets. Seed heads resemble miniature dandelions; each seed has a parachute of hairs that helps it blow for miles in the wind.

This plant is toxic if ingested.

VITAL STATISTICS
Maximum height: 120 centimetres
Flowering season: July to September

Top: Flowers are in flat-topped clusters. Middle: Plants are busy when in bloom. Bottom: The fern-like leaves have rounded lobes and teeth.

Aster family / Asteraceae

Canada lettuce

Native Species

Lactuca canadensis

Chicorée blanche, laitue du Canada, arrow-leaved lettuce

VITAL STATISTICS

Maximum height: 2.5 metres
Flowering season: July to August

HABITAT: Canada lettuce grows in disturbed habitats but also in open woodlands, thickets, and clearings throughout New Brunswick.

CHARACTERISTICS: Canada lettuce is a biennial. In the first season, it produces a rosette of low evergreen leaves; in the second, a tall non-branched stem with alternate leaves. The hairless waxy stem may be tinted red or purple. Leaves are lance-shaped to elliptical and pinnatifid with various sized deep lobes and sharp teeth; they may have hairs on the lower midvein. Upper stem leaves may be lance-shaped with smooth edges. This plant oozes a milky sap when cut.

Flowers are produced in narrow panicles. Flower heads are about 0.8 centimetres in diameter and composed of 12 to 20 light yellow ray florets. Phyllaries are 1 to 1.4 centimetres long. Seed heads look like miniature dandelions.

Prickly lettuce, *L. serriola*, a European species found in Albert and Westmorland counties, has bristle-edged clasping leaves and scattered stiff prickles along the midvein of the leaf undersides. The lower main stem has scattered bristles. Its panicle of pale yellow flowers is conical. Each flower head has five to 12 ray florets and four sets of overlapping phyllaries.

Top: The small flowers have 12 to 20 small light yellow ray florets. Middle: The pinnatifid leaves have a mixture of large and small lobes, all with sharp teeth. Bottom: Prickly lettuce has clasping leaves and bristle-tipped teeth.

Aster family / Asteraceae

Common nipplewort

Lapsana communis

Herbe aux mamelles, nipplewort

Introduced Species

HABITAT: Common nipplewort, a European species occasionally seen in waste areas and gardens, is most likely to be seen along the Saint John and St. Croix river systems.

CHARACTERISTICS: Common nipplewort is a slender annual or biennial which only branches near the flowers. The shallowly ridged stem, often red- or purple-tinted, has glandular hairs, especially near the base. Overwintering plants have a basal rosette; flowering plants, alternate stem leaves. The lower elliptical to ovate leaves may reach 15 centimetres in length. Each leaf has a large arrowhead-shaped terminal lobe and two smaller nipple-like lateral lobes which are widely separated from the terminal lobes. Leaf edges have hairs and large shallow teeth. The leaf surface is wrinkly with scattered hairs; hairs on the lower surface are confined to the veins. The petiole is fringed with hair and slightly winged. Upper stem leaves, smaller than the lower stem leaves, are unlobed and lanceolate to elliptical. Plants exude a white sap when cut.

Flowers are produced in an open panicle. Flower stems are hairless. Individual flower heads are 1.5 to 2 centimetres wide and composed of about 20 light yellow ray florets. Ray petals end in five fine teeth. Unlike many of the yellow composites found in Nova Scotia, this species does not have a tuft of hair at the tip of its seeds.

VITAL STATISTICS

Maximum height: 80 centimetres

Flowering season: July to August

Top: The ray florets end in five fine teeth. Bottom: Lower leaves are often ovate, with large teeth; the stems are often purple.

Aster family / Asteraceae

Fall dandelion

Leontodon autumnalis

Léontodon d'automne, autumn hawkbit

Introduced Species

VITAL STATISTICS

Maximum height: 30 centimetres

Flowering season: July to September

HABITAT: Fall dandelion, a European introduction, is well established in waste places, lawns, and gardens throughout the province.

CHARACTERISTICS: Fall dandelion is a rosette-producing plant with all basal leaves. Leaves, lance-shaped in outline, are either pinnatifid or have long thin well-spaced teeth often perpendicular to the leaf edge. Leaves and flower stems have scattered fine hairs. All parts of the plant ooze a milky sap when cut.

Flower stems, which are commonly branching, are leafless but have small scale-like bracts. Flower heads are in loose cymes. Stems thicken just below each flower head, which is 2.5 to 3.5 centimetres wide with yellow ray florets. Ray florets end in comb-like tips. Seed heads are like those of a dandelion but smaller and tawny rather than white.

Hairy cat's-ear, *Hypochaeris radicata*, is a rare introduction similar in appearance to fall dandelion. It also has pinnatifid basal leaves, but they are densely hairy and broader than those of fall dandelion. The naked flower stem is stouter than that of fall dandelion and it does not thicken immediately below the flower head.

Top: The flower stems are conspicuously thickened immediately below the flower. Middle: Fall dandelion produces a rosette of narrow pinnatifid leaves. Bottom: Hairy cat's-ear has hairy pinnatifid leaves.

Aster family / Asteraceae

Golden groundsel

Packera aurea (formerly *Senecio aureus*)

Séneçon doré, golden ragwort, heart-leaved groundsel

Native Species

HABITAT: Golden groundsel is common in damp meadows, thickets, and open woodlands throughout much of New Brunswick.

CHARACTERISTICS: Golden groundsel is a slender plant with non-branching stems. Most leaves are basal, oval- to heart-shaped, with fine teeth and long petioles and up to 10 centimetres long. Stem leaves are alternate, pinnatifid, and much smaller and narrower than basal leaves. Stem leaves usually clasp the stem. Leaves and stems are hairless, although young stems may have some tufts of hairs.

The flowers are in flat-topped corymbs atop slender stems. Each flower is about 2 centimetres wide with 8 to 13 golden-yellow ray florets surrounding many yellow disc florets. Phyllaries are usually purple-tipped. Seed heads resemble a small dandelion's.

The uncommon swamp ragwort, *P. schweinitziana* (*S. robbinsii*), is found in peaty meadows and swampy woodlands in southern and western New Brunswick. It is distinguished by narrow lance to triangular basal leaves, which have heart-shaped to rounded bases and sharp teeth. Flowers are pale yellow.

Balsam groundsel, *P. paupercula*, a bushy plant, under 50 centimetres tall, is uncommon in calcareous gravels and ledges along the upper Saint John and Restigouche rivers. Long-petioled basal leaves are oblanceolate, oblong to spatulate, and taper at the base, with sharp teeth. Lower stem leaves are sessile or short petioled, lance-shaped, and pinnatifid. Leaves and stems have scattered woolly tufts, especially at leaf axils and on leaf undersides. Flowers are produced in small, flat-topped corymbs.

VITAL STATISTICS

Maximum height: 100 centimetres

Flowering season: June to July

Top: Flowers are in flat-topped corymbs atop slender stems. Middle: Basal leaves are oval and heart-shaped with long petioles. Bottom: Balsam groundsel is smaller in stature with smaller flower clusters and spoon-shaped sharp-toothed basal leaves.

Aster family / Asteraceae

Orange hawkweed

Introduced Species

Pilosella aurantiaca (formerly *Hieracium aurantiacum*)
Bouquets rouges, marguerite rouge, devil's paintbrush

VITAL STATISTICS

Maximum height: 60 centimetres
Flowering season: June to August

HABITAT: Orange hawkweed is a European introduction found along roadsides, old meadows, and other previously disturbed areas throughout New Brunswick. Unlike other hawkweeds, it is not common on recently disturbed sites.

CHARACTERISTICS: A matted plant, orange hawkweed can form large colonies by producing leafy rooting stolons. Leaves, which are up to 12 centimetres long, are primarily basal and partly evergreen. Elliptical to obovate in outline, leaves are smooth-edged and covered in long hairs. The plant oozes a milky sap when cut.

Flowers are produced in a dense corymb at the end of generally leafless stems, which may occasionally have one or two alternately arranged leaves. The flower stem is also covered in long hairs. Individual flower heads are dandelion-like, about 2 centimetres in diameter, and deep orange with numerous ray florets but no disc florets. Ray florets are rectangular with comb-like tips. Phyllaries are covered in black glandular hairs. Seed heads are a smaller version of a dandelion's; dark-coloured seeds have an attached parachute that can carry them for many kilometres on the wind.

Top: The distinctive orange dandelion-like flowers.
Bottom: The basal leaves are elliptical and long-haired with smooth edges; flower stems also have long hairs.

Aster family / Asteraceae

Introduced Species

Meadow hawkweed

Pilosella caespitosa (formerly *Hieracium pratense/caespitosum*)

Éperviѐre des prés, king devil

HABITAT: A European species, meadow hawkweed is common on old pasturelands and meadows throughout New Brunswick.

CHARACTERISTICS: Meadow hawkweed forms mat-like colonies that increase rapidly through leafy rooting stolons. Leaves are basal and partly evergreen, elliptical to lance-shaped, up to 20 centimetres long, with either smooth or slightly toothed edges. Leaves are finely hairy with longer hairs along the edges and the midrib of the undersides. Flower stems are densely hairy and may have one to three alternately arranged leaves on its lower portion. All parts of the plant ooze a milky sap when cut.

Flowers are produced in a dense flattened corymb of five to 25 flowers. Individual flower heads are dandelion-like and 2 centimetres wide and composed of only ray florets, which are bright yellow and rectangular with comb-like tips. Phyllaries are covered in black glandular hairs. Fluffy seed heads resemble those of small dandelions.

Pale hawkweed, *P. floribunda* (*H. floribundum*), is similar to meadow hawkweed, but its leaves are usually hairless on their upper surfaces. Hairs are restricted to leaf edges and undersides.

Tall hawkweed, *P. piloselloides* (*H. florentinum* or *H. praealtum*), another look-alike, lacks long leafy stolons and has more leaves along its flowering stems.

VITAL STATISTICS

Maximum height: 50 centimetres

Flowering season: Late June to July

Top: Flowers are in a dense corymb. Middle: Plants produce leafy stolons and narrow long-haired basal leaves. Bottom: Pale hawkweed also has flowers in dense corymbs.

Aster family / Asteraceae

Mouse-ear hawkweed

Introduced Species

Pilosella officinarum (formerly *Hieracium pilosella*)

Oreille de souris, piloselle

VITAL STATISTICS

Maximum height: 25 centimetres

Flowering season: Mid-June to August

HABITAT: Mouse-ear hawkweed, a European species, is common in clearings, pastures, and fields throughout New Brunswick.

CHARACTERISTICS: Mouse-ear hawkweed is a mat-forming plant which can form large colonies through leafy rooting stolons. Leaves are basal, up to 8 centimetres long, oblong to spatulate, and smooth-edged with copious stiff hairs. Leaf undersides, especially those of young leaves, are whitened with a dense covering of fine tomentose hair. The entire plant oozes a milky sap when cut.

Flowers are solitary at the tips of wiry densely hairy stems. Individual flower heads are 2.5 to 3 centimetres wide with numerous ray florets but no disc florets. Pale lemon yellow ray florets are rectangular with comb-like tips. The undersides of the outermost ray florets are often striped in pale red. Phyllaries are covered in black glandular hairs. Seed heads are dandelion-like, but smaller: the dark seeds have an attached parachute that can carry them for several kilometres on the wind.

Whiplash hawkweed, *P. flagellaris* (*Hieracium flagellare*), is less common than mouse-ear hawkweed but occurs in similar habitats. It is distinguished by its green (not whitened) leaf undersides. Leaves may be longer, up to 15 centimetres, and the flower stem stouter, reaching 45 centimetres in length. Plants typically have two flowers per stem, but occasionally one or up to four flowers. Flowers are deep yellow.

Top: The solitary flowers have lemon yellow ray florets. Middle: Plants produce a mat-like growth with solitary flowers on leafless stems. Bottom: Whiplash hawkweed typically produces two flowers per stem rather than being solitary.

Aster family / Asteraceae

Black-eyed Susan

Rudbeckia hirta

Marguerite jaune, hairy coneflower

Native Species

HABITAT: Black-eyed Susan is often seen along roadsides and in old meadows and thickets, especially in the southern half of New Brunswick.

CHARACTERISTICS: Black-eyed Susan is a clumping plant with one to several upright stems. Plants have basal and alternately arranged stem leaves. All leaves are ovate to lance-shaped and coarsely toothed or smooth-edged; basal leaves are long petioled and stem leaves mostly sessile. The largest leaves may reach 15 centimetres in length. Stems and all leaves are rough and hairy.

Long-stemmed flowers are in loose cymes or, rarely, are solitary. Flower heads are 6 to 7.5 centimetres wide and composed of yellow ray florets and central dark brown disc florets. A ring of hairy green backward-bending phyllaries of irregular lengths is at the base of each flower.

Cut-leaved coneflower, *R. laciniata*, is a garden escape rarely encountered along ditches and trails near larger communities. The double-flowered cultivar golden glow is most often seen and grows to 2 metres high. Hairy or smooth leaves have three to seven large lobes and can reach 30 centimetres in length. Lower leaves have petioles; upper leaves are sessile. Stems end in a loose 6- to 7.5-centimetre-wide cluster of yellow flowers. Golden glow flowers often have several rows of ray florets with few or no disc florets. On the rarely seen wild form, ray florets arch down and yellow-green disc florets form a cone-like centre. Five green hairless leafy phyllaries grow beneath each flower.

VITAL STATISTICS

Maximum height: 100 centimetres
Flowering season: July and August

Top: Black-eyed Susan flowers have large golden yellow ray florets and a dense central cluster of dark brown disc florets. Middle: Leaves are covered in rough hairs; the base of the flower has a ring of green leafy phyllaries. Bottom: The double-flowered cut-leaved coneflower called golden glow is the most common naturalized form.

Aster family / Asteraceae

Seaside ragwort

Senecio pseudoarnica

Roi des champs, false arnica, beach groundsel

Native Species

VITAL STATISTICS

Maximum height: 100 centimetres

Flowering season: Mid-July to August

HABITAT: Seaside ragwort is extremely rare in New Brunswick, known only on Grand Manan Island and the adjacent islands of Charlotte County, where it grows along sandy and gravelly beaches.

CHARACTERISTICS: Seaside ragwort is a clumping plant with stout unbranched stems. Plants form colonies by their spreading rhizomes. Early leaves are densely arranged on short stems, appearing like a basal rosette. As stems elongate, they reveal alternate leaves which have short petioles at the base of the plants but are nearly sessile farther up. Leaves are fleshy, toothed, and elliptical to oblanceolate and covered in web-like hairs when they emerge. If the hairs on the upper surface wear away, the leaves become glossy. However, leaf undersides remain white with a dense coating of woolly hairs.

Flower heads are produced in a leafy corymb made up of a few flowers. Flower stems and buds are covered in white hairs. Individual flower heads are 5 to 8 centimetres wide with 10 to 20 yellow ray florets and numerous yellow disc florets. Tawny brown seed heads are much like those of a dandelion, except smaller. Seeds have a crown of hairs that enables them to drift many kilometres on the wind.

Top: The daisy-like flowers have long ray florets surrounding a central cluster of yellow disc florets.
Middle: Plants produce densely overlapping leaves; new leaves are covered in cobwebby hairs.
Bottom: Flowers are in leafy corymbs.

Woodland ragwort

Senecio sylvaticus

Séneçon des bois, woodland groundsel

Introduced Species

HABITAT: Woodland ragwort is a naturalized European species found primarily along the coasts of New Brunswick in moist disturbed habitats, upper beaches, and occasionally open woodlands.

VITAL STATISTICS
Maximum height: 100 centimetres
Flowering season: June to September

CHARACTERISTICS: Woodland ragwort is a low bushy annual or winter annual with sparsely branching stems. The plant is covered in soft slightly sticky hairs. Alternate leaves are soft, fleshy, oblong to lanceolate, pinnatifid or variously pinnately lobed and toothed. Lower leaves have petioles; upper leaves are sessile or clasp the stem. The plant emits a strong oily smell when bruised.

Flowers are produced in loose corymbs. Individual flowers are less than 1 centimetre wide with primarily yellow disc florets. Ray florets, when present, are small and curl backward. Seed heads are small puffballs that look like miniature dandelions.

Common ragwort, *S. vulgaris*, is similar to woodland ragwort but has fewer hairs, most of which are confined to the base of new leaves. It is also shorter (to 60 centimetres) and bushier, with a hollow stem and rayless flowers. The distinguishing feature of this species is black-tipped phyllaries on the outside base of the flower.

Sticky ragwort, *S. viscosus*, another look-alike, is covered in sticky hairs, which impart a grey-green appearance. It has distinct ray florets. Common ragwort and sticky ragwort are more widespread in New Brunswick than woodland ragwort.

Top: Woodland ragwort flowers are in loose corymbs and the small ray florets often curl backward. Middle: Common ragwort flowers have black-tipped phyllaries and rayless flowers. Bottom: Sticky ragwort has grey-green foliage and flowers with distinct ray florets.

Aster family / Asteraceae

Large-leaved goldenrod

Solidago macrophylla

Verge d'or à grandes feuilles

Native Species

VITAL STATISTICS

Maximum height: 100 centimetres
Flowering season: August to September

HABITAT: Large-leaved goldenrod, found in open shady woodlands and shaded ravines, especially among coniferous forest, is found throughout New Brunswick.

CHARACTERISTICS: Large-leaved goldenrod has a single stout upright stem with basal and stem leaves. Basal leaves, which reach 12 centimetres in length, are ovate, spatulate, or elliptical with rounded bases and elongate petioles; they are sharply toothed and are hairless except along the main underside veins. Stem leaves are alternate; upper leaves are more lanceolate than the lower and have short winged petioles or are sessile. Stem leaves may be smooth-edged or slightly toothed and are hairless or have scattered hairs.

Terminal and axillary flowers produced in a loose leafy raceme or panicle create a wand-like effect. Individual flower heads are about 0.5 centimetres wide with eight to 10 ray florets and a similar number of central disc florets. Unlike the flowers of many other goldenrods, those of large-leaved goldenrod are held outward.

Zigzag goldenrod, *S. flexicaulis*, is common in rich deciduous or mixed woodlands. It is distinguished by zigzagged stems, especially on the upper half of the plant, and long soft hairs on the upper portion of the main stem. Both the upper and lower leaves are ovate; the upper leaves often have longer teeth than the lower ones. Individual flowers have three to four ray florets.

Top: Large-leaved goldenrod has wand-like clusters of outward-facing flowers. Middle: The basal leaves are egg-shaped, toothed, and long petioled. Bottom: Zigzag goldenrod has all ovate leaves and an often kinked upper stem.

Aster family / Asteraceae

Multi-rayed goldenrod

Solidago multiradiata

Verge d'or à rayons nombreux, alpine goldenrod, Rocky Mountain goldenrod, northern goldenrod

Native Species

HABITAT: An extremely rare calciphile, multi-rayed goldenrod is restricted to gypsum cliffs of Albert Mine, Albert County.

CHARACTERISTICS: Multi-rayed goldenrod is a tufted leafy plant. Basal leaves, which are up to 12 centimetres long, are oblanceolate with rounded teeth and hairless except along the edges of the winged petioles. Stem leaves are alternate, sessile, and usually smooth-edged. Stems are hairless at the base but may have white hairs closer to the summit.

Flowers are produced in dense hemispherical corymbs. Stems are hairy close to the flowers. Individual flower heads are about 1.5 centimetres in diameter with 12 to 18 golden yellow ray florets and up to 30 disc florets. Seeds have a tuft of golden brown hair at their tips.

VITAL STATISTICS

Maximum height: 30 centimetres

Flowering season: July to August

Top: Flowers are in dense hemispherical corymbs.
Bottom: Plants are tufted with hairless round-toothed basal leaves.

Aster family / Asteraceae

Grey-stemmed goldenrod

Solidago nemoralis

Verge d'or des bois, grey goldenrod, field goldenrod, old field goldenrod

Native Species

VITAL STATISTICS

Maximum height: 75 centimetres
Flowering season: August to September

HABITAT: Grey-stemmed goldenrod is found in old meadows and along dry sandy roadsides primarily in the southwestern region of New Brunswick.

CHARACTERISTICS: Grey-stemmed goldenrod, a slender plant with unbranched stems, is covered in short grey hairs which impart a grey-green look. Plants have both basal and alternate stem leaves. Lower stem leaves and basal leaves are oblanceolate to spatulate with a petiole and slightly toothed edges; upper stem leaves are smaller than the lower leaves, sessile, and smooth-edged. Small leafy tufts often appear in the middle and upper leaf axils. The main stem may be red-tinted.

Lemon yellow flowers are in narrow wand-like panicles with short lateral branches. The flower heads of the side-branches are one-sided and upward-facing. The panicle tends to nod at the tip. Individual flower heads, which are about 0.6 centimetres in diameter, have three to six disc florets and five to 10 ray florets.

Downy goldenrod, *S. puberula*, is common in sterile dry soils of the province. This species has pubescent stems but its lanceolate leaves are primarily smooth. The wand-like golden yellow flower clusters are erect. The flower heads of the short side-branches are not one-sided. Flower heads have 10 ray florets that are, overall, larger than those of grey-stemmed goldenrod.

Top: Grey-stemmed goldenrod flowers are held in narrow wand-like panicles with one-sided short lateral branches. Bottom: Downy goldenrod flowers are also wand-like but its short side-branches are not one-sided and its ray florets are more noticeable than those of grey-stemmed goldenrod.

Aster family / Asteraceae

Rough-stemmed goldenrod

Solidago rugosa

Native Species

Verge d'or rugueuse, rough goldenrod, wrinkle-leaved goldenrod

VITAL STATISTICS

Maximum height: 2 metres
Flowering season: August to September

HABITAT: Rough-stemmed goldenrod occurs in damp woods, thickets, roadsides, old meadows, and other disturbed sites throughout New Brunswick.

CHARACTERISTICS: Rough-stemmed goldenrod is a clumping colonial plant with numerous unbranched stems. Alternate leaves are lanceolate, elliptical to narrowly ovate, nearly sessile, and sharply toothed. Leaves are crowded on the stems. Each leaf, which is up to 10 centimetres long, has a single central vein. Stems and leaves are covered in rough hairs.

Flowers are in terminal panicles which vary from wand-like to broadly pyramidal. Upward-pointing flower heads are on arching one-sided lateral branches. Each flower head is about 0.3 centimetres wide and composed of five to eight yellow ray florets and a similar number of yellow disc florets.

Canada goldenrod, *S. canadensis*, another look-alike, has two side veins that run parallel to the central vein. Its stem is finely hairy toward the flowers but smooth toward the base. It is common throughout the province except in the southwest.

Giant goldenrod, *S. gigantea*, looks like Canada goldenrod but forms large colonies, reaches up to 3 metres in height, and has smooth stems with a waxy whitened bloom. It is most often found in southern and western New Brunswick, where it grows in riverside meadows.

Top: Rough-stemmed goldenrod often has pyramidal panicles of many one-sided lateral branches. Middle: Canada goldenrod leaves have two lateral veins that run parallel to the midvein. Bottom: Giant goldenrod produces flowers in a loose pyramidal cluster.

Aster family / Asteraceae

Seaside goldenrod

Native Species

Solidago sempervirens

Verge d'or toujours verte, evergreen goldenrod, salt-marsh goldenrod

VITAL STATISTICS

Maximum height: 2 metres
Flowering season: July to September

HABITAT: Seaside goldenrod is restricted to brackish shorelines, marshes, and coastal dunes around New Brunswick's coastline.

CHARACTERISTICS: Seaside goldenrod is a clumping plant with several upright non-branching stems. The thick leaves are fleshy. Basal leaves, which are up to 30 centimetres long, are evergreen, elliptical, oblanceolate or spatulate, smooth-edged, and long petioled. Stem leaves are alternate and sessile, partly clasping the stem. Upper stem leaves are smaller, more lanceolate than the lower; upper leaves are sessile, partly clasping the stem.

Flowers, produced in dense pyramidal panicles, are held upright along side-branches. Individual flower heads are up to 0.8 centimetres wide with seven to 10 ray florets and a similar number of disc florets. Its seeds have the dense plume of hairs characteristic of all goldenrods.

Top: Flowers are in dense pyramidal clusters with upward-facing flower heads. Middle: Seaside goldenrod often forms dense clumps. Bottom: The hairless narrow leaves have smooth edges.

Coastal

Aster family / Asteraceae

Native Species

Bog goldenrod

Solidago uliginosa

Verge d'or des marais, northern bog goldenrod

VITAL STATISTICS

Maximum height: 100 centimetres
Flowering season: July to September

HABITAT: Bog goldenrod commonly occurs in peatlands, damp barrens, meadows, and woodlands throughout New Brunswick.

CHARACTERISTICS: An upright plant, bog goldenrod has one or a few unbranched stems. Plants have both basal and stem leaves, which are firm and lanceolate, oblanceolate, or elliptical. Basal leaves may reach 20 centimetres in length and are smooth-edged or slightly toothed and long petioled and partly clasp the stem. Stem leaves are alternate, smaller than basal leaves, smooth-edged, and sessile. Leaves and stems are usually hairless. The stems may be purple-tinted.

Flowers are produced in a dense panicle which varies from wand-like to broadly pyramidal. Flowering branches are at a narrow angle close to the main stem but are occasionally one-sided. Individual flower heads are 0.3 centimetres wide with one to eight (usually six to eight) golden yellow ray florets. Seed heads are tiny and fluffy; seed plumes help them travel on the wind.

Early goldenrod, *S. juncea*, common in southern and western New Brunswick, grows in old fields, on barrens, and along shorelines. Early goldenrod may have ciliate hairs along its leaf edges. In addition to its preference for dry sites, early goldenrod is distinguished by small leafy tufts in its upper leaf axils and a wide-spreading panicle of one-sided flowers that imparts a fireworks effect. Each flower head has up to 12 ray florets. It is among the earliest goldenrods to bloom in the province.

Top: Bog goldenrod may have narrow or broad flower clusters. Middle: Some bog goldenrod have narrow flower clusters; its leaves are often narrow and hairless. Bottom: Early goldenrod has wide-spreading panicles of flowers; the narrow foliage is similar to that of bog goldenrod.

Aster family / Asteraceae

Field sow-thistle

Sonchus arvensis

Laiteron des champs, perennial sow-thistle, corn sow-thistle

Introduced Species

VITAL STATISTICS

Maximum height: 120 centimetres
Flowering season: July to September

HABITAT: Field sow-thistle is a European introduction found in waste places and occasionally along gravelly coastal beaches throughout New Brunswick.

CHARACTERISTICS: A colonial plant, field sow-thistle spreads by extensively creeping rhizomes. It is upright with non-branching stems and hairless basal and alternate stem leaves. Basal leaves, up to 30 centimetres in length, are pinnatifid or pinnately lobed, oblanceolate in outline with soft spiny-toothed and deeply lobed edges like those of common dandelion. Stem leaves are clasping and much smaller than basal leaves. The main stem is hollow and smooth; elongate flower stems may have glandular hairs.

Flower heads are produced in loose terminal corymbs. Individual flower heads are 3 to 5 centimetres wide with numerous golden yellow ray florets and no disc florets. Seed heads look like those of a dandelion, but smaller.

Common sow-thistle, *S. oleraceus*, is an introduced slender annual scattered throughout the province. It reaches 100 centimetres in height. Its thin pinnatifid leaves have a terminal lobe that is larger than its lateral lobes. Stem leaves clasp the stem and have pointed auricles. Lemon yellow flower heads are 1.5 to 2.5 centimetres wide.

Prickly sow-thistle, *S. asper*, another scattered introduced look-alike, has leaves that may be oblanceolate to ovate, variously lobed, but always with stiff sharp spiny teeth. The leaves clasp the stem but have rounded auricles. The 1.5- to 2.5-centimetre-wide flower heads are pale yellow.

Top: Field sow-thistle flowers are in loose corymbs; flower and seed heads resemble those of small dandelions. Middle: Common sow-thistle has pinnatifid leaves with a large terminal lobe. Bottom: The leaf edges of prickly sow-thistle have sharp spiny teeth.

Aster family / Asteraceae

Common dandelion

Taraxacum officinale

Dent-de-lion, pissenlit, dumble-dor, blowballs, piss-n-the-beds

Introduced Species

HABITAT: Common dandelion grows in disturbed habitats and waste places, including lawns and gardens. It is abundant throughout New Brunswick.

VITAL STATISTICS

Maximum height: 40 centimetres

Flowering season: April to September

CHARACTERISTICS: Common dandelion is a low rosetted plant with a deep taproot and only basal leaves. Leaves, which are up to 45 centimetres long, are oblanceolate and mostly pinnatifid with deep, coarse lobes and teeth. Sometimes the leaves are only sharply toothed. Leaves taper into a long narrow-winged petiole and are sparsely covered in fine white hairs, especially along the central vein. The entire plant oozes a milky sap when cut.

The many solitary flower heads are at the ends of hollow pubescent stems. Flowers are up to 5 centimetres in diameter and composed of numerous ray florets but no disc florets. Seed heads are large and distinct: a globular mass of seeds with long-stalked plumes. The main flowering season is May and June, but plants flower sporadically through September.

Top: The many solitary flowers have numerous ray florets. Middle: Common dandelion are low-rosetted plants with only basal leaves. Bottom: Large plumed seed heads.

Aster family / Asteraceae

Meadow goatsbeard

Introduced Species

Tragopogon pratensis

Salsifis des prés, meadow salsify

VITAL STATISTICS

Maximum height: 100 centimetres
Flowering season: June to August

HABITAT: Meadow goatsbeard, a European species, is found in disturbed habitats. It is common throughout New Brunswick.

CHARACTERISTICS: Meadow goatsbeard is a slender biennial plant arising from a taproot. In the first season, plants produce a rosette of narrow lance-shaped to linear smooth-edged hairless leaves. Leaves may be up to 30 centimetres in length and have parallel veins. In the second season, one or a few stems arise with alternate lance-shaped to linear leaves which are sessile and clasp the stem. All parts of the plant exude a milky sap when cut.

Flowers are solitary on long stems from the axils of the upper leaves. Flower buds are long and tapered with a rounded base. Flower stems widen at the base of each flower head; flower heads are about 5 centimetres wide with numerous ray florets. Outer florets have larger rays than the inner florets; no disc florets are present. The base of each flower head has eight narrow green phyllaries that are almost as long as the outer ray florets. These heads close at night or during wet weather. The seed head resembles that of a dandelion.

Yellow or western goatsbeard, *T. dubius*, is very rare and found only along the Quebec border. It has pale yellow flowers and 13 narrow green phyllaries that extend beyond the outer ray florets. It also has waxy grey-green foliage.

Top: Hairless linear leaves clasp the stem. Middle: The seed heads are like a large version of a dandelion's seed head. Bottom: Yellow goatsbeard has green phyllaries that extend beyond the pale yellow ray florets.

Introduced Species

Aster family / Asteraceae

Coltsfoot

Tussilago farfara

Pas-d'âne, coughwort

HABITAT: Coltsfoot, of European origin, is found in damp waste areas throughout New Brunswick. It also invades open woodlands, swamps, and coastal rocky beaches, especially in limestone-rich areas.

CHARACTERISTICS: Coltsfoot is a ground-cover-like plant that forms large patches as it rapidly spreads by underground rhizomes. Leaves are primarily basal. Each leaf is toothed and palmately lobed, with five to 12 shallow lobes. New leaves are covered in white downy hairs which disappear from the upper surfaces as the season progresses; leaf undersides remain white with tomentose hairs. Leaves are up to 20 centimetres wide. Stems are white and woolly; alternate stem leaves are reduced to green bracts.

Plants produce numerous flower stems, each terminated by a single flower head. Individual flower heads are about 2.5 centimetres in diameter and composed of several overlapping rings of numerous narrow yellow ray florets, which surround numerous yellow disc florets.

Plants flower before they produce leaves; this makes them among the earliest wildflowers to bloom in New Brunswick. Flowers close on wet days or at night. The flower stem nods as the seeds develop but becomes erect as seeds are released from the small dandelion-like puffball. Seeds are released as leaves emerge.

VITAL STATISTICS

Maximum height: 45 centimetres

Flowering season: April to May

Top: Individual flower heads have several overlapping rings of narrow ray florets. Middle: Solitary flowers before the plant sends up leaves. Bottom: Palmately lobed leaves with many shallow lobes.

Aster family / Asteraceae

Common burdock

Introduced Species

Arctium minus

Bardane, tabac du diable, lesser burdock, stickly-buds

VITAL STATISTICS

Maximum height: 150 centimetres
Flowering season: June to September

HABITAT: A European species, common burdock is found in waste places, around buildings, and along roadsides, especially in shady areas throughout New Brunswick.

CHARACTERISTICS: Common burdock is a robust large-leaved biennial. In their first season, plants produce a rosette of large basal leaves, which are up to 60 centimetres long and look like rhubarb. Leaves are ovate to heart-shaped with long furrowed hollow petioles and smooth, often undulating, edges. The upper sides of the leaves are usually hairless; undersides are whitened with fine pubescent hairs. In the second year, plants produce a stout stalk with alternate stem leaves that are smaller than those produced in the first year and ovate in outline. Plants produce many flowering stems; these stems are whitened with finely pubescent hairs.

Upper stems end in dense raceme-like clusters of flower heads on short stalks. The globular flower heads are 1.5 to 2.5 centimetres wide with purple-pink disc florets but no ray florets. White styles, which extend beyond the pink corolla, create a pincushion effect. The phyllaries below the flower heads are strongly hooked, resulting in burrs that, when seeds are ripe, stick to animal fur or woolly clothing.

Greater burdock, *A. lappa*, is scattered throughout New Brunswick. The plant's petioles are solid, not hollow like those of common burdock. Flower heads are 3 to 4.5 centimetres in diameter and are in long-stalked corymbs. It prefers calcareous soils.

Top: The petal-less flowers are in dense racemes; the phyllaries have hooked tips. Middle: Leaves are large and heart-shaped with undulating edges. Bottom: Greater burdock has flowers with long stems.

Aster family / Asteraceae

Black knapweed

Centaurea nigra

Introduced Species

Centaurée noire, Spanish buttons, lesser knapweed, black starthistle

HABITAT: A European species, black knapweed is naturalized throughout New Brunswick along roadsides and in old pastures and other waste places.

VITAL STATISTICS

Maximum height: 80 centimetres
Flowering season: July to September

CHARACTERISTICS: Black knapweed is a bushy clumping plant with numerous upright and branching stems. Plants have both basal and alternate stem leaves which vary from elliptical to lanceolate. Leaves are generally smooth but wavy-edged; occasionally they may be slightly toothed or lobed. Basal leaves have petioles; stem leaves are usually sessile. Veins on the undersides of leaves are raised and ribbed. Hairs on the entire plant give it a grey-green appearance.

The rose-purple flower heads are held on long stems in an open corymb. Individual flower heads are about 3 centimetres wide with a globular base covered in dark brown fringed phyllaries. Flower heads are composed of only disc florets; close examination reveals five petals on each, although, from a distance, the flowers look like pincushions.

Brown knapweed, *C. jacea,* is occasionally seen in waste places of New Brunswick. It is quite similar to black knapweed but the showier flower heads have an outer ring of large disc florets that appear almost petal-like. Their phyllaries are light brown.

Top: The petal-less flowers have a globular base covered in brown fringed phyllaries. Middle: The basal leaves are occasionally lobed and toothed. Bottom: Brown knapweed has paler brown phyllaries and thin ray petals.

Aster family / Asteraceae

Canada thistle

Introduced Species

Cirsium arvense

Chardon du Canada, chaudron, field thistle, creeping thistle

Mixed Forest

Deciduous Forest

VITAL STATISTICS

Maximum height: 150 centimetres
Flowering season: July to August

HABITAT: Canada thistle is a European species found in disturbed habitats throughout New Brunswick.

CHARACTERISTICS: Canada thistle, a clumping plant, forms large colonies as it spreads through underground rhizomes. Plants have both basal and alternate stem leaves. Leaves are rigid, lanceolate to oblong, and pinnately lobed or pinnatifid with wavy, stiff, and spiny toothed edges. The upper sides of the leaves may be smooth, but the undersides have white woolly hairs. The uppermost leaves often clasp the stem. Stems have longitudinal ridges and scattered long white hairs. Upper stems are often purple-tinted.

Plants are dioecious, but male and female flowers look similar. Flower heads are produced in an open corymb. Each 1.5- to 2-centimetre-wide flower head is composed only of florets; close examination reveals that each floret has five distinct narrow petals. From a distance, however, the flowers look like pincushions. The base of each flower head is globular with spine-tipped purple-green phyllaries. Seeds have feathery plumes reminiscent of small dandelion seed heads.

Top: The pincushion-like petal-less flowers are in corymbs. Bottom: Canada thistle leaves have wavy spiny-toothed edges.

Disturbed

Introduced Species

Aster family / Asteraceae

Bull thistle

Cirsium vulgare

Piqueux, gros chardon, common thistle, Scotch thistle

HABITAT: Bull thistle, a European species, is found in waste places throughout New Brunswick.

CHARACTERISTICS: Bull thistle is a biennial plant with a solitary stout stem. First-year plants have evergreen basal leaves; second-year plants have alternate stem leaves. Pinnatifid leaves are lanceolate to elliptical with sharp spine-tipped lobes and teeth. Leaves have scattered hairs on their top surfaces but undersides are white and woolly. Stems have spiny wings.

The 3- to 5-centimetre-wide flower heads are in small corymbs. Flower bases are globular with 1- to 2-centimetre-long spiny phyllaries. Flowers, composed of only rose-purple disc florets, have a pincushion appearance. Seeds have plumed hairs and, when released, the seed heads resemble those of dandelion.

A slender biennial frequent in wet open woodlands, streamsides, and marshes, swamp thistle, *C. muticum*, is New Brunswick's only native species of thistle. Leaves are pinnatifid, more deeply lobed than those of bull thistle, and have fewer spines. Stems are smooth with scattered long hairs. The base of the 3-centimetre-wide flower heads is globular; phyllaries have sharp, rather than spiny, tips—more thorn-like than needle-like. They have distinct long white hairs among their phllaries.

Nodding thistle, *Carduus nutans*, is a biennial that resembles bull thistle but the flower heads are generally nodding and the phyllaries below the flower heads are broad, spiny-tipped, and purple-tinted. It is occasional in the eastern region.

VITAL STATISTICS

Maximum height:	150 centimetres
Flowering season:	Late July to September

Top: The globular petal-less flower heads have long-spined phyllaries. Middle: Swamp thistle phyllaries have sharp spines but its stems are smooth. Bottom: Nodding thistle has nodding flowers.

Aster family / Asteraceae

Spotted Joe-Pye weed

Native Species

Eutrochium maculatum (formerly *Eupatorium maculatum*)

Eupatoire maculée

VITAL STATISTICS

Maximum height: 2 metres
Flowering season: July to September

HABITAT: Spotted Joe-Pye weed occurs along streamsides, wet ditches, swamps, and marshes throughout New Brunswick.

CHARACTERISTICS: Spotted Joe-Pye weed is a robust clumping plant with multiple upright non-branching stems. Lance-shaped to ovate leaves are dark green, sharply toothed, slightly hairy, and in whorls of four or five, rarely three. Leaves taper gradually to the base of the short petiole. Stems are often purple-tinted.

Flower heads are produced in flat-topped dense corymbs that are up to 20 centimetres wide. Individual dusty rose to purple flower heads are 0.5 to 1 centimetre long and composed of eight to 20 disc florets. Overall, flower clusters look fluffy. The seeds have attached hairs that allow them to blow for many kilometres in the wind.

Top: Spotted Joe-Pye weed's fluffy flowers are in flat-topped clusters. Bottom: Leaves are in whorls.

Wetlands

Poppy family / Papaveraceae

Native Species

Pink corydalis

Capnoides sempervirens (formerly *Corydalis sempervirens*)

Corydale toujours verte, pale corydalis, rock harlequin

HABITAT: Pink corydalis is scattered in recently disturbed areas and burn sites and on gravelly shores throughout New Brunswick.

CHARACTERISTICS: Pink corydalis is a weakly ascending bushy biennial with multiple thin branches. The alternate leaves are bipinnately compound. Each leaflet is deeply lobed, resulting in a delicate fern-like leaf. The entire plant is hairless and waxy grey-green.

The flowers are produced terminally, in narrow panicles or racemes with two to eight flowers. Individual flowers are tubular, about 1.5 centimetres long, and pink with a yellow tip. The flower has four petals: two central petals are partly fused and house the six stamens and single style; the other two petals form an upper and lower lip. The uppermost petal has a pouch-like spur.

A similar slender native annual, common fumitory, *Fumaria officinalis*, reaches 30 centimetres in height. It also has delicate grey-green fern-like foliage. Its flowers are held in axillary racemes. Individual tubular flowers are about 0.7-0.9 centimetres long. The main floral tube is light purple with a dark purple tip. This European introduction is rare in the province.

VITAL STATISTICS

Maximum height: 60 centimetres

Flowering season: July to September

Top: Pink corydalis has tubular flowers with yellow tips.
Middle: The foliage is fern-like and waxy grey-green.
Bottom: The tubular purple-tipped flowers of common fumitory are in racemes.

Pea family / Fabaceae

American groundnut

Apios americana

Patates en chapelets, pénacs, American potato-bean, groundbean

Native Species

VITAL STATISTICS

Maximum height: 3 metres
Flowering season: Late July to August

HABITAT: American groundnut is found in moist soils along rivers, thickets, and bottomlands, primarily in the southern half of New Brunswick.

CHARACTERISTICS: American groundnut is a leafy twining vine arising from strings of edible tuberous roots. Alternate leaves are pinnately compound with three to seven elliptical to ovate smooth-edged leaflets. Leaves may reach 15 centimetres in length; stems and leaves are almost hairless.

Plants produce a dense raceme of axillary flowers. Each broad pea-like flower is maroon-purple to mauve, with a sweet fragrance, and is about 1 centimetre long. Flowers develop slender 6- to 12-centimetre-long seed pods.

American hog-peanut, *Amphicarpaea bracteata*, is an annual twining pea-family vine that may reach 250 centimetres in length. Long petioled leaves are trifoliate with ovate smooth-edged leaflets. The terminal leaflet has a distinct stalk; lateral leaflets are nearly sessile. Stems and leaves are finely pubescent. Plants have two types of flowers. The 1-centimetre-long upper flowers are pea-like, pale lilac to white, narrow, and produced in dense axillary racemes. Flowers develop scimitar-shaped seed pods that reach 7 centimetres in length. Lower flowers are petal-less and often push developing seed pods into the soil, similar to the seed pods of peanuts. American hog-peanut is found along shady thickets and riverbanks, primarily in southwestern New Brunswick.

Top: The pea-like flowers of American groundnut are in dense racemes. Middle: American groundnut has pinnate leaves with three to seven smooth-edged leaflets. Bottom: American hog-peanut is a twining vine with trifoliate leaves and small axillary clusters of pale lilac pea-like flowers.

Pea family / Fabaceae

Canada tick-trefoil

Desmodium canadense

Desmodie du Canada, showy tick-trefoil, Canada tick-clover

Native Species

HABITAT: Canada tick-trefoil is found along open riverbanks and in open woodlands and alluvial thickets throughout New Brunswick, especially along the Saint John River watershed.

VITAL STATISTICS

Maximum height: 80 centimetres

Flowering season: Late July to August

CHARACTERISTICS: Canada tick-trefoil is a slender upright plant. Stems are covered in fine white to brown hairs. Alternate short petioled leaves are trifoliate. Leaflets, which have short stems and rounded tips, are oblong to lanceolate and up to 8 centimetres long. Leaflets are smooth-edged but hairy, giving them a grey-green appearance.

Rose pink flowers grow in a panicle of elongate narrow racemes both in the upper leaf axils and at the ends of the stems. Individual pea-like flowers are up to 1.25 centimetres in length. The dorsal petal base has two pale spots outlined in deep purple. Flat elongate seed pods have three to five rounded segments and are covered in hooked hairs.

Large tick-trefoil, *D. glutinosum*, is extremely rare and found in rich shady deciduous woods at Jackson Falls, Carleton County. It is a bushy plant with long petioled trifoliate leaves. Ovate pointed leaflets, covered in fine hairs, have smooth edges. The terminal leaflet is larger than the two lateral ones and has a longer stem. Leaves are alternate to whorled. Stems have glandular hairs. Light pink pea-like flowers are produced in narrow branching terminal racemes. Their flattened seed pod has one to four triangular segments.

Top: The pea-like flowers of Canada tick-trefoil are in a panicle of racemes. Middle: Canada tick-trefoil's short petioled trifoliate leaves have narrow leaflets; the stems are covered in fine hairs. Bottom: Large tick-trefoil flowers are in elongate narrow racemes; the terminal leaflet of the trifoliate leaves is much larger than the lateral leaflets.

Pea family / Fabaceae

Alpine hedysarum

Native Species

Hedysarum alpinum

Sainfoin alpin, American sweet-vetch, alpine sweet-vetch

VITAL STATISTICS

Maximum height: 60 centimetres
Flowering season: July and August

HABITAT: Alpine hedysarum, an uncommon calciphile restricted to calcareous gravels and ledges in New Brunswick, is widely scattered in the western half of the province.

CHARACTERISTICS: Alpine hedysarum is a clumping plant with several low but arching stems arising from a deep taproot. The stems are leafy with alternate pinnately compound leaves composed of 13 to 23 oblong, smooth, or slightly pubescent leaflets.

The pink to magenta pea-like flowers are reflexed on a one-sided elongate raceme, 5 to 15 centimetres long, among the upper leaf axils. Individual flowers are 1.5 to 2 centimetres long. Seed pods resemble pea pods but are restricted between each seed, resulting in a string-of-pearls effect.

Top: The flowers are on a one-sided raceme. Bottom: Plants form mounds with arching stems.

Introduced Species

Pea family / Fabaceae

Red clover

Trifolium pratense

Trèfle rouge, purple clover

HABITAT: Red clover, a European introduction, grows in disturbed habitats and waste places throughout New Brunswick.

CHARACTERISTICS: Red clover is a clumping plant with many loosely ascending stems arising from a stout taproot. Plants have basal and alternate stem leaves that are trifoliate with ovate smooth-edged 1- to 3-centimetre-long sessile leaflets. Basal and lower leaves have long petioles; upper leaves are nearly sessile. The middle of each leaflet has a pale V-shaped chevron. Each leaf has a pair of ovate stipules at its base. Stems and leaves may be smooth or covered in fine pubescent hairs.

Flowers are produced in dense globular heads, which are 1.5 to 3 centimetres in diameter. A pair of sessile leaves grows below each head. The tiny narrow pea-like flowers are rose pink.

Rabbit's-foot clover, *T. arvense*, a low bushy annual, is found along sandy roadsides. Stems reach 40 centimetres in length. Hairy-edged trifoliate leaves have narrow sessile leaflets. The entire plant is covered in fine hairs. Flowers, in dense grey-pink fuzzy cylindrical 1- to 4-centimetre-long heads, bloom from July to September.

Crown vetch, *Securigera varia*, has pinnately compound leaves with 11 to 25 tiny oblong leaflets. Axillary flowers, produced in July, are in 3.5-centimetre-wide globular umbels of 10 to 25 two-tone pink pea-like blossoms. Widely scattered, it is considered an invasive species.

VITAL STATISTICS

Maximum height: 40 centimetres

Flowering season: June to September

Top: Red clover flowers are in dense globular heads; the trifoliate leaves have a pale V-shaped chevron. Middle: Rabbit's-foot clover has grey-pink fuzzy heads; the trifoliate leaves have narrow leaflets. Bottom: Crown vetch has pinnate leaves and flowers in globular umbels.

Milkwort family / Polygalaceae

Blood milkwort

Native Species

Polygala sanguinea

Polygala sanguin, purple milkwort, rose milkwort, field milkwort, common polygala

VITAL STATISTICS

Maximum height: 40 centimetres
Flowering season: Late June to October

HABITAT: Very rare and confined to the Saint John River watershed, blood milkwort grows in acidic fields, open woodlands, and burn sites.

CHARACTERISTICS: Blood milkwort is a slender leafy annual. Angled stems are hairless. Sessile hairless smooth-edged linear leaves may be opposite or alternate and up to 3.5 centimetres long.

Pink to purple flowers are produced in 2.5-centimetre-long cone-like racemes at the ends of branches. Each flower is composed of two large overlapping petal-like sepals at the bottom of the flower. Atop the sepals, three small petals, one of which has a yellow crest, form a tube.

Seneca snakeroot, *P. senega*, a woody-crowned leafy perennial with multiple single stems, grows to 50 centimetres. Lanceolate to elliptical alternate leaves have finely serrated edges. White flowers are in terminal narrow racemes. A pair of rounded, petal-like sepals is wide-spreading; the lowermost petal has fringes. It is very rare in calcareous woodlands and riverbanks in western regions.

Fringed milkwort, *Polygaloides paucifolia*, is extremely rare in moist acidic woodlands of Queens, Sunbury, and Charlotte counties. A crowded cluster of evergreen alternate ovate leaves are at the summit of 10 centimetre-long stems. One to four, 1.5- to 2.3-centimetre-long flowers are held just above the leaves. Each flower has two large purple-pink, spreading sepals, and a purple-pink floral tube created by three petals. A purple-pink fringe is at the end of the tube.

Top: Blood milkwort flowers are in cone-like racemes. Middle: Seneca snakeroot has white flowers in narrow, terminal racemes. Bottom: Fringed milkwort has a distinct pink fringe at the tip of its floral tube.

Balsam family / Balsaminaceae

Introduced Species

Purple jewelweed

Impatiens glandulifera

Balsamie de l'Himmalaya, policeman's helmet, Himalayan balsam

HABITAT: Purple jewelweed, a Himalayan species likely introduced as a garden ornamental, is locally common along the Bay of Fundy in Charlotte and Saint John counties. It is found in damp waste areas and roadside thickets and along streams.

CHARACTERISTICS: Purple jewelweed is a tall coarse annual with succulent stems that are square in cross-section, hairless, and often tinted purple. Lanceolate to elliptical leaves are opposite or in whorls of three; leaves are hairless with finely toothed edges and measure up to 18 centimetres in length.

Axillary flowers are produced in racemes of two to 14 flowers. Individual flowers, each 3 to 4 centimetres long, have three sepals and three petals. The lower sepal forms a pouch with a backward-pointing spur; the two upper sepals are small and insignificant. The upper petal forms a hood-like (the "helmet") structure; the lower pair of petals forms a landing pad for pollinating insects. Each of the lower petals has an upward-curling lobe near its base. Sepals and petals are coloured in shades of pink or purple-pink. Nodding and ridged elliptical seed capsules are up to 3.5 centimetres long and literally explode when touched.

Similar in appearance but with alternate leaves and erect racemes of straight-spurred, lemon yellow flowers is the small-flowered touch-me-not, *I. parviflora*, which is introduced and locally spreading within Fredericton.

Top: Flowers have three petals: the upper forms a hood, the lower pair hangs downward. Middle: The opposite or whorled leaves are narrow and finely toothed. Bottom: Small-flowered touch-me-not has pale yellow flowers and a straight spur.

VITAL STATISTICS	
Maximum height:	2 metres
Flowering season:	August to September

Wetlands

Disturbed

Mint family / Lamiaceae

Wild basil

Introduced Species

Clinopodium vulgare (formerly *Satureja vulgaris*)
Sarriette vulgaire, dogmint

VITAL STATISTICS

Maximum height: 60 centimetres
Flowering season: June to September

HABITAT: Wild basil is found in old pastures, open woods, damp rocky ravines, and waste places throughout New Brunswick.

CHARACTERISTICS: Wild basil is a clumping plant with numerous upright stems. Leaves are elliptical to ovate, opposite, shallowly toothed, and nearly sessile. Veins on leaf undersides are prominent and raised. Stems are square in cross-section. All parts of the plant are covered in soft hairs and emit a basil fragrance when bruised.

Pink to violet flowers are in dense terminal and axillary cymes and have densely hairy and bristle-tipped sepals. Tubular flowers, each about 0.8 to 1.5 centimetres long, end in five petals: two form an upper lip; three, a lower lip.

Top: The two-lipped flowers are in sessile axillary whorls; flowers may be violet. Middle: The opposite nearly sessile leaves have rounded teeth; flowers may be pale pink. Bottom: Flowers are also in dense terminal clusters; flowers may be pink.

Mint family / Lamiaceae

Introduced Species

Common hemp-nettle

Galeopsis tetrahit

Ortie royale, gratte, dog nettle, brittle-stemmed hemp-nettle

HABITAT: Common hemp-nettle and bifid hemp-nettle are European species found in recently disturbed habitats throughout New Brunswick. They are weeds in gardens and agricultural areas.

VITAL STATISTICS

Maximum height: 75 centimetres
Flowering season: June to September

CHARACTERISTICS: Common hemp-nettle is an upright leafy annual with a single stem and many branches. Stems and leaves are covered in bristly hairs. Stems are swollen below the joint of each opposite leaf pair and appear square in cross-section. Ovate to elliptical leaves are sharply toothed and have distinct petioles.

Flowers are held in dense axillary cymes. The five sepals are fused into a short tube and have conspicuous spiny tips that are 0.8 to 1.1 centimetres long. Petals, hairy on the outside, are fused into an elongate tube which is about 2 centimetres long. The upper two petals form a hood-like structure over the anthers and pistil; the lower three petals, a three-lobed lip. The central lobe of the lip is square. Flowers are white to deep pink, often with a darker blotch on each of the lateral lower lobes. The middle of the central lower lobe has a yellow blotch surrounded by a deeper pink.

Bifid hemp-nettle, *G. bifida*, is nearly identical in appearance to common hemp-nettle. Sepal spines are shorter, just 0.5 to 0.8 centimetres long; the lower central lobe of the lip is distinctly notched.

Top: The two-lipped flowers are in dense axillary whorls; the sepals are spine-tipped. Bottom: Bifid hemp-nettle has a distinctly notched lower lip.

Mint family / Lamiaceae

Purple dead-nettle

Introduced Species

Lamium purpureum

Lamier pourpre, red dead-nettle, red henbit

VITAL STATISTICS

Maximum height: 20 centimetres
Flowering season: July to October

HABITAT: Purple dead-nettle, a European species, is rare in newly disturbed areas of larger communities in the province.

CHARACTERISTICS: Purple dead-nettle is a mounding annual which freely branches from the base. The green or purple-tinted stem is square in cross-section and hollow. The 1- to 2.5-centimetre-long opposite leaves are ovate, covered in soft hairs, and have shallow-toothed edges. The veins on the undersides of the leaves are prominent and raised. Lower leaves have distinct petioles and are widely spaced; leaves closer to the flowers are nearly sessile and overlap. Upper leaves are often tinted purple, especially early and late in the growing season. The plant has a rank smell when bruised.

Nearly stemless flowers are in axillary whorls at the tips of the many branches. Sepals are fused and hairy with bristly tips. Petals fuse to form a 0.8- to 1.5-centimetre-long tube which ends in a mouth-like arrangement of fused petals. Two upper petals form a curved hood, which is hairy on the outer surface; the lower three, a lip which is pinched in appearance. The central lobe on the bottom itself has two lobes. Flowers are purple-red with darker spots on the lip.

Common dead-nettle or henbit, *L. amplexicaule*, is also a rare introduction. It is distinguished by its round to kidney-shaped leaves, which have large rounded teeth.

Top: The fuzzy leaves are often purple-tinted, especially early and late in the season. Middle: The lower lip of purple hemp-nettle has a pinched look. Bottom: Common dead-nettle has round leaves with large teeth.

Introduced Species

Mint family / Lamiaceae

Marsh hedge-nettle

Stachys palustris

Épiaire des marais, crapaudine, woundwort, marsh woundwort

HABITAT: Marsh hedge-nettle is a European species found throughout New Brunswick in damp waste places and along streams and shorelines near settlements.

VITAL STATISTICS

Maximum height: 100 centimetres
Flowering season: July to September

CHARACTERISTICS: Marsh hedge-nettle is a clumping upright sparingly branched plant that spreads through subterranean white tuber-like rhizomes. The stem, square in cross-section, is often tinted purple, especially near the top. Opposite leaves are lanceolate to elliptical, finely toothed, generally sessile, and up to 10 centimetres in length. The entire plant is covered in fine but stiff hairs; it has a rank smell when bruised.

Flowers are in 10- to 20-centimetre-long terminal spikes. Each spike has four to 12 whorls of stemless 1.5-centimetre-long rose-purple flowers. Each flower has a two-lipped appearance: the upper two petals are fused to form a hood or upper lip; the lower three form a three-lobed lip. The central lower lobe is larger than the two lateral lobes and usually mottled with paler and darker tones. The five hairy sepals are often purple-tinted and have pointed, but not sharp, tips.

Extremely rare, rough hedge-nettle, *S. hispida*, is native and found along the upper Saint John River. Petioled leaves and stem hairs confined to the angles of the stems are distinguishng features.

Hairy hedge-nettle, *S. pilosa*, is an uncommon native along streams and wet meadows in northern New Brunswick. It is also nearly identical to marsh hedge-nettle but the stem hairs are soft and its flowers shell pink.

Top: Whorls of stemless flowers are arranged in a raceme. Middle: Hairy hedge-nettle has pale pink flowers. Bottom: Canada germander is distinguished from marsh hedge-nettle by its split upper lip.

Mint family / Lamiaceae

Lemon thyme

Introduced Species

Thymus pulegioides (formerly *T. serpyllum* subsp. *chamaedrys*)

Thym faux-pouliot, thym serpolet, wild thyme, creeping thyme

VITAL STATISTICS

Maximum height: 20 centimetres
Flowering season: July to August

HABITAT: Lemon thyme, a European species originally grown as a garden ornamental in New Brunswick, is occasionally naturalized along roadsides, pasturelands, and waste places in Charlotte and Restigouche counties.

CHARACTERISTICS: Lemon thyme is a creeping matted evergreen that roots at the nodes as it creeps over the soil surface. Ascending stems are unbranched. Stems are square in cross-section and often purple-tinted and have hairs along their edges. Small opposite leaves, which are up to 1 centimetre in length, are ovate to elliptical, short petioled, smooth-edged, and hairless. The plant emits a lemony fragrance when bruised.

Flowers are produced in axillary clusters as well as densely arranged raceme-like terminal whorls. Individual flowers are about 0.6 centimetres long and tubular with a two-lipped appearance. The upper two petals form the upper lip; the lower three petals form a three-lobed lower lip. The inside of the flower is hairy and has four stamens. Flowers are generally purple-pink but can vary from pale pink to lavender to reddish-purple.

Top: The two-lipped flowers are in whorls arranged in racemes. Bottom: Lemon thyme forms mats with opposite elliptical smooth-edged leaves.

Native Species

Lopseed family / Phrymaceae

Lopseed

Phryma leptostachya

Phryma à épis grêles, American lopseed

HABITAT: Lopseed, found in rich hardwood forests, is often associated with butternut, *Juglans cinerea*. It is very rare in New Brunswick, mostly confined to the Saint John River watershed.

VITAL STATISTICS
Maximum height: 80 centimetres
Flowering season: June to August

CHARACTERISTICS: Lopseed is a leafy plant with unbranched stems. The stem is square in cross-section and finely pubescent. Opposite ovate leaves may reach 15 centimetres in length and have toothed edges and scattered soft hairs. The lowest leaves are the largest and have the longest petioles; upper leaves are smaller, with shorter petioles.

The flowers are produced on narrow leafless spikes, both terminally as well as from the axils of the upper leaves. The flowers are paired along the spike. Individual flowers are stemless and tubular, 0.6 to 0.8 centimetres long, with a two-lipped appearance. The upper lip is notched, shorter, and a deeper pink than the lower lip, which is three-lobed, longer, and pale pink. Each flower has four stamens and a single style with a bilobed stigma. Faded flowers and developing seed capsules hang down against the flower stalk.

Top: Flowers are paired along the raceme. Middle: Seed capsules hang down along the flower stalk. Bottom: Opposite ovate leaves have toothed edges.

Broomrape family / Orobanchaceae

Red bartsia

Introduced Species

Odontites vulgaris (formerly *O. serotina* or *O. verna*)

Odontite rouge

VITAL STATISTICS

Maximum height: 30 centimetres

Flowering season: July to September

HABITAT: Red bartsia is a European species occasionally found in disturbed areas of New Brunswick, primarily along the coast.

CHARACTERISTICS: Red bartsia is a slender multi-stemmed annual. Finely pubescent stems are square in cross-section. Plants are initially unbranched but, later in the season, produce both basal and upper branches. The stem and leaves are often purple-tinted; opposite leaves are narrow and lanceolate and sessile with short stiff hairs and sparse shallow teeth.

Flowers are produced in terminal one-sided racemes. A leaf-like bract, often tinted purple, is located at the base of each flower. Individual rose-red flowers are tubular and about 1 centimetre in length. The end of the floral tube has a two-lipped opening. The upper lip is notched; the lower is deeply three-lobed with a darker throat. Fine hairs fringe the edges of the petals. There are four stamens, and a single style extends beyond the end of the flower. Four green or purple-tinted sepals are finely pubescent.

Red bartsia, a hemiparasitic plant, obtains some of its nutrients from nearby plants.

Top: A leaf-like bract is located at the base of each flower on the one-sided racemes. Bottom: Stems and leaves are often purple-tinted.

Native Species

Lobelia family / Lobeliaceae

Cardinal-flower

Lobelia cardinalis

Lobélie du cardinal

HABITAT: Cardinal-flower is occasionally encountered in damp meadows and marshes and along shorelines. It is confined to southwestern New Brunswick.

CHARACTERISTICS: Cardinal-flower is an upright, slender plant with a few, non-branching, leafy stems. Leaves, which are alternate, lanceolate to elliptical, with irregularly toothed edges, may reach 20 centimetres in length and are essentially hairless.

The flowers are produced in an elongate, often one-sided, raceme that may reach 50 centimetres in length. Each flower has a green ribbon-like bract at its base. Individual flowers are 3 to 4.5 centimetres long with five vibrant red petals and a long exerted tube which has the stamens and stigma at its end. The two upper petals are narrow and spreading; the three lower petals are wider and form a three-lobed lip. This plant is almost exclusively pollinated by hummingbirds.

VITAL STATISTICS

Maximum height: 120 centimetres

Flowering season: August to September

Top: Brilliant red flowers are unmistakable. Bottom: The alternate leaves are lance-shaped and irregularly toothed.

Orchid family / Orchidaceae

Dragon's-mouth

Native Species

Arethusa bulbosa

Aréthuse bulbeuse, arethusa, swamp pink

VITAL STATISTICS

Maximum height: 30 centimetres
Flowering season: Mid-June to mid-July

HABITAT: Dragon's-mouth, which prefers sphagnum bogs and fens, is uncommon and widely scattered in New Brunswick.

CHARACTERISTICS: Dragon's-mouth is slender and not easily seen when out of flower. A single linear grass-like leaf arises from a bulb-like tuber. The hairless leaf elongates after flowering is complete.

The flower is solitary atop a leafless hairless stalk. The pink, rarely white, flower is 2.5 to 5 centimetres long; its length is greater than its width. Three narrow blunt-tipped sepals are erect or slightly outward-arching. Two narrow lateral petals arch forward and form a hood over the column and base of the lip; the base of the lip is erect but abruptly arches downward, causing it to appear tongue-like. The base of the lip is often paler than the rest of the flower, spotted, and streaked dark purple with three to five yellow or white-fringed crests running down the centre. The tip of the lip is fringed. Flowers have a sweet fragrance.

Top: Flowers are solitary on leafless stalks.
Bottom: The narrow grass-like leaves appear just as the flowers open.

Orchid family / Orchidaceae

Native Species

Grass pink

Calopogon tuberosus

Calopogon tubéreux, tuberous grass pink, swamp pink

HABITAT: Grass pink, uncommon and widely scattered in New Brunswick, grows in sphagnum bogs and fens or, occasionally, in swamps or along lakeshores.

VITAL STATISTICS
Maximum height: 30 centimetres
Flowering season: July

CHARACTERISTICS: Grass pink is slender and not easily seen when out of bloom. The plant produces a single, rarely paired, linear to lanceolate hairless leaf which looks like a blade of grass. It arises from a bulb-like tuber.

A raceme of two to 10 flowers is produced atop a slender leafless hairless stalk. The 2.5- to 4.5-centimetre-wide flowers are pink, or, rarely, white. Broad sepals have pointed tips, are held on the same plane, and may arch slightly backward. Broad petals arch slightly forward. The lip is uppermost—an unusual feature in New Brunswick's native orchids—and hinged at the base, allowing it to drop down to hit the outwardly arching column located in front of the lowermost sepal. The lip is narrow at the base but widens at the tip. A beard of white (lower) and yellow (upper) hairs occurs where the lip widens. These hairs look like anthers but are called pseudo-anthers as their only sexual function is to attract a pollinator.

Top: The lip is uppermost and has a cluster of hair-like pseudo-anthers. Bottom: Flowers are held in loose racemes on leafless stems.

Orchid family / Orchidaceae

Calypso

Calypso bulbosa

Calypso bulbeux, fairy-slipper, Venus' slipper

Native Species

VITAL STATISTICS

Maximum height: 20 centimetres
Flowering season: Mid-May to mid-June

HABITAT: Rare and localized in New Brunswick, calypso is found in mossy old-growth coniferous forests and at the base of white cedars in swamps overlying limestone.

CHARACTERISTICS: Calypso produces a solitary basal 2- to 6-centimetre-long oval leaf which is hairless with smooth but undulating leaf edges. The veins are distinct and the leaf has a pleated look. The leaf appears in late summer, remains green over winter, and shrivels shortly after flowering.

The magenta-pink flowers, each about 5 centimetres in diameter, are solitary on leafless stems that have a few sheathing bracts. The uppermost bract is pink and petaloid. The three narrow sepals are usually wide-spreading; the two narrow lateral petals point forward. The pouch-shaped lip points downward. The inside of the lip is pale pink and spotted and streaked purple-brown. The opening to the pouch has a tuft of yellow or white hairs. Two horn-like projections are located on the outside base of the lip.

Top: Two horn-like projections are found on the bottom of the lip. Middle: In side-profile, the flowers are shaped like a slipper. Bottom: Plants form loose colonies with a single oval basal leaf.

Native Species

Orchid family / Orchidaceae

Pink lady's-slipper

Cypripedium acaule

Sabot de la vierge, moccasin flower, pink moccasin flower

HABITAT: Pink lady's-slipper, found in open peaty barrens and acidic coniferous and mixed forests throughout New Brunswick, is its most common lady's-slipper.

CHARACTERISTICS: Pink lady's-slipper, a low clumping plant, has a pair of oblong to elliptical basal leaves. These leaves may reach 30 centimetres in length and have distinct folded parallel ribs and smooth edges. Leaves are finely pubescent.

Six-centimetre-long flowers are solitary on leafless finely pubescent stems. The dorsal sepal arches forward; the other two sepals unite to form one broad sepal behind the pouch. The two lateral petals arch downward, sometimes backward, and may be twisted. They have long hairs at their base. The downward-hanging lip is rose pink or, rarely, white and resembles an inflated sack. The opening of the pouch is groove-like. Sepals and petals are brownish- to greenish-purple. A single green leafy bract arches over the top of the flower parallel to the dorsal sepals.

VITAL STATISTICS

Maximum height: 30 centimetres
Flowering season: June to July

Top: The characteristic pink slipper-like pouch.
Bottom: Plants produce a pair of basal leaves and solitary flowers on leafless stems.

Orchid family / Orchidaceae

Small round-leaved orchid

Galearis rotundifolia (formerly *Amerorchis rotundifolia*)

Orchis à feuille ronde, round-leaved orchid

Native Species

VITAL STATISTICS
Maximum height: 25 centimetres
Flowering season: June to July

HABITAT: Small round-leaved orchid is confined to the calcareous bogs, fens, and cedar swamps of northern New Brunswick.

CHARACTERISTICS: Small round-leaved orchid produces a single basal smooth-edged leaf which has parallel veins. The leaf is ovate to elliptical and up to 8 centimetres in length.

A raceme of two to 12 flowers is produced atop a leafless stem. Each pink-shaded, rarely white, flower is 1 to 1.5 centimetres in diameter. The lateral sepals are wide-spreading, while the dorsal sepal and two lateral petals overlap and arch forward to form a hood over the lip. The lip has three lobes: two small lateral lobes and a larger central lobe with a bifid tip. The lip is variously spotted and streaked magenta. A short narrow spur extends behind the lip.

Showy orchis, *G. spectabilis*, is a very rare species found in Carleton and York counties along the Saint John River, where it grows in rich calcareous deciduous forest. Plants grow to 20 centimetres, with a pair of glossy basal leaves up to 12 centimetres in length. Leaves are ovate to elliptical with parallel veins. A raceme of three to 12 flowers is produced on a leafless stem. Each 2-centimetre-wide flower has a narrow leafy bract at its base. The lip is tongue-shaped and white; the rest of the flower is pink-shaded. The sepals and petals overlap and arch forward to form a hood over the lip. A blunt spur extends behind the lip. It blooms in late May through early June.

Top: The pale pink flowers are spotted with darker purple. Middle: Leafless flower stems arise from a single oval basal leaf. Bottom: Showy orchis' sepals and petals form a pink hood over the almost-white lip.

Native Species

Orchid family / Orchidaceae

Small purple fringed orchid

Platanthera psycodes

Platanthère papillon, butterfly orchid, lesser purple-fringed orchid

HABITAT: Small purple fringed orchid occurs in wetland areas such as fens, marshes, shorelines, and wet meadows throughout New Brunswick.

CHARACTERISTICS: Small purple fringed orchid is a slender plant with one or several non-branching stems. The alternate elliptical leaves are smooth-edged and hairless, have parallel veins, and clasp the stem. Each stem has two to five leaves. Lower leaves may be up to 20 centimetres long; upper leaves are shorter.

Plants produce a raceme of many 1.5- to 2-centimetre-wide lavender to rose-purple flowers. A narrow leafy bract is located at the base of each flower. Two broad lateral wide-spreading sepals often arch backward. The dorsal sepal and lateral petals arch forward to form a hood over the column. The lip is three-lobed and heavily fringed. Lateral lobes are smaller than the terminal lobe and often arch backward. A narrow spur extends behind the lip; the opening to the spur is rectangular.

Large purple fringed orchid, *P. grandiflora*, occurs in similar habitats as, and often grows with, small purpl fringed orchid, but it is very rare and widely scattered in the province. Plants are robust, reaching to 100 centimetres in height, and the flowers are twice the size of the small purple fringed orchid. The lateral lobes of the lip arch forward rather than backward. The opening to the nectar spur is rounded.

VITAL STATISTICS

Maximum height: 50 centimetres
Flowering season: July to August

Top: The heavily fringed lip of small purple fringed orchid is deeply trilobed; these lobes often arch backward. Middle: Flowers are held in a dense cylindrical raceme. Bottom: On large purple ringed orchid the lateral lobes of the fringed lip arch forward and the nectary opening is rounded.

Wetlands

Orchid family / Orchidaceae

Rose pogonia

Native Species

Pogonia ophioglossoides

Pogonie langue-de-serpent, snakemouth, beard-flower

VITAL STATISTICS

Maximum height: 30 centimetres
Flowering season: July to early August

HABITAT: Rose pogonia is common in peat bogs and, less frequently, along wet shorelines or wet meadows. It is well distributed in New Brunswick.

CHARACTERISTICS: A small plant, rose pogonia can form loose colonies as it spreads by slender subterranean rhizomes. Each non-flowering plant produces a single basal lanceolate to narrow ovate fleshy leaf that has a short petiole. The slender flowering stem has one elliptical clasping leaf partway up the stem and a single smaller leafy bract immediately below the flower. The entire plant is hairless.

Pink flowers, each 2 to 3 centimetres wide, are mostly solitary, rarely paired. Three narrow blunt sepals are wide-spreading. Two lateral petals arch forward to form a hood over the column and the base of the lip. The lip is fringed and bearded, with three rows of centrally located yellow hairs.

Top: The lip is heavily fringed and bearded; a leafy bract is located immediately behind the flower.
Bottom: Rose pogonia is often hidden among other peatland plants.

Bunchflower family / Melanthiaceae

Native Species

Red trillium

Trillium erectum

Trille dressé, wakerobin, purple trillium, stinking benjamin

HABITAT: Red trillium inhabits rich deciduous forests, especially on slopes. It is locally common in New Brunswick but uncommon along the east coast.

CHARACTERISTICS: Red trillium, a clumping plant, has non-branching stems and a whorl of three ovate sessile leaves which are up to 18 centimetres long. Leaf edges are smooth but often wavy. The entire plant is hairless.

A stem, which is up to 10 centimetres long, arises from the junction of the leaf whorl and holds a solitary flower. The blossom is often outward-facing or slightly nodding. Three narrow pointed sepals vary from green to brownish-purple. Three reddish-purple petals are the same length as the sepals but much broader; six large anthers and three recurved styles are present. Flower width varies from 4 to 9 centimetres. Flowers become small dark red poisonous berries when mature.

VITAL STATISTICS

Maximum height: 40 centimetres
Flowering season: Late May to early June

Top: Solitary flowers have three red petals alternating with three green sepals. Bottom: Each plant produces a whorl of three ovate sessile leaves.

Mustard family / Brassicaceae

American sea rocket

Native Species

Cakile edentula

Caquillier édentulé, sea rocket

VITAL STATISTICS

Maximum height: 50 centimetres
Flowering season: July to September

HABITAT: American sea rocket is common on coastal sandy to fine gravelly beaches and dunes along the coast of New Brunswick.

CHARACTERISTICS: American sea rocket is a bushy fleshy many-branched annual. Stems are prostrate or weakly ascending. Alternate leaves, averaging about 5 centimetres in length, are obovate to oblanceolate with rounded teeth, lobes, or smooth edges. The entire plant is hairless.

Flowers are in narrow 5- to 25-centimetre-long racemes. Individual flowers are 0.6 centimetres wide and composed of four lavender-pink or white petals, four green sepals, six stamens, and a single style. Only a few flowers are open on any raceme at a time.

Seed pods, which are up to 2 centimetres in length, are composed of two sections with a slight constriction between them. The lower section is globular and cylindrical; the upper, more lance-shaped and tapered. The upper section contains one seed; the lower, one or more seeds. When mature, the upper section breaks away and floats on the waves to wash up on another beach. The lower section remains attached to the parent plant and drops its seeds around the parent.

Top: The four-petalled lilac-pink flowers are held in a raceme. Middle: The seed capsule's two sections have a slight constriction between them; some plants have nearly white petals. Bottom: The spoon-shaped leaves have rounded teeth or lobes.

Mustard family / Brassicaceae

Introduced Species

Meadow bittercress

Cardamine pratensis

Cardamine des prés, cuckooflower, lady's smock, European field bittercress

HABITAT: Meadow bittercress, a European species found in damp meadows and along wet shorelines, is distributed throughout New Brunswick.

CHARACTERISTICS: Meadow bittercress is a slender but clumping plant with several upright non-branching stems. Plants have basal and alternate stem leaves, both of which are glossy. Basal leaves are pinnately compound with numerous rounded short-stemmed leaflets. The terminal leaflet is the largest and often has a few obscure teeth. Stem leaves are also pinnately compound but the leaflets are linear. The entire plant is hairless.

Flowers are initially produced in a compact raceme but, as the season advances, the raceme elongates. Fragrant flowers are 1 to 1.5 centimetres wide with four lavender-pink petals, six stamens, and a single style. The four sepals are often yellow-green or tinted purple. The seed capsule is thin, erect, and up to 3 centimetres long.

VITAL STATISTICS

Maximum height: 50 centimetres

Flowering season: Late May to mid-June

Wetlands

Top: The lavender-pink flowers are in a dense raceme, which elongates with time. Bottom: Meadow bittercress often grows with other wet meadow grasses and sedges.

Mustard family / Brassicaceae

Dame's rocket

Introduced Species

Hesperis matronalis

Julienne des dames, sweet rocket, dame's-violet, mother-of-the-evening

VITAL STATISTICS

Maximum height: 150 centimetres
Flowering season: June to July

HABITAT: Dame's rocket, a European species introduced to New Brunswick as a garden ornamental, is occasionally found in waste places and along roadsides, especially near settlements.

CHARACTERISTICS: Dame's rocket is a tall clumping biennial or short-lived perennial with multiple erect stems. In the first season, plants produce a rosette of evergreen lance-shaped leaves which are up to 12 centimetres long. Leaf edges are finely toothed and tips are long and narrow. Leaves are typically wider at the base. In the second and subsequent years, leaves are alternate along the stem and may either have a short petiole or be sessile. The entire plant is covered in coarse hairs.

Each stem is unbranched at the base but produces multiple upper branches that terminate in a raceme of purple, lavender-pink, or white flowers. Flowers are crowded at first but become more widely spaced as the raceme elongates later in the season. Flowers are fragrant, especially in the evening. Each blossom is about 2 centimetres in diameter with four petals; six stamens and a single style are often hidden within the petals. The seed capsule is narrow and up to 14 centimetres long.

Top: Flowers range from pale lilac-pink to deeper purple-pink; blossoms are in racemes. Bottom: Plants form large clumps with multiple stems and masses of flowers.

Native Species

Evening primrose family / Onagraceae

Fireweed

Chamerion angustifolium (formerly *Epilobium angustifolium*)

Bouquets rouges, great willowherb, rosebay willowherb

HABITAT: A conspicuous plant after forest fires, fireweed also occurs along roadsides and in thickets, open woodlands, and disturbed areas throughout New Brunswick.

CHARACTERISTICS: Fireweed is a tall slender leafy non-branching plant that forms large colonies. Alternate smooth-edged leaves are lanceolate, up to 20 centimetres long, and nearly sessile. Stems, especially their upper half, are often purple. The entire plant is nearly hairless.

Flowers are produced in long terminal racemes. Buds are reclined but become outward-facing when open. Individual flowers, each 3 to 4 centimetres wide, are rose-purple, including stems and sepals. Rarely, they may be white. Four narrow sepals are shorter than the four rounded petals; there are eight stamens and a single elongate style that ends in four recurved stigmas. The base of the pistil is hairy. Seed capsules are finely pubescent, slender, and 5 to 8 centimetres long, and, when ripe, split to release white silky-haired seeds.

VITAL STATISTICS

Maximum height: 2 metres

Flowering season: Mid-July to August

Top: The single elongate style has four recurved stigmas. Middle: Fireweed flowers are rarely white. Bottom: Flowers are in narrow racemes; stems are slender and non-branching.

Evening primrose family / Onagraceae

Northern willowherb

Epilobium ciliatum

Épilobe glanduleux, glandular willowherb

Native Species

VITAL STATISTICS

Maximum height: 100 centimetres
Flowering season: July to September

HABITAT: Northern willowherb appears throughout New Brunswick in damp to wet locations such as streamsides, seepage areas, coastlines, and disturbed areas, especially in shade. It is a weed in shady gardens.

CHARACTERISTICS: Northern willowherb is an upright leafy, often branched, plant. Stems are square in cross-section and often purple-tinted. Two subspecies are found in the province: stems of *ciliatum* are short-haired near the flowers; *glandulosum* has sticky hairs near the flowers. Leaves vary from lanceolate to ovate and are toothed, sessile, or short petioled with hairs along the lower veins. Leaves, mostly opposite but become alternate among the flowers, may reach 15 centimetres in length. Plants overwinter as a tight reddish-purple bulb-like rosette.

Flowers are crowded in terminal leafy racemes with axillary lowermost flowers. Individual flowers are 0.5 to 1 centimetre wide and held at the ends of long stalks. Each flower has four smaller green or purple-tinted sepals; four larger, deeply notched, white to rose-purple petals; eight stamens; and a single style with a knob-like stigma. Slender seed capsules are 4 to 8 centimetres long and finely pubescent and split when ripe to release white silky-haired seeds.

Purple-veined willowherb, *E. coloratum*, has more finely and numerous toothed leaves than northern wollowherb. Leaves are grey-green and rugose veined. Silky haired seeds are cinnamon-coloured. It is uncommon and found primarily in the southwest.

Top: Each flower has four notched petals and a central style with a knob-like stigma. Middle: Seed capsules are slender; flowers may be rose-purple. Bottom: Upper toothed leaves are alternate; flowers may be white with darker veins.

Evening primrose family / Onagraceae

Native Species

Marsh willowherb

Epilobium palustre

Épilobe palustre, swamp willowherb

HABITAT: Scattered in New Brunswick, marsh willowherb grows in bogs, ditches, seepage areas, and damp peaty barrens.

CHARACTERISTICS: Marsh willowherb is a slender plant with a few erect non-branching or sparingly branched stems. Stems and flower stalks are finely pubescent; upper leaf surfaces may or may not be pubescent. Sessile, linear to lanceolate, and smooth but revolute-edged leaves are mostly opposite but may be alternate toward the flowers. Plants often produce thin stolons after flowering.

Flowers are terminal, in loose racemes. Unopened buds often nod. Individual flowers are 0.4 to 0.8 centimetres wide with four deeply notched lilac, pink, or violet petals, eight stamens, and a single style with a knob-like stigma. The narrow erect seed capsule is finely pubescent and up to 9 centimetres long. It splits to release silky-haired seeds.

Bog willowherb, *E. leptophyllum*, resembles marsh willowherb, but is often more branched; its linear leaves are longer, pubescent on the upper surface, and mostly alternate. Unopened flowers are held erect. Flowers are pale pink to almost white. Plants have no, or short, stolons. This species is found in wetlands throughout the province.

Hornemann's willowherb, *E. hornemannii*, is square-stemmed, grows to 30 centimetres tall, and has opposite short elliptical to ovate leaves. Relatively large flowers reach 1.5 to 2 centimetres in diameter. It is very rare in cool coniferous forest seepages primarily in northern regions.

VITAL STATISTICS

Maximum height: 100 centimetres
Flowering season: July to August

Top: Marsh willowherb has nodding flowers. Middle: Bog willowherb has linear leaves and its unopened flowers are held erect. Bottom: Hornemann's willowherb has relatively short, broad leaves and relatively large flowers.

Purslane family / Portulacaceae

Carolina spring beauty

Native Species

Claytonia caroliniana

Claytonie de Caroline, northern spring beauty, wide-leaved spring beauty

VITAL STATISTICS

Maximum height: 12 centimetres
Flowering season: May to early June

HABITAT: Carolina spring beauty is found in rich open woodlands and slopes throughout most of New Brunswick.

CHARACTERISTICS: Carolina spring beauty is a dainty spring ephemeral that disappears by early summer. Plants arise from a rounded tuber. About halfway along the length of the stem is a pair of opposite and elliptical, oblong or broadly ovate leaves, which are up to 7.5 centimetres long. Leaves are fleshy with smooth edges and an obvious petiole. The entire plant is hairless.

Flowers are produced on a terminal raceme with two to 11 1.5- to 2-centimetre-wide five-petalled flowers. Buds are nodding but become erect when they open. Flowers are white or pale pink with dark pink veins and a small yellow patch at their bases. Each blossom has five stamens and a single style with a three-cleft stigma. Flowers close at night and during cloudy weather.

Top: Flowers are pale pink with darker veins; each petal has a yellow patch at its base. Bottom: Each plant has a single pair of hairless leaves.

Pink family / Caryophyllaceae

Deptford pink

Dianthus armeria

Oeillet arméria, field pinkyh

VITAL STATISTICS

Maximum height: 60 centimetres
Flowering season: May to July

HABITAT: Deptford pink is rarely found in dry fields and along roadsides in New Brunswick. It was introduced from Europe as a garden plant but has become naturalized.

CHARACTERISTICS: Deptford pink is a slender annual or biennial plant with several erect branching stems. Plants have opposite leaves that are linear, sessile, smooth-edged, and usually lightly pubescent. Leaves may reach 7 centimetres in length. A tuft of white hairs is found on the stem below each pair of leaves. The stem has a swelling at the node of each leaf pair.

Flowers are produced in small dense clusters with narrow pointed bracts at their base. The bracts, the tubular fused sepals, and the flower stems are all pubescent. Individual flowers are about 1 centimetre in diameter. The five petals are pink with white spots and have toothed edges. Flowers have 10 stamens with pink anthers and two styles.

Maiden pink, *D. deltoides*, is another rarely introduced garden escape. It has a mat-like habit with trailing stems and opposite linear leaves. The 1.5- to 2-centimetre-diameter flowers are solitary or in a few-flowered corymb at the end of 10- to 20-centimetre-long wiry stems. Flowers are shades of pink or magenta with darker central circles. Petal edges are toothed.

Top: Petals have toothed edges and fine white spots. Middle: The edges of the plant's opposite linear sessile leaves are smooth. Bottom: Maiden pink has a mat-like habit and wiry flower stems with one or a few flowers.

Pink family / Caryophyllaceae

Bouncing-bet

Saponaria officinalis

Herbe à savon, soapwort

Introduced Species

VITAL STATISTICS
Maximum height: 70 centimetres
Flowering season: July to September

HABITAT: Bouncing-bet, a European plant, was introduced to New Brunswick as a garden ornamental. It is occasionally encountered in waste places and along roadsides and trails near communities.

CHARACTERISTICS: Bouncing-bet, a stout clumping plant with multiple unbranched stems, is entirely hairless. Sessile leaves, which are 4 to 12 centimetres long, are opposite, lanceolate, and smooth-edged and often have three parallel veins. Stems are often purple-tinted.

Flowers are produced in dense terminal panicles. Individual flowers are 2.5 centimetres wide with five pink petals, 10 stamens, and two diverging styles. The base of each petal has two scale-like crests. Sepals are fused to form a narrow tube, which is often purple-tinted at the tip. Flowers are sweetly scented, especially in the evening. A double-flowered form is occasionally seen.

Top: Flowers are in dense terminal panicles. Middle: Sometimes a double-flowered form is encountered. Bottom: The opposite narrow leaves are sessile with smooth edges; stems are often purple-tinted.

Pink family / Caryophyllaceae

Introduced Species

Red campion

Silene dioica (formerly *Lychnis dioica*)

Silène rouge, compagnon rouge, red catchfly, red cockle

HABITAT: Red campion, a European plant, was introduced to New Brunswick as a garden ornamental. It is occasionally found along roadsides and trails around and near settlements.

CHARACTERISTICS: Red campion is a clumping biennial or short-lived perennial with multiple branching hairy stems. Opposite elliptical to ovate leaves have smooth edges and are covered in hairs. Some hairs are glandular, imparting a slight stickiness to the leaves and stems. Lower stem leaves and basal leaves, which are up to 12 centimetres long, have petioles; upper stem leaves, often 4 to 6 centimetres long, are sessile.

Plants are dioecious with the flowers produced in small cymes, terminally and from the upper leaf axils. Individual flowers are 2 to 2.5 centimetres in diameter with five deeply notched petals. The hairy calyx has 10 purple-tinted ribs. Male flowers have 10 stamens; female flowers have five styles. The seed capsule is globular.

Ragged robin, *Silene flos-cuculi*, another garden ornamental, is scattered and localized near settlements. It has spatulate basal leaves and lance-shaped stem leaves. The plant is hairy and glandular. Cymes are looser than those of red campion, and the flower's five rose pink petals have four deep wide-spreading lobes, giving it a distinct ragged appearance.

VITAL STATISTICS

Maximum height: 90 centimetres

Flowering season: July to August

Top: Each red campion flower has five deeply notched petals. Bottom: Each ragged robin flower has five petals, each with four deep wide-spreading lobes.

Pink family / Caryophyllaceae

Saltmarsh sand-spurrey

Native Species

Spergularia salina (formerly *S. marina*)

Spergulaire marine, marine sand-spurrey, lesser sand-spurrey

VITAL STATISTICS

Maximum height: 25 centimetres
Flowering season: July to September

HABITAT: A coastal plant, saltmarsh sand-spurrey is found on brackish shorelines and the upper tide line along the coast of New Brunswick. Rarely, it may be found inland near salt piles.

CHARACTERISTICS: Saltmarsh sand-spurrey is a mat-forming annual. Leaves, which reach 4 centimetres in length, are opposite, fleshy, linear, and pointed. Stems are usually prostrate and often purple-tinted, especially toward their base. Plants may be hairless or covered in sticky glandular hairs.

The flowers, which are 0.3 to 0.5 centimetres in diameter, are produced in cymes. They have five lilac-pink or, less commonly, white petals, five often sticky green sepals, two to five stamens, and three pistils.

Canada sand-spurrey, *S. canadensis*, often grows with saltmarsh sand-spurrey. The two are virtually identical except Canada sand-spurrey leaves have blunt tips and usually white flowers, which may be solitary or in loose cymes.

Red sand-spurrey, *S. rubra*, is a European introduction commonly found on disturbed sites throughout New Brunswick. It has non-fleshy linear pointed leaves that are often in a whorl of four. It is generally covered in glandular hairs. The flowers are pink, usually with 10 stamens.

Top: The paired linear leaves have pointed tips. Middle: Canada sand-spurrey often has solitary flowers and blunt-tipped linear leaves. Bottom: Red sand-spurrey has matted growth and appears on gravelly disturbed areas.

Knotweed family / Polygoniaceae

Native Species

Water smartweed

Persicaria amphibia (formerly *Polygonum amphibium*)

Renouée amphibie, water knotweed, amphibious bistort

HABITAT: Water smartweed is terrestrial and found along muddy or sandy shorelines, or aquatic and found in shallow ponds and slow-moving streams. It grows throughout New Brunswick.

VITAL STATISTICS	
Maximum height:	150 centimetres (floating stems)
Flowering season:	June to September

CHARACTERISTICS: Water smartweed, a low spreading plant, is weakly erect or floating aquatic. If terrestrial, leaves are lance-shaped, pointed, pubescent, and short petioled or sessile; stems root where they touch the soil. Aquatic forms have long petioled elliptical hairless leaves with rounded tips; petioles and stems are often pink-tinted. Both forms have alternate leaves up to 15 centimetres in length.

Flowers are in solitary dense terminal racemes which are 1 to 2 centimetres long. Individual flowers are 0.35 centimetres long with five deep pink petaloid sepals, five exerted stamens, and two styles.

Very rare along gravelly and muddy shorelines, dotted knotweed, *P. punctata*, has upright stems which reach 75 centimetres in height. Scarcely hairy leaves are narrow, lanceolate to elliptical, short petioled, and 3 to 9 centimetres long. Stems terminate in several 5- to 20-centimetre-long narrow racemes with a sparse arrangement of tiny white, rarely pale pink, flowers. Leaves have a peppery taste.

False waterpepper, *P. hydropiperoides*, is very rare and confined to southwestern New Brunswick. Similar to dotted knotweed, it has narrow linear to lanceolate leaves, which are 6 to 15 centimetres long, and narrow racemes of rose pink flowers.

Top: Water smartweed has floating leaves and dense spikes of pink flowers. Middle: Dotted knotweed has narrow racemes with widely scattered small white flowers. Bottom: False waterpepper produces narrow spikes of pink flowers.

Buckwheat family / Polygonaceae

Spotted lady's-thumb

Introduced Species

Persicaria maculosa (formerly *Polygonum persicaria*)

Fer à cheval, renouée persicaire, lady's-thumb, heart's-ease, redshank

VITAL STATISTICS

Maximum height: 100 centimetres
Flowering season: June to October

HABITAT: Spotted lady's-thumb, a European species found in moist waste places and disturbed areas throughout New Brunswick, can be a weed in vegetable gardens. It also occurs along gravelly riversides and shorelines.

CHARACTERISTICS: Spotted lady's-thumb is a bushy annual with both erect and wide-spreading stems. Alternate leaves are lanceolate with smooth edges, commonly 8 to 10 centimetres long, and short petioled; a dark purple blotch is usually seen on the middle, upper surface of the leaf. Smooth stems are often red-tinted. At the junction of the leaf and stem is a thin sheath, which is fringed in hairs. Stems have a jointed appearance.

Flowers are produced in dense cylindrical spike-like terminal and axillary racemes. Individual flowers are about 0.35 centimetres wide with five pink to white petaloid sepals, four to eight stamens, and two to three styles.

Pale smartweed, *P. lapthifolia*, is fairly common in the province and occurs in similar habitats to spotted lady's-thumb. It can reach 2 metres in height, but it may also be low and creeping. Leaves reach 20 centimetres in length and have pubescent or hairless undersides; they may have a purple blotch. Taller forms often have pendulous flowers. The distinguishing feature is a sheath at the base of the leaves, which lacks hairs; individual flowers usually have only four sepals.

Top: Spotted lady's-thumb has dense cylindrical racemes of small pink five-sepalled flowers. Middle: Spotted lady's-thumb leaves have a central dark purple blotch. Bottom: Pale smartweed is distinguished from spotted lady's-thumb by its four-sepalled flowers.

Buckwheat family / Polygonaceae

Native Species

Pennsylvanian smartweed

Persicaria pensylvanica (formerly *Polygonum pensylvanicum*)

Persicaire glanduleuse, renouée de Pennsylvanie, pinkweed, pink knotweed

HABITAT: Pennsylvanian smartweed occurs in moist cultivated areas and ditches and along shorelines throughout New Brunswick.

CHARACTERISTICS: Pennsylvanian smartweed is a bushy branching annual; the stem is often pink-tinted. Alternate leaves are lanceolate to elliptical with smooth edges and a short petiole. The sheath at the base of the leaf lacks hairs. Leaves may be smooth or have stiff hairs. Stems often have a jointed appearance.

This species is distinguished by its flower stems, which are covered in sticky glandular hairs. Flowers are produced in dense cylindrical spike-like racemes, both terminally and axillary. Individual flowers, about 0.3 centimetres wide, have five pink petaloid sepals, six to eight stamens, and two styles.

Marshpepper or common smartweed, *P. hydropiper*, is a European species found in high-fertility waste places such as cultivated fields or, less commonly, along shorelines. It rarely exceeds 50 centimetres in height. Its lanceolate wavy-edged leaves are up to 9 centimetres long and have a sharp peppery taste. The sheath at the leaf base may be hairless or have short hairs. The leaf node is often a darker red than the remainder of the stem. Flower racemes are narrow and often arching; flowers are more widely spaced along the raceme than on Pennsylvanian smartweed. Individual flowers commonly have four sepals; they are green with a pink tint and scattered minute dark spots.

VITAL STATISTICS

Maximum height: 120 centimetres
Flowering season: June to October

Top: Flowers are in dense cylindrical racemes. Middle: The pink-tinted stems have a jointed appearance. Bottom: Marshpepper has wavy-edged leaves and arching narrow racemes of widely spaced green pink-tipped flowers.

Knotweed family / Polygoniaceae

Arrow-leaved smartweed

Native Species

Persicaria sagittata

Gratte-cul, renouée sagittée, arrow-leaved tearthumb, arrow-leaved knotweed

VITAL STATISTICS

Maximum height: 150 centimetres
Flowering season: July to October

HABITAT: Arrow-leaved smartweed is found along shorelines and in rich alluvial thickets, bottomlands, shorelines, ditches, and wet meadows. It is common throughout New Brunswick.

CHARACTERISTICS: Arrow-leaved smartweed is a weakly ascending multiple branching annual. Stems are square in cross-section and covered in downward-pointing stiff prickles that help it climb neighbouring plants. Alternate leaves, each 3 to 10 centimetres long, are elliptical with two downward-pointing lobes at the base; this results in an arrowhead shape. Leaves are hairless and smooth-edged. Lower leaves have a petiole; upper leaves clasp the stem.

Flowers are produced in long-stemmed globular racemes, both terminally and from the upper leaf axils. Individual flowers are 0.4 centimetres long, with five pink-tinted or white petaloid sepals, eight stamens, and three stigmas.

Halberd-leaved smartweed, *P. arifolia*, is very rare, and confined to swamps in southern and eastern New Brunswick. Two diverging lobes on its lower leaves impart a triangular outline. Leaves are smooth-edged and pubescent. Globular flower clusters have white or pink flowers with four sepals, six stamens, and two stigmas. Flower stems are glandular and have prickles.

Top: Plants often grow in shallow, standing water.
Middle: Leaves have a pair of downward-pointing basal lobes; the flowers are in dense globular racemes.
Bottom: Each halberd-leaved smartweed leaf has two diverging lobes at its base, creating a triangular outline.

St. John's-wort family / Hypericaceae

Fraser's St. John's-wort

Hypericum fraseri

Millepertuis de Fraser, marsh St. John's-wort

Native Species

HABITAT: Fraser's St. John's-wort is common along muddy and boggy shores and beaches throughout New Brunswick.

CHARACTERISTICS: Fraser's St. John's-wort is a slender mostly non-branching plant, usually erect but sometimes leaning. Stems are often red-tinted. Oblong to ovate leaves are opposite, smooth-edged, and sessile to partly clasping the stem. Reaching 7.5 centimetres in length, leaves are dull and waxy and often have a blue-green or purple tint. Leaf undersides have minute dark spots. The entire plant is hairless.

Flowers, each 1 to 2 centimetres wide, are produced in small cymes at the ends of the stems and among the upper leaf axils. Blunt-tipped sepals, each 0.25 to 0.5 centimetres long, are half the length of the petals and form a green or purple-tinted cup at the base of the flower. The flower has five flesh pink petals, nine to 12 stamens, and a single 0.5- to 1.3-millimetre-long style. Flowers rarely open fully. Seed capsules are ovate-shaped and dark wine red.

VITAL STATISTICS
Maximum height: 80 centimetres
Flowering season: July to August

Top: Plants have pairs of sessile round leaves with smooth edges; the flesh pink five-petalled flowers are in small clusters. Bottom: Foliage is often waxy and purple-tinted; the dark wine red seed capsules are teardrop-shaped.

Mallow family / Malvaceae

Musk mallow

Malva moschata

Mauve musquée

Introduced Species

VITAL STATISTICS

Maximum height: 70 centimetres
Flowering season: July

HABITAT: Musk mallow is a garden escape occasionally seen along roadsides and in waste areas and old abandoned gardens throughout New Brunswick.

CHARACTERISTICS: Musk mallow is a bushy plant with several sparsely branched stiffly haired stems. Plants have both basal and stem leaves. Basal leaves are evergreen and overwintering, rounded in outline with five shallow lobes and rounded teeth. Stem leaves are alternate and round in outline but pinnatifid with deep lobes. Each individual lobe is bipinnately lobed. The overall effect is a finely dissected but round leaf. There are two small stipules at the base of each leaf. Leaves have fine hairs along the edges. The entire plant emits a musky fragrance when bruised.

Tissue-like flowers are produced in terminal racemes. Individual flowers have five pink or white widely notched petals similar in shape to a trout's tail. Flowers are about 5 centimetres in diameter. Five green sepals, which have scattered stiff hairs, enfold the developing seeds.

Vervain mallow, *M. alcea*, is a local garden escape found in Carleton County. Plants reach 125 centimetres in height. While palmately lobed, the individual lobes are less dissected than those of musk mallow. Flowers are often among the upper leaf axils but, overall, are in a raceme arrangement. Flowers are commonly pink with darker pink, rarely white, veins and are virtually identical in shape to those of musk mallow although the petal edges may be more ragged.

Top: The tissue-like flowers have five petals whose tips are broadly notched like a trout's tail. Middle: Less commonly, musk mallow flowers are white; flowers are in terminal racemes. Bottom: Vervain mallow petals often have a ragged-edged look.

Mallow family / Malvaceae

Dwarf mallow

Native Species

Malva neglecta

Fromagère, running mallow, cheese plant, common mallow

HABITAT: Dwarf mallow is a European introduction occasionally seen in waste areas and gardens throughout the province.

CHARACTERISTICS: Dwarf mallow is a mat-forming annual or biennial plant with trailing stems that reach to 60 centimetres in length. The round to heart-shaped 1.5- to 4-centimetre-long leaves have five to seven obscure lobes and sharp-toothed edges. Alternately arranged, leaves have a wrinkled appearance and long petioles. The entire plant is covered in short stiff hairs.

The flowers, which are pink with darker pink veins or white, are solitary or in groups of up to three flowers among the upper leaf axils. The centre of each flower has a knob-like cluster of stamens and stigma. Individual flowers are about 1.5 centimetres wide with five notched satiny petals. The petals are twice as long as the sepals. Sepals enfold the developing seeds.

Round-leaved mallow, *M. pusilla*, is rare in New Brunswick. It is similar to dwarf mallow, but the white petals are only about 1.5 times longer than the sepals and the flowers are less than 1 centimetre wide. Their sepals have long hairs. Leaves also differ from dwarf mallow slightly: they have five to nine shallow lobes and rounded teeth.

VITAL STATISTICS

Maximum height: 60 centimetres
Flowering season: June to October

Top: Dwarf mallow flowers have pink notched petals with darker veins and a central "knob" created by the stamens and stigma. Middle: Dwarf mallow's wrinkled leaves are round with five to seven shallow lobes and sharp teeth. Bottom: Round-leaved mallow has white flowers in small axillary clusters.

Pitcher plant family / Sarraceniaceae

Northern pitcher plant

Native Species

Sarracenia purpurea

Petits cochons, herbe-crapaud, common pitcher plant

VITAL STATISTICS

Maximum height: 60 centimetres
Flowering season: June to July

HABITAT: Northern pitcher plant is found on acidic sphagnum bogs throughout New Brunswick.

CHARACTERISTICS: Northern pitcher plant is a low clumping plant with rosettes of evergreen foliage. Leaves are hollow and pitcher-shaped, ranging from 10 to 30 centimetres in length. The outside leaf surfaces are leathery, hairless, green or purple-tinted and often red-veined. The "hood" or "lip" of the leaf has brown-red veins and downward-pointing stiff hairs. The inside of the leaf (the "pitcher") is smooth and contains water used to trap and drown insects. A "wing" extends down the length of the leaf's upper side. Leaves often turn completely wine-red in winter.

Plants produce several solitary globular 5-centimetre-wide nodding flowers at the ends of leafless stems. Five persistent leathery shiny purple-red sepals are petal-like and remain into the autumn months. Five wine-red petals are larger than the sepals, drooping, and relatively short-lived. The ovary is large and globular, surrounded by a ring of numerous stamens. The single style is capped by a five-angled umbrella-like body that houses the stigmas.

Northern pitcher plant is the provincial floral emblem for Newfoundland and Labrador.

Top: The nodding flowers have red-tinted petal-like sepals and larger red petals. Middle: Plants form clumps of basal leaves and produce several leafless flower stems with solitary nodding flowers. Bottom: The pitcher-shaped leaves often have distinct red veins.

Coniferous Forest

Mixed Forest

Native Species

Heath family / Ericaceae

Common pipsissewa

Chimaphila umbellata

Herbe à la clef, herbe à peigne, common prince's pine, pipsissewa

HABITAT: Common pipsissewa grows in dry mossy coniferous or mixed forests. It is uncommon and scattered throughout New Brunswick.

CHARACTERISTICS: This low colonial evergreen sub-shrub has unbranched stems. Common pipsissewa leaves are spatulate, dark green, and glossy with a leathery texture and toothed edges. They are 3 to 7 centimetres long and produced in whorls of three or four.

Plants produce a single flower stem that arises at the tip of the leafy stem. Five-petalled nodding white or pink blooms appear in an umbel of three to eight flowers. Each flower has 10 stamens and a single style. Petals often bend backward. The fruit is a globular capsule that often persists through winter.

VITAL STATISTICS
Maximum height: 30 centimetres
Flowering season: July

Top: Each flower has ten stamens, a single style, and five backward-arching petals. Middle: Flowers are in a small umbel atop a leafless stem. Bottom: The whorled leaves have sharp teeth along their edges.

Heath family / Ericaceae

Trailing arbutus

Native Species

Epigaea repens

Épigée rampante, fleur de mai, mayflower

VITAL STATISTICS

Maximum height: 10 centimetres

Flowering season: Early April to May

HABITAT: Trailing arbutus, a common forest-floor species throughout New Brunswick, occasionally occurs on open barrens. It is the provincial floral emblem for Nova Scotia.

CHARACTERISTICS: A prostrate broad-leaved evergreen sub-shrub, trailing arbutus branches are green to reddish-brown and hairy. Alternate leaves are reticulated, oval, and 2.5 to 7 centimetres in length. Stiff hairs cover leaf edges, top surfaces, and undersides, especially on younger leaves. Leaf edges are untoothed; leaf bases are cordate. Rich green leaves become an increasingly lighter yellow-green with exposure to the sun.

Clusters of 1.5-centimetre-diameter flowers grow at the ends of trailing stems as well as from the upper leaf axils. Each blossom's five petals fuse at the base to form a tube; this floral tube is hairy. Within the tube are 10 stamens and a single style. Spicily fragrant, flowers are white or pink.

Top: Each five-petalled flower has a tubular base. Middle: Terminal and axillary flowers are in tight clusters. Bottom: The leathery leaves have a heart-shaped outline.

Native Species

Heath family / Ericaceae

Pink pyrola

Pyrola asarifolia

Pyrole à feuilles d'asaret, pink-flowered wintergreen, pink wintergreen

HABITAT: Pink pyrola grows primarily in coniferous woodlands but is occasionally found in mixed forest or open barrens. It favours calcareous soils. Found throughout New Brunswick, it is most common in the northern, western and central regions.

VITAL STATISTICS
Maximum height: 30 centimetres
Flowering season: Late June to August

CHARACTERISTICS: Pink pyrola is a low rosetted plant that may produce small mats as it spreads through subterranean stolons. All leaves are basal, round to kidney-shaped, leathery, evergreen, shiny, and slightly toothed with rounded teeth. Long petioled leaves are up to 6 centimetres long. The entire plant is hairless.

Four to 20 flowers are produced in a cylindrical raceme at the end of a leafless, often pink-tinted, stem that may reach 30 centimetres in length. Individual flowers, each 0.8 to 1.2 centimetres wide, are bell-shaped and often nodding. The five petals are crimson to pale pink; 10 stamens arch upward; the single thick 0.5- to 1-centimetre-long style arches downward at the base and may arch upward at the tip, appearing similar in shape to an elephant trunk. The style projects beyond the petals. The stigma appears slightly five-lobed.

Lesser pyrola, *P. minor*, prefers old-growth coniferous forests. It is uncommmon in the north and along the Fundy coast. Round dull short-petioled evergreen leaves are up to 4 centimetres long. The cylindrical raceme grows on a pink-tinted stem which may reach 25 centimetres in height. Globular nodding flowers have five waxy white to light pink petals. The single style is about 0.1 centimetres long and hidden within the recurved petals.

Top: The style extends beyond the petals and its bent shape is like that of an elephant's trunk. Middle: The nodding flowers are in racemes atop leafless stems. Bottom: Lesser pyrola has globular pink-tinted flowers, and its stigma does not extend beyond the petals.

Myrsine family / Myrsinaceae

Sea milkwort

Native Species

Lysimachia maritima (formerly *Glaux maritima*)

Glaux maritime, saltwort, black saltwort, sea milkweed

VITAL STATISTICS

Maximum height: 20 centimetres

Flowering season: Mid-June to July

HABITAT: Sea milkwort is commonly found in coastal salt marshes around the entire coast of New Brunswick.

CHARACTERISTICS: Sea milkwort is a low clumping plant with semi-upright stems from a creeping rootstock. Opposite leaves are fleshy, linear to oblong, sessile, and smooth-edged. Leaves are small, usually 1 centimetre in length, and densely arranged along the stem. The entire plant is hairless and exudes a milky sap when cut.

Small stemless 0.4- to 0.6-centimetre-wide flowers are cup-shaped and solitary among the upper leaf axils. They have no petals but five petaloid sepals which vary from white through shades of pink, lavender, and crimson. They have five stamens and a single style.

Top: Each flower has five stamens and a single style that extend beyond the five petaloid sepals. Middle: Flowers are solitary among the upper leaf axils. Bottom: The opposite fleshy leaves are densely arranged along the stems.

Primrose family / Primulaceae

Mistassini primrose

Native Species

Primula mistassinica

Primevère du lac Mistassini, bird's-eye primrose, dwarf Canadian primrose

HABITAT: Mistassini primrose is a calciphile restricted to calcareous ledges, cliffs, meadows, and shorelines, primarily along the Saint John and Restigouche rivers.

CHARACTERISTICS: Mistassini primrose is a small tufted plant. All leaves are basal and oblanceolate to spatulate with irregularly toothed edges. Leaves are usually 2 to 3 centimetres in length and smooth but may have some white powdery scales called farina, especially on the undersides.

An umbel of two to five flowers sits atop a slender leafless stem. Sepals are covered in white farina. The five lilac-pink notched petals are fused into a tube at their base. The five anthers and single style are located with this floral tube. Plants may have long or short styles. Flowers are 1 to 2 centimetres in diameter and have a distinct yellow eye.

Laurentian primrose, *P. laurentiana*, is an extremely rare calciphile only found on limestone ledges within Albert County. It is more robust than Mistassini primrose, with stouter flower stems and umbels of up to 15 flowers. Plants are heavily covered in farina.

VITAL STATISTICS

Maximum height: 15 centimetres
Flowering season: June to July

Top: Mistassini primrose has slender stems and fewer flowers per umbel than Laurentian primrose. Middle: Mistassini primrose stems lack farina; pictured here is the rare white form. Bottom: Laurentian primrose produces small umbels of flowers atop stems covered in white powder-like farina; spoon-shaped leaves are in basal rosettes

Orpine family / Crassulaceae

Garden stonecrop

Hylotelephium telephium (formerly *Sedum telephium*)

Orpin pourpre, vit-toujours, live-forever, live-longs

Introduced Species

VITAL STATISTICS

Maximum height: 60 centimetres

Flowering season: July to September

HABITAT: Garden stonecrop, a European plant originally introduced in New Brunswick as a garden ornamental, is scattered throughout the province and is occasionally encountered in damp shady waste places or along roadsides near settlements.

CHARACTERISTICS: Garden stonecrop is a clumping plant with many unbranched stems. Stems and leaves are thick, succulent, and hairless. Alternate, opposite, or occasionally whorled leaves are oblong, elliptical, or spatulate with toothed edges. The largest leaves may reach 10 centimetres in length.

Flowers are produced in compact panicles, terminally as well as in the upper leaf axils. Individual starlike flowers are about 1 centimetre in diameter with five pointed pink petals, 10 stamens, and five pointy styles. Rarely, the flowers may be creamy white. Seed capsules are five-pointed and starlike.

Top: Flowers are held in dense panicles at the ends of the stems and from the upper leaf axils. Bottom: Each flower is star-shaped with five pointed pink petals and five pointed styles.

Rose family / Rosaceae

Native Species

Marsh cinquefoil

Comarum palustre (formerly *Potentilla palustris*)

Comaret, argentine rouge, marsh five-fingers, purple cinquefoil

HABITAT: Marsh cinquefoil is found in fresh- and saltwater marshes throughout New Brunswick.

CHARACTERISTICS: Marsh cinquefoil is a clumping or mat-forming plant with stout sprawling stems that often root along their length; flowering stems, however, are held relatively upright. Alternate leaves are pinnate with five to seven lanceolate to elliptical sharply toothed leaflets. Leaflets, which are up to 10 centimetres in length, are covered in fine hairs and often blue-green or purple-tinted. Stems are commonly pink or purple-tinted and have fine hairs, which may be glandular, on their upper sides.

Flowers are produced in a loose cyme. Individual flowers, each about 2 centimetres wide, have five pointed sepals which are hairy on the outside and strongly tinted purple-red and appear almost petaloid. The five petals are much shorter than the sepals, rendering them almost inconspicuous, and are rich purple-wine. The centre of the flower is a mass of purple-red stamens and styles. A small leafy bract is located between each sepal.

VITAL STATISTICS

Maximum height: 40 centimetres
Flowering season: July

Top: Each flower has five small wine red petals and five much larger purple-red-tinted sepals. Bottom: Leaves are pinnate with five or seven narrow toothed leaflets.

Wetlands

Rose family / Rosaceae

Water avens

Geum rivale

Benoîte des ruisseaux, purple avens, chocolate root

Native Species

VITAL STATISTICS

Maximum height: 50 centimetres
Flowering season: June

HABITAT: Water avens grows in swamps, wet meadows, and seepages throughout New Brunswick.

CHARACTERISTICS: Water avens is a clumping leafy plant arising from a thick rhizome. It has several upright non-branching flower stems with a few alternately arranged leaves; most leaves, however, are basal. Basal leaves are pinnately compound with five to nine coarsely toothed leaflets. The terminal leaflet, which is often tri-lobed, is larger than the others. Smaller leaflets are often interspersed among the larger. Stem leaves are usually trifoliate and have a pair of stipules at their base. The entire plant is covered in hairs.

Flowers are nodding and produced in loose cymes. Flowering stems are usually dark purple. Individual flowers are about 2 centimetres wide with five conspicuously veined dull red to pale pink-purple petals with numerous yellow anthers and pistils. The five hairy sepals are the same length as the petals. A small linear bract is located between each sepal. As seeds develop, flowers become erect. The seeds are produced in a spiky globular head; each seed has an elongate hooked spine that enables it to stick to animal fur.

Top: The nodding flowers' sepals and petals are of equal length. Bottom: Basal leaves are pinnate with alternating large and small leaflets.

Introduced Species

Lythrum family / Lythraceae

Purple loosestrife

Lythrum salicaria

Salicaire, boquet violet, spiked loosestrife

HABITAT: Purple loosestrife, a European species introduced in New Brunswick as a garden ornamental, is found along roadside ditches, streams, and lakeshores and in swamps and marshes throughout the province. It is spreading rapidly and considered an invasive species.

CHARACTERISTICS: Purple loosestrife is a tall slender clumping plant with non-branching stems, which are commonly tinted red or purple and square in cross-section. Sessile opposite or whorled leaves are lanceolate and up to 10 centimetres in length. The entire plant is usually downy, but the degree of hairiness varies. Leaf edges are smooth and leaf bases are rounded.

Stemless flowers are produced in narrow wand-like racemes. Individual flowers are 1 to 2 centimetres wide with six, less commonly five, narrow magenta petals. Sepals are often purple-tinted and hairy. The length of the 10 or 12 stamens and single style varies among the three types of flowers.

VITAL STATISTICS

Maximum height: 150 centimetres

Flowering season: July to September

Top: Each flower has five narrow petals; flower stems are downy with short hairs. Middle: Flowers are held in wand-like racemes. Bottom: Purple loosestrife can form large colonies.

Shamrock family / Oxalidaceae

Common wood-sorrel

Native Species

Oxalis montana

Surette, paine de lièvre, mountain wood-sorrel, white wood-sorrel

VITAL STATISTICS

Maximum height: 10 centimetres
Flowering season: June to July

HABITAT: Common wood-sorrel is primarily restricted to shady mossy old-growth coniferous or mixed forests throughout New Brunswick.

CHARACTERISTICS: Common wood-sorrel grows as patches which are connected by subterranean rhizomes. All leaves are basal and trifoliate and composed of three heart-shaped leaflets. Each leaflet is 1.5 to 3 centimetres wide, hairless, and smooth-edged. Leaflets fold and unfold depending on light conditions.

Early flowers are solitary on leafless stems that arise to 10 centimetres. These 2-centimetre-diameter flowers have slightly notched, white to pink petals with darker purple-pink veins. Near the base of each petal is a purple band, imparting a purple ring in the centre of the flower. Below this purple ring, each petal has a yellow patch. Flowers have 10 stamens and five styles. Later season flowers lack petals, and self-pollinate.

Top: Each flower is white with pink veins and has a yellow blotch at the base of each petal. Middle: The veins on the petals create a ring within the flower. Bottom: The trifoliate leaves have heart-shaped leaflets.

Geranium family / Geraniaceae

Native Species

Herb-Robert

Geranium robertianum

Herbe à Robert, herbe à l'esquinancie, Robert's geranium, red robin

HABITAT: Herb-Robert is found in shady ravines, rocky woods, and gravelly shorelines, primarily near the Fundy coast of New Brunswick.

VITAL STATISTICS

Maximum height: 40 centimetres

Flowering season: May to September

CHARACTERISTICS: Herb-Robert is a creeping annual or biennial. Thin branching stems are wide-spreading or weakly ascending. Basal and opposite stem leaves are palmately compound with three to five pinnatifid leaflets. The terminal leaflet has a stalk; others are sessile. The entire plant is sparsely hairy. Stems and leaves are often red-tinted.

Long-stalked flowers grow in pairs from the leaf axils. One-centimetre-wide flowers have five green or purple-tinted hairy pointed sepals; five pink-red, rarely white, slightly notched petals; 10 stamens; and a single style with five recurved stigmas. Seeds are produced at the bottom of a bill-like structure; when the seeds are ripe, part of the bill curls back, catapulting them.

Bicknell's geranium, *G. bicknelii*, uncommon on recently burned or cleared sites, is scattered in New Brunswick. Plants are sprawling; all leaflets on the sparsely hairy leaves are sessile. One-centimetre-wide pale pink flowers are either solitary or in pairs and grow from the upper leaf axils.

Common storksbill, *Erodium cicutarium*, a European species, grows in dry open areas. It is uncommon and widely scattered. Plants have sticky sparsely hairy pinnately compound fern-like leaves. One-centimetre-wide rose pink flowers grow in few-flowered axillary umbels. Flowers have five anthers.

Top: Herb-Robert has palmately compound leaves with pinnatifid leaflets and axillary pink flowers.
Middle: Bicknell's geranium has pale pink flowers; all leaflets of the palmately compound leaves are sessile.
Bottom: Common storksbill has pinnately compound leaves with deeply lobed leaflets; flowers are in umbels.

Dogbane family / Apocynaceae

Spreading dogbane

Apocynum androsaemifolium

Herbe à la puce, creeping dogbane

Native Species

VITAL STATISTICS

Maximum height: 50 centimetres
Flowering season: July to September

HABITAT: Spreading dogbane, found in open sandy barrens and dry meadows and along roadsides, is common throughout New Brunswick.

CHARACTERISTICS: Spreading dogbane is a colonial plant that spreads by subterranean rhizomes. Stems are branching, smooth, and purple-tinted. Ovate to elliptical opposite leaves are up to 7 centimetres long and smooth-edged; short petioles make the leaves appear sessile. The top surfaces of leaves are hairless and shiny; undersides may be pubescent. Leaves often have a droopy appearance. The plant exudes a milky sap when cut.

Fragrant flowers are in small cymes, both terminally and axillary. Individual flowers, each up to 1 centimetre wide, are nodding and bell-shaped. They have five light pink recurved petals with darker veins on the inside. Stamens are fused to form a pointed structure. There is no visible style. The length of the sepals is half that of the petals. The pendant two-pronged seed capsules, up to 15 centimetres long, are narrow and cylindrical and split to release tawny-haired seeds.

Indian hemp, *A. cannabinum*, is found province-wide in open gravelly sites, particularly on limestone. It is most common along the Saint John River watershed. Its long ascending leaves with distinct petioles distinguish it from spreading dogbane. The greenish-white bell-like flowers are 0.5 centimetres wide, more numerous than those of spreading dogbane, always terminal, and point upward. Sepals are as long as the petals.

Top: The nodding bell-shaped flowers of spreading dogbane are pink with darker veins. Middle: The shiny, opposite leaves are often drooping. Bottom: The white flowers of Indian hemp flowers are in larger clusters, always terminal, and upward-pointing.

Dogbane family / Apocynaceae

Native Species

Common milkweed

Asclepias syriaca

Herbe à coton, petits cochons, silkweed, silky milkweed

HABITAT: Common, especially in the southern half of New Brunswick, common milkweed is encountered on sandy meadows and in thickets and waste places.

VITAL STATISTICS

Maximum height: 120 centimetres
Flowering season: July

CHARACTERISTICS: Common milkweed is a tall slender plant with several unbranched stems. Opposite oblong to ovate leaves are up to 20 centimetres long, smooth-edged, hairless on the upper surface, and velvet hairy on the lower. Stems and flower stalks are finely pubescent. All parts of the plant exude a milky sap when cut.

Flowers are produced in long-stemmed dense spherical umbels, both terminally and axillary. Pale flesh pink to dull purple flowers are highly fragrant. Each flower, which is nearly 1 centimetre wide, has five strongly reflexed petals. The reproductive parts are fused and appear thickened and starlike, resembling a flower atop a flower. The reproductive portion of the flower has five horn-like projections. Softly prickled seed capsules, which may reach 10 centimetres in length, are cylindrical but swollen on a sharply elbowed stem. They split to release silky-haired seeds.

Swamp milkweed, *A. incarnata*, is locally common in southern New Brunswick. It prefers damp to wet shorelines and thickets; leaves are more lance-shaped than those of common milkweed, and usually hairless. The umbels of purple-pink flowers are terminal and bloom in August. Cylindrical seed capsules are on erect stems.

Top: Petals arch backward from the flower's starlike reproductive parts. Middle: Common milkweed flowers are in spherical umbels among the upper leaves. Bottom: Swamp milkweed has terminal umbels of bright pink flowers.

Disturbed

Honeysuckle family / Caprifoliaceae

Twinflower

Linnaea borealis

Linnée boréale, northern twinflower, pink bells

Native Species

VITAL STATISTICS

Maximum height: 8 centimetres
Flowering season: Late June to July

HABITAT: Twinflower is a predominant wildflower in coniferous and mixed forests and open areas throughout New Brunswick.

CHARACTERISTICS: A low trailing broad-leaved evergreen sub-shrub, twinflower's paired short petioled round leaves are about 1 centimetre long with a few rounded teeth and scattered hairs on both surfaces.

As its name suggests, twinflower produces a pair of nodding bell-like flowers atop a thin wiry 5- to 8-centimetre-long stalk. Highly fragrant blossoms are light pink with dark pink stripes and hairy inner surfaces. Flowers consist of five petals, which are fused to form the distinct bell-like shape, four stamens—two on short stems, two on longer—and a single style.

Top: The nodding pink bell-shaped flowers are in pairs.
Middle: Twinflower forms a low mat on the forest floor.
Bottom: The trailing stems produce opposite round leaves.

Introduced Species

Valerian family / Valerianaceae

Common valerian

Valeriana officinalis

Herbe aux chats, valériane officinale, garden valerian, garden heliotrope

HABITAT: Common valerian, a European plant introduced as a garden ornamental, has escaped and is scattered in the province, occasionally found in waste areas and along roadsides and trails near communities.

CHARACTERISTICS: Common valerian is a coarse but slender plant with unbranched grooved stems. Plants have basal and opposite stem leaves; all are pinnate with five to 12 pairs of irregularly toothed or smooth-edged sessile leaflets. Leaflet undersides, leaflet edges, and leaf stems are hairy. Basal leaves have wider lanceolate leaflets; upper stem leaves have more linear leaflets.

Fragrant flowers are terminal and in several corymbs which combine into a rounded panicle. Individual flowers are about 0.4 centimetres wide with five roseate petals fused at their base. Flowers have three stamens that extend beyond the petals and a single style with a two-lobed stigma.

Marsh valerian, *V. dioica*, is native and extremely rare in New Brunswick; it inhabits moist, calcareous woodlands in Restigouche County. Basal leaves are lanceolate to oblong, with long petioles. Stem leaves are pinnate with the terminal leaflet much larger than the other two to six pairs. The plant is hairless. Flowers resemble those of common valerian but plants have fewer corymbs. It reaches 70 centimetres in height.

Swamp valerian, *V. uliginosa*, is very rare in cedar-larch swamps, primarily near the Maine and Quebec borders. Leaflets have hairs along their margins. White flowers are 0.5 to 0.7 centimetres wide. Plants may reach 100 centimetres in height.

Top: Pale pink flowers in multiple corymbs create a rounded panicle. Middle: Plants produce opposite pinnate leaves with narrow leaflets. Bottom: Flowers of swamp valerian are pure white.

VITAL STATISTICS	
Maximum height:	150 centimetres
Flowering season:	Mid-July to mid-August

Cabomba family / Cabombaceae

Watershield

Brasenia schreberi

Brasénie de Schreber, purple wendock

Native Species

VITAL STATISTICS

Maximum height: n/a
Flowering season: June to September

HABITAT: Found in shallow nutrient-rich pools, watershield is scattered primarily in southwestern New Brunswick.

CHARACTERISTICS: Watershield is a floating aquatic plant whose alternate long petioled leaves arise from creeping rhizomes. Ovate leaves form a mat on the surface of the water; their petioles are attached to the centres of the leaf undersides. Leaves are smooth-edged, hairless, and 2 to 10 centimetres in diameter. They resemble miniature water-lily leaves. All underwater parts are covered in a thick clear mucilage.

Solitary flowers are axillary on long stems that extend a few centimetres above the water's surface. Flowers have 12 to 18 stamens, four to 18 styles, three or four sepals, and three or four petals; dull purple-pink sepals and petals look alike. Flowers last two days. On the first day, flowers extend above the water's surface and are functionally female. That night, flowers recede below the surface and emerge the second day as a functionally male flower, releasing their pollen to the wind. The flower then recedes below the surface again, where seeds develop.

Top: The solitary flowers arise just above the water's surface. Bottom: The round leaves float on the water's surface.

Native Species

Lily family / Liliaceae

Eastern rose twisted-stalk

Streptopus lanceolatus (formerly *S. roseus*)

Rognons de coq, streptope rose, rose twisted-stalk, rose mandarin

HABITAT: Eastern rose twisted-stalk grows in acidic coniferous and mixed forests and bottomlands throughout New Brunswick.

CHARACTERISTICS: Eastern rose twisted-stalk has a stout stem with forking sparsely hairy branches. The 5- to 10-centimetre-long alternate leaves are sessile and elliptical to lanceolate. Leaves are corrugated with distinct parallel veins and smooth but ciliate-haired edges.

One-centimetre-long flowers are solitary and hang from the upper leaf axils on thin hairy stems. Each flower has six pink tepals with darker purple streaks and spots and slightly recurved tips. The stigma has a three-cleft tip. Flowers become bright red globular berries.

VITAL STATISTICS

Maximum height: 50 centimetres
Flowering season: Late May to June

Top: The nodding solitary flowers have pink lily-like flowers with darker markings on the inside.
Middle: Flowers are solitary from each leaf axil.
Bottom: The elliptical leaves are ribbed and sessile; flowers develop into red berries later in summer.

Aster family / Asteraceae

Philadelphia fleabane

Erigeron philadelphicus

Érigéron de Philadelphie, common fleabane, Philadelphia daisy

Native Species

VITAL STATISTICS

Maximum height: 50 centimetres

Flowering season: June to August

HABITAT: Philadelphia fleabane is found in old moist meadows and on damp slopes. It is uncommon and widely scattered in the province.

CHARACTERISTICS: Philadelphia fleabane is an upright clumping plant with few branches, except near the top. Plants produce several evergreen overwintering rosettes of oblong to spatulate leaves. Up to 10-centimetre-long stem leaves are alternate and oblong to lanceolate and clasp the stems. Leaf edges have small widely spaced teeth. Leaves are usually hairless but may have fine hairs along their edges; stems have scattered white hairs.

Flowers, produced in a loose corymb, are nodding in bud but become erect upon opening. Individual flowers are about 2 centimetres wide and composed of 100 or more threadlike ray florets which surround a mass of yellow disc florets. Ray florets vary from white to pale pink to purple-pink. Little hairs on seeds allow them to be blown on the wind.

Top: Each flower head has numerous threadlike ray florets surrounding a central cluster of yellow disc florets. Bottom: The narrow leaves clasp the stem.

Violet family / Violaceae

Labrador violet

Native Species

Viola labradorica (formerly *Viola conspersa*)

Violette du Labrador, violette décombante, northern blue violet, alpine violet, American dog violet

HABITAT: Labrador violet is locally common in moist pastures and swamps and less common in open woodlands. It is found throughout the province.

CHARACTERISTICS: Labrador violet is a tufted plant with trailing leafy stems, a feature that separates it from the previous group of blue violets. Alternate leaves, which are up to 6 centimetres in length, are ovate to heart-shaped, with rounded teeth. Stems and leaves are generally hairless; the top leaf surface may have a few hairs.

Two-centimetre-wide flowers, produced from the leaf axils, are solitary atop stems that are up to 8 centimetres long. Flowers have five pale violet to violet-blue petals. The two lower lateral petals have beards; the lowermost petal has a spur which is about 0.6 centimetres long. Plants produce non-petalled flowers later in the season.

Early blue violet, *V. adunca*, is uncommon and widely scattered. It grows along brooksides and wet slopes and in cold woods. It is similar to Labrador violet but smaller and more tufted. Leaves are covered in fine hairs; leaf edges are rolled back. Petioles have winged edges.

VITAL STATISTICS

Maximum height: 20 centimetres
Flowering season: May to June

Top: Labrador violet often has paler violet-blue flowers than other blue violets. Middle: Labrador violet has leafy trailing stems and a tufted habit. Bottom: Early blue violet has a tighter, more tufted habit than Labrador violet.

Violet family / Violaceae

Tufted blue violet

Viola species

Native Species

VITAL STATISTICS

Maximum height: 20 centimetres
Flowering season: May to July

HABITAT: Six species of tufted blue violets with short thick rhizomes occur in damp to wet meadows and pastures, swamps, marshes, stream and pond shorelines, and moist open woodlands in New Brunswick.

CHARACTERISTICS: These blue violets are tufted plants with basal leaves arising from a small stout rhizome. Leaves are generally long petioled, with ovate to heart-shaped blades and generally rounded teeth; they are pubescent or hairless.

Flowers often overtop the leaves. Two-centimetre-wide solitary flowers have five violet-blue petals, which often have white bases. Darker veins are usually evident at the base of the petals. The upper two petals often arch backward; the lower three arch forward; the two lateral side petals often have beards; and the lower petal has a short spur. Non-petalled flowers are produced later in the season.

The following key may help in species identification:

1a. Lateral petals hairless: *V. selkirkii*

1b. Lateral petals bearded: move to step 2

2a. Beard hairs have swollen tips: *V. cucullata*

2b. Beard hairs have tapering tips: move to step 3

3a. Edges of sepals hairless: move to step 4

Top: The base of marsh blue violet's lateral petals is bearded. Middle: Marsh blue violet has heart-shaped leaves. Bottom: Northern bog violet has heart-shaped leaves with rounded teeth; it is best identified by its preference for limestone.

3b. Edges of sepals with ciliate hairs: move to step 5

4a: Leaf blade longer than wide; beards only on lateral petals: *V. novae-angliae*

4b: Leaf blade as wide as or wider than long; beards on lateral petals and hairs also present on spurred petal: *V. nephrophylla*

5a. Leaf blade is arrow-shaped and 1.5 to 3 times longer than wide; lower leaves pubescent; pointed teeth on leaf edge: *V. sagittata*

5b. Leaf blade as wide as or wider than it is long; lower leaves pubescent; teeth rounded: *V. sororia* (includes *V. septentrionalis*)

Specific locations and habitats of each species:

- *V. cucullata*, marsh blue violet: various wetlands; common; provincial floral emblem for New Brunswick.
- *V. nephrophylla*, northern bog violet: calcareous wetlands; mainly Saint John and Restigouche rivers; uncommon.
- *V. sagittata*, arrow-leaved violet: drier open sites; localized in southwestern region; extremely rare.
- *V. selkirkii*, great spurred violet: rich, deciduous, woodlands; uncommon.
- *V. sororia* (includes *V. septentrionalis*), woolly blue violet: moist, but not wet, open sites; common, particularly in the southern half of the province.

Top: Great spurred violet is distinguished by its beardless lateral petals. Middle: Woolly blue violet has long hairs on its beard and soft hairs on its leaves and flower stems. Bottom: Arrow-leaved violet is easily distinguished by its narrow leaves.

Pea family / Fabaceae

Alpine milk-vetch

Native Species

Astragalus alpinus

Astragale alpin, Brunet's milk-vetch

VITAL STATISTICS
Maximum height: 15 centimetres
Flowering season: June to August

HABITAT: Within New Brunswick, alpine milk-vetch is an uncommon calciphile of limestone gravels and ledges along the upper Saint John and Restigouche rivers.

CHARACTERISTICS: Alpine milk-vetch is a mat-forming plant with creeping stems radiating 20 to 40 centimetres from a central rootstock. The alternate leaves are pinnate with five to 11 pairs of 0.4- to 0.5-centimetre-long elliptical leaflets. Leaf undersides are hairy; upper sides have scattered hairs. Hairs are white.

Compact racemes of flowers are produced from the upper leaf axils and are held above the foliage. Pea-like flowers, 1.5 centimetres long, are light violet-blue with darker tips on the standard and keel. The sepals and the small seed pods are covered in white or black hairs.

Elegant milk-vetch, *A. eucosmus*, is a very rare calciphile restricted to the same region as alpine milk-vetch. Elegant milk-vetch has prostrate stems which are up to 60 centimetres in length. Pinnate leaves have four to eight pairs of elliptical 1- to 2.5-centimetre-long leaflets; leaf undersides have stiff hairs but top sides are usually hairless. Flowers, each 0.8 centimetres long, are deep purple with a few white streaks on the standard. Sepals and small seed pods are covered in white or black hairs.

Top: Pea-like flowers are light violet-blue with darker tips on the standard and keel. Middle: Plants are mat-like with pinnate leaves. Bottom: Elegant milk-vetch flowers are deep purple with a few white streaks on the standard.

Native Species

Pea family / Fabaceae

Beach pea

Lathyrus japonicus

Pois de mer, sea pea, sea vetchling

HABITAT: Beach pea grows just above the upper tide zone in gravelly to sandy beaches around the coast of New Brunswick.

CHARACTERISTICS: Beach pea is a clumping tangled plant whose tendrils twine around themselves. Leaves are blue- to grey-green, alternate, and pinnately compound with four to 10 ovate to elliptical leaflets. Smooth or pubescent 2.5- to 5-centimetre-long leaflets are opposite or alternate. Leaves end in a branching tendril. The base of each leaf has a pair of leafy ovate stipules which are as large as the leaflets.

Tight racemes of six to 10 pea-like flowers are produced from the upper leaf axils. The flower stem is generally shorter than the petiole of the accompanying leaf. Individual flowers are 1.5 to 2 centimetres long; standards vary from purple to violet-blue, the wings are paler. The 3- to 7-centimetre-long seed pod is like a miniature pea pod.

Marsh vetchling, *L. palustris*, is a slender upright plant found throughout the province in wet coastal marshes or damp meadows. Its pinnate leaves have two to five pairs of opposite elliptical leaflets and a terminal tendril. Plants are smooth or pubescent. Its purple-pink to violet-blue flowers are not as crowded as those of beach pea; marsh vetchling is also distinguished by its winged stem, arrowhead-like stipules, and its flower stem, which is longer than the petiole of the accompanying leaf.

VITAL STATISTICS
Maximum height: 150 centimetres
Flowering season: July to September

Top: A beach pea flower often has a two-toned effect: its banner and wings are usually slightly different colours. Middle: Beach pea flowers are on compact one-sided racemes; its pinnate leaves have rounded leaflets. Bottom: Marsh vetchling has fewer and more widely spaced flowers on its raceme than beach pea; leaflets are narrow.

Pea family / Fabaceae

Large-leaved lupine

Introduced Species

Lupinus polyphyllus

Lupin perenne, garden lupine

VITAL STATISTICS

Maximum height: 120 centimetres

Flowering season: Late June to early August

HABITAT: Large-leaved lupine grows in dry disturbed areas such as roadsides, embankments, and waste places. This western North American introduction has been firmly naturalized.

CHARACTERISTICS: A stout clumping plant with many non-branching stems arising from a thick rootstock, large-leaved lupine has both basal and alternate stem leaves. Long petioled basal leaves are palmately compound with nine to 18 6- to 13-centimetre-long lanceolate to elliptical leaflets. Leaflets have white hairs below and ciliate hairs along their edges. Stems and upper leaf surfaces are generally hairless. Stem leaves are smaller than basal leaves and have shorter petioles.

Stems terminate in a raceme, which is up to 70 centimetres long, of pea-like flowers. Individual 1.5-centimetre-long flowers are usually blue-purple but may be white to shades of blue-purple or pink, often with contrasting white or yellow patches on their standards. Flowers develop pea-like seed pods up to 8 centimetres long and covered in velvety white hairs. Pods turn brown-black when ripe.

Top: Large-leaved lupine flowers are held on a dense cylindrical raceme. Middle: Flowers may be two-toned blue and white. Bottom: Pink flowers are less common.

Introduced Species

Pea family / Fabaceae

Alfalfa

Medicago sativa

Luzerne, lucerne

VITAL STATISTICS
Maximum height: 100 centimetres
Flowering season: June to August

HABITAT: Alfalfa, a central Asian species introduced to New Brunswick as a fodder crop, is naturalized along dry roadsides and in old meadows and waste places throughout much of the province.

CHARACTERISTICS: Alfalfa is an upright bushy plant with multiple branching stems from a stout taproot. Alternate leaves are trifoliate, each leaflet oblanceolate to oblong and sharply toothed along its outer half. Each leaflet may reach 2.5 centimetres in length. The terminal leaflet has a distinct stem. The leaflet's top surface is hairless; the underside is lightly pubescent. Petioles are finely pubescent. A pair of triangular stipules is present at the base of each leaf.

Flowers are produced in axillary globular to cone-shaped racemes. Pea-like flowers, each 0.7 to 1.2 centimetres long, are blue-violet to purple, rarely white. Seed pods are coiled.

Top: The globular to cone-shaped racemes are among the upper leaf axils. Middle: Less commonly, flowers are white. Bottom: The terminal leaflet of the trifoliate leaves has a distinct stem; the other leaflets are sessile.

Pea family / Fabaceae

Saint John River locoweed

Oxytropis campestris var. johannensis

Oxytrope du fleuve Saint-Jean, Newfoundland oxytrope

Native Species

VITAL STATISTICS
Maximum height: 30 centimetres
Flowering season: June to August

HABITAT: Within New Brunswick, Saint John River locoweed is an uncommon calciphile restricted to limestone gravels and cliffs of the upper Saint John and Restigouche rivers.

CHARACTERISTICS: Saint John River locoweed is a tufted to mat-forming plant with prostrate stems radiating from a central taproot. Leaves are alternate and pinnately compound with 15 to 31 linear to lanceolate leaflets, which may be alternate or paired along the length of the leaf. Stems and leaves are covered in white pubescent hairs. At the base of each leaf is a pair of stipules.

Flowers are produced in dense round terminal racemes. Individual purple to violet-blue flowers are 0.5 to 0.7 centimetres in length. The standard has a large purple-striped white patch. Sepals and seed pods are covered in pubescent hairs.

Foliose locoweed, *O. deflexa*, is extremely rare and restricted to calcareous gravels of Victoria County. Pinnate leaves have 15 to 29 ovate to elliptical opposite leaflets and are mostly basal. Flower stems are long with a terminal cluster of deep violet, 0.8- to 1-centimetre-long flowers. The entire plant is covered in soft hairs and the petioles and flower stalks are often wine red.

Top: Flowers are in rounded racemes. Middle: The matted plants have pinnate leaves with many small narrow leaflets. Bottom: The flowers of foliolose locoweed are dark purple and the leaves are covered in silky hairs.

Introduced Species

Pea family / Fabaceae

Tufted vetch

Vicia cracca

Jargeau, cow vetch, bird vetch, Canada pea

HABITAT: Tufted vetch, a European species naturalized throughout New Brunswick, grows in disturbed habitats.

CHARACTERISTICS: Tufted vetch is a delicate climbing vine that clings to neighbouring vegetation. Stems are ridged along their length. Alternate 6- to 12-centimetre-long leaves are pinnately compound with eight to 12 pairs of oblong to linear leaflets. Leaves end in a forking tendril and have a pair of small narrow stipules at their bases. Leaflets may be smooth or finely pubescent.

One-sided axillary racemes have 10 to 30 reflexed blossoms. Individual pea-like flowers are blue-violet to purple and 1 to 1.3 centimetres long. Pea pods reach 2 to 3 centimetres in length and contain up to eight seeds.

Common vetch, *V. sativa*, is an annual with paired axillary, nearly sessile, showy 1.5- to 3-centimetre-long flowers. Standards are purple; wings are violet-red to magenta. Narrow pea pods may reach 8 centimetres in length.

Scattered in waste places, four-seed vetch, *V. tetrasperma*, is a slender annual which reaches 40 centimetres in length. Pinnate leaves have three to five pairs of narrow leaflets. Axillary 0.8-centimetre-long flowers are solitary or in groups of two or three. Flowers are pale lilac-blue with dark purple-blue veins on the standard and a dark-tipped keel. The seed pod reaches 1.3 centimetres.

VITAL STATISTICS
Maximum height: 2 metres
Flowering season: Late June to August

Top: Tufted vetch flowers are held in one-sided racemes. Middle: Common vetch's purple banner and violet-red wings create a two-toned blossom. Bottom: Four-seed vetch flowers, held in small groups, are pale lilac-blue with dark purple-blue veins on its banners.

Borage family / Boraginaceae

Common viper's bugloss

Echium vulgare

Vipérine, bluedevil, blueweed

Introduced Species

VITAL STATISTICS
Maximum height: 80 centimetres
Flowering season: June to September

HABITAT: Common viper's bugloss, a European introduction, is naturalized but localized along roadsides and in old meadows and other dry waste places throughout New Brunswick.

CHARACTERISTICS: Common viper's bugloss is a slender biennial. In the first season, plants produce a flat rosette of elongate lanceolate leaves which are up to 15 centimetres long. Leaves often have raised white spots; leaf edges are smooth but may be undulating. In the second year, plants produce several upright stems. Stem leaves are also narrow and lanceolate but sessile and smaller than the basal leaves. The entire plant, including the five narrow sepals, is covered in stiff white hairs.

Early in the flowering season, blooms appear in wand-like spikes. Close examination reveals that flowers are produced in axillary one-sided cymes, many of which are produced along the upper stems. Each cyme has a small narrow leaf or bract at its base. As the season progresses, the cymes elongate to become side-branches, giving plants a bushier appearance. Funnel-shaped flowers, composed of five fused petals, are 0.9 to 1.2 centimetres in diameter and open as pink buds but quickly turn vivid blue. The five stamens extend beyond the petals; they have blue pollen and contrasting red filaments. A single threadlike style has a pair of stigmas.

Top: The stamens extend beyond the funnel-shaped blue flowers. Middle: Each side-branch of the wand-like flower cluster is created by a one-sided scorpioid cyme. Bottom: First-season plants produce a basal rosette of long narrow leaves.

Introduced Species

Mint family / Lamiaceae

Ground ivy

Glechoma hederacea

Lierre terrestre, creeping Charlie, gill-over-the-ground, run-away-robin

HABITAT: Ground ivy is a European introduction found in damp and shaded waste areas throughout much of New Brunswick.

CHARACTERISTICS: Ground ivy is a trailing matted plant. Stems, square in cross-section, trail along the ground and usually root at their nodes. Opposite long petioled leaves are round or fan-shaped with rounded teeth; they are 2 to 3 centimetres in diameter. Upright flowering stems also have opposite rounded leaves, which may be smooth or have scattered stiff hairs. Leaves and stems are usually purple-tinted. Plants emit a minty fragrance when bruised.

Violet-blue flowers are sessile, usually in two groups of two to three flowers among the upper leaf axils. Individual tubular flowers, each about 2 centimetres long, have five petals arranged in a two-lipped fashion. Two petals fuse to form a two-lobed upper lip; the other three, a three-lobed lower lip. The middle lower lobe is the largest and is often two-lobed. This lower lobe and the throat of the flower are mottled with dark veins. The inside of the throat is hairy.

VITAL STATISTICS

Maximum height: 30 centimetres
Flowering season: May to October

Top: Each flower is tubular; the middle lobe of the trilobed lower lip is the largest. Bottom: The fan-shaped leaves are in pairs and the flowers axillary.

Mint family / Lamiaceae

American pennyroyal

Native Species

Hedeoma pulegioides

Hédéoma faux-pouliot, American false pennyroyal, pudding-grass

VITAL STATISTICS	
Maximum height:	30 centimetres
Flowering season:	August to September

HABITAT: American false pennyroyal is very rare on rocky ledges and gravelly soils in the southern region of New Brunswick.

CHARACTERISTICS: American pennyroyal is a branched or unbranched annual. Stems are square in cross-section and pubescent. Opposite small leaves, each reaching 2.5 centimetres in length, are elliptical to oblong with a few hairs. Short petioled leaves have smooth edges or scattered obscure teeth. The plant emits a mint-like fragrance when bruised.

Flowers are produced in small axillary clusters of two to four flowers. Individual flowers are about 0.5 centimetres long. Tubular flowers have a two-lipped appearance with two fused petals forming an upper lip and three a lower lip. The lowermost petal is often notched. Flowers are pale violet-blue with a darker blue throat.

Top: The axillary two-lipped flowers are pale blue with a darker throat. Bottom: The small elliptical leaves are opposite and covered in fine hairs.

Mint family / Lamiaceae

Field mint

Native Species

Mentha arvensis (formerly *M. canadensis*)

Menthe du Canada, baume, wild mint, common mint, Canada mint, corn mint, field mint

VITAL STATISTICS
Maximum height: 60 centimetres
Flowering season: July to September

HABITAT: Field mint is found in open damp meadows and along roadsides and shorelines throughout New Brunswick.

CHARACTERISTICS: Field mint is a bushy plant with upright or ascending stems from a creeping rhizome. Stems, square in cross-section, have downward-facing pubescent hairs and are often tinted red. Opposite, sharply toothed leaves are ovate, elliptical, or lanceolate with short petioles. Leaves, covered in long pubescent hairs, especially on the undersides, vary from 2 to 8 centimetres in length. All parts of the plant emit a minty fragrance when bruised.

Sessile flowers are produced in dense clusters among the upper leaf axils. The 0.4-centimetre-long funnel-shaped lilac-pink to purple flowers have a two-lipped appearance. The upper lip is shallowly lobed and wider than the lower lip's three lobes. Four stamens and single style with a two-forked stigma extend beyond the petals. The throat of the flower is hairy.

Red mint, *M. X gentilis* (also known as *M. gracilis*), prefers wet sites and is distinguished by its almost hairless leaves and often purple-tinted stems. Spearmint, *M. spicata*, is also found in wet sites. Its flowers are in narrow terminal spikes and its leaves appear rugose. Peppermint, *M. X peperita*, also inhabits wet places and is distinguished by its short terminal spikes.

Top: Field mint has sessile flowers in the leaf axils of the upper leaves. Middle: Red mint has hairless leaves. Bottom: Peppermint has short terminal spikes.

Mint family / Lamiaceae

Common self-heal

Native Species

Prunella vulgaris

Herbe au charpentier, carpenter weed, heal-all, self-heal

VITAL STATISTICS

Maximum height: 30 centimetres
Flowering season: June to September

HABITAT: Common self-heal occurs in waste places as well as on pastures and lawns and along roadsides throughout New Brunswick.

CHARACTERISTICS: Common self-heal is a tufted plant with loosely ascending stems. Prostrate rhizomes, often purple-tinted, root at the nodes. Stems, square in cross-section, are hairy when young but often hairless as they mature. Opposite toothed leaves are lanceolate and oblong or ovate and may reach a length of 9 centimetres. Leaves may be hairless or have scattered hairs and often appear crinkled.

Flowers are produced in club- or cone-like clusters. Each cluster has a pair of leaves at its base. The base of each flower has a small scale-like bract. Sepals are white, hairy, and often purple-tinted. Tubular 0.8- to 1.5-centimetre-long flowers have five fused petals that give them a two-lipped appearance. The upper two petals fuse to form a hood; the lower three petals, a three-lobed lip. The lowest lobe is the largest; it is shallowly notched with a fringed edge. Flowers are violet-blue to lavender with four stamens and a single style hidden within the tube.

Top: Individual flowers appear two-lipped; the upper petals form a hood, the lower is trilobed.
Bottom: The base of each flower has a scale-like bract; flowers are in terminal cone-shaped racemes.

Native Species

Mint family / Lamiaceae

Marsh skullcap

Scutellaria galericulata

Toque, tertianaire, common skullcap

HABITAT: Marsh skullcap grows along rocky shorelines and streamsides throughout New Brunswick.

CHARACTERISTICS: Marsh skullcap is a clumping plant with narrow, usually unbranched, stems arising from creeping rhizomes. Stems are square in cross-section with hairs along their corners. Opposite leaves, each up to 8 centimetres in length, are lance-shaped to oblong with rounded teeth and a rounded base. Leaves are rugose and glossy on the upper surfaces but have finely hairy undersides; they have short petioles or are sessile.

Tubular two-lipped flowers are trumpet-shaped and 1.5 to 2 centimetres long. They are produced in nearly sessile one-sided pairs from the axils of the upper leaves. The fused petals are blue to violet and covered in fine hairs. Upper petals form a narrow hood over the wider lower lip. The throat of the flower is white with darker blue spots; the sepals are often purple-tinted.

Mad-dog or blue skullcap, *S. lateriflora*, is bushier than marsh skullcap, although it occurs in similar habitats and blooms at the same time. It has ovate, usually hairless, leaves, which are up to 10 centimetres long. Leaves have rounded bases, coarse teeth, and distinct petioles. Flowers are produced in axillary or terminal one-sided racemes, which are up to 15 centimetres long. Each flower is 0.8 centimetres long with a small broad bract at its base.

VITAL STATISTICS
Maximum height: 100 centimetres
Flowering season: Mid-July to August

Top: The paired tubular flowers appear two-lipped; the flower's throat is white with darker blue spots. Middle: Marsh skullcap's paired leaves are sessile and its stems square. Bottom: Blue skullcap produces flowers in one-sided axillary racemes; its leaves have petioles.

Plantain family / Plantaginaceae

Striped toadflax

Introduced Species

Linaria repens

Linaire rampante, linaire striée, pale toadflax

VITAL STATISTICS
Maximum height: 50 centimetres
Flowering season: July to September

HABITAT: Striped toadflax, a European species now naturalized in disturbed habitats such as roadsides, fields, and waste places, is locally common but overall uncommon and widely scattered in New Brunswick.

CHARACTERISTICS: A slender plant, striped toadflax forms loose colonies as plants spread through subterranean rhizomes. Stems may be branched or unbranched. The numerous leaves are waxy, blue-tinted, linear, and sessile. Lower leaves are whorled; upper are alternate. The entire plant is hairless.

Flowers are produced in narrow terminal racemes. Individual flowers, each 0.8 to 1.5 centimetres long, are shaped like those of snapdragon (Antirrhinum) and have a two-lipped appearance. The upper bilobed lip is composed of two fused petals; the lower three-lobed lip has three fused petals. Lips are pale lilac with dark violet stripes. The base of the lower lip often has a pale cream or yellow swelling that closes the "mouth." The lower lip has a 0.2- to 0.3-centimetre-long spur at its base. Flowers have four stamens and a single style.

Top: The pale lilac flowers have darker stripes and are produced in a terminal raceme. Bottom: The numerous narrow linear leaves are sessile.

Plantain family / Plantaginaceae

Native Species

Canada toadflax

Nuttallanthus canadensis (formerly *Linaria canadensis*)

Linaire de Canada, old field toadflax, blue toadflax

HABITAT: Canada toadflax occurs in waste places and along roadsides, especially sandy sites. It is uncommon and scattered, primarily in southern and eastern New Brunswick.

VITAL STATISTICS
Maximum height: 80 centimetres
Flowering season: May to September

CHARACTERISTICS: Canada toadflax is a slender annual or biennial. Overwintering plants have several flat rosettes, which arise in spring as non-branching stems. Four-centimetre-long stem leaves are linear, opposite on the lower stem and alternate on the upper stem. The stem is often purple-tinted; stems and leaves are hairless.

Light blue to blue-violet flowers are produced in a loose narrow terminal raceme. Individual 1-centimetre-wide flowers are snapdragon-like: two petals are fused to form a two-lobed upper lip; three petals form a larger three-lobed lower lip. The throat of the flower is white with two raised ridges. A thin curving 0.2- to 0.6-centimetre-long spur is located behind the lower lip. Five fused sepals form a pubescent tube behind the flower.

Dwarf snapdragon, *Chaenorrhinum minus*, is an introduced multiple branching annual scattered in waste places, especially in western New Brunswick. Plants reach 40 centimetres in height. Linear to oblong leaves are generally alternate but occasionally opposite. Leaves, stems, and flowers are covered in glandular hairs. Flowers are solitary among the upper axils and form leafy racemes. Individual lilac-coloured snapdragon-like flowers are 0.5 to 0.8 centimetres wide with a paler lilac throat. Flowers have short stout spurs.

Top: Canada toadflax's snapdragon-like flowers are blue-violet with a paler throat and in racemes.
Bottom: Dwarf snapdragon has solitary flowers in the upper leaf axils; the plant is covered in fine sticky hairs.

Plantain family / Plantaginaceae

American speedwell

Native Species

Veronica americana

Véronique Américaine, American brooklime

VITAL STATISTICS

Maximum height: 60 centimetres
Flowering season: June to September

HABITAT: American speedwell, common throughout New Brunswick, occurs in wet habitats such as streamsides, shorelines, thickets, and ditches.

CHARACTERISTICS: American speedwell is a trailing matted plant whose stem tips are often ascending. Stems often root at their nodes. Opposite leaves are lanceolate, elliptical to ovate, shallowly toothed, and petioled on the lower part of the stem, but sessile and clasping closer to the flowers. Leaves may reach 7 centimetres in length. Stems and leaves are hairless.

Flowers are produced in axillary racemes from the upper leaves. These racemes may reach 15 centimetres in length. Flowers, each about 0.5 centimetres wide, are composed of four pale violet-blue petals, the uppermost of which is the widest. The petal base has dark blue-violet veins. Each flower has two exerted stamens and a single style.

Marsh speedwell, *V. scutellata*, is a thinner, weaker plant than American speedwell and has long stolons. Stems may reach 75 centimetres in length. Sessile opposite leaves are linear to lanceolate, with smooth edges or fine teeth. Widely spaced white or lilac to lavender-blue flowers are produced in axillary racemes on a zigzag stem. The upper stem and new leaves are often red or purple-tinted. It blooms from mid-June to September and is common throughout the province.

Top: American speedwell flowers are pale blue with darker veins and in racemes. Middle: American speedwell has trailing stems; its opposite leaves are hairless. Bottom: Marsh speedwell often has white flowers with pale blue veins.

Plantain family / Plantaginaceae

Introduced Species

Long-leaved speedwell

Veronica longifolia

Véronique à longues feuilles, garden speedwell

HABITAT: Long-leaved speedwell, a European species originally grown in New Brunswick as a garden ornamental, is occasionally naturalized along roadsides.

VITAL STATISTICS
Maximum height: 100 centimetres
Flowering season: July to August

CHARACTERISTICS: Long-leaved speedwell is a slender clumping plant with unbranched lower stems and a few upper flowering branches. Stems and leaves may be hairless or have a fine, pale pubescence. Opposite or whorled leaves are lanceolate, short petioled, and sharply toothed.

Stems end in long narrow racemes, which may occupy nearly one-third of the plant's height. Individual deep violet-blue flowers are 0.6 to 0.8 centimetres wide and have four petals: a single upper and three wide-spreading lower petals. Flowers also have two exerted stamens and a single style that give a bottlebrush look to the racemes.

Top: Flowers are in many narrow racemes.
Bottom: The flowers have a bottlebrush appearance; its opposite leaves are narrow and sharply toothed.

Plantain family / Plantaginaceae

Common speedwell

Introduced Species

Veronica officinalis

Thé d'Europe, common gypsyweed

VITAL STATISTICS

Maximum height: 20 centimetres

Flowering season: July to August

HABITAT: Common speedwell, a European species commonly found throughout New Brunswick in disturbed places such as roadsides, old pasturelands, woodland trails, and lawns, is especially fond of shady rich soils.

CHARACTERISTICS: A trailing mat-forming plant, common speedwell's opposite leaves reach 5 centimetres in length; they vary from ovate, oblong, to elliptical and have short petioles and fine teeth. The entire plant is covered in soft hairs.

Ten- to 20-centimetre-high erect flower stems are produced from leaf axils near the ends of the stems. Flowers are produced in a dense raceme. Individual flowers are about 0.8 centimetres wide with four petals. The lower petal is narrower than the other three; all are lilac to lavender-blue with dark veins. Flowers have two stamens and a single style. The throat of the flower is hairy. The developing seed capsules have a heart-like shape.

Germander speedwell, *V. chamaedrys*, occurs in similar habitats to common speedwell, but it is less common and widely scattered. Although trailing, it produces more erect stems than common speedwell, to 40 centimetres tall; round leaves are essentially sessile with larger, rounder teeth. It blooms from May to July; the bright blue flowers in axillary racemes have dark blue veins. Individual flowers are up to 1.2 centimetres wide.

Top: The lavender-blue flowers are in narrow racemes; the lowermost petal is narrower than the other petals. Middle: Common speedwell stems are trailing with opposite oval leaves. Bottom: Germander speedwell has rounder leaves with larger rounded teeth than common speedwell; its axillary flowers are bright blue.

Plantain family / Plantaginaceae

Introduced Species

Thyme-leaved speedwell

Veronica serpyllifolia

Véronique à feuilles de serpolet

HABITAT: A European species, thyme-leaved speedwell is found in damp disturbed areas throughout the province.

CHARACTERISTICS: Thyme-leaved speedwell is an evergreen mat-forming plant. Stems are trailing and often root at their nodes. Opposite leaves, up to 1.5 centimetres in length, are sessile and ovate, with obscure rounded teeth. Leaves and stems are usually hairless.

Flowers are produced on upright terminal racemes. Each has a leafy bract at its base. Individual flowers are 0.6 to 0.8 centimetres wide with four pale blue petals veined in a darker blue. The lower petal is narrower than the other three. Flowers have two stamens and a single style. The developing seed capsules are heart-shaped.

Corn speedwell, *V. arvensis*, is a narrow annual that grows to a height of 30 centimetres with small opposite toothed leaves. Lower stem leaves are round and short-stalked; the upper, sessile. Stems and leaves have long hairs. Sessile 0.2- to 0.3-centimetre-wide violet-blue flowers are produced on narrow racemes, each with a narrow leafy bract at their base.

Bird's-eye speedwell, *V. persica*, is another long-haired annual but its 0.8- to 1.2-centimetre-wide violet-blue flowers with white centres are solitary in the leaf axils and held on thin stems. Petioled leaves are ovate to round with coarsely toothed edges. Both corn and bird's-eye speedwells are European species widely scattered in disturbed habitats and bloom from June to September.

VITAL STATISTICS	
Maximum height:	20 centimetres
Flowering season:	Mid-May to October

Top: Thyme-leaved speedwell has upright racemes of pale blue flowers with darker veins, especially on the uppermost petal; leaves are round and almost smooth along their edges. Middle: Corn speedwell's sessile flowers are partly hidden among the many narrow hairy bracts. Bottom: Bird's-eye speedwell has solitary flowers among the upper leaf axils; the violet-blue flowers have white centres.

Wetlands

False pimpernel family / Linderniaceae

Yellow-seed false pimpernel

Lindernia dubia

Lindernie douteuse, slender false pimpernel, moist-bank pimpernel

Native Species

VITAL STATISTICS

Maximum height: 30 centimetres

Flowering season: Late June to October

HABITAT: Yellow-seed false pimpernel is found primarily on the shores of muddy rivers and lakes but is seen occasionally in moist disturbed areas such as roadsides and seepages. It is uncommon and widely scattered in the province.

CHARACTERISTICS: Yellow-seed false pimpernel is a low bushy, but open, annual with arching stems. Stems are square in cross-section and often tinted red. Opposite leaves are up to 3.5 centimetres long, elliptical to ovate, with smooth or slightly toothed edges. They are either sessile or nearly sessile. The entire plant is hairless.

Flowers, which are 0.5 to 1 centimetre long, are solitary in the upper leaf axils. Produced at the ends of 2.5-centimetre-long slender pedicles, the pale violet-blue flowers are tubular with a two-lipped appearance: the upper lip is two-lobed and hoodlike, the lower, three-lobed and wide-spreading. Inside the floral tube are four stamens and a single style.

Top: The solitary pale violet-blue flowers appear two-lipped; the lower lip has three wide-spreading lobes. Bottom: The hairless leaves are opposite, sessile, and only slightly toothed.

Disturbed

Lopseed family / Phrymaceae

Square-stemmed monkeyflower

Native Species

Mimulus ringens

Mimule à fleurs entrouvertes, blue monkeyflower, Allegheny monkeyflower

HABITAT: Square-stemmed monkeyflower, common throughout New Brunswick, grows in wet marshes and along shorelines and streams.

CHARACTERISTICS: Square-stemmed monkeyflower is a slender clumping plant with stems arising from stoloniferous rhizomes. Stems are square in cross-section. Opposite leaves, which are up to 10 centimetres in length, are lanceolate to elliptical, sessile or clasping, with toothed edges. Leaves and stems are hairless.

Long petioled flowers are solitary among the upper leaf axils. The 2.5-centimetre-long pale blue-violet flowers have a two-lipped snapdragon-like appearance. The upper two petals are fused into an erect two-lobed lip; the lower three petals form a wide-spreading three-lobed lower lip. The base of the lowermost petal has two yellow ridges that lead into the hairy throat. The outside surface of the petals is covered in fine glandular hairs; inside the throat are four stamens and a two-lobed stigma. Fused sepals form a five-ridged tube with five pointed teeth at its end.

VITAL STATISTICS

Maximum height: 120 centimetres
Flowering season: July to August

Top: The flowers appear two-lipped; the base of the lower lip has two yellow ridges. Bottom: The narrow opposite leaves are sessile with toothed edges and the flowers axillary.

Bladderwort family / Lentibulariaceae

Common butterwort

Pinguicula vulgaris

Grassette vulgaire

Native Species

VITAL STATISTICS

Maximum height: 12 centimetres

Flowering season: June to early August

HABITAT: Common butterwort prefers wet calcareous gravels, open seepages, and wet shorelines. It is extremely rare in New Brunswick, restricted to the Restigouche River.

CHARACTERISTICS: Common butterwort is a small rosetted plant. Basal spatulate to elliptical leaves are fleshy and yellow-green and have smooth upward-curling edges. Insects adhere to its sticky and greasy upper leaf surface. Leaves may reach 5 centimetres in length.

Purple funnel-shaped flowers are solitary and arise on leafless glandular stems, which reach 12 centimetres in length. Each rosette produces up to nine flowers. Individual flowers are up to 1.5 centimetres wide and have a two-lipped appearance: the upper lip is two-lobed; the lower, three-lobed. A narrow downward-curving spur extends behind the lower lip. The inside of the throat has long white hairs. The five sepals are often dark purple-tinted and covered in glandular pubescence. Inside the throat are two stamens and a single disc-shaped stigma.

Top: The funnel-shaped flowers appear two-lipped; the inside of the flower has long white hairs. Middle: Plants produce a low rosette of yellow-green leaves with smooth upward-curling edges. Bottom: Solitary flowers arise on leafless stems.

Native Species

Bellflower family / Campanulaceae

Water lobelia

Lobelia dortmanna

Lobélie de Dortmann, water gladiole

VITAL STATISTICS
Maximum height: 30 centimetres
Flowering season: August

HABITAT: Water lobelia grows in gravelly or rocky-bottomed ponds and slow-moving streams throughout New Brunswick. It is usually restricted to water less than 150 centimetres in depth.

CHARACTERISTICS: Water lobelia is an aquatic plant with a tuft of evergreen linear leaves. Its hollow leaves are fleshy, curving, and 2.5 to 7.5 centimetres long.

One to 11 widely spaced flowers are produced in a raceme at the end of a leafless hairless stem that arises up to 30 centimetres above the water's surface. Each flower has a narrow 1- to 2-centimetre-long floral tube and five petals. The flower opening has a two-lipped appearance. The upper lip has two narrow lobes that curve backward; the lower lip has three larger wide-spreading lobes. Petals are pale blue or almost white. Inside the floral tube are five stamens and a single style.

Kalm's or bog lobelia, *L. kalmii*, is found in damp calcareous wetlands. It has slender 15- to 30-centimetre-high stems, spatulate to obovate and slightly toothed basal leaves, alternate linear stem leaves, and a loose one-sided raceme of 0.7- to 1.6-centimetre-long flowers. Flowers have five petals: two small narrow backward-curving petals form an upper lip; three larger, broader petals, a three-lobed lower lip. Flowers are blue with a conspicuous white eye on the lower lip. It is uncommon and most often found in the western and northern regions of the province.

Top: Petal bases are fused into a tube; the pale blue flowers appear two-lipped. Middle: Water lobelia flowers are on narrow leafless racemes that arise directly from the water. Bottom: Kalm's lobelia flowers are blue with conspicuous white eyes.

Bellflower family / Campanulaceae

Indian tobacco

Lobelia inflata

Lobélie gonflée, herbe à l'asthme, wild tobacco

Native Species

Mixed Forest | Deciduous Forest | Barrens | Disturbed

VITAL STATISTICS
Maximum height: 100 centimetres
Flowering season: July to August

HABITAT: Indian tobacco grows along roadsides or in open woodlands and waste places throughout New Brunswick.

CHARACTERISTICS: Indian tobacco is a tall leafy annual or biennial. Overwintering plants have a basal rosette of ovate leaves. Flowering plants have alternate elliptical to ovate sessile leaves with toothed edges. Leaves may reach 8 centimetres in length. The stem and leaf undersides are hairy.

Pale violet flowers are produced in terminal and axillary racemes among the upper leaves. Individual 0.7- to 1-centimetre-long flowers have a two-lipped appearance created by the fusing of five petals. The upper lip has two narrow erect lobes; the lower, three larger wide-spreading lobes. The base of the lower lip has a pale yellow patch with white hairs. Each flower has a stalk and a small leaf or leafy bract at its base. This plant is toxic if ingested.

Top: The pale violet flowers appear two-lipped, with two narrow upper lobes and three wide-spreading wider lobes. Bottom: Indian tobacco flowers are in racemes that are both terminal and from the upper leaf axils.

Pickerelweed family / Pontederiaceae

Pickerelweed

Pontederia cordata

Pontédérie cordée

Native Species

HABITAT: Pickerelweed is found in shallow water or along muddy shores in southwestern New Brunswick.

CHARACTERISTICS: Pickerelweed is a stout clumping plant that forms large colonies as plants spread via thick rhizomes. The waxy leaves are basal, arising directly from the rhizome, and held on hollow petioles which reach 60 centimetres in length. Leaf bases are often submersed. Leaf blades, which are up to 18 centimetres in length, vary from ovate, oblong, to lanceolate, with smooth edges and a heart-shaped base. Leaves and petioles are hairless.

Thick flower stems have one stem leaf. Above this leaf is a spathe from which a dense spike of flowers, which is up to 12 centimetres long, emerges. The stem above the spathe, as well as the sepals, is covered in glandular hairs. Individual flowers are 1.5 to 2 centimetres wide. Flowers have six blue-violet tepals, three arched upward and three arched downward, imparting a two-lipped effect. The uppermost tepal has a distinct yellow spot at its base. Flowers have six anthers of varying lengths, usually three long and three short, and a single style.

VITAL STATISTICS
Maximum height: 50 centimetres
Flowering season: June to September

Top: The uppermost petal has a central yellow blotch. Middle: Flowers are in dense racemes; the smooth leaves are commonly heart-shaped. Bottom: Leaves have long petioles and arise directly from the water.

Wetlands

Iris family / Iridaceae

Blue flag

Native Species

Iris versicolor

Clajeux, iris sauvage, harlequin blue flag, northern blue flag

VITAL STATISTICS
Maximum height: 80 centimetres
Flowering season: June to July

HABITAT: Blue flag occurs in wet to damp habitats throughout New Brunswick.

CHARACTERISTICS: Blue flag is a clumping grass-like plant. Leaves are basal, strap- or sword-like, hairless, and smooth-edged. Their bases are often purple-tinted.

Flowers are produced on stout leafless stems. Stems may be single or have two to three branches, each producing one to three flowers. Deep blue or blue-violet flowers are showy, each about 10 centimetres wide; they have three downward-arching broad sepals (the falls) and three erect narrower petals (the standards). The base of the sepals is white to yellow with blue-violet veins. Both sepals and petals may have darker veins. The standards are about half as long as the sepals. The thick cylindroid seed capsule is three-angled and has a nipple-like beak at its terminus.

Beach-head iris, *I. hookeri*, is confined to peaty shores, headlands, and salt marshes near the coast. It is only half the size of blue flag, reaching a maximum height of 50 centimetres. Its flowers have tiny narrow standards, rounded falls, and more globular seed capsules without a terminal beak. It blooms slightly earlier than blue flag.

Top: Each blue flag flower has three large falls, the base of which is often yellow with dark veins, and three smaller standards. Middle: Blue flag produces large grass-like clumps with broad sword-shaped leaves. Bottom: Beach-head iris flowers have three rounded falls and three minute standards.

Gentian family / Gentianaceae

Spurred gentian

Halenia deflexa

Halénie défléchie

Native Species

HABITAT: Found throughout much of New Brunswick, spurred gentian grows on peaty coastal headlands, and in thickets and moist open woods. It prefers calcareous soils.

CHARACTERISTICS: Spurred gentian is a tufted leafy annual or biennial. Its leaves are opposite, sessile, smooth-edged, fleshy, and spoon- to lance-shaped. Leaves, often purple-tinted, have three distinct veins. The entire plant is hairless. The stem is square in cross-section.

Flowers are in crowded, both terminal and axillary, cymes. Flowers vary in length from 0.8 to 1.5 centimetres; individual flowers have four narrow green sepals and four pointed petals, which vary from purple to bronze to yellow-green. Each petal has a perpendicular spur at its base. Flowers rarely open fully.

Marsh felwort, *Lomatogonium rotatum*, is an extremely rare annual or biennial found in South Wolf Island, Charlotte County, where it grows along wet shorelines. A slender annual or biennial, it reaches 25 centimetres in height. Opposite leaves are lance-shaped, sessile, and fleshy. Stems are often purple-tinted. Four or five sepals are narrow, leaf-like, and longer than the same number of porcelain-blue petals. Starlike flowers bloom from July to September.

VITAL STATISTICS

Maximum height: 30 centimetres
Flowering season: July to September

Top: Each flower, which never opens fully, has four petals with perpendicular spurs; shown here are two colour extremes. Middle: Shown here is the usual spurred gentian flower colour; flowers are clustered at the tip and among the upper leaf axils. Bottom: The sepals of marsh felwort are a little longer than the porcelain-blue petals.

Madder family / Rubiaceae

Azure bluets

Native Species

Houstonia caerulea

Houstonie bleue, mountain bluets, Quaker-ladies

VITAL STATISTICS

Maximum height: 20 centimetres

Flowering season: Mid-May to mid-June

HABITAT: Azure bluets are encountered in damp meadows, lawns, and open hillsides, primarily in southwestern New Brunswick.

CHARACTERISTICS: Azure bluets is a small tufted annual or short-lived perennial with both basal and stem leaves. The former are spatulate to elliptical and up to 1.5 centimetres in length. Stem leaves are opposite, lance-shaped to linear, and smaller than the basal leaves. They are hairless or may have fine hairs. Unbranched stems are thin and threadlike.

Flowers are solitary on the ends of thin wiry stems. Individual flowers are about 1 centimetre wide with four pale blue petals set at the end of a narrow tube. Each flower has a yellow eye, four stamens, and a single style with a bifid stigma. Some flowers have long stamens and a short style; others, short stamens and a long style. This is known as dimorphism or dimorphous flowers.

Top: Each flower is solitary with four pale blue petals, and each centre has a yellow eye. Bottom: Plants are low and tufted, often with small oval leaves.

Introduced Species

Buttercup family / Ranunculaceae

European columbine

Aquilegia vulgaris

Ancolie vulgaire, gants de Notre-Dame, garden columbine

HABITAT: European columbine, a garden escape originally introduced as a garden ornamental, is found along roadsides and trails and in waste areas near settlements throughout the province.

CHARACTERISTICS: European columbine is a tufted plant. The long petioled leaves are basal and biternately compound. Leaflets are lobed with rounded teeth. The lower stem leaves, which are alternately arranged, are similar, with shorter petioles than the basal leaves; upper stem leaves are trifoliate and sessile. Upper leaf surfaces are smooth and waxy; undersides are finely hairy.

Nodding flowers, produced in loose clusters, are up to 5.5 centimetres wide. Flowers have five petals, each with a hooked spur at the basal end, five petal-like sepals, numerous stamens, and five styles. Flowers are usually violet-blue but may also be pale blue, wine red, pink, or white. Petals may be white or paler at their tips, imparting a bi-coloured effect to blossoms. Each flower develops five pointy-tipped narrow tubelike capsules that are joined at the base.

VITAL STATISTICS
Maximum height: 120 centimetres
Flowering season: Late May to June

Top: Each flower has five petal-like sepals and five petals with hooked spurs at their basal end. Middle: Flowers, which are nodding, vary from blue to wine-red (shown here) to pink to white. Bottom: Leaves are mostly basal and biternately compound; leaflets are lobed with rounded teeth.

Plumbago family / Plumabaginaceae

Sea lavender

Limonium carolinianum

Lavande de mer, marsh rosemary

VITAL STATISTICS
Maximum height: 60 centimetres
Flowering season: Mid-July to September

HABITAT: Sea lavender occurs in salt marshes and peaty seashores. It is common along the coasts of New Brunswick.

CHARACTERISTICS: Sea lavender is a leafy tufted plant arising from a thick rootstock. Hairless smooth-edged leaves are oblong and spatulate to elliptical. Leaves are basal and commonly 20 to 30 centimetres in length with long petioles, and they have a leathery texture.

Numerous flowers are produced in airy spray-like panicles of one-sided racemes atop relatively stout leafless stems. Sepals are finely pubescent at their base; flowers are about 0.3 centimetres wide with five lavender petals. Inside the flower are five stamens and five styles.

Top: The tiny flowers are in open panicles; each blossom has five small lavender-blue petals. Middle: The elliptical leaves are basal, creating a tufted habit. Bottom: Plants have a tufted appearance with large airy panicles of flowers.

Geranium family / Geraniaceae

Introduced Species

Meadow geranium

Geranium pratense

Géranium des prés, meadow cranesbill

HABITAT: Meadow geranium, a European plant introduced as a garden ornamental, is occasionally found in waste areas and along trails and roadsides near settlements throughout New Brunswick.

VITAL STATISTICS

Maximum height: 70 centimetres
Flowering season: June to August

CHARACTERISTICS: Meadow geranium is a clumping plant with multiple unbranched stems arising from a thickened rhizome. Basal leaves have long petioles. Leaves are palmately lobed with seven to nine divisions; each division is subsequently deeply lobed and each lobe has large rounded teeth. Stem leaves are opposite and short-stalked or sessile. Leaves and stems are pubescent. Upper stems and flower stalks are often purple-tinted.

Flowers are produced in loose branching corymbs. Buds are nodding before they open. Flower stems and pedicles are slightly sticky with glandular hairs. Three- to 4-centimetre-wide flowers are saucer-shaped; they have five violet-blue petals with pale veins, five pointed finely hairy green sepals, 10 stamens, and a single style with a five-parted thin starlike stigma. Seeds are produced at the bottom of a bill-like structure. When seeds are ripe, part of the bill curls back, catapulting the seeds.

Top: Unopened flowers typically nod; open outward-facing flowers have five violet-blue petals with pale veins. Middle: White-flowered plants are less common. Bottom: Leaves are palmately lobed with seven to nine divisions, each of which is lobed and toothed.

Gentian family – Gentianaceae

Autumn dwarf gentian

Native Species

Gentianopsis amarelle

Gentiane amarelle, northern gentian, felwort gentian

VITAL STATISTICS

Maximum height: 30 centimetres
Flowering season: July to September

HABITAT: Autumn dwarf gentian, an extremely rare calciphile found on limestone gravels and shallow peaty pockets overlying limestone, is widely scattered in New Brunswick.

CHARACTERISTICS: Autumn dwarf gentian is a slender annual or biennial. Its opposite sessile lanceolate leaves are widely spaced and often purple-tinted. Leaves are hairless with smooth edges.

Violet to lilac flowers are produced as a terminal leafy raceme or as axillary clusters or racemes among the upper leaves. Individual flowers are tubular with a flaring star-shaped opening composed of five, rarely four, petals. A distinct central ring of fringed hair is located at the opening to the floral tube.

Narrow-leaved gentian, *Gentiana linearis*, is extremely rare in Northumberland and York counties, where it grows in damp thickets and peaty lowlands. Plants reach 70 centimetres in height with opposite sessile lanceolate hairless leaves with smooth edges. Flowers are produced in a terminal cluster, less commonly from the upper leaf axils. Individual bottle-shaped flowers are bright blue to blue-violet and measure 2.5 to 3.5 centimetres in length. Flowers are composed of five petals fused into a floral tube. The end of the floral tube has five lobes, but the flowers never fully open.

Top: A distinct central ring of fringed hairs is at the opening to the floral tube. Middle: Violet to lilac flowers are produced as a terminal leafy raceme or as axillary clusters among the upper leaves. Bottom: The blue tubular flowers of narrow-leaved gentian are produced in terminal clusters.

Dogbane family / Apocynaceae

Introduced Species

Lesser periwinkle

Vinca minor

Pervenche mineure, running myrtle, common periwinkle

HABITAT: Lesser periwinkle is a European species that was introduced to New Brunswick as a garden plant. It is now found occasionally along roadsides, trails, and the edges of deciduous and mixed forests near larger communities throughout the province.

CHARACTERISTICS: Lesser periwinkle is an evergreen groundcover with 1.5- to 3-centimetre-long opposite leaves that are glossy, hairless, and smooth-edged. Plants produce upright flowering stems with three to five pairs of leaves, as well as elongate non-flowering creeping stems that often root along their length.

Flowers are solitary from each pair of leaves along the upright stems. Each flower is 1.5 to 3 centimetres wide with five blue-violet petals that are fused at their base into a tube.

VITAL STATISTICS

Maximum height: 30 centimetres
Flowering season: May and June

Top: Flowers are solitary; the five blue-violet petals are fused at their base. Bottom: The glossy leaves are paired and hairless with smooth edges; plants form evergreen groundcovers.

Nightshade family / Solanaceae

Bittersweet nightshade

Solanum dulcamara

Morelle douce-amère, climbing nightshade

Introduced Species

VITAL STATISTICS

Maximum height: 3 metres
Flowering season: July to September

HABITAT: Bittersweet nightshade is an introduced species that is native throughout Europe and Asia. It typically grows in urban areas, along roadsides, and on scrubland. It is most common in the southern half of New Brunswick.

CHARACTERISTICS: Bittersweet nightshade is technically a woody vine, but, as this is not always apparent, it is included here as a wildflower. The plant's intertwining stems reach 2 to 3 metres in height. Young stems are green to purple; older wood becomes grey-brown.

The 4- to 12-centimetre-long leaves come in two shapes: some are ovate, others have two large lobes at their base, which give them an almost trifoliate appearance. The edges of both leaf types are untoothed. Foliage has a rank smell when bruised and is without significant fall colour.

Purple five-petalled 1-centimetre-diameter flowers have strongly recurved petals. Yellow anthers produce a central beak-like extension in the blooms. Flowers are produced in loose clusters of three to 20 blossoms from July until the first frost. In autumn, flowers develop into 1-centimetre-long egg-shaped shiny red berries in autumn.

Bittersweet nightshade fruit resembles tiny tomatoes (a plant to which this species is related). The berries are mildly poisonous to humans but palatable to fruit-eating birds.

Top: Leaves commonly have two large lobes at their bases. Middle: The purple star-like flowers have a yellow "beak" created by the stamens. Bottom: The fruit appear like small tomatoes.

Introduced Species

Borage family / Boraginaceae

Oysterleaf

Mertensia maritima

Sanguine de mer, sea lungwort

HABITAT: Oysterleaf is common on sandy or gravelly shorelines along the Fundy coast and the far northeastern coast of New Brunswick.

CHARACTERISTICS: Early in the season, oysterleaf has tufted basal leaves; later, plants become trailing and mat-like. Their leaves are waxy, fleshy, and blue-grey to grey-green. Basal leaves are petioled and ovate to spatulate; stem leaves are alternate, short petioled to sessile, and ovate to elliptical. All leaves are hairless and smooth-edged. The upper-outer portion of all leaves often has small bumps on its surface.

Flowers are produced in terminal leafy cymes. Individual flowers, which are up to 0.9 centimetres long, are bell-like with five lobes. Flowers are pink when they open but quickly turn bright blue. Within the bell are five stamens and a single style.

VITAL STATISTICS
Maximum height: 20 centimetres
Flowering season: Mid-June to August

Top: Blue bell-shaped flowers open from pink flower buds. Middle: Trailing flowering stems end in leafy cymes. Bottom: Young plants and early-in-the-season plants have tufted basal leaves; leaves are typically blue-tinted.

Coastal

Borage family / Boraginaceae

Small forget-me-not

Native Species

Myosotis laxa

Myositis laxiflore, small-flowered forget-me-not, bay forget-me-not, tufted forget-me-not

VITAL STATISTICS

Maximum height: 40 centimetres
Flowering season: June to September

HABITAT: Small forget-me-not is common along slow-moving streams and pond shorelines, muddy ditches, and wet meadows throughout the province.

CHARACTERISTICS: Small forget-me-not is a matted semi-aquatic plant with weak rounded trailing stems. Alternate lanceolate leaves, which are up to 10 centimetres in length, are nearly sessile with smooth edges. The upper leaf surface has short bristly hairs. Trailing stems do not root at their nodes; plants do not produce stolons.

Flowers are produced at the ends of branches on one-sided cymes. As they mature, cymes become more raceme-like and the flowers are widely spaced. Unopened flowers are held in a tight coil. Each five-petalled flower is 0.2 to 0.5 centimetres wide and bright blue with a yellow eye. The bases of the petals form a floral tube which is shorter than or equal to the length of each petal.

European or large forget-me-not, *M. scorpioides*, has stolons and squared stems that root at the nodes. Leaves are oblong and wider and shorter (to 5 centimetres) than those of small forget-me-not. Flowers are up to 0.5 to 1 centimetre wide, and the length of the floral tube is greater than that of an individual petal. Flowers are closer together than those of small forget-me-not. It is scattered throughout the province but locally common along the Saint John River watershed.

Top: Small forget-me-not leaves are smooth-edged and sessile; flowers are on one-sided cymes. Bottom: European forget-me-not has larger flowers and broader leaves than small forget-me-not.

Borage family / Boraginaceae

Introduced Species

Woodland forget-me-not

Myosotis sylvatica

Myosotis des bois, garden forget-me-not

HABITAT: Woodland forget-me-not, introduced from Europe as a garden ornamental, is occasionally naturalized in waste areas near settlements in the province.

CHARACTERISTICS: Woodland forget-me-not is a tufted biennial or short-lived perennial plant. Basal leaves are oblong to elliptical with smooth edges and winged petioles. Stem leaves are alternate and sessile. Stems, leaves, and sepals are covered in short soft hairs. The stems may be purple-tinted.

Flowers, which are 0.6 to 0.8 centimetres wide, are produced on one-sided cymes that elongate to become more raceme-like. Individual flowers have five clear blue, rarely pink or white, petals which are fused at their base to produce a floral tube. Flowers have a central yellow eye, five stamens, and a single style.

Rough forget-me-not, *M. arvensis*, is similar to woodland forget-me-not but only reaches 40 centimetres in height; flowers are just 0.3 to 0.4 centimetres wide. It blooms mid-May through September. Plants are covered in hairs.

Stickseed, *Lappula squarrosa*, is a related annual with forget-me-not-like flowers produced in elongate racemes on plants up to 60 centimetres tall. Their flowers are commonly more cupped than those of true forget-me-not. The entire plant is rough-haired; seeds have hooked bristles that stick to fur and clothing. Both rough forget-me-not and stickseed are widely scattered in the province.

VITAL STATISTICS

Maximum height: 50 centimetres
Flowering season: June to July

Top: Woodland forget-me-not is a bushy tufted plant with sessile elliptical leaves; stems may be purple-tinted. Middle: Rough forget-me-not has hairy sepals. Bottom: Stickseed has long white-haired sepals and cup-shaped flowers.

Borage family / Boraginaceae

Prickly comfrey

Symphytum asperum

Consoude âpre

Introduced Species

VITAL STATISTICS

Maximum height: 150 centimetres
Flowering season: Mid-June to July

HABITAT: Prickly comfrey, a European species likely introduced as a garden ornamental, is found in waste areas, especially near settlements along the Fundy coast and the Maine border.

CHARACTERISTICS: Prickly comfrey is a robust leafy plant that forms large clumps. Stems and leaves are covered in rough prickly hairs. Alternate leaves are elliptical and petioled, with smooth but often undulating edges. They are rugose with distinct veins. The lowermost leaves may reach 20 centimetres in length.

Nodding flowers are produced in one-sided cymes, both terminally and axillary from the upper leaf axils. Five fused petals produce a tubular flower, which is up to 1.5 centimetres long, with a bell-like end. Flowers are pink when they open but rapidly turn blue; they also have five stamens hidden within the floral tube and a single thread-like style that extends beyond the petals.

Common comfrey, *S. officinale*, occurs in similar habitats as prickly comfrey, primarily along the Fundy coast. Hairs are not as stiff as those on prickly comfrey and the upper leaves have winged petioles. Flower colours include dirty white, pale straw yellow, or dull purple.

Top: Prickly comfrey's pink buds open into blue bell-like flowers; leaves are rugose with undulating smooth edges. Bottom: Common comfrey's nodding flowers are commonly dirty white to straw yellow.

Verbena family / Verbeniaceae

Native Species

Blue vervain

Verbena hastata

Verveine bleue, American blue vervain, false vervain, swamp verbena, simpler's-joy

HABITAT: Blue vervain is seen along river bottoms, shore- and streamsides, and wet meadows throughout much of New Brunswick.

CHARACTERISTICS: Blue vervain is a tall clumping plant. Stems are square in cross-section, slightly hairy, and often purple-tinted. Opposite leaves, which up to 15 centimetres long, are narrow and lanceolate with coarsely toothed edges, a veiny appearance, and a short petiole. Lowermost leaves may have a pair of short lobes at their base.

Flowers are produced in a panicle of numerous dense narrow racemes up to 12 centimetres in length. Individual flowers are about 0.6 centimetres wide with five violet-blue petals that are fused at the base to form a short tube.

White vervain, *V. urticifolia*, is rare along the upper Saint John River. It is a slender plant to 150 centimetres in height with ovate to elliptical coarsely toothed opposite leaves that are hairy along their lower veins. Stems are square in cross-section. Flowers are produced in narrow, arching spikes at the ends of the many upper stem branches. Individual flowers have five white petals and are about 0.3 centimetres wide.

VITAL STATISTICS

Maximum height: 150 centimetres

Flowering season: August to September

Top: Flowers are in dense racemes. Middle: The paired narrow leaves are coarsely toothed and petioled. Bottom: White vervain has tiny white flowers on branching racemes.

Bellflower family / Campanulaceae

Gieseck's harebell

Native Species

Campanula gieseckiana (formerly *Campanula rotundifolia*)
Campanule à feuilles rondes, common bluebell, Scottish bluebell

VITAL STATISTICS

Maximum height: 40 centimetres
Flowering season: Mid-June to September

HABITAT: Common harebell grows along coastal headlands, coastal meadows, rocky roadsides, and gravelly streamsides throughout New Brunswick.

CHARACTERISTICS: Common harebell forms colonies by thin subterranean rhizomes. Usually less than 15 centimetres tall, this tufted, creeping plant occasionally reaches 40 centimetres. Round to heart-shaped toothed basal leaves have narrow petioles and develop in late summer, overwinter, and shrivel before flowering commences. Leaves on the upright non-branching stems are alternate, linear, often smooth-edged, and primarily sessile. The entire plant is hairless.

Nodding bell-shaped flowers are solitary or, more commonly, in loose racemes. The 1.5-centimetre-long flowers have five pointed violet-blue, rarely white, lobes; five threadlike sepals; five stamens; and one style with a three-lobed stigma.

Marsh bellflower, *C. aparinoides*, is uncommon and grows on riverbanks and wet meadows mainly in southern New Brunswick. Slender, branching plants reach 100 centimetres in length; linear sessile leaves have hairy undersides and hairy widely toothed edges. Solitary, often nodding, bell-like 1- to 1.5-centimetre-long flowers have five white or pale blue pointed lobes.

Creeping bellflower, *C. rapunculoides*, has unbranched stems up to 100 centimetres long and narrow heart-shaped coarsely toothed leaves. Nodding 2.5-centimetre-long violet-blue bell-like flowers bloom on one-sided racemes in July and August.

Top: Common harebell has linear stem leaves and loose racemes of nodding bell-shaped flowers. Middle: Marsh bellflower's weak stems have a few pale blue bell-like flowers. Bottom: Creeping bellflower has nearly sessile flowers on dense one-sided racemes.

Amaryllis family / Amaryllidaceae

Wild chives

Allium schoenoprasum

Ciboulette, brûlotte, chives

Native Species | Introduced Species

HABITAT: Both native and European varieties of chives are found within New Brunswick. European forms are generally found along roadsides near settlements; native forms are found along gravelly shorelines particularly in calcareous areas.

CHARACTERISTICS: Wild chives is a clumping, grass-like plant arising from a cluster of small bulbs. All leaves are basal, linear, terete, and hollow with a distinctive onion smell when bruised. All parts of the plant is hairless.

Flower stems are leafless and stiffer and taller than the leaves. Before flowers open, they are encased in a thin purple or pink-tinted sheath, which splits to reveal a hemispherical umbel of flowers 2.5 to 4 centimetres in diameter. Individual flowers have six narrow purple tepals. Leaves of the European form are usually longer than flower stems.

Wild leek, *A. tricoccum*, is very rare in rich deciduous woodlands and bottomlands of the southern counties and near the Maine border in Carleton County. From a cluster of bulbs arise 10- to 30-centimetre-long elliptical to lanceolate smooth fleshy leaves which shrivel by the time flowering begins in late June and July. Atop 15- to 40-centimetre-high leafless flower stems is a hemispherical cluster of white six-tepaled flowers.

Wild garlic, *A. canadense*, is extremely rare in thickets and meadows of Madawaska, York, and Kings counties. It has linear flattened leaves, stiff flower stems 30 to 50 centimetres long, and an umbel of small bulbs with a few six-tepaled white- or pink-tinted flowers.

VITAL STATISTICS

Maximum height: 50 centimetres

Flowering season: Late June to July

Top: Flowers are in dense hemispherical umbels; note the papery remains of the "skin" that protected the unopened buds. Middle: Wild leek has a cluster of white flowers. Bottom: Wild garlic's umbel of small bulbs has a few pale pink flowers.

Iris family / Iridaceae

Strict blue-eyed grass

Native Species

Sisyrinchium montanum (formerly *S. angustifolium*)

Bermudienne montagnarde, herbe aux yeux bleus, common blue-eyed grass, mountain blue-eyed grass

VITAL STATISTICS

Maximum height: 35 centimetres
Flowering season: Late May to July

HABITAT: Strict blue-eyed grass is commonly found in meadows and along roadsides; it is less common in open woodlands and along shorelines. It is found province-wide.

CHARACTERISTICS: Strict blue-eyed grass is a tufted grass-like plant. Leaves are basal, linear, flattened, grass-like, and smooth-edged.

Flowers stems, which are taller than the leaves, are stiff, winged, and non-branching and have two leaf-like bracts, one below the flowers and the other overtopping the flowers. Flowers are produced in an umbel of two to five flowers. Individual flowers are 1.5 to 2.5 centimetres wide with six deep violet-blue, bristle-tipped tepals. Each flower has a central yellow eye, six stamens, and a single style. Flowers later develop into 0.4- to 0.7-centimetre-diameter globular seed capsules which turn dark brown when seeds are ripe.

Top: Each flower has six deep violet-blue bristle-tipped petals and a central yellow eye. Bottom: Strict blue-eyed grass produces clumps of grass-like foliage and straight flower stems.

Buttercup family / Ranunculaceae

Native Species

Round-lobed hepatica

Anemone americana (formerly *Hepatica americana*)

Anemone d'Amérique, hépatique d'Amérique, round-leaved hepatica

HABITAT: Round-lobed hepatica is very rare in dry, deciduous, or mixed woodlands, primarily in the southwestern region of the province.

CHARACTERISTICS: Round-lobed hepatica is a tufted woodland plant. Leaves, each about 7.5 centimetres wide, are wider than they are long; they are basal, tri-lobed, leathery, and evergreen and turn purple-brown through the winter months. The petiole is 10 to 15 centimetres long and covered in long soft hairs. The top sides of leaves are hairless; the undersides have long hairs, which are often lost as the season progresses. The leaf edges are smooth with fine hairs. New leaves, which may be mottled purple-brown, appear after the plant flowers.

Flowers are solitary at the ends of hairy purple-tinted stems. Flowers usually have six or seven (but up to 12) sepals which are petaloid and lavender-blue, pink, or white. Flowers are 1.5 to 2.5 centimetres wide and have numerous stamens and pistils at their centres. Flowers close, and often nod at night or on cloudy days. Each flower has three purple-green sepal-like bracts below their colourful sepals.

VITAL STATISTICS

Maximum height: 15 centimetres
Flowering season: May

Top: Plants often produce solitary flowers with seven or more petaloid sepals. Middle: Flowers are often pink; the flower stems have long hairs. Bottom: Leaves are tri-lobed and often mottled when they unfurl.

Aster family / Asteraceae

Wild chicory

Cichorium intybus

Chocorée, blue sailors, chicory, wild chicory

Introduced Species

VITAL STATISTICS

Maximum height: 100 centimetres
Flowering season: July to September

HABITAT: Wild chicory is a European plant found in disturbed habitats such as roadsides and waste places throughout New Brunswick.

CHARACTERISTICS: Wild chicory is a slender biennial or short-lived perennial arising from a taproot. Early in the season, first-year plants form a flat rosette of lanceolate, sharply toothed, sharply lobed, or pinnatifid leaves, similar to those of dandelion. Alternate stem leaves are similar but have smaller, widely spaced teeth and are sessile or partly clasp the stem. Hairs grow along the lower central vein of each leaf. The stem is grooved, green or purple-tinted, hairy on the lower portion but often hairless above. All parts of the plant ooze a milky sap when cut.

Flowering stems appear spike-like or as an open branching panicle. The widely spaced flowers are produced in clusters of two to three along mostly leafless stems. Individual flower heads are 2.5 to 3.5 centimetres wide with 10 to 20 bright blue ray florets. Each ray floret ends in five teeth and is finely hairy on the outside. Flower heads have no disc florets; the base of each ray floret has a tubular blue stamen and a single style with a bifid, curled stigma. Flowers close during sunny afternoons. Seed tips have a tuft of hairs.

Top: Each flower has several blue ray but no disc florets; each floret ends in five teeth. Bottom: Deeply lobed and sharply toothed leaves appear like those of dandelion.

Native Species

Aster family / Asteraceae

Low rough aster

Eurybia radula (formerly *Aster radula*)

Aster rude, rough aster, rough wood aster

HABITAT: Low rough aster grows on peaty barrens and in damp forest clearings and damp thickets throughout the province.

VITAL STATISTICS

Maximum height: 90 centimetres
Flowering season: July to September

CHARACTERISTICS: Low rough aster is a slender plant with non-branching stems arising from cord-like subterranean rhizomes. Alternate sessile leaves, up to 8 centimetres long, are lanceolate to elliptical with sharp teeth. Leaf surfaces are covered in short stiff hairs; leaves appear veined.

Flowers are produced in a loose corymb but, in exposed locations, may be solitary. Each 2.5- to 3.5-centimetre-wide flower head is composed of 20 to 30 pale violet-blue ray florets and a similar number of yellow disc florets that turn red with age. Seeds have a tuft of tawny hairs at their tips.

Large-leaved aster, *E. macrophylla*, is found in dry open woods and clearings throughout New Brunswick. Growing to 100 centimetres in height and blooming from July to September, this plant forms leafy clumps. The lowermost leaves are heart-shaped, long petioled, and up to 20 centimetres long; upper leaves are smaller and become sessile. All leaves are alternate, sharp-toothed, and rough textured. Flowers are produced in a loose corymb. Individual flower heads are 2 to 2.5 centimetres wide with nine to 16 narrow pale violet-blue ray florets. Flower stems have glandular-tipped hairs.

Top: Each flower has about 20 lavender-blue ray florets surrounding a central cluster of yellow disc florets. Middle: Stems of low rough aster are generally unbranched and the narrow sessile leaves have sharp teeth. Bottom: Large-leaved aster's heart-shaped lower leaves have petioles; its flowers are in open corymbs.

Aster family / Asteraceae

Flax-leaved aster

Native Species

Ionactis linariifolia (formerly *Aster linariifolius*)

Aster à feuilles de linaire, flat-leaved whitetop aster, flax-leaved ankle-aster, stiff aster, spruce aster

VITAL STATISTICS

Maximum height: 45 centimetres

Flowering season: August and September

HABITAT: Flax-leaved aster is confined to the sandy roadsides and dry fields of Gloucester, Northumberland, and Kent counties of New Brunswick.

CHARACTERISTICS: Flax-leaved aster is a clumping plant with multiple non-branching stems which may be erect or sprawling. Stems, tinted red or purple, are covered in fine grey hairs. The leaves are numerous and alternate but so crowded they appear whorled. Each sessile leaf is linear, stiff, about 3 centimetres long, and has a distinct central vein. Leaves are smooth on top and finely grey hairy below.

Flowers are produced in terminal corymbs. Individual flower heads, 2 to 3 centimetres in diameter, have 10 to 20 lavender or pale blue-violet ray florets surrounding many yellow disc florets. Each flower head stem has many small narrow leafy bracts. Faded flowers eventually release tiny seeds, each with an attached tuft of white hairs.

Top: Flowers are in open corymbs. Bottom: Leaves are linear and densely crowded along the stem.

Aster family / Asteraceae

Native Species

Tall blue lettuce

Lactuca biennis

Laitue bisannuelle, wild blue lettuce, biennial lettuce, blue wood lettuce

HABITAT: Tall blue lettuce, which is found in disturbed areas such as roadsides and waste places, is scattered throughout the province.

CHARACTERISTICS: Tall blue lettuce is a slender but coarse biennial plant. In the first season, plants produce a flat rosette of nearly elliptical leaves, which are up to 30 centimetres in length. These leaves are pinnatifid, deeply divided into several wide coarsely toothed lobes with pointed tips and have distinct winged petioles. Alternate stem leaves are smaller than those in the rosette, less divided, and sessile. Stems and leaf undersides are slightly hairy. The stem is non-branching except near its top. All parts of the plant exude a milky sap when cut.

Flowers are densely packed into multiple branched panicles. Individual flower heads are 0.6 to 0.7 centimetres wide with 15 to 30 pale blue ray florets. The base of each floret has a tubular blue stamen and a single style with a curled bifid stigma. The phyllaries often have purple-tinted tips. Flower heads develop into small dandelion-like seed heads. Each seed has a tuft of white hairs at its top.

VITAL STATISTICS

Maximum height: 200 centimetres
Flowering season: July to September

Top: Each flower has 15 or more blue ray florets but no disc florets; phyllaries often have purple-tinted tips. Bottom: Stem leaves are sessile and pinnatifid with deeply cut lobes.

Aster family / Asteraceae

Bog aster

Native Species

Oclemena nemoralis (formerly *Aster nemoralis*)

Asater des bois, leafy bog aster

VITAL STATISTICS

Maximum height: 70 centimetres
Flowering season: August to September

HABITAT: Bog aster grows in wetland habitats and on peaty barrens, primarily in the southern and eastern regions of New Brunswick and especially near the coasts.

CHARACTERISTICS: A slender plant with non-branching thin stems, bog aster forms loose colonies via subterranean rhizomes. Its numerous closely spaced alternate leaves are linear to narrow lanceolate. Up to 6 centimetres long, leaves are sessile with revolute slightly toothed edges, and a rugose appearance. Leaves and stems are slightly hairy.

Flower heads are solitary or in loose corymbs with fewer than 10 flower heads. Each 2.5- to 4-centimetre-diameter flower head has 15 to 25 lilac-purple ray florets and a similar number of yellow disc florets that turn red with age. Each flower stem has three to eight narrow bracts. Seed tips have tufts of golden hairs.

Whorled wood aster, *O. acuminata*, a woodland species found province-wide, grows to a height of 50 centimetres and blooms in August and September. Its upper leaves are larger than the lower; alternate upper leaves are closely spaced and appear to be whorled. Leaves are lance-shaped to elliptical and sessile with sharply toothed edges, and they have scattered hairs along the lower midvein. Plants produce a globular corymb of flower heads. Each 2.5- to 4-centimetre-diameter flower head has 10 to 18 narrow partially twisted white or pale lilac ray florets. Disc florets change from yellow to red as they age.

Top: Bog aster flowers may be solitary. Middle: Bog aster has numerous closely spaced linear leaves. Bottom: Whorled wood aster produces its elliptical leaves in a whorl-like cluster.

Aster family / Asteraceae

Native Species

Heart-leaved aster

Symphyotrichum cordifolium (formerly *Aster cordifolius*)

Aster à feuilles cordées, common blue wood aster

HABITAT: Heart-leaved aster is common in New Brunswick. It grows along roadsides and in clearings, thickets, and old meadows.

CHARACTERISTICS: Heart-leaved aster is a clump-forming plant. Stems are non-branching, except near the flowers, and often tinted red. The stem is usually smooth; rarely it may have a few fine hairs. The basal and lower alternate stem leaves may reach 12 centimetres in length; they are heart-shaped and sharply toothed with scattered hairs and relatively long petioles.

Flowers are produced in a many-flowered dense panicle. Individual flower heads are 1.5 to 2 centimetres wide with 10 to 16 pale violet-blue or white ray florets and a similar number of creamy yellow disc florets that become red with age. Each flower head stem has a few small narrow bracts. Seeds have a tuft of white to pink-tinted hairs at their ends.

Lindley's aster, *S. ciliolatum*, is found throughout the province; it is distinguished by its winged petioles and hairy leaf edges. Although lower and basal leaves are heart-shaped, the upper leaves are lanceolate. Lindley's aster produces 2.5- to 3.5-centimetre-wide flowers, which are often on narrower panicles than those of heart-leaved aster.

VITAL STATISTICS

Maximum height: 90 centimetres

Flowering season: August to October

Top: Leaves are heart-shaped with fine teeth and relatively long petioles; flowers are in dense panicles. Middle: Some populations of heart-leaved aster have white flowers. Bottom: Lindley's aster flowers are often in more narrow panicles than those of heart-leaved aster.

Aster family / Asteraceae

New York aster

Native Species

Symphyotrichum novi-belgii (formerly *Aster novi-belgii*)

Aster de la Nouvelle-Belgique, Michaelmas daisy

VITAL STATISTICS

Maximum height: 100 centimetres
Flowering season: July to October

HABITAT: New York aster is common along coastal New Brunswick, including shorelines, headlands, and salt marshes. It is also found along roadsides and in old meadows and thickets.

CHARACTERISTICS: New York aster is a clumping plant that may be slender in sheltered sites or dense in exposed habitats. Stout stems are usually hairless and often tinted red or purple. Basal leaves have winged petioles; alternate stem leaves are sessile and partly clasp the stem. Leaves, which are up to 20 centimetres long, are narrow lanceolate to elliptical, generally hairless, with smooth or slightly toothed edges. Basal leaves have generally withered by the time flowering commences. In sheltered sites, plants reach 100 centimetres in height, but in their more usual exposed habitats near the coast, plants are less than 30 centimetres tall.

Flowers are produced in open or dense panicles at the ends of upper branching stems. Individual flower heads, which are 2.5 to 4 centimetres in diameter, have 15 to 35 violet-blue ray florets and about twice as many yellow disc florets that become reddish-brown with age. Seeds have a tuft of yellow-brown hairs attached to their tops.

Very rare along calcareous rocky shores of the upper Saint John and Restigouche rivers is Anticosti aster, *S. anticostense*, which looks like a slender, narrow- and long-leaved version of New York aster. Its flowers are in looser, smaller clusters than New York aster and individual flowers sit atop relatively long stems.

Top: Each flower has many narrow violet-blue ray florets surrounding a central cluster of disc florets; disc florets redden as they age. Middle: The narrow leaves are hairless and plant stems often tinted red or purple. Bottom: Anticosti aster has long, narrow leaves.

Aster family / Asteraceae

Purple-stemmed aster

Native Species

Symphyotrichum puniceum (formerly *Aster puniceus*)

Aster ponceau, red-stemmed aster, swamp aster, rough aster

HABITAT: Purple-stemmed aster is found along streamsides, roadside ditches, and swamps throughout New Brunswick.

CHARACTERISTICS: Purple-stemmed aster is a coarse tall clumping plant. It is the tallest of the blue-violet asters in the province. Stems are stout, distinctly purple or red-purple, and variably hairy. Basal and alternate stem leaves are lanceolate, stiff-haired, and up to 20 centimetres long. Lower, larger leaves have widely spaced teeth along their edges; upper, smaller leaves may be smooth-edged. All stem leaves clasp the stem. Basal leaves, which have petioles, shrivel by the time flowering commences.

Flowers are produced in open panicles at the ends of wide-spreading branches. Individual flower heads are 2.5 to 3.5 centimetres in diameter with 20 to 50 violet-blue ray florets and a similar number of yellow disc florets that age to red-purple. Seeds have a tuft of white hairs at their ends.

New England aster, *S. novae-angliae*, is widely scattered in the province. It is as tall as or taller than purple-stemmed aster, but it prefers drier sites. Crowded lanceolate leaves are smooth-edged and hairy and clasp the stem. The main stem is also finely hairy. Flowers are produced in dense corymbs. Individual flower heads have 40 to 50 violet-purple ray florets surrounding yellow disc florets that age to red-purple. Its phyllaries curl back, a feature that distinguishes it from purple-stemmed aster, whose phyllaries are straight.

VITAL STATISTICS	
Maximum height:	200 centimetres
Flowering season:	Late July to September

Top: The upper narrow leaves are mostly smooth-edged and clasp the stem. Middle: Flowers are in open panicles and the stems often purple-tinted. Bottom: New England aster has crowded narrow leaves that clasp the stem; its flowers are in a dense corymb.

GLOSSARY

alternate (leaves): leaves borne one at a time along the length of a stem

annual: living for only one year

anther: the tip of the stamen; anthers produce pollen

auricle: a small ear-like appendage

awn: a slender bristle

axil: the angle created by (and between) two leaves

axillary: located in the axil (of leaves)

beard: a cluster of long or stiff hairs

biennial: living for two years; generally flowering and fruiting in the second year

bipinnate (leaf): a pinnate leaf whose leaflets are also pinnate

biternate (leaf): a ternate (trifoliate) leaf whose leaflets are also ternate, resulting in each leaf being composed of nine leaflets

bottomland: intervale; low-lying land, especially along a river

bract: a leaf (often modified) located immediately under a flower

bracteole: a small bract

branchlet: a smaller side-branch that grows out of a larger branch

bristle: a stiff hair

burr: a seed or fruit with short stiff bristles or hooks

calcareous: containing lime

calciphile: a plant that thrives on lime-rich soil

calyx: the combined sepals of a flower, which often protects the flower in the bud stage

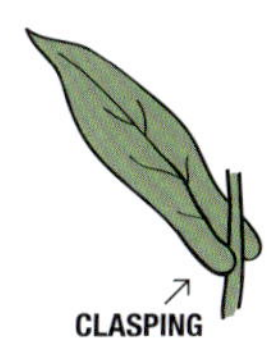

clasping: embracing or surrounding, usually refers to a leaf base around a stem

colonial: plants that form colonies (groups) via underground stems (rhizomes)

compound leaf: a leaf composed of two or more leaflets

compound umbel: a flower cluster in which each stalk of the umbel produces a smaller umbel of flowers; inflorescence typical of members of the parsley family (Apiaceae)

cordate: heart-shaped

corolla: combined flower petals; often the coloured portion of a flower

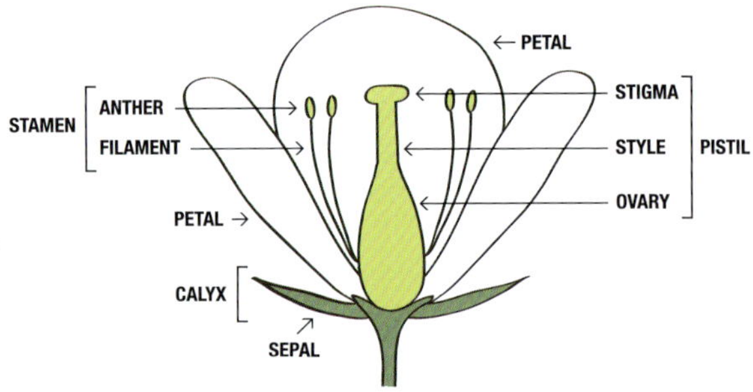

corymb: a flat-topped flower cluster in which individual flower stalks grow upward from various points on the main stem to approximately the same height

crenate: having rounded teeth along the leaf edge

cyme: a flower cluster in which the main axis and each branch end in a flower that opens before the flowers below or to the side of it

deltoid: triangular in outline

dioecious: unisexual plants in which male and female flowers are on separate plants

dimorphic (flowers): have flowers of two forms

disc floret: any of the small tubular flowers at the centre of a flower head in members of the aster family (Asteraceae)

disjunct: a plant whose population is far removed from the main population of that plant

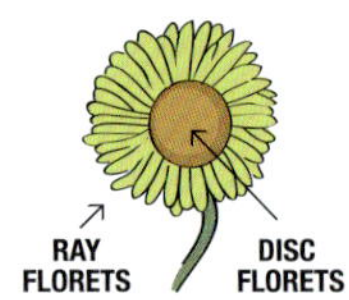

division (of a leaf): a sub-unit of a leaf such as a leaflet or deep lobe

elliptical: in the shape of an ellipse, broadest in the middle and tapering at each end

elongate(d): long or lengthened

endemic: plant populations that are confined to a single and relatively small geographic area

ephemeral: appearing for a short period of time

escape: a non-native species that has become naturalized

exerted: protruding or projecting

farina: a powder-like substance

felted: densely covered in fine hairs

filament: the stalk of a stamen, to which the anther is attached

flower head (daisy): an aster family (Asteraceae) flower head that is composed of many separate unstalked flowers packed closely together; the outer flowers have one conspicuous large petal (ray floret) and the central disk is formed of flowers with smaller petals (disc floret)

flower head (non-daisy): a dense cluster of sessile or nearly sessile flowers

glandular: having glands that excrete a substance that makes stems or leaves sticky

glandular-tipped: having glands, at the tips of hairs, that excrete a substance that makes stems or leaves sticky

globular: rounded

hemiparasitic: a plant that obtains some nourishment from its host but is also capable of photosynthesis

herbaceous: plants with stems that die back in the winter

inflorescence: the flowering part of a plant

intervale: a tract of low-lying land along a river

lanceolate: lance-shaped

leaflet: a small leaf; one of the segments of a compound leaf

linear: long and narrow with parallel edges

lobe: a rounded division of a leaf

localized: confined to a small area

midrib: the central or main rib of a leaf, which runs from stem to tip

monoecious: species in which male and female flowers grow on the same plant

nectar spur: part of a sepal or petal that develops into an elongated hollow spike extending behind the flower and contains nectar

net veins: distinct veins that form a net-like pattern

nodding: an upright stem or structure that droops at the tip

non-stoloniferous: not bearing stolons

nutlet: a small nut

oblanceolate: lance-shaped with the widest part of the leaf at the tip (farthest from the stem)

oblong: two to three times longer than broad, with parallel sides

obovate: inverted egg-shaped: narrowest at the base, widest at the terminal end

old meadows: areas once cultivated but left fallow for many years

opposite (leaves): leaves that are borne two at a time (paired) along the length of a stem

orbicular: circular

ornamental: species that are planted to beautify gardens

ovate: egg-shaped

palmate: a lobed leaf with a hand-like silhouette

panicle: a branched raceme, with each branch having a smaller raceme of flowers; the terminal bud of each branch continues to grow, producing more side shoots and more flowers, resulting in a cluster of flowers

pedicle: the stem of an individual flower

pendant: hanging downward from a stem

petal: a division of the corolla

petaloid: coloured and resembling a petal

petiole: the stalk of a leaf

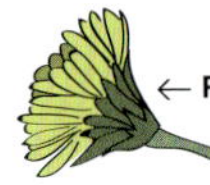

phyllaries: modified bracts located at the base of a flower head of flowers of the aster family

pinnate (leaf): a leaf composed of many smaller leaflets on either side of the main axis

pinnatifid (leaf): a dissected leaf that is pinnately deeply cleft; appears pinnately compound but does not have separate leaflets

pistil: the entire female portion of a flower, composed of an ovary (where seeds are produced), a style (stalk), and a stigma (pollen-receptive tip)

plumose: feather-like

prickle: a sharp slender outgrowth from bark that is thinner than a thorn and not anchored as deeply in the branch

prostrate: growing flat along the ground

pubescent: covered in short downy hairs (not as dense as "felted")

raceme: a flower spike; the flowers have stalks of equal lengths, and the tip of the stem continues to grow and produce more flowers

ray floret: any of the small strap-shaped ("petalled") flowers in the flower head of certain flowers of the aster family (Asteraceae)

recurved: curving downward

reflexed: curled back toward the stem

reniform: kidney-shaped

reticulated: covered with veins that interconnect in a net-like pattern

revolute: rolled under (usually referring to the leaf edge)

rhizome: a prostrate or underground stem

rhombic: square-shaped

rosette (leaves): a cluster of leaves at the base of a plant

rugose: wrinkled

seepage: an area, usually on a slope, through which water slowly trickles, either on or just below the surface

seed head: a dense cluster of seeds

sepal: a division of the calyx; a small leaf under the flower

sessile: lacking flower stems or leaf stems

silique: a two-chambered seed capsule which is longer than wide; it is confined to the mustard family (Brassicaceae)

spadix: a flowering spike with a fleshy stem, indicative of the arum family (Araceae)

spathe: a large bract enclosing an inflorescence

spatulate: spatula or narrow spoon-shaped

spike: a group of sessile flowers arising from the main stem

stamen: the male portion of a flower, composed of a filament (stalk) and an anther

standard: the uppermost petal on flowers of the pea family (Fabaceae)

stigma: the pollen-receptive tip of the pistil (the female part of a flower)

stipule: a small leaf-like appendage at the base of a regular leaf

stolon: a runner or low-lying branch that tends to root itself

stoloniferous: bearing stolons

style: the narrow elongate portion of the pistil (the female part of a flower)

substrate: a plant's growing medium

suckering: producing vegetative shoots from underground roots and rhizomes

swale: a low, moist tract of land

taproot: a plant's main or primary root

tendril: a threadlike structure climbing plants use to wrap around or hook a support

tepal: the name for a "petal" on flowers (such as tulips) in which petals (corolla) and sepals (calyx) look alike

terminal: located at the end

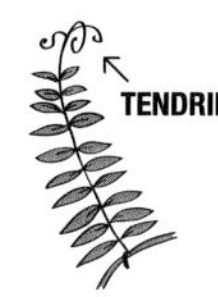

ternate: composed of three parts, such as a leaf with three leaflets

thorn: a sharp woody outgrowth from a stem that is anchored more deeply—and is often thicker—than a prickle

trifoliate: a leaf composed of three leaflets

triternate (leaf): a biternate leaf whose divisions are ternate, resulting in a triangular-shaped leaf with approximately 27 leaflets

tuber: a swollen root-like stem located below the ground

twining: twisting

umbel: a flower cluster in which all flower stalks are of the same length, so that the flower head is rounded like an umbrella

umbellet: a smaller, secondary umbel

undulated: with a wavy edge

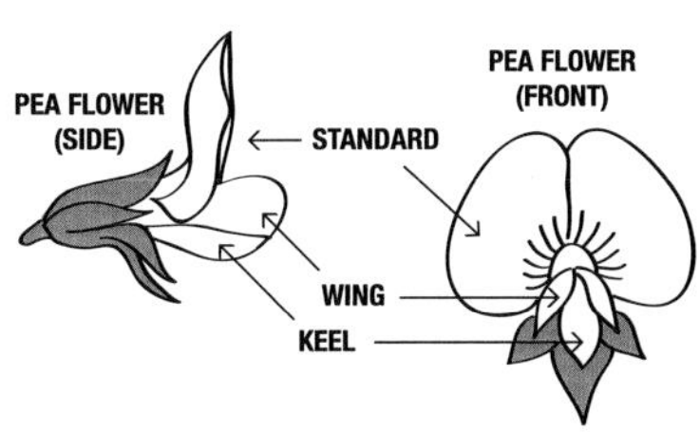

villous: having long silky hairs

wide-spreading: held horizontal, like outspread arms

wing: one of the two side petals on flowers of the pea family (Fabaceae)

whorled (leaves): having three or more leaves originating from the same point on a stem

NEW BRUNSWICK WILDFLOWERS BY FAMILY

This section lists the New Brunswick wildflowers (native and introduced) described in this field guide, grouped by family.

Acoraceae	Sweetflag family
Acorus americanus	American sweetflag
Alismataceae	Water-plantain family
Alisma triviale	northern water-plantain
Sagittaria cuneata	northern arrowhead
Sagittaria graminea	grass-leaved arrowhead
Sagittaria latifolia	broad-leaved arrowhead
Alliaceae	Onion family
Allium canadense	wild garlic
Allium schoenoprassum	wild chives
Allium tricoccum	wild leek
Amaranthaceae	Amaranth family
Amaranthus albus	white amaranth
Amaranthus retroflexus	redroot amaranth
Atriplex glabriuscula	glabrous saltbush
Atriplex patula	common orach
Chenopodium album	common lamb's-quarters
Chenopodium glaucum	oak-leaved goosefoot
Salicornia depressa	Virginia glasswort
Salicornia maritima	sea glasswort
Salsola kali	saltwort
Suaeda maritima	sea-blite
Apiaceae	Parsley family
Aegopodium podagraria	goutweed
Angelica atropurpurea	purple-stemmed angelica
Angelica lucida	seacoast angelica
Angelica sylvestris	woodland angelica
Anthriscus sylvestris	wild chervil
Carum carvi	wild caraway
Cicuta bulbifera	bulbous water-hemlock

Cicuta maculata	spotted water-hemlock
Conioselinum chinense	hemlock-parsley
Daucus carota	Queen Anne's lace
Heracleum mantegazzianum	giant hogweed
Heracleum maximum	American cow parsnip
Heracleum sphondylium	common hogweed
Hydrocotyle americana	American water pennywort
Ligusticum scothicum	Scotch lovage
Osmorhiza berteroi	mountain sweet cicely
Osmorhiza claytonii	hairy sweet cicely
Osmorhiza longistylis	smooth sweet cicely
Pastinaca sativa	wild parsnip
Pimpinella saxifraga	burnet saxifrage
Sanicula marilandica	black snakeroot
Sanicula odorata	yellow snakeroot
Sium suave	common water-parsnip
Zizia aurea	golden alexanders
Apocynaceae	Dogbane family
Apocynum androsaemifolium	spreading dogbane
Apocynum cannabinum	Indian hemp
Vinca minor	lesser periwinkle
Araceae	Arum family
Arisaema triphyllum	Jack-in-the-pulpit
Calla palustris	wild calla
Symplocarpus foetidus	eastern skunk cabbage
Araliaceae	Ginseng family
Aralia hispida	bristly sarsaparilla
Aralia nudicaulis	wild sarsaparilla
Aralia racemosa	American spikenard
Panax trifolius	dwarf ginseng
Aristolochiaceae	Birthwort family
Asarum canadense	Canada wild ginger
Asclepiaceae	Milkweed family
Asclepias incarnata	swamp milkweed
Asclepias syriaca	common milkweed
Asparagaceae	Asparagus family
Asparagus officinalis	garden asparagus
Convallaria majalis	European lily-of-the-valley
Maianthemum canadense	wild lily-of-the-valley
Maianthemum racemosum	large false Solomon's-seal

Maianthemum stellatum	star-flowered false Solomon's-seal
Maianthemum trifolium	three-leaved false Solomon's-seal
Medeola virginiana	Indian cucumber-root
Polygonatum pubescens	hairy Solomon's-seal
Asteraceae	**Aster family**
Achillea millefolium	common yarrow
Achillea millefolium var. *lanulosa*	woolly yarrow
Achillea ptarmica	sneezeweed
Ageratina altissima	white snakeroot
Ambrosia artemisiifolia	common ragweed
Ambrosia trifida	giant ragweed
Anaphalis margaritacea	pearly everlasting
Antennaria howellii subsp. *neodioica*	northern pussytoes
Antennaria parlinii	Parlin's pussytoes
Anthemis cotula	stinking chamomile
Arctium lappa	greater burdock
Arctium minus	common burdock
Arnica lanceolata	lance-leaved arnica
Arnica lonchophylla	long-leaved arnica
Artemisia biennis	biennial wormwood
Artemisia campestris	field wormwood
Artemisia stelleriana	beach wormwood
Artemisia vulgaris	common wormwood
Bidens beckii	water beggarticks
Bidens cernua	nodding beggarticks
Bidens connata	purple-stemmed beggarticks
Bidens frondosa	devil's beggarticks
Bidens hyperborea	estuary beggarticks
Bidens vulgata	tall beggarticks
Carduus nutans	nodding thistle
Centaurea jacea	brown knapweed
Centaurea nigra	black knapweed
Cichorium intybus	wild chicory
Cirsium arvense	Canada thistle
Cirsium muticum	swamp thistle
Cirsium vulgare	bull thistle
Doellingeria umbellata	flat-top white aster
Erechtites hieraciifolia	eastern burnweed
Erigeron annuus	annual fleabane
Erigeron canadensis	horseweed
Erigeron hyssopifolius	hyssop-leaved fleabane
Erigeron philadelphicus	Philadelphia fleabane
Erigeron strigosus	rough fleabane

Eupatorium perfoliatum	common boneset
Eurybia macrophylla	large-leaved aster
Eurybia radula	low rough aster
Euthamia graminifolia	grass-leaved goldenrod
Eutrochium maculatum	spotted Joe-Pye weed
Galinsoga quadriradiata	hairy galinsoga
Gnaphalium uliginosum	low cudweed
Helianthus giganteus	giant sunflower
Helianthus tuberosus	Jerusalem artichoke
Helianthus X laetiflorus	beautiful sunflower
Hieracium murorum	wall hawkweed
Hieracium scabrum	rough hawkweed
Hieracium umbellatum	narrow-leaved hawkweed
Hieracium vulgatum	common hawkweed
Hypochaeris radicata	hairy cat's-ear
Inula helenium	elecampane
Ionactis linariifolia	flax-leaved aster
Jacobaea vulgaris	tansy ragwort
Lactuca biennis	tall blue lettuce
Lactuca canadensis	Canada lettuce
Lactuca serriola	prickly lettuce
Lapsana communis	common nipplewort
Leontodon autumnalis	fall dandelion
Leucanthemum vulgare	oxeye daisy
Matricaria discoidea	pineappleweed
Nabalus altissimus	tall rattlesnakeroot
Nabalus racemosus	purple rattlesnakeroot
Nabalus trifoliolatus	three-leaved rattlesnakeroot
Oclemena acuminata	whorled wood aster
Oclemena nemoralis	bog aster
Omalotheca sylvatica	woodland cudweed
Packera aurea	golden groundsel
Packera paupercula	balsam groundsel
Packera schweinitziana	swamp ragwort
Petasites frigidus	Arctic sweet coltsfoot
Pilosella aurantiaca	orange hawkweed
Pilosella caespitosa	meadow hawkweed
Pilosella flagellaris	whiplash hawkweed
Pilosella floribunda	pale hawkweed
Pilosella officinarum	mouse-ear hawkweed
Pilosella piloselloides	tall hawkweed
Pseudognaphalium obtusifolium	rabbit tobacco
Rudbeckia hirta	black-eyed Susan
Rudbeckia laciniata	cut-leaved coneflower
Senecio pseudoarnica	seaside ragwort
Senecio sylvaticus	woodland ragwort

Senecio viscosus	sticky ragwort
Senecio vulgaris	common ragwort
Solidago bicolor	white goldenrod
Solidago canadensis	Canada goldenrod
Solidago flexicaulis	zigzag goldenrod
Solidago gigantea	giant goldenrod
Solidago hispida	hairy goldenrod
Solidago juncea	early goldenrod
Solidago macrophylla	large-leaved goldenrod
Solidago multiradiata	multi-rayed goldenrod
Solidago nemoralis	grey-stemmed goldenrod
Solidago petiolaris	downy ragged goldenrod
Solidago puberula	downy goldenrod
Solidago rugosa	rough-stemmed goldenrod
Solidago sempervirens	seaside goldenrod
Solidago uliginosa	bog goldenrod
Sonchus arvensis	field sow-thistle
Sonchus asper	prickly sow-thistle
Sonchus oleraceus	common sow-thistle
Symphyotrichum anticostense	anticosti aster
Symphyotrichum boreale	rush aster
Symphyotrichum ciliolatum	Lindley's aster
Symphyotrichum cordifolium	heart-leaved aster
Symphyotrichum lanceolatum	white panicled aster
Symphyotrichum lateriflorum	calico aster
Symphyotrichum novae-angliae	New England aster
Symphyotrichum novi-belgii	New York aster
Symphyotrichum puniceum	purple-stemmed aster
Symphyotrichum racemosum	smooth white oldfield aster
Symphyotrichum tradescanti	Tradescant's aster
Tanacetum huronense	Lake Huron tansy
Tanacetum parthenium	feverfew
Tanacetum vulgare	common tansy
Taraxacum officinale	common dandelion
Tragopogon dubius	yellow goatsbeard
Tragopogon pratensis	meadow goatsbeard
Tripleurospermum inodorum	scentless chamomile
Tussilago farfara	coltsfoot
Xanthium strumarium	rough cockleburr
Balsamaceae	Balsam family
Impatiens capensis	spotted jewelweed
Impatiens glandulifera	purple jewelweed
Impatiens pallida	pale jewelweed

Berberidaceae	**Barberry family**
Caulophyllum thalictroides	blue cohosh
Boraginaceae	**Borage family**
Echium vulgare	common viper's bugloss
Lappula squarrosa	stickseed
Mertensia maritima	oysterleaf
Myosotis arvensis	rough forget-me-not
Myosotis laxa	small forget-me-not
Myosotis scorpioides	European forget-me-not
Myosotis sylvatica	woodland forget-me-not
Symphytum asperum	prickly comfrey
Symphytum officinale	common comfrey
Brassicaceae	**Mustard family**
Alliaria petiolata	garlic mustard
Armoracia rusticana	horseradish
Barbarea orthoceras	erect-fruited wintercress
Barbarea vulgaris	bitter wintercress
Boechera stricta	Drummond's rockcress
Brassica nigra	black mustard
Brassica rapa	field mustard
Cakile edentula	American sea rocket
Capsella bursa-pastoris	shepherd's-purse
Cardamine diphylla	two-leaved toothwort
Cardamine pensylvanica	Pennsylvania bittercress
Cardamine pratensis	meadow bittercress
Descurainia sophia	flixweed
Draba arabisans	rock draba
Draba incana	twisted draba
Draba norvegica	Norway draba
Erucastrum gallicum	common dog mustard
Erysimum cheiranthoides	wormseed mustard
Hesperis matronalis	dame's rocket
Lepidium campestre	field peppergrass
Lepidium densiflorum	common peppergrass
Nasturtium microphyllum	small-leaved watercress
Raphanus raphanastrum	wild radish
Rorippa palustris	marsh yellowcress
Rorippa sylvestris	creeping yellowcress
Sinapsis arvensis	wild mustard
Sisymbrium altissimum	tall tumble mustard
Sisymbrium officinale	common tumble mustard
Thlaspi arvense	field penny-cress

Scientific name	Common name
Cabombaceae	Cabomba family
Brasenia schreberi	watershield
Callitrichaceae	Water-starwort family
Callitriche heterophylla	large water-starwort
Callitriche palustris	spring water-starwort
Campanulaceae	Bellflower family
Campanula aparinoides	marsh bellflower
Campanula gieseckiana	Gieseck's harebell
Campanula rapunculoides	creeping bellflower
Lobelia cardinalis	cardinalflower
Lobelia dortmanna	water lobelia
Lobelia inflata	Indian tobacco
Lobelia kalmii	Kalm's lobelia
Cannabaceae	Hemp family
Humulus lupulus	hops
Caprifoliaceae	Honeysuckle family
Linnaea borealis	twinflower
Caryophyllaceae	Pink family
Cerastium arvense	field chickweed
Cerastium fontanum subsp. *vulgare*	common mouse-ear chickweed
Cerastium semidecandrum	five-stamen mouse-ear chickweed
Cerastium tomentosum	snow-in-summer
Dianthus armeria	deptford pink
Dianthus deltoides	maiden pink
Honckenya peploides	seabeach sandwort
Moehringia lateriflora	grove sandwort
Sagina nodosa	knotty pearlwort
Sagina procumbens	procumbent pearlwort
Saponaria officinalis	bouncing-bet
Silene dioica	red campion
Silene flos-cuculi	ragged robin
Silene latifolia	white campion
Silene noctiflora	night-flowering catchfly
Silene vulgaris	bladder campion
Spergula arvensis	corn spurrey
Spergularia canadensis	Canada sand-spurrey
Spergularia rubra	red sand-spurrey
Spergularia salina	saltmarsh sand-spurrey
Stellaria alsine	bog stitchwort
Stellaria calycantha	northern starwort
Stellaria graminea	grass-leaved starwort

Stellaria longifolia	long-leaved starwort
Stellaria longipes	long-stalked starwort
Stellaria media	common chickweed
Celastraceae	Bittersweet family
Parnassia glauca	fen grass-of-Parnassus
Colchicaceae	Autumn-crocus family
Uvularia sessilifolia	sessile-leaved bellwort
Convolvulaceae	Morning-glory family
Calystegia sepium	hedge bindweed
Convolvulus arvensis	field bindweed
Cuscuta cephalanthi	buttonbush dodder
Cuscuta gronovii	swamp dodder
Cornaceae	Dogwood family
Cornus canadensis	bunchberry
Crassulaceae	Orpine family
Hylotelephium telephium	garden stonecrop
Rhodiola rosea	roseroot
Cucurbitaceae	Gourd family
Echinocystis lobata	wild cucumber
Droseraceae	Sundew family
Drosera anglica	English sundew
Drosera rotundifolia	round-leaved sundew
Drosera intermedia	spoon-leaved sundew
Ericaceae	Heath family
Chimaphila umbellata	common pipsissewa
Epigaea repens	trailing arbutus
Gaultheria hispidula	creeping snowberry
Hypopitys monotropa	pinesap
Linnaea borealis	twinflower
Moneses uniflora	one-flowered wintergreen
Monotropa uniflora	Indian pipe
Orthilia secunda	one-sided wintergreen
Pterospora andromedea	pine-drops
Pyrola americana	round-leaved pyrola
Pyrola asarifolia	pink pyrola
Pyrola chlorantha	green-flowered pyrola
Pyrola elliptica	shinleaf
Pyrola minor	lesser pyrola

Eriocaulaceae	Pipewort family
Eriocaulon aquaticum	seven-angled pipewort
Euphorbiacae	Spurge family
Euphorbia maculata	spotted spurge
Euphorbia polygonifolia	seaside spurge
Euphorbia vermiculata	wormseed spurge
Fabaceae	Pea family
Amphicarpaea bracteata	American hog-peanut
Apios americana	American groundnut
Astragalus alpinus	alpine milk-vetch
Astragalus eucosmus	elegant milk-vetch
Desmodium canadense	Canada tick-trefoil
Desmodium glutinosum	large tick-trefoil
Hedysarum alpinum	alpine hedysarum
Lathyrus japonicus	beach pea
Lathyrus palustris	marsh vetchling
Lathyrus pratensis	meadow pea
Lotus corniculatus	bird's-foot trefoil
Lupinus polyphyllus	large-leaved lupine
Medicago lupulina	black medick
Medicago sativa	alfalfa
Meliolotus albus	white sweet-clover
Meliolotus officinalis	yellow sweet-clover
Oxytropis campestris var. *johannensis*	Saint John River locoweed
Oxytropis deflexa	foliose locoweed
Securigera varia	crown vetch
Trifolium arvense	rabbit's-foot clover
Trifolium aureum	yellow clover
Trifolium campestre	low hop clover
Trifolium dubium	small hop clover
Trifolium hybridum	alsike clover
Trifolium pratense	red clover
Trifolium repens	white clover
Vicia cracca	tufted vetch
Vicia sativa	common vetch
Vicia tetrasperma	four-seed vetch
Gentianaceae	Gentian family
Bartonia paniculata	branched bartonia
Gentiana linearis	narrow-leaved gentain
Gentianopsis amarella	autumn dwarf gentian
Halenia deflexa	spurred gentian
Lomatogonium rotatum	marsh felwort

Geraniaceae	Geranium family
Erodium cicutarium	common storksbill
Geranium bicknelii	Bicknell's geranium
Geranium pratense	meadow geranium
Geranium robertianum	herb-Robert
Hemerocallidaceae	Daylily family
Hemerocallis fulva	orange daylily
Hemerocallis lilioasphodelus	yellow daylily
Hippuridaceae	Mare's-tail family
Hippuris vulgaris	common mare's-tail
Hypericaceae	St. John's-wort family
Hypericum canadense	Canada St. John's-wort
Hypericum ellipticum	pale St. John's-wort
Hypericum fraseri	Fraser's St. John's-wort
Hypericum mutilum	dwarf St. John's-wort
Hypericum perforatum	common St. John's-wort
Iridaceae	Iris family
Iris hookeri	beach-head iris
Iris pseudacorus	yellow iris
Iris versicolor	blue flag
Sisyrinchium montanum	strict blue-eyed grass
Juncaginaceae	Arrowgrass family
Triglochin maritima	seaside arrowgrass
Triglochin palustris	marsh arrowgrass
Lamiaceae	Mint family
Clinopodium vulgare	wild basil
Galeopsis bifida	bifid hemp-nettle
Galeopsis tetrahit	common hemp-nettle
Glechoma hederacea	ground ivy
Hedeoma pulegioides	American pennyroyal
Lamium amplexicaule	common dead-nettle
Lamium purpureum	purple dead-nettle
Lycopus americanus	American water-horehound
Lycopus uniflorus	northern water-horehound
Mentha arvensis	field mint
Mentha spicata	spearmint
Mentha X gentilis	red mint
Mentha X piperata	peppermint
Prunella vulgaris	common self-heal
Scutellaria galericulata	marsh skullcap

Scutellaria lateriflora	mad-dog or blue skullcap
Stachys hispida	rough hedge-nettle
Stachys palustris	marsh hedge-nettle
Stachys pilosa	hairy hedge-nettle
Thymus pulegioides	lemon thyme
Lentibulariaceae	Bladderwort family
Pinguicula vulgaris	common butterwort
Utricularia cornuta	horned bladderwort
Utricularia intermedia	intermediate bladderwort
Utricularia macrorhiza	common bladderwort
Liliaceae	Lily family
Clintonia borealis	corn lily
Erythronium americanum	yellow trout lily
Lilium bulbiferum	orange lily
Lilium canadense	Canada lily
Streptopus amplexifolius	clasping-leaved twisted-stalk
Streptopus lanceolatus	eastern rose twisted-stalk
Linderniaceae	False pimpernel family
Lindernia dubia	yellow-seed false pimpernel
Lythraceae	Lythrum family
Lythrum salicaria	purple loosestrife
Malvaceae	Mallow family
Malva alcea	vervain mallow
Malva moschata	musk mallow
Malva neglecta	dwarf mallow
Malva pusilla	round-leaved mallow
Melanthiaceae	Bunchflower family
Trillium cernuum	nodding trillium
Trillium erectum	red trillium
Trillium undulatum	painted trillium
Veratrum viride	green false hellebore
Menyanthaceae	Bog buckbean family
Menyanthes trifoliata	bog buckbean
Nymphoides cordata	little floatingheart
Molluginaceae	Carpetweed family
Mollugo verticillata	green carpetweed

Myrsinaceae	Myrsine family
Lysimachia ciliata	fringed yellow loosestrife
Lysimachia maritima	sea milkwort
Lysimachia nummularia	creeping yellow loosestrife
Lysimachia punctata	spotted yellow loosestrife
Lysimachia terrestris	swamp yellow loosestrife
Lysimachia thyrsiflora	tufted yellow loosestrife
Lysimachia vulgaris	garden yellow loosestrife
Trientalis borealis	northern starflower
Nymphaceae	Waterlily family
Nuphar microphylla	small yellow pond-lily
Nuphar variegata	yellow pond-lily
Nymphaea odorata	fragrant water-lily
Onagraceae	Evening-primrose family
Chamerion angustifolium	fireweed
Circaea alpina	small enchanter's-nightshade
Circaea canadensis	large-leaved enchanter's-nightshade
Epilobium ciliatum	northern willowherb
Epilobium coloratum	purple-veined willowherb
Epilobium hornmannii	Hornemann's willowherb
Epilobium leptophyllum	bog willowherb
Epilobium palustre	marsh willowherb
Ludwigia palustris	marsh seedbox
Oenothera biennis	common evening-primrose
Oenothera parviflora	small-flowered evening-primrose
Oenothera perennis	perennial evening-primrose
Orchidaceae	Orchid family
Arethusa bulbosa	dragon's-mouth
Calopogon tuberosus	grass pink
Calypso bulbosa	calypso
Corallorhiza maculata	spotted coralroot
Corallorhiza trifida	early coralroot
Cypripedium acaule	pink lady's-slipper
Cypripedium parviflorum	yellow lady's-slipper
Cypripedium reginae	showy lady's-slipper
Dactylorhiza viridis	frog orchid
Epipactis helleborine	broad-leaved helleborine
Galearis rotundifolia	small round-leaved orchid
Galearis spectabilis	showy orchis
Goodyera oblongifolia	Menzie's rattlesnake-plantain
Goodyera repens	dwarf rattlesnake-plantain
Goodyera species	rattlesnake-plantain

Goodyera tesselata	checkered rattlesnake-plantain
Liparis loeselii	Loesel's twayblade
Malaxis monophyllos var. *brachypoda*	white adder's-mouth orchid
Malaxis unifolia	green adder's-mouth orchid
Neottia auriculata	auricled twayblade
Neottia australis	southern twayblade
Neottia convallarioides	broad-leaved twayblade
Neottia cordata	heart-leaved twayblade
Platanthera aquilonis	tall northern green orchid
Platanthera blephariglottis	white fringed orchid
Platanthera clavellata	club-spur orchid
Platanthera dilatata	tall white bog orchid
Platanthera flava	tubercled orchid
Platanthera grandiflora	large purple fringed orchid
Platanthera hookeri	Hooker's orchid
Platanthera huronensis	Lake Huron orchid
Platanthera lacera	ragged fringed orchid
Platanthera macrophylla	large round-leaved orchid
Platanthera obtusata	blunt-leaved orchid
Platanthera orbiculata	lesser round-leaved orchid
Platanthera psycodes	small purple fringed orchid
Pogonia ophioglossoides	rose pogonia
Spiranthes casei	Case's ladies'-tresses
Spiranthes cernua	nodding ladies'-tresses
Spiranthes lacera	northern slender ladies'-tresses
Spiranthes lucida	shining ladies'-tresses
Spiranthes ochroleuca	yellow ladies'-tresses
Spiranthes romanzoffiana	hooded ladies'-tresses
Orobanchaceae	Broomrape family
Conopholis americana	American cankerroot
Epifagus virginiana	beechdrops
Euphrasia nemorosa	common eyebright
Euphrasia randii	Rand's eyebright
Euphrasia stricta	stiff eyebright
Odontites vulgaris	red bartsia
Orobanche uniflora	one-flowered broomrape
Rhinanthis minor	little yellow rattle
Oxalidaceae	Shamrock family
Oxalis dillenii	slender wood-sorrel
Oxalis montana	common wood-sorrel
Oxalis stricta	European wood-sorrel
Papaveraceae	Poppy family
Capnoides sempervirens	pink corydalis

Chelidonium majus	greater celandine
Dicentra cucullaria	Dutchman's breeches
Fumaria officinalis	common fumitory
Sanguinaria canadensis	bloodroot
Penthoraceae	Ditch stonecrop family
Penthorum sedoides	ditch-stonecrop
Phrymaceae	Lopseed family
Erythranthe moschata	musk monkeyflower
Mimulus ringens	square-stemmed monkeyflower
Phryma leptostachya	lopseed
Plantaginaceae	Plantain family
Chaenorrhinum minus	dwarf snapdragon
Chelone glabra	white turtlehead
Gratiola aurea	golden hedge-hyssop
Gratiola neglecta	clammy hedge-hyssop
Linaria dalmatica	dalmatian toadflax
Linaria repens	striped toadflax
Linaria vulgaris	butter-and-eggs
Nuttallanthus canadensis	Canada toadflax
Plantago lanceolata	narrow-leaved plantain
Plantago major	common plantain
Plantago maritima	seaside plantain
Veronica americana	American speedwell
Veronica arvensis	corn speedwell
Veronica chamaedrys	germander speedwell
Veronica longifolia	long-leaved speedwell
Veronica officinalis	common speedwell
Veronica persica	bird's-eye speedwell
Veronica scutellata	marsh speedwell
Veronica serpyllifolia	thyme-leaved speedwell
Plumabaginaceae	Plumbago family
Limonium carolinianum	sea lavender
Polygalaceae	Milkwort family
Polygala sanguinea	blood milkwort
Polygala senega	seneca snakeroot
Polygaloides paucifolia	fringed milkwort
Polygonaceae	Knotweed family
Fallopia cilinodis	fringed black bindweed
Fallopia convolvulus	Eurasian black bindweed
Fallopia japonica	Japanese knotweed

Fallopia sachalinensis	giant knotweed
Fallopia scandens	climbing false buckweed
Rumex acetosa	garden sorrel
Rumex acetosella	sheep sorrel
Rumex brittanica	greater water dock
Rumex crispus	curled dock
Rumex obtusifolius	blunt-leaved dock
Persicaria amphibia	water smartweed
Persicaria arifolia	halberd-leaved smartweed
Persicaria hydropiper	marshpepper smartweed
Persicaria hydropiperoides	false waterpepper
Persicaria lapthifolia	pale smartweed
Persicaria maculosa	spotted lady's-thumb
Persicaria pensylvanica	Pennsylvanian smartweed
Persicaria punctata	dotted knotweed
Persicaria sagittata	arrow-leaved smartweed
Polygonum aviculare	common knotweed
Polygonum fowleri	Fowler's knotweed
Rumex pallidus	seabeach dock
Rumex triangulivalvis	willow-leaved dock
Pontederiaceae	Pickerelweed family
Pontederia cordata	pickerelweed
Portulacaceae	Purslane family
Claytonia caroliniana	Carolina spring beauty
Portulaca oleracea	common purslane
Potamogetonaceae	Pondweed family
Potamogeton species	pondweed
Primulaceae	Primrose family
Primula laurentiana	Laurentian primrose
Primula mistassinica	Mistassini primrose
Ranunculaceae	Buttercup family
Actaea pachypoda	doll's eye
Actaea rubra	red baneberry
Anemone americana	round-lobed hepatica
Anemone canadensis	Canada anemone
Anemone multifida	cut-leaved anemone
Anemone parviflora	small-flowered anemone
Anemone quinquefolia	woodland anemone
Anemone virginiana	Virginia anemone
Aquilegia vulgaris	European columbine
Caltha palustris	marsh marigold

Coptis trifolia	goldthread
Halerpestes cymbalaria	seaside buttercup
Ranunculus abortivus	kidney-leaved buttercup
Ranunculus acris	tall buttercup
Ranunculus aquatilis	white water buttercup
Ranunculus flammula var. *flammula*	lesser spearwort
Ranunculus gmelinii	small yellow water buttercup
Ranunculus pensylvanicus	Pennsylvania buttercup
Ranunculus recurvatus	hooked buttercup
Ranunculus repens	creeping buttercup
Thalictrum confine	northern meadow-rue
Thalictrum pubescens	tall meadow-rue
Rosaceae	Rose family
Agrimonia gryposepala	hooked agrimony
Agrimonia striata	woodland agrimony
Alchemilla filicaulis	thin-stemmed lady's mantle
Comarum palustre	marsh cinquefoil
Drymocallis arguta	tall cinquefoil
Filipendula rubra	queen-of-the-prairie
Filipendula ulmaria	queen-of-the-meadow
Fragaria vesca	woodland strawberry
Fragaria virginiana	wild strawberry
Geum aleppicum	yellow avens
Geum canadense	white avens
Geum laciniatum	rough avens
Geum macrophyllum	large-leaved avens
Geum rivale	water avens
Geum urbanum	wood avens
Potentilla anserina	common silverweed
Potentilla argentea	silvery cinquefoil
Potentilla intermedia	downy cinquefoil
Potentilla norvegica	rough cinquefoil
Potentilla recta	sulphur cinquefoil
Potentilla simplex	old field cinquefoil
Rubus chamaemorus	cloudberry
Rubus pubescens	dewberry
Rubus repens	dewdrop
Sanguisorba canadensis	Canada burnet
Sibbaldia tridentata	three-toothed cinquefoil
Rubiaceae	Madder family
Galium asprellum	rough bedstraw
Galium mollugo	smooth bedstraw
Galium palustre	marsh bedstraw
Galium species	bedstraw

Galium tinctorium	Dyer's bedstraw
Galium trifidum	three-petalled bedstraw
Galium triflorum	three-flowered bedstraw
Houstonia caerulea	azure bluets
Mitchella repens	partridgeberry
Santalaceae	Sandalwood family
Comandra umbellata	bastard toadflax
Geocaulon lividum	northern comandra
Sarraceniaceae	Pitcher plant family
Sarracenia purpurea	northern pitcher plant
Saxifragaceae	Saxifrage family
Chrysosplenium americana	American golden-saxifrage
Mitella nuda	naked mitrewort
Saxifraga paniculata	white mountain saxifrage
Micranthese virginiensis	early saxifrage
Tiarella cordifolia	heart-leaved foamflower
Scrophulariaceae	Figwort family
Scrophularia lanceolata	lance-leaved figwort
Scrophularia nodosa	knotty figwort
Verbascum blattaria	moth mullein
Verbascum thapsus	common mullein
Solanaceae	Nightshade family
Solanum dulcamara	bittersweet nightshade
Solanum physalifolium	ground-cherry
Solanum ptychanthum	eastern black nightshade
Tofieldiaceae	Tofieldia family
Triantha glutinosa	sticky tofieldia
Urticaceae	Nettle family
Laportea canadensis	Canada wood nettle
Urtica dioica	stinging nettle
Valerianaceae	Valerian family
Valeriana dioica	marsh valerian
Valeriana officinalis	common valerian
Valeriana uliginosa	swamp valerian
Verbeniaceae	
Verbena hastata	blue vervain
Verbena urticifolia	white vervain

Violaceae	Violet family
Viola adunca	early blue violet
Viola arvensis	European field pansy
Viola blanda	sweet white violet
Viola cucullata	marsh blue violet
Viola labradorica	Labrador violet
Viola lanceolata	lance-leaved violet
Viola macloskeyi	small white violet
Viola nephrophylla	northern bog violet
Viola novae-angliae	New England blue violet
Viola pubescens	downy yellow violet
Viola renifolia	kidney-leaved violet
Viola sagittata	arrow-leaved violet
Viola selkirkii	great spurred violet
Viola sororia	woolly blue-violet
Viola species	tufted blue violet
Viola tricolor	Johnny-jump-up

INDEX / PLANTS BY LATIN NAME

Species listed are included in this book with a full-page description or are mentioned in the description of another species. Former (but still familiar) Latin names mentioned in the book are also included.

INDEX / PLANTS BY COMMON NAME

Species listed are included in this book with a full-page description or are mentioned in the description of another species.

PHOTO CREDITS

All plant photographs by Todd Boland except those by the following photographers, whom we acknowledge with appreciation. A number after the flower name indicates that the photograph appears (1) at the top of the page, (2) in the middle, or (3) at the bottom.

Per Aasen: oak-leaved goosefoot, marsh willowherb (1), common mare's-tail (2), marsh skullcap (2), common valerian (2), greater celandine (2)

Clare Beelman: blunt-leaved orchid (2)

Donald Cameron: Northern meadow-rue, estuary beggarticks (1), Anticosti aster

Gerald D. Carr, Oregon State University: tall beggarticks

Toni Corelli: seabeach dock

Alan Cressler: yellow bartonia, Loesel's twayblade, green adder's-mouth orchid (1), Canada germander

Layla Dishman: eastern burnweed (1, 2)

George Dixon: fringed yellow loosestrife

Jim Fowler: woodland anemone, showy orchis, hooker's orchid (2), northern slender ladies'-tresses

Jennifer Garrett/MA NHESP: Plymouth gentian (2)

Peter Gorman: purple-stemmed angelica (1)

Aaron Gunnar: golden hedge-hyssop (2)

John Hagstrom: Canada tick-trefoil (1)

Arthur Haines, New England Wildflower Society: Pennsylvania buttercup

Mary Ellen Harte: Robbin's milk-vetch (1, 2, 3)

Scott Hecker: Indian cucumber-root (2)

Patricia Henschen: little floatingheart (1, 2)

Gene Hertzberg: round-leaved sundew (1), small round-leaved orchid (2), large round-leaved orchid

Charlie Hickey: Indian tobacco (2)

Sonnia Hill: Pennsylvanian smartweed (2)

Jason Hollinger: blue cohosh (1), dwarf rattlesnake-plantain, common wood-sorrel (2)

William Hull: wild cucumber (2)

Neill Kenmuir: common hogweed

Cindy Kilpatrick: kidney-leaved violet

Olivia Kwong: hairy sweet cicely

Louis M. Landry: American spikenard, bulbous water-hemlock, swamp dodder (1), bog willowherb, tall blue lettuce (2), Canada lettuce (2), Indian tobacco (1), downy goldenrod, corn spurrey (2), calico aster, heart-leaved foamflower (2), Fraser's St. John's-wort (2), nodding trillium (1), European field pansy (1), rough hawkweed (2, 3), common viper's bugloss (3), grass-leaved arrowhead

Matt Lavin: square-stemmed monkeyflower (2)

Ryan LeBlanc: auricled twayblade

Glen Lee: water beggarticks

Uli Lorimer: trailing arbutus (2), whorled wood aster, tall rattlesnakeroot, golden hedge-hyssop (1), two-leaved toothwort (2), large tick-trefoil, fringed milkwort

Alain Maire: biennial wormwood, beechdrops (2), common pipsissewa (3), pale St. John's-wort, flax-leaved aster, shinleaf, zigzag goldenrod, shining ladies'-tresses, fen grass-of-Parnassus (2)

Susan Meades: marsh bellflower, creeping snowberry (1), large-leaved aster, Lindley's aster

Jason S. Morris: common pipsissewa (1, 2)

Walter Muma: early goldenrod

Brian O'Brien: tubercled orchid, yellow snakeroot

Bruce Patterson: estuary beggarticks (2)

Douglas Alden Peterson: white panicled aster

Tom Potterfield: American hog-peanut, cut-leaved toothwort

Homer Edward Price: wild sarsaparilla (3), wild chicory (2), Philadelphia fleabane (2), painted trillium (3)

Corey Raimond: branched bartonia, pink corydalis, Pennsylvania bittercress (2), northern comandra (1), American water pennywort (1), heart-leaved twayblade (2), smooth sweet cicely, clammy hedge-hyssop, swamp valerian (1), Pennsylvania buttercup (1)

Jay Ross: water beggarticks

Andree Reno Sanborn: dewdrop (1, 2), calico aster (2)

Jennifer Schlick: two-leaved toothwort, American golden saxifrage (1), Carolina spring beauty (2), kidney-leaved buttercup, broad-leaved arrowhead (1), heart-leaved foamflower (1)

Al Schneider, www.swcoloradowildflowers.com: foliose locoweed

Melanie Schori: hooked buttercup

David Smith: heart-leaved aster

Forest and Kim Starr: black mustard, woodland ragwort

Will Stuart: white goldenrod (2)

Superior National Forest: Bicknell's geranium

Robert Svvenson: prickly comfrey

Mike Turner: halberd-leaved smartweed

Giles Watson: American sweetflag (1)

Doug Waylett: early coralroot, naked mitrewort (2), green-flowered pyrola, lesser pyrola

Wayne Webber: tall tumble mustard

Western New Mexico University Department of Natural Sciences: Indian hemp, spotted water-hemlock, wild basil (2), wormseed spurge, common dead-nettle, dwarf mallow (2), field mint, peppermint, green carpetweed (1, 2), dotted knotweed, common purslane (1, 2), European black nightshade (1), American speedwell (1, 2), prickly lettuce

Mary Winter: small yellow water buttercup

Kerry M. Woods: Fraser's St. John's-wort (1)

Andrey Zharkikh: lance-leaved figwort (1), seaside buttercup, Drummond's rockcress (2)

ABOUT THE AUTHOR

Todd Boland is the author of *Wildflowers of Nova Scotia*, *Trees & Shrubs of Newfoundland and Labrador*, *Trees & Shrubs of the Maritimes*, and *Wildflowers of Fogo Island and Change Islands*. He is the Research Horticulturist at the Memorial University of Newfoundland Botanical Garden.

Boland has written about and lectured nationally and internationally on various aspects of horticulture and native plants. He is a founding member of the Newfoundland and Labrador Wildflower Society (1990) and an active website volunteer with the North American Rock Garden Society.

Born and raised in St. John's, Newfoundland and Labrador, Boland graduated from Memorial University of Newfoundland with an M.Sc. in Biology and a specialization in Plant Ecology. Alpine plants are his longstanding outdoor gardening passion; indoors, he maintains an ever-increasing orchid collection. Photography and bird watching occupy any non-gardening downtime.